the forest

who's who

FOREST

compiled by tony matthews

a britespot publication

THE FOREST WHO'S WHO
A Britespot Publication

First Published in Great Britain by
Britespot Publishing Solutions Limited, Chester Road, Cradley Heath, West Midlands, B64 6AB

February 2004
© Tony Matthews 2004

Request

In a text document with such a huge amount of data, I have tried hard to eradicate mistakes. Football writing in the past has been prone to error, many carried through the years from book to book, volume to volume, chapter to chapter, story to story.

I have found that a players' date of birth has been two years earlier and some times two years later than initially thought. A birthplace is different, a Christian name is wrong (E for Edwin and not Edward, or H for Henry and not Harold) and the spelling of a name is also debatable. In summary, a great deal of effort has gone into checking and double-checking all the thousands of facts and figures in this book, and also to confirm the many queries that have arisen. However, while every care has been taken, it is inevitable that some where between the pages, the lines, the words, some errors have slipped through the net. I am only human and the great WC Fields and even George Bernard Shaw got somethings wrong! Corrections, additions, will be welcome and I would also love to hear from anyone who

has any memorabilia, old photographs, programmes, scrapbooks which I could borrow, look at, even buy. Anything on Forest would be appreciated - so that the next publication on the club and its players can be even better.

ISBN 1 904103 20 0

Design and layout © Britespot Publishing Solutions Limited.
Pictures © Empics and Colorsport

Printed and bound in Great Britain by
Cromwell Press Ltd, Aintree Avenue, White Horse Business Park, Trowbridge, Wiltshire BA14 0XB

Acknowledgments

I acknowledge the assistance afforded to me by Fraser Nicholson (Forest Press office), David Barber (of the Football Association) and Zoe Ward (FA Premier League). Thank you, too - and 'sorry' darling for the inconvenience caused - to my loving wife Margaret who once again has had to put up without me for hours upon end whilst I've been sat tapping away on the computer keyboard, thumbing through old reference books, matchday programmes and soccer magazines, checking and re-checking the thousands of statistics and stories as well as travelling up and down the country from sunny Devon.

Last but by no means least I must give a sincere thank you to everyone who has worked on the book at Britespot Publishing, especially to Roger Marshall, Paul Burns, Chris Russell and Linda Perkins, and a final thank you to Ian Nannestad for proof reading.

•Appearances are for Premiership, Football League, FA Cup, League Cup (various guises), European Cup, Inter-Cities Fairs Cup, UEFA Cup, European Super Cup, World Club Championship, Football Alliance, United Counties League, Simod Cup, FA Charity Shield, Texaco Cup, Anglo-Scottish Cup, Zenith Data Systems Cup & Mercantile Credit Trophy. Appearances made during WW1 & WW2 are not included in the player's first-class record but are listed in his write-up if deemed necessary. Substitute appearances have been made since 1965.

•My facts & figures (i.e appearance totals and goals scored) may differ slightly from those printed in previous history/statistical books published on Nottingham Forest. I have done a fair bit of research myself and my calculations, although not outrageously different, are my own findings.

Bibliography

I have referred to several books to clarify certain relevant statistics including facts and figures, individual players' details and, indeed, stories and match reports from past seasons regarding Nottingham Forest FC. There is some conflicting information in these sources and we have made judgement as to which is likely to be correct, here is a list:

- Nottingham Forest: A Complete Record: 1865-1991
- Nottingham Forest Football Club: Centenary 1865-1965
- AFS Who's Who: 1902, 1903, 1907 & 1909
- English Internationals Who's Who: 1872-1972
- Football League Directory: 1985-89
- The PFA Premier & Football League Players': 1946-1998
- Rothmans Yearbook (Vols. 1-33) 1970-2003

- The Essential History of Nottingham Forest, 2002
- Association Football & The Men Who Made It (4 vols) 1905
- The Encyclopaedia of Association Football 1969
- FA Official Yearbooks: 1951-2000
- Football League Players' records: 1888-1939 (M Joyce)
- Footballers' (PFA) Factfile (B J Hugman/AFS) 1995-2003
- Where Are They Now? (A Pringler & N Fissler) 1996

Others

- AFS Football Recollections & AFS Bulletins (various)
- Nottingham Forest handbooks

- Nottingham Forest 'home' programmes (various) 1947-2003
- Nottingham Forest 'away' programmes (various) 1947-2003

I have referred to several newspapers (especially those from the East Midlands area), thumbed through numerous club histories & various Who's Who publications, certain autobiographies and biographies of individual players and managers and quite a number of football reference books in general for confirmation of certain factual points.

CONTENTS

Pinnacle
Insurance

I am positively certain that all supporters of Nottingham Forest Football Club, young and old, male and female, have, at some time or another, been involved in an argument concerning a player, whether from the past or present!

I know from experience that in numerous pubs and clubs, inside street cafes, bars and restaurants, at schools and colleges, at home, in office blocks, on the work floor, at various grounds, in cars, on trains and buses, even when travelling in an aircraft or walking down the road, perhaps sitting on the beach, discussions have taken place about certain players (and a few managers) who have been associated with Forest down the years.

Some of these for sure have turned into heated arguments, with questions being asked but no definite answer given. As a result wagers have been laid as to who is right and who is wrong!

Some questions revolve round the obvious, such as (a) When did he join the club and where from? (b) How many goals did he score? (c) Where did he go after leaving Forest? (d) Did he play for England (or Wales etc)? (e) Was he a defender or midfielder, a left or right-winger? or (f) Did he play in a Cup final?

Hopefully this Who's Who can answer most, if not all of those questions, as well as offering you a lot more information besides. It will also satisfy that laudable curiosity without a shadow of doubt.

On the following pages you will find multitudinous authentic personal details of every single player who has appeared for Forest in a competitive League and Cup match from 1889 (when the club entered the Football Alliance) right up to the end of the 2002-03 season.

There are details, too, of several footballers who guested for the club during the two World War periods (1915-19 & 1939-46). There is also information about the men who have managed Forest down the years and there have been over 20 all told, with Brian Clough the longest-serving with 18 years in the 'hot seat.'

For easy reference, all personnel have been listed in A-Z order, with the date and place of birth and death given, if clarified, although occasionally it has only been possible to ascertain a certain year with regards to when he was actually born and when he died. Also included in the pen-picture portraits are details of the junior and non-League clubs that the player served, any transfer fees involved (if known), honours won at club and international level, plus the respective senior appearance and goalscoring records (for Forest) which appears at the head of each individual players write-up. An asterisk (i.e *) alongside any figures, indicates that the player was still adding to his appearance and/or goals tallies at the time the book was published.

Virtually throughout this book, the name of the club - Nottingham Forest is referred to, in the main, as (the) Forest or the Reds. Very few abbreviations have been used, but among the more common ones are the obvious: FC (Football Club), FAC (FA Cup), FLC (Football League Cup), apps (appearances), sub (substitute), cs. Close Season.

Where a single year appears in the text (when referring to an individual players career), this indicates, in most cases, the second half of a season: i.e. 1975 is 1974-75. However, when the figures (dates) such as 1975-80 appear, this means seasons 1975-76 to 1979-80 inclusive and not 1974-80.

If you spot any discrepancies, errors, even omissions, I would appreciate it very much if you could contact me (via the publishers) so that all can rectified in any future publications appertaining to Nottingham Forest Football Club. If you have anything to add, this too, would be welcome as people tend to reveal unknown facts from all sources when football is the topic of conversation.

NB - Several supporters have verbally stated that there were errors, omissions, discrepancies etc. in certain previous Forest books - but very few have come forward with a list of what they were. I have diligently checked through several other reference books (including a number of similar Who's Who publications which have been produced on other clubs) and I am now hopeful that most, if not all, the facts and figures revealed on the forthcoming pages are correct.

Tony Matthews

A

AAS, Einar Jan
Defender: 24 apps. one goal
Born: Norway, 12 October 1955
Career: FKmoss, Bayern Munich, FOREST (March 1981); FKmoss
Einar Aas, a Norwegian international central defender, was signed to replace Larry Lloyd at the heart of the Forest defence after some impressive displays in the Bundesliga with Bayern Munich. He left the City Ground at the end of the 1981-82 season after failing to recover from injury, suffered against Sunderland at Roker Park in November 1981. He later became a bank clerk back in Norway.

ABBOTT, Harry
Defender: 7 apps.
Born: Nottingham circa 1873.
Career: FOREST (August 1894 to May 1896)
Defender Harry Abbott, who was basically a reserve to the likes of Stewart and MacPherson, spent two seasons with Forest in the mid-1890s, making his debut against Blackburn Rovers in January 1895. He did not figure in competitive football after leaving the Reds.

ADDISON, Colin
Inside-forward: 176 apps. 69 goals
Born: Taunton, Somerset, 18 May 1940
Career: York City (juniors, July 1955, professional May 1957), FOREST (£12,000, January 1961), Arsenal (£45,000, September 1966), Sheffield United (£40,000, December 1967), Hereford United (as player-manager, October 1971-May 1974), Durban City/South Africa (manager, January 1975), Notts County (assistant-manager, December 1975 to October 1976), Newport County (manager, January 1977 to May 1978), West Bromwich Albion (assistant-manager, July 1978 to May 1979), Derby County (manager, May 1979 to January 1982), Newport County (manager, January 1982 to May 1985); coaching in Kuwait & Qatar; then Celta Vigo/Spain (manager-coach, April 1986 to April 1987), West Bromwich Albion (assistant-manager, September 1987 to October 1988), Atletico Madrid (assistant-manager/coach, October 1988, then manager December 1988 to June 1989), FC Cadiz/Spain (coach, March-July 1990), Hereford United (manager, July 1990 to May 1991), Al Arabi (coach, 1991-92), Merthyr Tydfil (two spells as manager, from October 1994 & from July 1996), Yeovil Town (manager), Swansea City (manager, autumn 2001-March 2002), Forest Green Rovers (manager, October 2002).
Inside-forward Colin Addison spent five-and-a-half years with Forest before transferring to Arsenal. A very positive player, aggressive with good ball control, he was forced to retire in 1973 after breaking his leg. He had an excellent career, amassing well over 400 League and Cup appearances and scoring more than 230 goals. He was, in fact, Forest's top marksman three seasons out of four

during the 1960s. He guided Hereford to that magnificent FA Cup victory over Newcastle in 1972 and later did well on the coaching circuit abroad. He was with Ron Atkinson at both West Brom and Atletico Madrid. Addison, who became Merthyr's fourth manager in 15 months when he joined the Welsh club in 1994, and Swansea's eighth in 10 years when he moved into the hot-seat at the Vetch Field in 2001.

ALEXANDER, Dennis Leslie
Inside-forward: 20 apps. 4 goals
Born: Nottingham, 19 February 1935
Career: FOREST (juniors April 1950, amateur June 1952, professional June 1955), Brighton & Hove Albion (March 1958), Gateshead (October 1958 to April 1959).
A League debutant against Liverpool in 1955, inside-forward Dennis Alexander struggled to gain regular first team football with Forest and after leaving the City Ground failed to get a first team outing with Brighton.

ALLAN, Stanley James E
Inside/centre-forward: 22 apps. 3 goals
Born: Wallsend 28 December 1886.
Died: Wallsend 4 May 1919.
Career: Wallsend FC, Sunderland, Newcastle United (June 1908), West Bromwich Albion (May 1911), FOREST (June 1912). Retired in May 1913, joined RAMC at outbreak of WW1 and served his country throughout the hostilities.
A fringe player at Newcastle (six goals scored in 16 games) Jack Allan was a fast, strong, old-fashioned centre-forward who later helped WBA reach the 1912 FA Cup final. He did reasonably well in his only season with Forest before struggling with injury. He sadly died of pneumonia at the age of 32.

ALLEN, Herbert Anthony
Inside-forward: 4 apps. one goal
Born: Nottingham, 27 October 1924
Career: Beeston Boys Club, FOREST (professional, November 1945), Notts County (August 1949) Corby Town (July 1954), Grantham Town (May 1956).
Tanner Allen was a well-built, strong-kicking full-back who, after leaving Forest, made 30 League appearances for neighbours Notts County. His debut in the red shirt of Forest was against Aston Villa in a Football League (South) game in December 1945 and his senior bow followed a month later against Watford in the 3rd round of the FA Cup when he scored in a 1-1 draw. He made 12 appearances in that transitional FLS campaign.

ALLEN, Christopher Anthony
Wing-forward: 28 apps. 3 goals
Born: Oxford, 18 November 1972.
Career: Oxford United (YTS, June 1989, professional, May 1991), FOREST (on loan, February 1996, signed

permanently July 1996), Luton Town (on loan, November 1997), Cardiff City (on loan, October 1998), Port Vale (free transfer, March 1999), Oxford United (free transfer, August 1999), Stockport County (free transfer, October 1999), Slough Town (June 2000). Brighton HA (March 2001) Dover Athletic, (September 2001) Aldershot Town. (March 2002).

An England Under-21 international left-winger (two caps gained) Chris Allen was quick and lively, but unfortunately he failed to produce the goods at the highest level despite gaining international recognition.

ALLOU, Anoh Bernard
Midfielder: 10 apps. 2 goals
Born: Cocody, Ivory Coast, 19 June 1975
Career: Paris St Germain; Grampus 8 (Japanese J-League), FOREST (March 1999, Rwdmolenbeek (August 2001).

Capped 24 times by France at Under-21 level, wide midfielder Bernard Allou never really settled at the City Ground and, indeed, he faded quickly from the scene. Seven of his ten outings for the Reds came as a substitute.

ALLSOPP, Dennis Watkin
Goalkeeper: 245 apps.
Born: Derby, 13 February 1871. Died: Derby, 6 October 1921
Career: Derby Junction FC, FOREST (August 1892-May 1900). Dan Allsopp was a very capable goalkeeper, standing over 6ft tall and weighing around 14 stones. He showed uncanny ability between the posts and made almost 250 senior appearances for Forest during his eight-year association with the club, gaining an FA Cup winners medal in 1898 when he pulled off several important saves against his boyhood heroes Derby County. He lost his place following the emergence of Harry Linacre.

ALSFORD, Walter John
Wing-half/centre-half/inside-forward: 31 apps.
Born: Edmonton, 6 November 1911.
Died: Bedford, 3 June 1968
Career: Tottenham Hotspur (junior, 1928, amateur May 1929), Cheshunt (on loan), Northfleet (on loan), Tottenham Hotspur (professional, August 1930), FOREST (January 1937). Retired from League football in May 1938, but returned as a wartime guest for Forest in 1941-42 while also assisting Aldershot, Arsenal and Doncaster Rovers during the hostilities.

The versatile Wally Alsford could play in a variety of positions, preferring the right-half berth in the main. He appeared in exactly 100 first-class games for Spurs and, after doing exceedingly well in an international trial match, he gained his one and only England cap, lining up against Scotland in April 1935 before moving to Forest halfway through the 1936-37 season. It was then found that he was suffering from osteomyelitis, a bone marrow inflammation, and was told not to play again, taking retirement in the summer of 1938. However, he returned to the game to guest for Forest (and other clubs) during WW2 and later became a licensee in Nottingham, Brighton and finally Bedford. He was only 56 when he died.

ANDERSON, John
Half-back: 43 apps. one goal
Born: Salford, 11 October 1921.
Career: Adelphi Lads' Club, Brindle Heath Lads' Club, Manchester United (amateur, March 1938, professional December 1938), Plymouth Argyle (WW2 guest, also served in Royal Navy), FOREST (October 1949), Peterborough United (August 1952). Retired from playing in 1954 and was appointed trainer-coach at London Road, remaining with Posh until the summer of 1962

The son of a former Swinton Rugby League player, half-back John Anderson gained an FA Cup winners medal with Manchester United in 1948 (v. Blackpool) and scored twice in 39 games for the Old Trafford club before moving to Forest. An assured performer he helped the Reds win the Third Division South championship (making eight appearances) and later served with Peterborough (in various ways) for almost a decade.

A driving, authoritative half-back, Anderson did excellent work with Posh and was with them when they gained Football League status.

ANDERSON, Vivian Alexander
Right-back: 425+5 apps. 22 goals
Born: Nottingham, 29 August 1956.
Career: FOREST (apprentice November 1972 professional August 1974), Arsenal (£250,000, July 1984), Manchester United (£250,000, July 1987), Sheffield Wednesday (January 1991), Barnsley (player-manager, July 1993), Middlesbrough (assistant-manager, 1994-July 2001, left the Riverside Stadium when Steve McClaren took over as manager).

Viv 'Spider' Anderson appeared in almost 600 League games during his first-class career. A skilful attacking right full-back, he signed apprentice forms at the City Ground after representing Nottingham Schools and working as a printer. The first black footballer to win a full England cap (doing so v. Czechoslovakia in November 1978) he went on to star in 30 senior internationals for his country (11 as a Forest player), also gaining one Under-21 and seven 'B' caps as well as representing the Football League. As a Forest player, he was a member of the League championship-winning side (1978), triumphed in two League Cup finals (1978 & 1979) and also celebrated two European Cup final victories (1979 & 1980) as well as tasting Super Cup glory (also in 1980), Second Division promotion in 1977, Anglo-Scottish success, also in 1977, and a League Cup final defeat v. Wolves, again in 1980. He played in more than 400 first-class games during his ten years at the City Ground and after adding more than 150 outings to his tally with the Gunners he switched to

Old Trafford, the fee being agreed by an independent tribunal. Approaching his 31st birthday, Anderson certainly gave a good account of himself, before moving to Hillsborough. Two-and-a-half years later, having helped the Owls win promotion and reach two Cup finals at Wembley, he became player-manager at Oakwell before his appointment as player/assistant-manager (to Bryan Robson) at Middlesbrough - remaining at the Riverside Stadium for seven years during which the Teeside club reached the Premiership.

ANDREWS, Gary Michael

Full-back: 0+1 appearance.
Born: Nottingham, 12 May 1968
Career: FOREST (apprentice, June 1984, professional September 1985), Peterborough United (August 1988 to May 1990).
A reserve full-back, Gary Andrews' only senior outing for Forest came as a substitute in the League Cup game v. Brighton at home in October 1986. He went on to appear in 43 League matches for Posh.

ANTHONY, Walter

Outside-left: 7 apps. one goal
Born: Basford, 21 November 1879. Died: 1950.
Career: Osmanton FC, Heanor Town, FOREST (August 1903), Brighton & Hove Albion (May 1905), Blackburn Rovers (February 1907), Stalybridge Celtic (season 1914-15).
A reserve left-winger, Walter Anthony made just a handful of first-team appearances for Forest. After leaving the Reds he did well at Brighton before doing even better with Blackburn, scoring 14 goals in 163 senior outings for Rovers during his seven years at Ewood Park.

ARDRON, Walter

Centre-forward: 191 apps. 124 goals
Born: Swinton-on-Dearne, 19 September 1918.
Died: 1978.
Career: Kilnhurst Colliery, LNER (Engine Department), Denaby United, Rotherham United (a part-time professional, December 1938), Denaby United (full-time professional, September 1939), Rotherham United (£100 initially, November 1941, with a further £750 being paid later), Halifax Town & Sheffield Wednesday (WW2 guest), FOREST (£10,000, July 1949). Retired in May 1955 and returned to Rotherham where he worked in a steelworks (his first week's wage packet was bigger and healthier than any he had earned as a footballer). For four seasons, 1959-63, he was trainer/physio at Doncaster Rovers and the following five years worked as a scout around Yorkshire for Carlisle United. During that time he was appointed to the post of head messenger with the National Westminster Bank (Rotherham) and he also ran his own part-time business of physiotherapy and chiropody in which he qualified whilst with Forest. He was trainer of Rawmarsh Welfare FC for three years in the 1960s and then became a travelling supporter of the Centralians team in which his two sons both played. He also ran his own youth club, first from his home and then at the Swinton Manor Youth Club.

Wally Ardron was a soccer super star of the 1940s. A dynamic centre-forward, he was able to strike fear into the heart of all opposing defences, and he found the net virtually every week, making him one of the most prolific marksmen the game has known.

After netting 94 goals in 122 League games for Rotherham (plus 129 in 149 WW2 games), he continued to cause major headaches for defenders and goalkeepers alike by adding well over 120 more to his tally (in close on 200 games) with Forest. He had topped the Third Division North scoring charts in 1948-49 (with 20 goals) when Forest manager Billy Walker swooped to bring him to the City Ground - and what a great asset he turned out to be. He responded magnificently and was instrumental in helping Forest regain their Second Division status in 1950-51 (as champions) when he topped the Third Division South's scoring charts with a club record 36 goals, having netted 25 the previous season. Many of his goals came from headers, the crosses being supplied mainly by Fred Scott. Ardron, who grabbed six hat-tricks during his days at the City Ground (five in the League, one in the FA Cup) ended his career in 1955 with 221 League goals in his locker in 305 appearances - a superb strike-record. He was top-scorer for Forest four seasons running: 1949-53.

As a teenager Ardron trained with weights. He was an extremely extra ordinary fit man and a member of the Doncaster Plant Athletics Club, competing nationally in track and field events until 1939 when his becoming known as a professional footballer disqualified him from AAA meetings.

NB - Ardron's son was born on the morning of 13 February 1947... in the afternoon he went out and scored four goals for the Millers against Carlisle United to celebrate the occasion!

* Ardron's son Keith was registered with Forest but never made the grade.

ARMSTRONG, John

Goalkeeper: 22 apps.
Born: Airdrie, Scotland 5 September 1936
Career: Calderbank FC (Lanarkshire), Bellshill FC (Glasgow), Barrow (March 1958), FOREST (November 1958), Portsmouth (February 1963), Southport (August 1967 to cs. 1971).
Goalkeeper John Armstrong, 5ft 9ins tall and weighing less than 11 stones, made 165 League appearances after leaving the City Ground. He had been brought in as initial cover for Chick Thomson but found it difficult to get into the side, especially when Peter Grummitt arrived on the scene. He made on average five first-team appearances a year, although he did have two separate spells of 11 and eight League games in a row - in early 1960 and late 1962

respectively. He later became a representative for a frozen food firm.

ARMSTRONG, John

Wing-half: 460 apps. 10 goals
Born: Willington, 4 February 1884.
Died: Tollerton, 9 November 1963
Career: Keyworth United, Keyworth Town, FOREST (August 1905), Sutton Town (1923).
Wing-half Jack Armstrong appeared in more than 530 first-team games for Forest (460 at competitive level with 432 coming in the Football League and 75 during WW1). He was given his League debut v. Everton (home) two days before Christmas, 1905 and remained a regular in the side (injuries permitting) until 1922, captaining the team from 1919, the year he and Forest won the Victory Shield. He also gained Second Division championship medals in 1907 and 1922. He actually appeared in every position for Forest except goal, although on the training ground he often took over between the posts to show what he could do. His best position was wing-half (either right or left) and he was described as being a 'light-framed player with an exceptional turn of speed and some neat skills.' He took over from Grenville Morris as Forest's leading appearance-maker in League football in 1922 but he could have played in many more games had not WW1 intervened when it did. Away from football, Armstrong ran a poultry farm in Keyworth and was regarded as one of the country's leading experts on the subject of chickens!
* Armstrong's son, Jack junior, was also registered with Forest.

ARMSTRONG, Richard Johnstone

Half-back/inside-forward: 17 apps
Born: Newburn, 31 August 1909. Died: 1969.
Career: Willington, FOREST (April 1929), Bristol City (July 1935-May 1940)
A versatile player, able to occupy both wing-half positions and also that of inside-right, Dick Armstrong did not have the greatest of starts with the Reds, making his debut in a 6-0 defeat at Stoke in March 1930. He never made more than seven League appearances in any one of his six full seasons at the City Ground but after leaving Forest he scored 19 goals in 115 League games for Bristol City.

ARMSTRONG, Steven Craig

Left-back: 31+18 apps. one goal
Born: South Shields, 23 May 1975.
Career: FOREST (trainee June 1991, professional, June 1992), Barnsley (on loan, December 1994), Bristol Rovers (on loan, two spells: January 1996 & March 1996), Gillingham (on loan, October 1996), Watford (on loan, two spells: January 1997 & March 1997), Huddersfield Town (£750,000, February 1999), Sheffield Wednesday (£100,000, February 2002).
An attacking left-back, Craig Armstrong took quite some time before gaining a place in Forest's first XI - and when

he did (in 1997-98) he earned himself a First Division championship medal. Also able to play in midfield, he was called into the England Under-21 squad in 1998 but never got into the action. He became Huddersfield's most expensive defender when he joined the Terriers in 1999.

ASHMAN, George Alan

Centre-forward: 12 apps 3 goals
Born: Rotherham, 30 May 1928.
Died: Walsall, 30 November 2002.
Career: Sheffield United (amateur during WW2), FOREST (wartime football briefly, then professional April 1946), Carlisle United (£5,500, June 1951). Retired in May 1958 (with knee problems); worked on a poultry farm and managed Penrith until February 1963, Carlisle United (manager, February 1963-May 1967), West Bromwich Albion (manager, June 1967 to May 1971), Olympiakos/Greece (coach, season 1971-72), Carlisle United (manager, August 1972-October 1975), Workington (manager, December 1975-February 1977), Manchester United (scout, season 1977-78), Walsall (manager, August 1978-February 1979), Derby County (chief scout 1979-82, then assistant-manager), Hereford United (assistant-manager 1983-87), Plymouth Argyle (scout), Notts County (scout), Mansfield Town (scout), Derby County (scout), Telford United (scout), Aston Villa (scout to 2000).
Alan Ashman, a centre-forward with plenty of dash and shooting power, failed to establish himself with Forest but after leaving the City Ground he scored almost a goal every two games for Carlisle - netting 101 in 206 in the Football League alone.
The poultry farm he worked on was owned by a future Carlisle director and when he got onto the board he asked Ashman to become United's manager. At the time the Cumbrians were bottom of the Third Division and were in fact eventually relegated. But he quickly got them promoted and in 1964-65 they won the Third Division title. Two seasons later United finished third in Division Two. His achievements had been all the more creditable as attendances at Brunton Park were so low and therefore the club was unable to buy any new players. His success attracted the attentions of WBA and he became their manager in 1967, taking over from Jimmy Hagan. At the end of his first season in charge Albion won the FA Cup; the following season they lost in the semi-finals and reached the quarter-final stage of the European Cup Winners Cup, following up in 1970 with an another Wembley appearance, this time as losing finalists in the League Cup. Unfortunately after a rather disappointing 1970-71 season Ashman lost his job, replaced by Don Howe. He then went to Greece and guided Olympiakos to runners-up spot in the League. He returned to Carlisle for a second spell and after a disappointing start he amazed everyone by taking the team into the First Division and, in fact, at one point in 1974-75 they topped the table.

Ashman resigned in the autumn of 1975 and after brief flurries with Workington and Walsall, he served as a scout and/or and assistant-manager before quitting football in 2000 through poor health. He lived in Walsall until his death at the age of 74.

ASHMORE, Richard A
Centre-half/inside-right: 12 apps. one goal
Born: Rotherham, 28 November 1892.
Career: Bristol Rovers, Barnsley, FOREST (August 1920), Doncaster Rovers (cs, 1922), Scunthorpe & Lindsey United (late 1923), Denaby United.
Dick Ashmore made a scoring League debut for Forest v. Wolves in February 1921 when he replaced Fred Parker at centre-half. He made a further nine appearances in the side that season but figured only twice in 1921-22 and he was then transferred to Doncaster, where he was an ever present in 1922-23 when they finished runners-up in the Midland League.

ASHTON, Percy
Goalkeeper: 189 apps
Born: Bolton-on-Dearne, 21 March 1909.
Died: Nottingham, 19 March 1985
Career: West Melton Excelsior FC, FOREST (August 1930), Grantham FC (season 1939-40). He did not play after WW2.
Signed as cover for Alf Dexter, Percy Ashton made his League debut for Forest as a 20 year-old v. Stoke City in a second Division game a month after joining the club. However, despite an impressive start, he had to wait three years before finally securing a regular first team place. He was a consistent goalkeeper, but always prone to the odd mistake.

ASHWORTH, Joseph Ernest
Outside-left: 3 apps
Born: Warrington, 28 January 1902.
Career: Everton (trialist, season 1924-25), FOREST (July 1925), Blackpool (August 1926).
Joe Ashworth was a reserve left-winger who failed to get a senior game with either Everton or Blackpool. He made his Forest debut against his future club (Blackpool) when he partnered the regular flank player Jack Burton in a 1-1 draw in September 1925.

BADGER, Herbert Osborne
Right-half/centre-forward: 2 apps.
Born: Islington, London, 4 October 1882.
Died Colchester, 1965.
Career: Colchester Town, Ilford, Tottenham Hotspur (November 1903), Woolwich Arsenal (September 1904), Watford (July 1906), Brentford (August 1908), FOREST (September 1909), Brentford (September 1910-May 1911).
Reserve wing-half Bert Badger's only senior outings for

Forest were against Bury and Chelsea during the second half of the 1909-10 season when he deputised firstly for Edwin Hughes and then for George Needham. An amateur throughout his career, Badger did very well in Southern League circles with Watford and Brentford.

BAILEY, Walter George
Inside-forward: 4 apps.
Born: Thame, 9 February 1890.
Died: Weymouth, 20 July 1974.
Career: Thame United, FOREST (July 1909), Oxford City (August 1911), Reading (cs. 1919), Boscombe FC (cs. 1922).
Joe Bailey was a strong-looking player who was mainly a reserve with Forest, acting as cover for Harry Lockett and Gren Morris. He scored 17 goals in 41 League games for Reading.

BAILY, Edwin Francis
Inside-forward: 76 apps. 17 goals
Born: Clapton, London, 6 August 1925.
Career: Tottenham Juniors, Finchley (on loan), Tottenham Hotspur (juniors), Chelsea (juniors), Tottenham Hotspur (part-time professional, February 1946,full professional October 1946), Port Vale (£7,000, January 1956), FOREST (£7,000, October 1956), Leyton Orient (December 1958) He returned to White Hart Lane as coach and assistant to manager Bill Nicholson (a former playing colleague) in October 1963. Later acted as scout for West Ham United and was also England's regional scout in the south.
Eddie Baily appeared in 296 League games for Spurs and in 381 first-team matches overall (including friendlies). He scored 90 goals (69 in League and Cup). Nicknamed 'The Cheeky Chappie', he made his League debut in January 1947 and became a star performer in Spurs' 'push and run' team, gaining successive Second Division and Football League championship medals in 1950 and 1951 when he partnered Les Medley on the left-flank.
A positive little player, always seeking to create openings for his colleagues, he won three England 'B' caps, appeared in nine full internationals (his debut coming in the heat of Rio de Janeiro against Spain in the 1950 World Cup finals). He also represented the Rest of the uk against Wales, played for the Football League on five occasions and in 1957 starred in the eve of Cup final encounter for England against Young England.
He was sold by Vale to Forest in 1956 because he was 'too much of an individualist'. At the City Ground he linked up well with Doug Lishman, Jim Barrett and Tommy Wilson and was always looking to get left-winger Stuart Imlach into the game with some smart passes. He scored twice on his home debut for the club in a 5-1 win over Bury and in all gave Forest a shade over two years excellent service, helping them win promotion to the First Division in 1957.

* Baily was reported missing during WW2 while serving with the Royal Scots Fusiliers. Spurs, on hearing the news, did not re-register him as a player ...until he walked into White Hart Lane to show his face.

BAINES, Stephen John

Defender: 2 apps.

Born: Newark, Notts, 23 June 1954

Career: FOREST (apprentice, June 1970, professional June 1972), Huddersfield Town (July 1975), Bradford City (March 1978), Walsall (£50,000, July 1980), Bury (on loan, December 1981), Scunthorpe United (player-coach, August 1982), Chesterfield (July 1983), Matlock Town (1987), Alfreton, Gainsborough, Burton Albion, retiring in May 1988 with an arthritic neck. He immediately took up refereeing and by 1995 had won a place on the Football League list.

Steve Baines made a total of 441 League appearances during his senior career (42 goals scored). He helped Scunthorpe gain promotion to the Third Division in 1983 and Chesterfield take the Fourth Division title in 1985. He had only two first-team outings for Forest, deputising for Sammy Chapman in successive Second Division away matches against Preston and Blackpool in April 1973.

BAIRD, Douglas Francis Hogg

Right-back: 37 apps

Born: Falkirk, 26 November 1935.

Career: Matilda FC (Glasgow), Partick Thistle, FOREST (September 1960), Plymouth Argyle (October 1963), Tavistock Town (1968).

Capped once by Scotland at Under-23 level, Doug Baird also represented the Scottish League XI as a Partick Thistle player. He deputised in four League games for Roy Patrick in his first season with Forest and after two moderate campaigns when he occupied both full-back berths, he was transferred to Plymouth (signed by manager Andy Beattie) for whom he made over 150 senior appearances, a few in the centre of the defence.

BAKER, David Henry

Centre-half: 3 apps

Born: Penzance, Cornwall 21 October 1928

Career: Brush Sports FC, FOREST (October 1949), Notts County (1950-51).

Cornishman David Baker deputised in three Third Division South games for Horace Gager during the second half of the 1949-50 season. He did not make a first-team appearance for County.

BAKER, Joseph Henry

Centre-forward: 134+1 apps. 49 goals

Born: Liverpool 17 July 1940

Career: Coltness United, Armadale Thistle (Edinburgh), Hibernian (1956), AC Torino/Italy (May 1961), Arsenal (record fee of £70,000, July 1962), FOREST (record fee

of £65,000, March 1966), Sunderland (July 1969), Hibernian (1971), Raith Rovers (1974), Albion Rovers (manager-coach).

An England international with a strong Scottish accent, Joe Baker gained eight full caps (1959-66) and six at Under-23 level. He was a sharp-shooting striker, confident, aggressive when he had to be, dashing with his head-on style, whose career brought him almost 200 goals, including 146 in 302 League matches. He was hugely popular with the Forest fans, especially the females, and was nicknamed 'The King' at the City Ground. After netting a goal every three games for the Reds, including 21 in season 1967-68, there was uproar when manager Matt Gillies sold Baker to Sunderland and soon afterwards Gillies departed too!

Baker, who continued in football until 1978, later worked in the building trade and was also mine host of a pub in Craigneuk (Lanarkshire). He is now an after dinner speaker and also a part-time coach at various youth clubs and schools in and around the Motherwell area. He suffered a heart attack in 1994, but fortunately has made a good recovery.

* Baker once kept goal against Leicester and was beaten five times! Playing for Arsenal in 1963 he took over between the posts after regular 'keeper Jack McClelland was carried off after 22 minutes with the Gunners already 2-0 down. Joe let in another five as City won 7-2. "My first and positively my last appearance in goal" said Joe afterwards.

BALL, Geoffrey Hudson

Right-back: 3 apps

Born: Nottingham, 2 November 1944

Career: Ericsson's Electronic FC, FOREST (June 1961, professional February 1963), Notts County (November 1967), Ilkeston Town (cs.1972).

Reserve full-back during his six years at the City Ground, Geoff Ball's three senior outings all came against London clubs - Arsenal and Chelsea in October 1964 and Spurs in April 1966, the first two following an injury to Joe Wilson. He went on to play in 112 League games for County.

BANHAM, Royston

Right-back/centre-half: 2 apps.

Born: Nottingham, 30 October 1936

Career: Hyson Green Boys Club, FOREST (juniors 1952, professional November 1953), Peterborough United (July 1958), Bedford Town (1962).

Reserve defender who deputised for Bob McKinlay when making his Football League debut against Leeds United (away) in October 1955.

BANKS, Frederick William

Outside-right/left & inside-forward: 76 apps. 5 goals

Born: Aston, Birmingham 9 December 1888.

Died: Nottingham, 1957

Career: Park Road, Myrtle Villa, Birmingham (August 1909), Stourbridge (briefly, 1910), Wellington Town (April 1911), FOREST (September 1911), Stalybridge Celtic (July 1914), FOREST (August 1915), Worksop Town (September 1920), Notts County (trainer, 1929-30). Fred 'Sticker' Banks made his senior debut for Forest a week after joining the club from non-League football, occupying the left-wing berth against Grimsby Town. A week later he was joined in the team by his pal Bob Firth who had moved from Birmingham to the City Ground with him. Banks settled down quickly on the left flank before losing his place to a revitalized and fit again Jack Ford. An adaptable forward, he occupied four different positions in 1912-13 but the following season he was not such a regular performer and moved off to Stalybridge, only to return to the fold in 1915, going on to appear in 111 games for Forest during the hostilities.

BANNISTER, Gary

Striker: 32+5 apps. 10 goals

Born: Warrington, 22 July 1960

Career: Coventry City (apprentice, July 1976, professional May 1978), Sheffield Wednesday (£100,000, August 1981), Queen's Park Rangers (£200,000, August 1984), Coventry City (£300,000, March 1988), West Bromwich Albion (£250,000, March 1990), Oxford United (on loan, March 1992), FOREST (free transfer, August 1992), Stoke City (free, March 1993), Hong Kong Rangers (free, summer 1994), Lincoln City (free, September 1994), Darlington (free, August 1995, later appointed player-coach & assistant-manager). He is now involved in the running of two B&B establishments in Cornwall.

An England Under-21 international striker (one cap gained) Gary Bannister had a fine career, scoring 172 goals in 517 League games for his nine English clubs. His best efforts, without doubt, came at QPR where he netted 72 times in 172 games. An asset to every team he served, his off-the-ball running, sharpness both inside and outside the penalty area always caused defenders problems. His one season with Forest saw him link up splendidly at times with Nigel Clough and Roy Keane, likewise with Ian Woan on the wing and Scot Gemmill. He retired from the game due to a serious neck injury in July 1996.

BARBOUR, Alexander

Utility: one app.

Born: Dumbarton, 7 June 1862.

Died: 29 December 1930.

Career: Dalry Primrose, Dalry Albert, Dundee, Renton (four seasons 1884-88), Bolton Wanderers (August 1888-November 1889), Renton, Accrington (1890-91), Bolton Wanderers (September 1891), Glossop (briefly), FOREST

(April-May 1893)

Mainly regarded as a centre-forward north of the border, the versatile Alex Barbour could also play on the right-wing and in emergency turned out as a centre-half. A powerful footballer who flourished at Renton where he responded in 'great fashion' to the promptings of the stars then illuminating that fine side. He was capped by Scotland v. Ireland in 1885 and helped Renton reach successive Scottish Cup finals in 1885 and 1886, gaining a winners' medal in the first. His only game for Forest was against West Bromwich Albion (in place of the injured Jack MacPherson) on the last day of the 1892-93 season. Barbour played and scored for Bolton in the Lancashire club's first-ever game in the Football League v. Derby County on 8 September 1888.

* Barbour's brother, Arthur, also played for Accrington - although several reference books have the respective players' statistics mixed up.

BARKS, Edwin

Wing-half: 73 apps. 7 goals

Born: Ilkeston, 1 September 1921. Died: 1989

Career: Heanor Town, FOREST (April 1939), Mansfield Town (January 1949 to May 1955).

Eddie Barks was one of the game's larger than life characters who simply hated the boredom of training but whose perpetual motion displays at half-back on match days belied the fact. With his broad grin, he was certainly an efficient, hard-working wing-half whose career was severely disrupted by WW2. Nevertheless he scored 12 goals in 71 games for Forest during the conflict and after leaving the City Ground in 1949 he went on to make 225 League and Cup appearances for the Stags (seven goals scored), serving under four different managers. Barks was manager Billy Walker's first signing when the ex-Aston Villa player took over the hot seat at the City Ground in 1939.

BARNETT, William Thomas

Inside-right/centre-forward: 2 apps.

Born: Sherwood, circa 1879.

Career: Beeston Rovers, FOREST (seasons: 1900-02).

Tom Barnett played twice in Forest's League side, against Stoke (home) in October 1900, replacing Jack Calvey as leader of the attack and then against Notts County (away) a year later when he deputised for Arthur Capes.

BARNSDALE, John Davison

Right-half/centre-forward: 26 apps

Born: Nottingham, 25 May 1878. Died: 1960.

Career: FOREST (seasons 1903-05)

A versatile player, able to fill in as a half-back or forward, Jack Barnsdale had one excellent spell with Forest (between April-December 1904) when he produced some fine displays in the middle of the park, playing mainly alongside Sammy Timmins.

BARNWELL, John
Wing-half/inside-forward: 192+9 apps. 25 goals
Born: High Heaton, Newcastle-upon-Tyne, 24 December 1938.
Career: Bishop Auckland (as an amateur, 1953), Arsenal (amateur, August 1955, professional, November 1956), FOREST (£30,000, March 1964), Sheffield United (April 1970). Retired in June 1971; Hereford United (coach, summer 1972, remaining at Edgar Street for 13 weeks), Peterborough United (coach 1974, then manager from May 1977-November 1978), Wolverhampton Wanderers (manager, November 1979-January 1982), Saudi Arabia (coaching in 1982-83), AEK Athens (manager-coach, August 1983 - banned from working in Greece, January 1984), Notts County (manager, June 1987-December 1988), Walsall (manager, January 1989-March 1990), Northampton Town (consultant to player-manager Phil Chard, 1992-93). Later appointed Chief Executive of the Football League Managers Association (July 1996) while also controlling team affairs at Grantham Town.

As a player, John Barnwell was a powerful, workmanlike inside-left who scored 24 goals in more than 160 games for the Gunners before having by far his best spell in the game with Forest whom he served splendidly for six years, making over 200 first-class appearances. When he retired in 1971 he had netted almost 50 goals in 327 League games and had gained England Youth and Under-23 international honours (winning one cap in the latter category) while also representing the Army during his National Service with the RASC in the 1950s. After that Barnwell developed into a very efficient manager, leading Wolves to victory in the 1980 League Cup final (over Forest) and to the FA Cup semi-finals the year before. In 1979 he almost his lost his life in a horrific car crash in which he suffered a fractured skull. He was also involved in to two huge transfers - selling Steve Daly from Wolves to Manchester City for £1.43 million and then signing Andy Gray from Aston Villa for £1.15 million in the space of a week at the start of the 1979-80 season. He was voted 'Midland Sports Personality of the Year' in 1979-80.

BARRATT, Percy Marriott
Full-back: 229 apps. 17 goals
Born: Annesley, 6 October 1898. Died: 6 July 1974
Career: Annesley St Alban's FC, FOREST (1919), Grantham Town (1930).
Percy Barratt was spotted by Forest playing local football soon after WW1. A natural full-back, sure-footed with a strong kick (in both feet), he made great strides in his first season at the City Ground. However, after losing his place to a fit-again Harry Bulling he played only 18 games during the next four years before re-establishing himself in the side during the 1924-25 campaign, going on to form an excellent partnership with Bill Thompson. He was the club's regular penalty-taker and missed only twice from the spot during his time with Forest. An injury sustained

against Grimsby Town in January 1929 eventually resulted in him quitting top-class football in 1930. His brother Fred Barratt was a fast bowler for Nottinghamshire CCC.

BARRETT, Colin
Full-back: 86+8 apps. 8 goals
Born: Stockport, 3 August 1952
Career: Cheadle Town, Manchester City (May 1970), FOREST (March 1976), Swindon Town (June 1980-April 1981).
Colin Barrett was a competent full-back whose best season with Forest came in 1977-78 when he helped the team win the First Division title and reach the League Cup final. Although he didn't play in the final at Wembley, he made up for that disappointment by playing in the winning side v. Southampton a year later. He also helped the Reds gain promotion from Division Two in 1977 and win the Anglo-Scottish Cup that same year when he netted twice in a 4-0 second leg final victory over Leyton Orient. He made 53 League appearances during his time at Maine Road.

BARRETT, James Guy
Forward: 117 apps. 69 goals
Born: West Ham, London, 5 November 1930.
Career: West Ham United (June 1946, professional February 1949), FOREST (£7,500, December 1954), Birmingham City (October 1959), West Ham United (player-manager of 'A' team, August 1960-May 1968), Millwall (coach, under Benny Fenton, 1968-70). He later became a publican at the Napier Arms, Halstead, Essex.
'Young' Jim Barrett top-scored for Forest three seasons running: 1954-57. He had football in his blood, for his father (Jim senior) had been a prominent player with West Ham before WW2. Young Jim was nurtured through the junior ranks at Upton Park, making his debut for the Hammers in February 1949, the first of 87 senior appearances for the London club (25 goals scored). He immediately showed his goalscoring prowess in a Forest shirt and in 1956-57 had his best haul in a season (30 in League and Cup) as the Reds gained promotion to the First Division. Unfortunately he did not last the pace and missed out on Forest's FA Cup triumph in 1959. He didn't settle down at all with Birmingham despite hitting four goals in 10 games.
* Jim Barrett's father ('Big Jim') spent 13 years with West Ham (1925-38) making 467 appearances and scoring 53 goals.

BARRINGTON, James
Left-back: 228 apps. one goal
Born: Lower Ince, Wigan, Lancashire 15 November 1901.
Died: 1968
Career: Wigan United (as a junior, 1918), Bradford City (professional, August 1920), Hamilton Academical (1922), Wigan Borough (1925), FOREST (£90, July 1929). Retired in May 1937.

Slightly-built full-back Jimmy Barrington had failed to make much of an impression with Bradford or indeed with Hamilton but he did score once in 59 League games for Wigan Borough. He wanted to play at a higher level and as a result wrote to Forest for a trial. He was successful and was duly signed by the club in 1929. He quickly made his mark and went on to serve the Reds for six years, making well over 200 appearances before receiving a free transfer at the end of the 1936-37 campaign. He failed to get another club and called it a day, settling in the Ruddington area, continuing to scout for Forest until the later 1950s.

BARRON, James

Goalkeeper: 180 apps.

Born: Tantobie, County Durham, 19 October 1943.

Career: Newcastle West End FC, Wolverhampton Wanderers (amateur June 1960, professional, November 1961), Chelsea (April 1965), Oxford United (March 1966), FOREST (£35,000, July 1970), Swindon Town (August 1974), Connecticut Bi-Centennials/NASL (briefly in 1977), Peterborough United (August 1977-May 1981), Mansfield Town (assistant-manager, briefly), Wolverhampton Wanderers (coach/assistant-manager, 1981-83, then coach/caretaker-manager 1988-89), Cheltenham Town (manager, November 1989-October 1990, while also running a goalkeeping school in Gloucestershire); Everton (reserve team manager & goalkeeping coach under Howard Kendall, 1991-92), Aston Villa (assistant-manager/coach 1992-93, Sheffield United (assistant-manager, 1996-98), Birmingham City (coach, November 1998, joint caretaker-manager/coach, October 2001, until appointment of Steve Bruce); Crystal Palace (assistant-manager/coach: 2002-03).

Following in his father's footsteps (he too was a goalkeeper with Blackburn Rovers and Darlington) Jim Barron junior developed into a fine custodian, making eight senior appearances for Wolves at the start of his career which eventually spanned 20 years during which time he played in a total of 416 League games. He was also an FA Youth Cup winner during his time at Molineux where he understudied Malcolm Finlayson before moving to Stamford Bridge. He didn't make much headway there but played over 150 times for Oxford and then spent eight excellent years at the City Ground, taking over between the posts from the inured Alan Hill. A safe, unspectacular 'keeper he only missed 13 League games in his four years with Forest.

* Jim's son played in goal for Cheltenham Town when he was manager of the then Vauxhall Conference club.

BARRY, Leonard James

Outside-left: 16 apps. one goal

Born: Sneinton, Nottingham, 27 October 1901.

Died: Mapperley, 17 April 1970

Career: RAF, Notts County (May 1920, professional October 1924), Leicester City (September 1927), FOREST (August 1933-May 1935).

Len Barry was initially an amateur with Notts County while completing his RAF service at Cranwell, Lincs. In fact, he was capped by England at that level v. Ireland in 1923-24. He later added five more caps to his collection (in 1928-29) when he helped set up 10 of the 20 goals scored by his country in those internationals. An old-fashioned dribbler, Barry helped Leicester finish third and then second in the First Division during the 1920s, when he featured in a star-studded forward-line along with Hugh Adcock, Ernie Hine, Arthur Chandler and Arthur Lochhead. He scored 26 goals in 214 games for the Foxes before joining Forest when almost 32 years of age. He figured only briefly in the Reds' struggling Second Division side. Barry was a very keen motorist and once contemplated being a racing driver!

BART-WILLIAMS, Christopher Gerald

Midfielder: 237+8 apps. 35 goals

Born: Freetown, Sierra Leone, 16 June 1974.

Career: Leyton Orient (trainee July 1990, professional July 1991), Sheffield Wednesday (£275,000, November 1991), FOREST (£2.5 million, July 1995), Charlton Athletic (on loan, November 2000, signed permanently on a free transfer, February 2001).

An England Under-21 international (16 caps won) Chris Bart-Williams also played in Youth and 'B' team games. He made over 40 appearances for Orient and more than 150 for the Owls before joining Forest. A hard-worker, strong tackler, with added ingredients of aggression and commitment, he was a key member of the Reds' First Division championship winning side of 1998. He was used mainly as a defensive midfielder during the latter stages of his career at the City Ground.

BARTON, Anthony Edward

Forward: 24 apps. 2 goals

Born: Sutton, Surrey, 8 April 1937.

Died: Southampton, 20 August 1993

Career: Sutton United, Fulham (juniors, June 1952, professional, May 1954), FOREST (December 1959), Portsmouth (£5,000, December 1961-May 1967, then player-coach at Fratton Park); Aston Villa (coach and assistant-manager to Ron Saunders, then manager, February 1982-May 1984), Northampton Town (manager, July 1984-April 1985), Southampton (assistant-manager to Chris Nicholl, September 1985-May 1986), Portsmouth (assistant-manager to Alan Ball, then caretaker-manager February-June 1991 until the appointment of Jim Smith). Later acted as a scout for several clubs including Southampton and Bournemouth.

Tony Barton won one England schoolboy and five youth caps as a teenager. One of a family of nine, he never really settled down at the City Ground, having his best spell towards the end of the 1959-60 season when he played in

13 League games, mainly on the right-wing. He was in charge of Aston Villa when they triumphed in the 1982 European Cup Final (v. Bayern Munich) and soon afterwards saw them lift the Super Cup. He died of a heart attack at the age of 56.

BAXTER, James Curran

Left-half/inside-left: 49+1 apps. 3 goals

Born: Hill of Beath, Fife, Scotland, 29 September 1939. Died: Glasgow, 14 April 2001.

Career: Crossgates Primrose FC, Raith Rovers (£200, April 1957), Glasgow Rangers (£27,000, June 1960), Sunderland (£72,500, May 1965), FOREST (£105,000, December 1967), Glasgow Rangers (May 1969). Retired in November 1970.

Brilliant Scottish international wing-half/midfielder (34 full caps gained) 'Slim Jim' Baxter also played for his country's Under-23 side, represented the Scottish League XI and played for the FIFA & Europe XI (v. England) in the FA Centenary match at Wembley in 1963. Blessed with boundless talent, Baxter was unquestionably one of the greatest ball players in Scottish football history. A law unto himself, he stroked the ball around the pitch to devastating effect, always composed and reading the game marvellously. Baxter was certainly a one-off original and as a Rangers player was a European Cup Winners Cup finalist in 1961, won three Scottish League championship medals (1961-63-64), gained three Scottish Cup winners' medals (1962-64 inclusive), and collected four Scottish League Cup trophies during the early 1960s.

During his career, north and south of the border, 'Slim Jim' appeared in well over 400 competitive games (98 for Sunderland). Unfortunately after hanging up his boots and becoming a licensee his life was ruined by years of drinking and gambling which eventually led to his demise at the age of 61.

* Baxter's cousin was the Scottish international full-back Willie Cunningham who played Preston North End (v. WBA) in the 1954 FA Cup final.

BAXTER, William Amelius

Centre-half: 18 apps

Born: Nottingham, 6 September 1917. Died: 1992.

Career: Berridge Road Institute, FOREST (December 1936), Notts County (October 1946), Grantham Town (May 1954).

Bill Baxter, whose senior debut for Forest came against Watford in the 3rd round of the FA Cup in January 1946, made 133 appearances for the Reds during WW2 (from November 1942 onwards) and after leaving the City Ground in 1946, he played in 140 League games for County. He was a tough-tackling defender, strong in the air, who had Bob Davies, Tom Graham and George Pritty to contend with for the pivotal position.

BEASANT, David John

Goalkeeper: 153+1 apps.

Born: Willesden, 20 March 1959

Career: Edgware Town (1976), Wimbledon (£1,000, August 1979), Newcastle United (£800,000, June 1988), Chelsea (£275,000, January 1989), Grimsby Town (on loan, October 1992), Wolverhampton Wanderers (on loan, January 1993), Southampton (£300,000, November 1993), FOREST (free transfer, August 1997), Portsmouth (free, August 2001), Tottenham Hotspur (free, November 2001), Portsmouth (January 2002), Bradford City (Free, September 2002) Wigan Athletic (October 2002), Brighton & Hove Albion (January 2003), Fulham (August 2003).

England international (two full caps gained, plus seven at 'B' team level) Dave Beasant was the star of Wimbledon's 1988 FA Cup final victory when he saved John Aldridge's penalty-kick. He helped the Dons win the Fourth Division Championship in 1983 and gain promotion (as runners-up) from Division Three a year later. Then, in 1986, he was in fine form when the London club climbed into the top-flight (finishing 3rd in the table). In 1990 he was a Full Members Cup winner with Chelsea and in 1998 helped Forest clinch the First Division title. At 6ft 4ins tall and 14st 3lbs in weight, Beasant has precisely the right build for a goalkeeper and has done superbly well during his Football League career, which is now 24 years old. He reached the double personal milestone of 850 senior and 750 League appearances during the 2001-02 season. He became Wigan's and then Brighton's oldest player and in his four years with Forest he starred in over 150 first-class matches, having his best campaign in 2000-01 when he missed only one League fixture. He is the oldest player to appear for Forest (42 years, 47 days v. Tranmere, May 2001).

BEAUMONT, Leonard

Outside-right/left: 36 apps. 3 goals

Born: Huddersfield, 4 January 1915.

Died: Nottingham, 23 July 2002.

Career: Huddersfield Town (amateur November 1931, professional, August 1932), Portsmouth (July 1936), FOREST (July 1938); in WW2 he guested for Mansfield Town (1939-42), Portsmouth & Lincoln City (1944-45); then with Peterborough United (season 1946-47).

During WW2 (from January 1942 onwards) Len Beaumont appeared in more than 90 games for Forest and scored 32 goals. Prior to that he had been a reserve right-winger with Huddersfield (12 appearances) and Pompey (six games). It was unfortunate that the hostilities came when they did, for he looked impressive during the last pre-war campaign when he made 34 League appearances. After leaving football Beaumont had a spell as chief scorer for Nottinghamshire CCC, charting their progress during the glory years of the 1980s. At the time of his death he was the second oldest surviving Pompey player.

BECK, Mikkel Venge
Striker: 5 apps. one goal
Born: Aarhus, Denmark, 12 May 1973
Career: B1909 FC (Denmark), Kolding FC (Denmark), Fortuna Cologne (Germany), Middlesbrough (free transfer, September 1996), Derby County (£500,000, March 1999), FOREST (on loan, November-December 1999), Queen's Park Rangers (on loan, February-March 2000), Aalborg BK/Denmark (on loan, April-May 2000), OSC Lille/France (July 2000)
A Danish international striker (22 caps gained) Mikkel Beck (6ft 2ins tall, 12st 9lbs in weight) drew up a fine scoring record with Middlesbrough (32 goals in 105 games). Sadly he failed to make much of an impression at Derby and his only goal for Forest during his loan spell at the City Ground, came in a 2-0 home win over Portsmouth on 24 November 1999 after being recruited following the departure of Ian Wright. He was surprisingly recalled to the Danish national team for the Euro 2000 finals after previously falling from grace after a series of poor performances.

BEDFORD, Henry Alfred
Utility forward: 20 apps. 9 goals
Born: Calow near Chesterfield, 15 October 1899.
Died: Derby, 24 June 1976
Career: Grassmoor Ivanhoe FC (Chesterfield), FOREST (October 1918), Blackpool (£1,500, March 1921), Derby County (£3,000, September 1925), Newcastle United (£4,000, December 1930), Sunderland (£3,000, January 1932), Bradford Park Avenue (May 1932), Chesterfield (June 1933), Heanor Town (player-trainer, August 1934), Newcastle United (trainer, October 1937), Derby County (masseur, May 1938), Belper Town (manager, January 1954), Heanor Town (manager, March 1955-March 1956). Bedford was also a licensee in Derby and for 23 years was employed by the Rolls Royce fire service.
Able to play at inside-right, centre-forward (where he made his name) or inside-left, Harry Bedford, who was recommended to Forest by the club's former goalkeeper Sam Hardy, was a great dribbler, an ideal forager and a tremendous marksman with a strong right-foot shot. An ex-miner, he gained two full England caps during an excellent career that saw him score well over 300 goals in 486 League appearances over a period of 15 years, actually netting his 300th in September 1933. Standing 5ft 9ins tall and weighing 12st 4lbs, he was Derby's leading marksman five seasons running, averaging 30 goals per campaign. Highly under-rated in an era when there was a galaxy of noted strikers, he also represented the Football League, celebrating the occasion with four goals against the Irish League in 1924.

BELL, John James
Centre-forward/inside-left: 59 apps. 7 goals
Born: Basford, Notts, 2 March 1891.
Career: Sherwood Foresters, St Bartholomew's FC, Christchurch FC, FOREST (on trial, August-September 1909), Sutton Town, Royal Engineers, Reading (1911-12), Plymouth Argyle (August 1912), FOREST (December 1913), South Shields (August 1919), Merthyr Town (October 1919), Grimsby Town (March 1921), FOREST (April 1921), Loughborough Corinthians (August 1921), Rotherham County (February 1922), Jack Bell was 18 when he had a trial with Forest. It was another four years before he returned to the club and, although his progress was disrupted by WW1, he made over 100 first-team appearances for the Reds (with almost 50 of them coming during the hostilities). He also played in several representative matches for the Army. A player who preferred the cultured approach, Bell would always try to deliver a studied pass rather than give the ball the thoughtless big boot downfield. He helped Plymouth win the Southern League title in 1913.

BELL, Matthew
Full-back: 88 apps. one goal
Born: West Hartlepool, 8 July 1897.
Died: Hull, 27 January, 1962
Career: Army football (1916-18), West Hartlepool, Hull City (August 1919), FOREST (August 1931). Retired May 1934; Heracles FC/Holland (manager/coach to WW2). Returned to live in Hull in 1939.
Matt 'Ginger' Bell appeared in more than 400 League and Cup games for Hull City (many of them as captain) before joining Forest at the age of 35. He was a prominent member of the celebrated Tigers' defence which also featured goalkeeper Billy Mercer and his fellow full-back Jock Gibson. His tackling was aptly said to be as fiery as his ginger hair. He had other defensive requirements too, being strong in the air with exceptional positional sense. A loyal clubman to Hull, he also gave Forest excellent service for three years. Bell later ran a tobacconist's shop in the Anlaby district of Hull.

BELTON, John
Right-half/centre-forward: 347 apps. 17 goals
Born: Loughborough, 1 May 1895.
Died: Barrow on Sour, 15 January 1952.
Career: Quorn Emmanuel FC, Loughborough Corinthians, FOREST (on trial, September 1914, signed as a professional October 1914), Loughborough Corinthians (September 1928-May 1930)
Jackie Belton was a prolific goalscorer with Loughborough Corinthians before joining Forest as a trialist in 1914. He did well under supervision, was soon taken on full-time, but before he could show what he was made of WW1 broke out. Belton returned to the club in 1919 and remained a regular in the side until 1927-28, producing

many fine performances both at home and away as he powered on towards the milestone of 350 appearances while also helping the Reds win the Second Division title in 1922. One can only imagine what sort of record he would have accumulated had the war not intervened. A fine footballer.

BENALI, Francis Vincent
Full-back: 15 apps.
Born: Southampton, 30 December 1968
Career: Southampton (trainee, June 1985, professional November 1987), FOREST (on loan, January-April 2001). With Forest still in with a chance of making the play-offs experienced defender Francis Benali was recruited by manager David Platt to fill the troublesome left-back position - and he did an excellent job before returning to the St Mary's Stadium. When he arrived at the City Ground Benali, a former England schoolboy international had already amassed well over 350 senior appearances for Saints before losing his place to Wayne Bridge.

BENBOW, James A C
Inside-right: 2 apps
Career: Oswestry United (1895), FOREST (seasons 1897-99). Jim Benbow was a reserve forward with Forest for two seasons. He made his League debut in a 3-1 home win over Bury in April 1898 when he replaced Sammy Richards.

BENBOW, Leonard
Centre-forward: 62 apps. 20 goals
Career: Burslem Port Vale (briefly), Oswestry United, Shrewsbury Town, FOREST (1897), Stoke (season 1900-01), Northampton Town (1901-06).
A determined centre-forward, quick and alert, Len Benbow spent three seasons with Forest, amassing a very useful scoring record and gaining an FA Cup winners medal in 1898 (v. Derby County). He made his debut for the Reds v. Sheffield United (home) in September 1897 and hit his first goal in a 3-1 local derby win over neighbours Notts County the following month. He later had over 20 outings with Stoke.

BENNETT, Alfred
Goalkeeper: 88 apps
Born: Clowne, Derbyshire, 13 November 1898.
Career: Clowne Rising Star FC, FOREST (August 1919), Port Vale (May 1927-May 1929).
Alf Bennett (6ft tall, 12st 10lbs in weight) spent eight years with Forest. He made his debut (in place of Joshua Johnson) in a 0-0 draw with Barnsley in December 1920, but the following season had Sam Hardy as his challenger for a first-team place. The loyal Bennett hung in there and finally gained a regular slot in the side during the 1924-25 campaign. He made his debut for Vale against his former club, Forest, in a 2-2 draw on 27 August 1927 and remained first choice for the first of his two seasons with the Valiants.

BETTS, Arthur R
Outside-right: 68 apps. 10 goals
Born: Huthwaite, 17 May 1916.
Career: Huthwaite CWS, FOREST (July 1935 to May 1939).
Arthur Betts bided his time at Forest before taking over on the right flank during the last third of the 1936-37 season, having earlier made his League debut in a 2-1 defeat at Bradford City in the December as a replacement for John Getty. Quick and lively, he held his position throughout the following campaign and was first choice during the first half of 1938-39 when he also played a few games as an inside-forward.

BEVERIDGE, Robert
Centre-forward: 33 apps. 7 goals
Born: Polmadie, Glasgow, circa 1872.
Died: 11 October 1901
Career: Maryhill Harp, Third Lanark, FOREST (July 1899), Everton (September 1900 until his sudden death). Craggy centre-forward Bob Beveridge had done well north of the border before Forest recruited him to take over from Len Benbow as leader of the attack. He did a good job playing in between Jack Calvey and Gren Morris, but was then whisked away by Everton. He died suddenly at the age of 29 after just a handful of outings for the Merseysiders.

BIGGINS, James
Defender: one app.
Born: Nottingham, 6 June 1985
Career: FOREST (junior, June 2001, professional June 2003).
Jim Biggins developed steadily through the youth and second teams at The City Ground before making his first team debut in the Coca-Cola Cup in 2003.

BIRCH, William
Outside-right or left: 14 apps. 2 goals
Born: Rainford near St Helens 1887.
Died: Eccleston, 14 June 1968
Career: Blackpool (July 1907), FOREST (February 1908), Reading (August 1909), Eccles Borough (August 1910), Grimsby Town (July 1912), Gainsborough Trinity (May 1914), FOREST (WW1 guest), Rotherham County (1918-19).
Bill Birch (5ft 8ins tall) was a speedy right or left-winger, an adroit dribbler with the ability to centre accurately. Several big-named clubs watched him as a Blackpool player and it was Forest who won the race, but he never really fitted in with the Reds and after leaving the club he made 35 appearances for Grimsby. Returning to the City Ground as a guest in WW1, Birch duly helped Forest win the Victory Shield v. Everton in 1919.

BIRTLES, Garry
Inside/centre-forward: 278+5 apps 96 goals
Born: Nottingham, 27 July 1956.
Career: Long Eaton Rovers, Long Eaton United (1974), FOREST (£30,000, December 1976), Manchester United (£1.25 million, October 1980), FOREST (£275,000, September 1982), Notts County (free transfer, June 1987), Grimsby Town (free, July 1989 to May 1992), Ilkeston Town (free, August 1992), Gresley Rovers (assistant-manager to Paul Futcher, season 1993-94, then manager, season 1994-95).
Centre-forward Garry Birtles netted Forest's first-ever goal in the European Cup competition, obliging against Liverpool (home) in September 1978.
In no time at all - after taking over from the departed Peter Withe - he rose from non-League football to a quality marksman and tormented many a defence with his surging runs and capital finishing. Fast and dangerous, he gave Forest splendid service and during his time at the City Ground (first time round) gained three full England caps (his debut was as a sub against the reigning World champions Argentina in May 1980), plus two at Under-21 and one at 'B' team levels. He also won two European Cup winners medals (1979 & 1980), a League Cup winners medal in 1979 (when he netted twice v. Southampton), a runners-up prize in the same competition v. Wolves (1980) and collected a Super Cup winners medal in 1980 (v. Barcelona). He formed a tremendous partnership in attack with Tony Woodcock, then Trevor Francis and later with Ian Wallace. He was also voted the Midland Sports Writer's 'Young Player of the Year' for season 1978-79. After leaving Forest for Manchester United he took some time to settle in at Old Trafford, failing to score in his first 29 games for the club. He finally broke his duck in an FA Cup 3rd round replay v. Brighton. He had arrived on the verge of greatness, but was undoubtedly grateful and relieved to get away from two years of misery and under achievement with United. Later in his career he played as a defensive midfielder and then as a central defender for the Mariners. He later became a football pundit for local radio in the Nottingham area.

BLACK, Kingsley Terence
Winger/striker: 128 apps. 20 goals
Born: Luton, 22 June 1968
Career: Luton Town (juniors June 1982, professional July 1986), FOREST (£1.5 million, September 1991), Sheffield United (on loan, March 1995), Millwall (on loan, September 1995), Grimsby Town (£25,000, July 1996), Lincoln City (on loan, October 2000, signed on a free transfer, July 2001; retired October 2002).
Kingsley Black scored 30 goals in 156 outings for Luton before his big money transfer to Forest in 1991. A former England Schoolboy international, he went on to gain 30 full caps for Northern Ireland as well earning others at 'B' and Under-21 levels, and was a League Cup winner with

Luton in 1988. After helping Forest win the Zenith Data Systems Cup in 1992 but lose the League Cup final (to Manchester United) he was instrumental when promotion to the Premiership was gained in 1994 and four years later was a Second Division play-off winner with Grimsby.
A player with excellent close control, intricate passing skills and a strong shot (when allowed to let fly) Black's first three seasons with Forest were excellent but then he lost his way somewhat in 1994-95 and after loan spells at Bramall Lane and the Den he was transferred to Grimsby Town in readiness for the 1996-97 campaign. He passed the milestone of 500 senior appearances during 2002.

BLACKMAN, Ronald Henry
Centre-forward: 11 apps 3 goals
Born: Cosham near Portsmouth, 2 April 1925.
Career: Gosport Borough, Reading (March 1947), FOREST (£8,000, June 1954), Ipswich Town (July 1955-May 1958), Tonbridge (season 1958-59).
Ronnie Blackman had scored 167 goals in 240 competitive games for Reading before moving to Forest in the summer of 1954. He is still the most prolific scorer in the Berkshire club's history and had the honour of netting a hat-trick on his League debut v. Leyton Orient in February 1949, six months before he signed full-time forms at the age of 24. He netted 39 times in 1951-52 and cracked in 158 League goals in total, both Reading records. Although he had a powerful shot in both feet, his main asset was his lethal heading ability and a fair proportion of his goals came from exquisitely timed or well-directed headers. He was a tough player who feared no-one, yet he was a gentleman both on and off the field. Blackman didn't want to leave Reading but had to for financial reasons. He was never the same player at the City Ground, admitting that he hadn't settled in Nottingham, and after three seasons with Ipswich Town he rounded off his career with Tonbridge before taking employment in a post office. He now lives in quiet retirement in Fareham, Hants.

BLAGG, Edward Arthur
Centre-half: 61 apps.
Born: Shireoaks, 9 February 1918.
Died: Sheffield, 28 October 1976.
Career: Wood End FC, FOREST (February 1938), Southport (November 1948), Worksup Town (cs.1949)
Ted Blagg was a solid and more than useful centre-half who had to wait until September 1946 before making his League debut for Forest. During WW2, Blagg had appeared in 116 Regional League and Cup matches for the club (from August 1942). He also played one first class match for Nottinghamshire in 1948

BLAKE, Robert James
Midfielder/striker: 12 apps. one goal
Born: Middlesbrough, 4 March 1976
Career: Darlington (trainee, June 1992, professional July 1994), Bradford City (£300,000, March 1997), FOREST (on loan, August-September 2000), Burnley (£1 million, January 2002).
Robbie Blake netted 23 goals for Darlington and 29 for Bradford City before joining Forest on loan at the start of the 2000-01 season. Able to play as a right-sided midfielder or an out-and-out attacker, he did well at the City Ground before returning to the Bantams.

BLATHERWICK, Stephen Scott
Defender: 15 apps.
Born: Hucknall, Notts 20 September 1973.
Career: Notts County (YTS), FOREST (professional, August 1992), Wycombe Wanderers (on loan, February 1994), Hereford United (on loan, September 1995), Reading (on loan, March 1997), Burnley (£150,000, July 1997), Chesterfield (on loan, September 1998, signed for £50,000, December 1998).
A 6ft 1in, 14st 6lbs central defender, Steve Blatherwick had another Steve (Chettle) to contest the pivotal position with at Forest. Chettle won the race for first-team occupancy and after three separate loan spells with lower division clubs, Blatherwick was transferred to Burnley after spending five years at the City Ground, averaging just three outings per campaign.

BLYTHE, J R
Centre-forward: one app.
Born: circa 1891
Career: FOREST (season 1911-12).
Centre-forward, Blythe's only senior game for Forest was against Chelsea (at Stamford Bridge) in a League match on 14 October 1911 when he deputised for Frank Saunders in a 2-0 defeat.

BOARDMAN, Craig George
Central-defender: 0+1 app.
Born: Barnsley, 30 November 1970
Career: FOREST (YTS, June 1987, professional May 1989), Peterborough United (August 1993), Halifax Town (November 1993), Scarborough (August 1995, Stalybridge Celtic (May 1996).
A six-foot strong defender, son of a former Barnsley player (George), Craig Boardman was seemingly a permanent reserve with Forest before having spells with Posh, Halifax and then Scarborough. His time at the latter club was blighted by injury problems and a three-month absence, due to a hernia operation, severely restricted his opportunities.

BOHINEN, Lars
Midfielder: 69+6 apps. 10 goals
Born: Vadso, Norway, 8 September 1969
Career: Valerenga, FC Viking/Stavanger (Norway), Young Boys/Berne (Switzerland), FOREST (£450,000, November 1993), Blackburn Rovers (£700,000, October 1995), Derby County (£1.45 million, March 1998), FC Lyngby/Denmark (January 2001), Farum BK (January 2002).
At 5ft 11ins tall and 12st 6lbs in weight, Lars Bohinen was a strong, hard-working midfielder, able to occupy any position across the centre area of the park. He was already an established Norwegian international when he joined Forest in 1993 and went on to gain a total of 30 full caps for his country. As well as being a creative player, he could also score goals and he had an excellent first two seasons at the City Ground, helping Forest win a place in the Premiership in 1994, before the arrival of Chris Bart-Williams saw him depart to Ewood Park After 66 games for Rovers, he then had a horrid 1999-2000 season with Derby (out for three months with a damaged knee) before finally returning to Scandinavia with over 200 senior appearances under his belt in English soccer.

BONALAIR, Thierry
Midfielder: 65+15 apps. 4 goals
Born: Paris, France, 14 June 1966
Career: FC Amiens, FC Nantes, AJ Auxerre, Lille OSC (all in France), Neuchatel Xamax (Switzerland), FOREST (free transfer, July 1997). FC Zunich (July 2000).
Experienced midfielder Thierry Bonalair had already made 265 League appearances in French football and a further 68 in Switzerland before joining Forest on a free transfer. Capped by his country at Under-21 level, he helped Forest win the First Division title in his first season at the City Ground, producing some useful performances in a variety positions. After shaking off an Achilles injury he had a difficult first campaign in the Premiership but his work-rate and effort could not be faulted.

BOOT, Leonard George William
Goalkeeper: 2 apps
Born: West Bromwich, 4 November 1899.
Died: West Bromwich 23 November, 1937
Career: York City (April 1923), Huddersfield Town (October 1923), Fulham (August 1925), Bradford City (July 1926), FOREST (November 1927), Caernarvon Town (August 1928) Worcester City (September 1928).
Len Boot was a reserve goalkeeper at every club he served. He made only 28 League appearances during his professional career, 10 with Huddersfield whom he helped win successive League championships in the 1920s, nine with Fulham and seven with Bradford. He made his debut for Forest in a 5-0 defeat at Preston in March 1928 and then conceded two more goals in his next game v. Grimsby Town. His early death was the result of a motorcycle accident.

BOOTH, Colin
Inside-forward: 99 apps. 43 goals
Born: Manchester, 30 December 1934
Career: Wolverhampton Wanderers (juniors, 1949, professional January 1952), FOREST (October 1959), Doncaster Rovers (August 1962), Oxford United (July 1964 to May 1966).
A player with film-star looks, Colin Booth was a fine marksman who scored a total of 145 goals in 301 League games during his senior career that spanned 14 years. He gained one England Under-23 cap during his stay at Molineux where he battled hard to gain regular first-team football owing to the presence of star players like Peter Broadbent, Dennis Wilshaw, Roy Swinbourne and Ted Farmer. At Forest he came into a Cup winning side and scored eight goals in 24 League games in his first season when he played very well alongside centre-forward Tom Wilson, and then in the next two campaigns (1960-62) he did even better, netting more than a goal every two games when linking up with Geoff Vowden and Johnny Quigley and benefiting immensely from the wing-play of Dick le Flem and Trevor Hockey. He moved on following the arrival of Colin Addison.

BOPP, Eugene
Midfielder: 33+17 apps. 6 goals
Born: Kiev, Ukraine, 5 September 1983.
Career: FOREST (YTS, June 1999, professional September 2000).
Widely regarded as one of the brightest midfield talents to emerge from Forest's successful academy, Eugene Bopp made a positive start to his career in League football, making 19 appearances in the First Division in 2001-02, but his 2002-03 campaign was disrupted by injury.

BOWDEN, Oswald
Inside-forward: 14 apps. 3 goals
Born: Byker, Newcastle upon Tyne, 7 September 1912.
Died: Newcastle upon Tyne, 20 May 1977
Career: Newcastle United Swifts, Newcastle United (amateur 1929), Derby County (May 1930), Nottingham Forest (June 1935), Brighton & Hove Albion (June 1937), Southampton (June 1938 to September 1939). Did not play after WW2.
Ossie Bowden spent most of his career playing reserve team football. His best spell came at Forest although WW2 did disrupt his stay at the Dell. He made his debut for Forest in September 1935 in a 6-0 defeat at Fulham, having earlier appeared in just ten games for the Rams.

BOWERY, Bertram Nathanial
Forward: 5 apps. 2 goals
Born: St Kitts West Indies 29 October 1954
Career: Ilkeston Town, Worksop Town, FOREST (January 1975), Lincoln City (on loan, February-March 1976), Boston Minutemen/USA (April-August 1976),

Team Hawaii/USA (April-June 1977)
Bert Bowery was handed a belated Christmas present by Forest boss Brian Clough - and he certainly made the most of it, scoring twice on his Football League debut in a 4-1 win at Blackburn on 27 December 1975. After three more League appearances - and an outing as a sub in the 1977 Anglo-Scottish Cup final win over Leyton Orient - he failed to consolidate himself in the squad and after two separate spells in the USA, was released after two-and-a-half years with the club. A giant striker, he was loaned out to Lincoln (with Tony Woodcock) and scored on his debut for the Imps in a 6-0 win over Southport. He has remained in the Nottingham area and featured for Arnold Town Veterans in the mid-1990s.

BOWLES, Stanley
Inside-forward: 23 apps. 2 goals
Born: Manchester, 24 December 1948.
Career: Manchester City (apprentice June 1965, professional January 1967), Bury (on loan, July 1970), Crewe Alexandra (September 1970), Carlisle United (October 1971), Queen's Park Rangers (September 1972), FOREST (£225,000, December 1979), Leyton Orient (July 1980), Brentford (October 1981 to May 1984). Later returned to Griffin Park as a part-time coach (mid-1990s).
A Very skilful inside-forward/striker who gained five full England caps and also represented the Football League, Stan Bowles had already scored well over 100 goals in almost 400 senior games before he joined Forest in 1979. He never really adapted to life at the City Ground and although he showed plenty of class - as always - he chose to leave the club after just seven months, having gained a European Super Cup winners medal in the process. When he quit top-class football in 1984, Bowles boasted a proud record of 127 goals in 507 matches in League competition. Hot-headed at times he always gave 100 percent effort out on the park and at one point was regarded as one of the finest footballers in the country.

BOWYER, Ian
Midfielder: 539+23 apps. 97 goals
Born: Little Sutton, Cheshire, 6 June 1951
Career: Manchester City (apprentice, June 1966, professional August 1968), Leyton Orient (£25,000, June 1971), FOREST (£40,000, October 1973), Sunderland (£50,000, January 1981), FOREST (£50,000, January 1982), Hereford United (free transfer, July 1987, then player-manager from October 1987, to May 1990), Cheltenham Town (coach, February 1991), Plymouth Argyle (assistant-manager to Peter Shilton, 1994-95), Rotherham United (coach, September 1996), Birmingham City (coach, under manager Trevor Francis, 1997-2001), FOREST (coach, July 2002).
Ian Bowyer was a workaholic in the engine-room, a grafter to the last whose playing career lasted for 23 years during

which time he amassed 780 club appearances and scored 139 goals. He helped Forest win the First Division title and the League Cup in 1978, the European Cup twice in 1979 and 1980 and finish runners-up in the League Cup in 1980 (v. Wolves) as well as toasting success in the Anglo-Scottish Cup final and gaining promotion from Division Two in 1977, having earlier collected his first League Cup winners' prize with Manchester City in 1970. Bowyer's son was the cause of him leaving Hereford - he refused to sign him as a professional so that they could obtain a fee for him when he moved to Forest in 1990. Hereford had not achieved a great deal when he was in charge, survival being the name of the game.

* On 21 April 1990 Bowyer made a little bit of soccer history when he played in the same Hereford side as his son, Ian, the first time this had happened at League level since 1951 when the Herds, father Alec and his son David, played for Stockport County.

BOYMAN, Walter William Richard
Centre-forward/inside-left: 13 apps. 3 goals
Born: Richmond-on-Thames, Surrey 10 August 1891. Died: 1970.
Career: Cradley Heath (1915), Aston Villa (August 1919), FOREST (October 1921), Stourbridge (January 1923), Kidderminster Harriers (August 1924).
After a bright start to his Football League career, Dick Boyman, who scored a hat-trick in his second game for Villa versus Middlesbrough, had the ill-luck to miss the 1920 FA Cup final. He was injured frequently during his playing days and never really looked the part with Forest although he did help the team win the Second Division title in 1922.

BRADSHAW, Thomas Dickinson
Winger/inside-forward: 21 apps.
Born: Humbleton, Lancashire 15 March 1879.
Career: Lostock Hall, Preston North End (April 1896), Blackpool (December 1896), Sunderland (May 1897), FOREST (January 1898), Leicester Fosse (March 1899), New Brighton Tower (July 1900), Swindon Town (July 1901), Reading (October 1901), Preston North End (August 1902), Wellingborough (1903), Southport Central (1904), Accrington Stanley (late 1904), Leicester Fosse (October 1905), Glossop (May 1907-May 1908).
One of soccer's great wanderers, Tom Bradshaw, 6ft 2ins tall and 14st in weight, travelled all over the country but surprisingly during his lengthy career he amassed just over 100 League appearances (43 of them with Leicester). At times he tended to lose concentration and his temperament was always suspect. He was suspended by Glossop (for whom he never played a competitive game) when criminally charged and found guilty of wife-beating in 1908. He made his Forest debut against Stoke a week or so after arriving at the club from Sunderland and his last appearance came against Burnley four days before he left.

Bradshaw was also a cricket professional with Preston CC and a coach at Harrow School.

BRENNAN, James Gerald
Left-back/left-wing back: 131+6 apps. one goal
Born: Toronto, Canada, 8 May 1977
Career: Sora Lazio FC (Canada), Bristol City (October 1994), FOREST (£1.5 million, October 1999), Huddersfield Town (on loan, March 2001), Norwich City (July 2003). Norwich City (December 2003).
After more than 60 first-team games for Bristol City, Canadian full and Under-21 international and 2000 Gold Cup winner Jim Brennan joined Forest. He had a useful first season at The City Ground but then lost his form before returning from a loan spell with Huddersfield Town to play exceedingly well during the 2001-02 campaign when he hardly missed as match.

BRENTNALL, Arthur Arnold Harrison
Right-back: 2 apps.
Born: Basford, Nottinghamshire, 1875
Career: FOREST (August 1899 to April 1901).
A full-back who had two League outings for Forest, both in April 1900, deputising for Teddy Peers. He made his debut in a 2-0 defeat by Manchester City.

BRIDGETT, Raymond Alwyn
Full-back: 2+2 apps
Born: Walsall, 5 April 1947
Career: FOREST (juniors July 1962, professional May 1964 to April 1970).
reserve full-back Ray Bridgett spent eight years at the City Ground and made the first of his four League appearances for Forest as a substitute against Southampton at the Dell in September 1967. His last came at Burnley in February 1970. He was a committed second XI player.

BRIGHAM, Harry
Right-back: 39 apps. 2 goals
Born: Selby, Yorkshire, 19 November 1914. Died: 1978
Career: Frickley Colliery FC, Stoke City (May 1936), FOREST (November 1946), York City (July 1948-May 1950).
A strong-tackling full-back, Harry Brigham made over 100 League appearances for Stoke City before joining Forest 12 games into the first peacetime season after WW2 when injury sidelined Geoff Thomas. Injuries then affected Brigham's progress the following campaign and after being replaced by a fit-again Thomas, he moved to York City for whom he played 60 senior matches in two seasons.

BRINDLEY, John Charles
Right-back: 8+8 apps. one goal
Born: Nottingham, 29 January 1947.
Career: FOREST (apprentice, June 1962, professional

February 1964), Notts County (May 1970), Gillingham (July 1976 to May 1977), Ilkeston Town (manager from cs.1994).

Bill Brindley - an England Schoolboy & Youth international - did tremendously well with Notts County after leaving the City Ground where he had struggled to gain a first-team place owing to the form displayed by Joe Wilson and then Peter Hindley. In fact, he appeared in 223 League games for the Magpies before moving to Gillingham.

He now works as a sales manager for a cleaning company.

BRODIE, John Charles

Inside-right: 16 apps. 10 goals
Born: Crosshouse near Kilmarnock, circa 1868. Died: 1901.
Career: Hurlford, Kilmarnock, Burnley (season 1890-91), Kilmarnock, Third Lanark, Kilmarnock, FOREST (September 1893), Kilmarnock (April 1894), Kilmarnock Athletic. Retired through ill-health in 1899.

Jock Brodie made a great start to his Forest career, scoring on his League debut against Darwen in December 1893. He netted four more goals before the end of that season (plus another three in the United Counties League). But then he lost his place in the front-line to Tommy Rose and quickly returned to Scotland, joining Kilmarnock for a fourth time.

BROMAGE, Enos

Outside-left: one app
Born: Mickleover, Derbyshire, 22 October 1898.
Died: Derby, 20 April 1978
Career: Stapleton Town, Sheffield United (1922), Derby County (August 1923), Gillingham (August 1927), West Bromwich Albion (March 1928), FOREST (January 1929), Chester (May 1930), Wellington Town (season 1931-32). Retired through injury.

Despite his height of 5ft 6ins, Enos Bromage was a sturdy left-winger who travelled around quite a bit, his best spell coming with Derby (four seasons). His only game for Forest was against his former club, WBA, in October 1929.

BROUGHTON, Matthew

Outside-right: 28 apps. 5 goals
Born: Grantham, 8 October 1880.
Died: Grantham, 23 January 1957
Career: Grantham, FOREST (September 1901), Grantham (May 1903), Notts County (October 1904), Watford (November 1904), Grantham (1907).

Matt Broughton, fast and direct, made his League debut for Forest against Wolves in December 1901, taking over on the right-wing from Fred Forman. He retained his place in the team until the end of that season but then found it difficult to stay in the side with a fit again Forman and Ross Fielding also contesting the same position.

BROWN, Albert Richard

Outside-right/left: 21 apps. 2 goals
Born: Pegswood, 14 February 1911.
Career: Alnwick United, Rochdale (August 1928), Sheffield Wednesday (briefly, September 1930), Blyth Spartans (November 1930), Morton, Queen's Park Rangers (July 1932), Northampton Town (seasons 1934-36), FOREST (April 1936-May 1939). He did not figure after WW2. Dick Brown was a speedy winger who scored 10 times in 40 League games for Rochdale; failed to make an impression at Hillsborough, did reasonably well at a lower level with Blyth, netted 20 goals in 60 League outings for QPR and found the net on 27 occasions in 90 appearances for the Cobblers before having a rather disappointing three-year spell with Forest. He lost his place in the first XI following the emergence of Arthur Betts.

BROWN, Albert Roy

Outside-right/left: 59 apps. 8 goals
Born: Sneinton, Nottingham, 14 August 1917.
Career: Sneinton FC, FOREST (February 1936), Wrexham (June 1939), Mansfield Town (July 1947-May 1948).

An efficient, hard-working winger with good pace and neat control, Roy Brown replaced Billy Simpson on Forest's left-wing during the latter part of the 1936-37 season, having made his League debut in a 4-0 defeat at Norwich in mid-April 1936. He scored four goals in 28 peacetime games for Wrexham and two in 17 League matches for the Stags.

BROWN, H N

Right-half: 6 apps.
Born: Nottingham, circa 1867
Career FOREST (1889-90)

A right-half who thrived on hard work, Brown played for Forest in six of their Football Alliance League games during the 1889-90 season, displaying plenty of aggression.

BROWN, Oliver Maurice

Centre-forward: 9 apps. 6 goals
Born: Burton-on-Trent, Staffs, 10 October 1908.
Died: London, 17 January 1951
Career: Trent Villa, Robirth Athletic, Burton Town, FOREST (August 1930), Norwich City (December 1931), West Ham United (briefly in August 1933), Brighton & Hove Albion (four seasons: September 1933 to April 1937).

An exuberant character, Oliver 'Buster' Brown committed himself well in the days of telling tackles. He was a very efficient, hard-working centre-forward who grabbed plenty of goals throughout his career, although he never really settled down at the City Ground. He scored 33 times in 51 League games for Norwich and followed up by netting 38 goals in just 58 League appearances for Brighton, top scoring for the Hove club in 1933-34 while playing in only eight matches!

BROWN, Robert Alan John
Inside or outside-left/centre-forward: 50 apps. 17 goals
Born: Gorleston, 7 November 1915.
Career: Gorleston Town (1932-34), Charlton Athletic (August 1934); served with in the RAF and the Greenwich Auxiliary Police and also guested for East Fife, Leicester City, Manchester City, Millwall, Newcastle United, West Ham United, Wolves and York City during WW2; FOREST (£6,750, May 1946), Aston Villa (£10,000, October 1947), Gorleston Town (player-coach, June 1949, then player-manager from August 1949 to May 1956, retiring as a player in 1954. During his last two years at Gorleston he also scouted for Aston Villa. He also indulged in a sports-shop business (1954-59) and later, in partnership with his former Charlton colleague Joe Jobling, he took charge of a betting shop in Gorleston, arranging sporting events at a holiday centre in the town for five years. His last job was that of a timber merchant which involved driving a 10-ton truck. He finally retired (from work) in 1982.

'Sailor' Brown, with his balding head and ambling action, was a powerful goalscoring forward who did well with every club he served. He toured South Africa with the FA party in May-June 1939; skippered the RAF team in Norway, Denmark and Sweden during the hostilities, gained two League South Cup winners; medals with Charlton in 1944 and Millwall a year later, and played for England in seven wartime/Victory internationals (1945-46). He made his League debut for Forest against Norwich City in April 1936 and three years later played his last game in that competition for the club, also v. Norwich in May 1939.

BROWN, William
Right-half: 1 apps.
Born: circa 1905
Career: FOREST (two seasons: 1928-30)
A well-built, strong-tackling wing-half, Billy Brown was basically a reserve at the City Ground for two seasons during which time he made just one first team appearence.

BROWN, William
Goalkeeper: 58 apps.
Born: Nottinghamshire: circa 1870.
Career: FOREST (August 1890), Notts County (August (1894).
Goalkeeper in Forest's first-ever League game versus Everton in September 1892, Bill Brown had previously served as the club's last line of defence in over 30 Alliance games, helping the Reds win the championship of that competition in 1891-92 when he missed only one match. Well built, with strong wrists, and quite erratic at times, he enjoyed fly-kicking the ball to safety and often got good distance with his clearances..

BROWN, William
Right-half: 4 apps.
Born: Cambuslang, Scotland, 10 May 1897.
Career: Flemington Hearts, Cambuslang Rangers, Partick Thistle, Everton (as an amateur August 1913, professional July 1914), FOREST (for a 'nominal fee', May 1928), Liverpool Cables FC (player-coach, August 1930).
An engineer's fitter by trade, Willie Brown made 179 League and Cup appearances for Everton either side of WW1 before joining Forest. A product of the famous Cambuslang nursery he was a key member of Everton's classic middle-line of the 1920s and made his Football League debut at the age of 17. He was well past his best when he joined Forest but his experience rubbed off on several of the club's younger players. He was unlucky not to win a full cap for Scotland.

BUCKLEY, Alan Paul
Inside/centre-forward: 16+3 apps. one goal
Born: Mansfield, 20 April, 1951
Career: FOREST (apprentice June 1967, professional April 1968), Walsall (August 1973), Birmingham City (October 1978), Walsall (July 1979, then manager at Fellows Park from July 1979 to July 1981 and again from May 1982 to August 1986), Stourbridge (as a player, September 1986), Tamworth (October 1986), Kettering Town (manager, November 1986), Grimsby Town (manager, June 1988), West Bromwich Albion (manager October 1994), Grimsby Town (manager, May 1997), Lincoln City (manager, February 2001 to May 2002), Rochdale (manager, May 2003).
After failing to gain a regular place in the Forest line-up, Alan Buckley, a short, stocky inside-forward with an eye for goal, turned out be one of the Walsall's best-ever signings, scoring over 200 goals in some 500 games for the Saddlers during his two spells with the club. He took Walsall to the brink of promotion several times before achieving success with Grimsby. He had just one good season at St Andrew's. As a manager he did wonders for Grimsby Town, leading the Mariners up from the Fourth to the Second Division in double-quick time (1990-91). Unfortunately he failed to do the business at the Hawthorns and after rejoining Grimsby, he inspired the Blundell Park club to a Wembley double in 1998 when they lifted the Auto-Windscreen Shield and clinched promotion by winning the Second Division Play-off final. However, after some poor results he left the Cleethorpes-based club and was out of football for a short while, before re-entering the fray as manager at Sincil Bank. His brother Steve played for Luton Town, Derby County & Lincoln City and one of his two sons, Adam, also made his mark in League football.

BULL, Gary William
Striker: 6+11 apps. one goal
Born: West Bromwich, 12 June, 1966
Career: Swindon Town (schoolboy forms, 1981), Paget Rangers (August 1982), Southampton (October 1986), Cambridge United (March 1988), Barnet (March 1989), FOREST (July 1993), Birmingham City (on loan, September 1994), Brighton & Hove Albion (on loan, August 1995), Birmingham City (signed on a free transfer, December 1995), York City (March 1996), Scunthorpe United (July 1998), Wolverhampton Wanderers (briefly), Grantham Town (June 2000).

Prior to joining Forest, striker Gary Bull had been with Barnet when they entered the Football League as GM Vauxhall Conference champions in 1991, and after helping the Reds reach the Premiership (in 1994) he left the City Ground for St Andrew's, duly assisting Blues clinch the Second Division championship the following year. Cousin of Wolves' ace marksman Steve Bull, Gary was a very useful marksman himself. He scored 37 goals in 83 League games for Barnet and during his career in the Football League he netted 65 times in 253 appearances. He was used mainly as a substitute during his time with Forest.

BULLING, Harold Montague
Full-back: 199 apps. 2 goals
Born: Horncastle, 29 September, 1890.
Died: West Bridgford 9 November 1933.
Career: Heanor Town (as a professional), Watford (August 1911), FOREST (July 1915-May 1925), Shirebrook FC (season 1925-26).

Harry Bulling was a very confident, strong-kicking defender who formed a splendid full-back partnership at Forest with Harry Jones. Prior to his arrival he had spent four excellent seasons at Cassio Road with Watford, making over 100 appearances in the Southern League. He was an ever-present in Forest's Second Division championship-winning season of 1921-22 and continued to produce the goods until the emergence of Bill Thompson in 1925. Besides his near-200 first-class games for Forest, Bulling also made over 60 appearances for the Reds during WW1, helping them win the Victory Shield in 1919. He remained in Nottingham after retiring and his death in 1933 came as a great shock to all Forest supporters. His younger brother, James (who died in 1992) played for Leicester City and Wrexham during the 1930s, making 133 senior appearances for the Welsh club.

BULLOCK, John Henry
Inside-right/right-half: 2 apps
Born: circa 1870.
Career: FOREST (seasons 1891-93)
Reserve utility player, Jack Bullock made his first appearance for Forest on 28 April 1892 against Grimsby Town in the final game of the Alliance League programme

and almost a year later he lined up at right-half in the away First Division game at Bolton.

BURDITT, George Leslie
Outside-right/inside-right/centre-forward: 21 apps. 10 goals
Born: Ibstock, Leics, 22 July 1910. Died: 1981
Career: Ibstock Rovers (1919), Norwich City (briefly, on trial), FOREST (March 1934), Millwall (January 1937), Wrexham (November 1937), Doncaster Rovers (July 1939). Did not play after WW2.

George Burditt scored over 70 goals for Ibstock Rovers before moving into League football with Forest following an unsuccessful trial with Norwich. After leaving the City Ground he notched 35 goals in 67 League games for Wrexham. He started the 1934-35 season as Forest's centre-forward but failed to command a regular place with Jack Dent and Tom Peacock pushing him hard. His brother Ken Burditt, also played as a forward for Norwich City and Millwall as well as for Notts County and Colchester United, scoring over 80 goals in almost 250 League and Cup appearances.

BURGIN, Meynell
Inside-forward: 22 apps. 11 goals
Born: Sheffield, 29 November 1911. Deceased.
Career: Rossington Main Colliery (May 1919), Sheffield Wednesday (on trial), Huddersfield Town (trialist), Bradford City (trialist), Wolverhampton Wanderers (May 1933), Tranmere Rovers (on loan, October 1934), Bournemouth (May 1935), FOREST (July 1936), West Bromwich Albion (£1,065, May 1938); guested for Chesterfield and Sheffield Wednesday during WW2. Retired due to cartilage trouble in May 1943.

Meynell Burgin was a powerfully built inside-forward, hard and aggressive whose body-strength enabled him to withstand the fiercest of challenges. Difficult to knock off the ball, he loved to be involved in the action and only the conflict of WW2 prevented him from becoming a really top-class player. He gained a Welsh Cup winners medal with Tranmere in 1935 and all told amassed over 70 senior appearances and scored more than 40 goals. He failed to get into Wolves' first team, however.

BURKE, Stephen James
Winger: 0+1 app.
Born: Nottingham, 29 September 1960.
Career: FOREST (apprentice, June 1976, professional March 1978), Queen's Park Rangers (September 1979), Millwall (on loan, October 1983), Notts County (on loan, October 1984), Lincoln City (on loan, August 1985), Brentford (on loan, March 1986), Doncaster Rovers (transfer, August 1986), West Bromwich Albion (on loan), Stockport County (on loan, October-November 1987).

Capped by England at Youth team level, Steve Burke failed to make the required breakthrough at the City Ground and after just one substitute appearance (v. Ayr United in the 1st leg of the semi-final of the Anglo-Scottish Cup in October 1976) he left the club for pastures new. Over a period of 11 years (from 1977-88) he made a total of 156 League appearances and scored 15 goals, including five in 67 outings for QPR and eight in 57 matches for Doncaster.

BURKITT, John Orgill

Left-half: 503 apps. 12 goals
Born: Wednesbury, Staffordshire, 19 January 1926.
Died: Brighouse, Yorkshire 12 September 2003.
Career: Darlaston, FOREST (professional, May 1947). Retired in May 1962 to take up a coaching position with the club; Notts County (manager, April 1966-February 1967); later Derby County (as trainer, when Brian Clough was manager at the Baseball Ground, September 1967-May 1969).
Jack Burkitt started out as a centre-half before developing into a splendidly efficient left-half, earning a reputation as one of the most consistent players in the club's history. A great servant to Forest, he was also an inspirational captain who skippered the side for many seasons, leading the Reds to FA Cup glory in 1959, eight years after gaining a Third Division South championship medal and two years after helping the team clinch promotion to the top flight. He gained a regular place in the side (at left-half) in 1948-49 and with strength in the tackle aided by determination and dedication, he remained in control of the number six jersey until 1960-61 when he handed over his duties to Jim Iley. Only four players, fellow defenders Stuart Pearce (622), Steve Chettle (526) and Bobby McKinlay (686), midfielder Ian Bowyer (564) and winger John Robertson (514) have made more senior appearances for Forest than Jack Burkitt.

BURNS, John Christopher

Midfielder: 4+1 apps.
Born: Dublin, 4 December 1977
Career: Belvedere Youth Club, FOREST (December 1994), Bristol City (£100,000+ November 1999, Carlisle United (August 2002), Burton Albion, (November 2002), Hucknall Town (January 2003).
A creative, hard-tackling midfielder, John Burns was dubbed the new Roy Keane by Forest fans but sadly he never established himself in the first XI and after almost five years of trying at the City Ground he was transferred to Bristol City. He was capped by the Republic of Ireland at both Youth and Under-21 levels (two outings in the latter category).

BURNS, Kenneth

Defender/centre-forward: 196 apps. 15 goals
Born: Glasgow, 23 December, 1953
Career: Glasgow Rangers (schoolboy forms), Birmingham City (apprentice, June 1970, professional July 1971), FOREST (£150,000, July 1977), Leeds United

(£400,000, October 1981), Derby County (on loan, March 1983 and again in February 1984, signing permanently in March 1984), Notts County (on loan, February 1985), Barnsley (August 1985), IF Elfsborg/Sweden (March 1986), Sutton Town (August 1986, then player-manager March 1987), Stafford Rangers (player, July 1987), Grantham Town (player-coach season 1988-89), Gainsborough Trinity (player-coach 1989), Ilkeston Town (player-coach 1990-93); Oakham United (player-coach), Telford United (assistant-manager July 1993-94). Later Nottingham Forest corpoate department.
A Scottish international (20 full and two Under-23 caps gained - 12 of the former coming with Forest over a period of three years: May 1978 to May 1981) Kenny Burns was a rare talent, a player able and willing to perform in any outfield position with equal effect. Initially a central defender, he was successfully converted into an out-and-out striker after Bob Latchford had departed from St Andrew's and his aggressive, all-action play and superb heading ability made him a player feared by many. But he always wanted to get back to defend and it was here that he won most of his honours at club and international level. He helped Birmingham gain promotion in 1972 and after joining Forest (signed by Brian Clough) gained two European Cup winners' medals (1979 & 1980), a First Division championship medal (1978), two Football League Cup prizes (winners in 1978 and runners-up in 1980), a European Super Cup triumph (also in 1980) and was named 'Footballer of the Year' 1978 before joining his country for that summer's World Cup finals in Argentina. Despite a dubious disciplinary record (which deterred a handful of managers from signing him when he was with Birmingham) he still amassed in excess of 500 senior appearances as a professional, 424 coming in the Football League, 170 of them with Blues (45 goals scored) and 137 for Forest (13 goals) Burns is now a publican in the Stoke-on-Trent area, having previously held a similar position in Ilkeston.

BURTON, Bruce Brian

Outside-left: 3 apps.
Born: Nottingham, 28 December 1932
Career: Basford Boys Club, FOREST (junior 1949, professional July 1951-May 1955)
Brian Burton was a reserve with Forest and was handed only three first-team outings on the left-wing, owing to the form and consistency of Colin Collindridge, and after that Hugh McLaren. He was released after spending six years at the City Ground.

BURTON, Frederick E

Inside-forward/outside-left: 17 apps. 5 goals
Born: Nottingham, circa 1858
Career: Notts County, FOREST (July 1887). Retired in May 1891 through injury.

One of the early utility forwards, Fred Burton made his debut for Forest on the left-wing in the 3rd qualifying round of the FA Cup v. Notts County in November 1887, scoring in a 2-1 win. He also played in both inside-forward positions and was capped by England against Ireland at Everton in March 1889.

BURTON, John William
Full-back: 40 apps
Born: Shirebrook, Derbyshire, 1 April 1908. Died: 1975.
Career: Mansfield Woodhouse Albion, Woodhouse Comrades, Sutton Junction, FOREST (August 1930), Brighton & Hove Albion (July 1936), Bilsthorpe Colliery (season 1938-39). Did not feature after WW2.
Billy Burton, a well-built defender, made his debut for Forest in the left-back berth in the home League game with Bury in December 1931. He had to wait until January 1935, however, before claiming a regular place in the side and then after some gritty performances, he was replaced by Dan Edgar and eventually transferred to Brighton.
In 1933 he was described as being a 'gallant defender with plenty of class.'

BURTON, Noah
Inside-forward: 320 apps. 62 goals
Born: Old Basford, Nottinghamshire, 18 December 1896.
Died: Nottingham, 16 July 1956.
Career: Bulwell St Alban's FC, Ilkeston United, Derby County (amateur, December 1915); guested for FOREST during WW1; Derby County (as a professional, August 1919), FOREST (June 1921). Retired in May 1932.
As a guest for Forest during WW1, Noah Burton made over 50 first-team appearances and scored the all-important goal v. Everton that won the Victory Shield in 1919. On returning to Derby he was the Rams' leading scorer in the first season after the hostilities (13 goals) and at that point several clubs were interested in signing him. It wasn't until the summer of 1921, however, that the move was made to Forest and over the next decade he gave the Reds supreme service. He was instrumental in helping Forest win the Second Division title in 1922 and despite his ungainly frame, he was certainly the most popular player in the side throughout the 'twenties. A fine sprinter, he displayed tremendous versatility, showing great skill in whatever position he filled, and he had the ability to hoodwink referees by gaining penalties! A marvellous character, both on and off the pitch, he was the dressing room comedian and likewise on the team coach travelling to away matches. For many years after his retirement Burton ran his own tobacconists shop in Nottingham.

BUTLER, Richard
Wing-half: 2 apps.
Born: Shepshed, Leicestershire, 1885
Career: Shepshed Albion, FOREST (August 1906), Leicester Fosse (December 1910-May 1912).

A reserve wing-half with Forest, Dick Butler made only two appearances in the first XI during his four years with the club, his debut coming against Burnley in January 1907 (won 2-0). He did a shade better with Fosse, making 28 senior appearances before leaving Filbert Street in the summer of 1912.

BUTLIN, Barry Desmond
Striker: 85+3 apps. 20 goals
Born: Rosliston, Derbyshire, 9 November 1949
Career: Derby County (apprentice, June 1965, professional January 1967), Notts County (on loan, January-October 1969), Luton Town (£50,000, November 1972), FOREST (£122,000, October 1974), Brighton & Hove Albion (on loan, September 1975), Reading (on loan, January 1977)), Peterborough United (August 1977), Sheffield United (August 1978-May 1981).
During his professional career Barry Butlin scored over 80 goals in almost 300 League appearances. His opportunities at the Baseball Ground were limited due to the consistency of John O'Hare and Kevin Hector and much of his early experience was gained from an extended loan spell at Meadow Lane. He moved to Kenilworth Road for a record in-coming fee for the Rams and met with some success with the Hatters, being their top-scorer when they won promotion to the First Division in 1974. He settled in reasonably quickly with Forest and performed decent enough in his first two seasons when playing up front with first Neil Martin and later with his former Derby colleague O'Hare, helping the Reds win promotion from Division Two in 1977. Then Peter Withe arrived on the scene and at that juncture Butlin's first-team outings became non-existent. He was subsequently transferred to Peterborough and then on to Bramall Lane before quitting League football at the end of the 1980-81 season

BUTTERWORTH, Ian Stewart
Defender: 33+1 apps.
Born: Crewe, 25 January 1964
Career: Coventry City (apprentice, July 1980, professional August 1981), FOREST (£250,000, June 1985), Norwich City (on loan, September 1986, signed permanently for £160,000, December 1986-May 1994).
Central defender Ian Butterworth had 90 League appearances to his name when he joined the Reds from Coventry in 1985. He went straight into the first team at the City Ground, lining up alongside Des Walker, but injuries disrupted his progress and after returning to the side at right-back (following a loan spell at Carrow Road) he failed to re-establish himself long term, and was eventually transferred on contract to the Canaries. He did very well with Norwich, making 289 League and Cup appearances before leaving the club in 1994.
He was capped eight times by England at Under-21 level (six as a Forest player). Ian has remained in the game and most recently has been assistant-manager of Cardiff.

BYWATER
Goalkeeper: One app.
Born: circa 1870.
Career: FOREST (season 1891-92)
Reserve goalkeeper Bywater - deputising for Brown - made his only senior appearance between the posts for Forest in a Football Alliance game at Walsall on 2 April 1892 (lost 3-0).

CALDERWOOD, Colin
Defender: 6 apps.
Born: Glasgow, 20 January 1965.
Career: Mansfield Town (juniors, June 1980, professional March 1982), Swindon Town (£30,000, June 1985), Tottenham Hotspur (£1.25 million, July 1993), Aston Villa (£225,000, March 1999), Nottingham Forest (£70,000, March 2000-May 2001). Notts County (on loan, March 2001). Northampton Town (manager, season 2003-04).
Despite being a Scotsman and representing his country in schoolboy internationals, centre-back Colin Calderwood surprisingly started his professional career with Mansfield Town. Three years and 117 games later he left Field Mill for Swindon. He did well at the County Ground, accumulating a splendid record of over 400 games for the Robins, whom he helped win the Fourth Division championship in 1986, followed by promotion from Division Three a year later, a play-off spot in 1989 and promotion from Division Two in 1993 - and he also represented the Football League Division Two XI in 1992. His performances with Swindon didn't go unnoticed and he was duly signed by Gerry Francis, manager of Premiership side Tottenham Hotspur. He quickly gained the first of his 36 full caps for his country and went on to play almost 200 games for the London club before transferring to Villa Park in 1999. After a bright start, when he formed part of a three-man defence along with Ugo Ehiogu and Gareth Southgate, Calderwood then lost his place to young Gareth Barry. He became unsettled and after 30 appearances for the club was eventually sold to Nottingham Forest - signed by ex-Villa star David Platt! Unfortunately injuries ruined his stay at the City Ground and he was forced to retire at the end of the 2000-01 season.

CALVEY, John
Inside-right/centre-forward: 150 apps. 57 goals
Born: South Bank, Middlesbrough 23 August 1876.
Died: Poplar, London January 1937.
Career: South Bank Juniors, Millwall Athletic (May 1895), FOREST (August 1899), Millwall Athletic (September 1904-May 1905).
Stocky Jack Calvey was Forest's top-scorer three seasons running: 1899-1902. An England international (one cap gained v. Ireland in Belfast in March 1902) he scored a goal roughly every three games for the Reds during his four seasons with the club, including one on his League debut v. Preston North End in September 1899 (won 3-1). Prior to joining Forest he gained eight gold medals and four Southern League championship badges with Millwall as well as playing in an international trial (the South v. the North at Crystal Palace in February 1899). Described as 'fast and plucky with an excellent shot' he later returned to the Lions and despite being somewhat overweight he still gave them useful service for another season, taking his tally of goals with them to an impressive 98 in 152 outings, having scored a hat-trick on his Southern League debut v. Ilford in February 1896. He twice claimed 33 goals in a season (in 1896-97 & 1898-99). Calvey worked in the London dockyard after retiring.

CAMERON, David Franklin
Centre-half/left-half: 21 apps. one goal
Born: Partick, 25 June 1902.
Career: Cameron Highlanders (1917-18), Akeld FC (briefly), Queen's Park, Chelsea (June 1920), Helensburgh (December 1926), Heart of Midlothian (August 1927), Dunfermline Athletic (briefly), FOREST (August 1928), Colwyn Bay (May 1930).
A tall, commanding defender, with black wavy hair, David Cameron's promising career was marred by injury almost as soon as he arrived at Chelsea. He battled on gamely and made a total of 81 first-class appearances for the London club before moving back to Scotland in the winter of 1926. His spell with Forest lasted just two seasons and although he produced some quality performances he was short of pace and suffered a few more injuries in the process. In 1919, one reporter declared that there was '...no better defender in Scottish football than the wily Cameron'.
* Cameron was only 15 years of age when he went to war.

CAMPBELL, David Anthony
Midfielder: 39+8 apps. 5 goals
Born: Eglington, Londonderry, Northern Ireland, June 1965
Career: FOREST (apprentice, June 1981, professional June 1983), Notts County (on loan, February 1987), Charlton Athletic (October 1987), Plymouth Argyle (on loan, March 1989), Bradford City (March 1989), Derry City (December 1990) Shamrock Rovers, Rotherham United (non-contract, November 1992), West Bromwich Albion (non-contract) February 1993, Burnley (March 1993), Lincoln City (on loan, February 1994), Wigan Athletic (non-contract, July 1994), Cambridge United (non-contract, January-May 1995).
Capped ten times by Northern Ireland (seven with Forest) David Campbell had an interesting professional career which saw him serve with 12 different clubs over a period of 12 years during which time he scored 11 goals in almost 150 League games. His best spell came at Forest and although he was never a regular choice in the first team, owing to the presence of Messrs Metgod, Hodge, Webb and Bowyer, he did give value for money during the

second half of the 1985-86 season and the opening three months of the following campaign when he had a run of 27 outings in the First Division. He later suffered a broken leg on his Cambridge debut leading to his retirement.

CAMPBELL, Kevin Joseph
Striker: 95+1 apps. 35 goals
Born: Lambeth, London, 4 February 1970
Career: Arsenal (apprentice, June 1986, professional, February 1988), Leyton Orient (on loan, January 1989), Leicester city (on loan, November 1989), FOREST (£3 million, July 1995), Trabzonspor/Turkey (£2.5 million, August 1998), Everton (£3 million, March 1999).
Capped once by England 'B' and on four occasions by the Under-21 side, striker Kevin Campbell is a powerful and intelligent leader of the attack. He did superbly well at Highbury, scoring 59 goals in 228 games for the Gunners, helping them win the FA Youth Cup in 1988, the League Cup and FA Cup double in 1993 and the European Cup Winners Cup in 1994. He then did just as well with Forest, teaming up with fellow front men Jason Lee, Dean Saunders and the Dutchman Pierre Van Hooijdonk in that order while helping the Reds gain promotion to the Premiership in 1998. Indeed, he rattled in 23 goals in 1998 to help steer the Reds into the Premiership before leaving for a spell in Turkey. A niggling back injury has interrupted his progress at Goodison Park but he has still managed to net 50 goals for the Merseysiders in less than 140 senior appearances (up to May 2003).

CANNING, Leslie Daniel
Goalkeeper: 5 apps.
Born: Pontypridd, 21 February 1926.
Career: Abercynon, Cardiff City (professional, July 1945), Swansea Town (January 1949), FOREST (July 1951-May 1952), Yarmouth (August 1952), Newport County, (August 1955-April 1956). When goalkeeper Danny Canning arrived at the City Ground he had already appeared in 127 League games, having been an ever-present between the posts in successive seasons for Cardiff and helped the Swans gain promotion from Division Three South. Signed as cover for Harry Walker, he was drawn into service in just five senior matches, making his Forest debut in a 2-0 win at Birmingham in September 1951.

CAPEL, Thomas
Inside-left: 162 apps. 72 goals
Born: Chorlton, Manchester, 27 June, 1922
Career: Droylsden FC, Manchester City (November 1941), Chesterfield (October 1947), Birmingham City (June 1949), FOREST (£14,000, November 1949), Coventry City (June 1954), Halifax Town (October 1955), Heanor Town (July 1956-62). Served in the Marines during WW2 with Eddie Quigley (Blackburn Rovers & Preston North End) and Ken Oliver (Derby County & Exeter City).

Tommy Capel was a powerful, bustling player who scored plenty of goals in a fine career. He did very well initially at Maine Road, especially during WW2. He netted more than a goal every three games for Chesterfield and after a brief spell with Birmingham he arrived at the City Ground full of confidence, eager to feature in the promotion push. He had a wonderful 1950-51 campaign, claiming 24 goals as Forest duly climbed back into the Second Division as champions of the Third South. He faltered somewhat after that but still bagged his fair share of goals. He joined Coventry City with his wing-partner Colin Collindridge and went on playing until 1962. During his League career he hit 120 goals in 276 appearances. He played with his full-back brother Fred at Chesterfield

CAPES, Adrian
Inside-forward: 34 apps. 5 goals
Born: Burton-on-Trent, Staffs, 18 April 1873.
Died: Stoke-on-Trent, 29 September 1955
Career: Burton Wanderers (September 1894), FOREST (July 1896), Burton Swifts (September 1897), Burslem Port Vale (November 1900), Stoke (November 1905), Burslem Port Vale (December 1908). Retired with a knee injury in April 1911. He remained with the Vale as a training supervisor until August 1919, but continued working with the club's backroom staff until May 1934.
Adrian Capes was a dashing, all-purpose player who spent just over a season with Forest, lining up alongside his brother Arthur (q.v). He made his debut for the Reds v. Derby County in September 1896 and it was a surprise to a lot of people when he left the club after appearing in the first match of the 1897-98 campaign. He gave the Vale excellent service after that, scoring 69 goals in 181 League and FA Cup matches, hardly missing a match in five years.

CAPES, Arthur John
Inside/centre-forward/outside-right: 191 apps. 42 goals
Born: Burton-on-Trent, 23 February 1875.
Died: Burton-on-Trent, 26 February 1945.
Career: Burton Wanderers (September 1894), FOREST (July 1896), Stoke (August 1902), Bristol City (June 1904), Swindon Town (August 1905).
Arthur 'Sailor' Capes, like his brother, was a wonderful footballer whose senior career realised almost 100 goals in some 350 appearances. He joined Forest with Adrian (one wouldn't come without the other - such was the bond between them) and they made their debuts for the Reds together. After Adrian had left, Arthur continued to please the fans with some superb displays of all-action forward play and as time went by he became more of a goal-maker than goal-taker. He scored twice when Forest beat Derby in the 1898 FA Cup final, was capped once by England (v. Scotland in April 1903) and also represented the Football League.

CARGILL, James

Outside-right/inside-left; 10 apps. one goal
Born: Arbroath, 21 November 1914.
Career: Arbroath Rosslea, Arbroath Woodside, FOREST (June 1934), Brighton & Hove Albion (July 1936), Barrow (August 1939). Did not play League football after WW2.

Jimmy Cargill - signed as cover for Arthur Masters - made his debut for Forest in the Nottingham derby at Meadow Lane in September 1934 and played well in a 5-3 victory. After a run of four matches he bided his time in the reserves and made only six more first-team appearances before his departure to Brighton in the summer of 1936.

CARGILL, James Gordon

Goalkeeper: one app.
Born: Alyth near Perth, Angus, 22 September 1945
Career: Balbeggie Juniors, FOREST (juniors July 1961, professional September 1962), Notts County (July 1966-May 1967).

Goalkeeper Jimmy Cargill gained Scotland Schoolboy honours before joining Forest. He spent, in total, five years at the City Ground, acting as reserve in the main to Peter Grummitt. His only first-team outing was against Arsenal at Highbury in October 1964 when Forest won 3-0 before 35,000 spectators. He later made ten League appearances for Notts County.

CARNELLY, Albert

Inside-forward: 63 apps. 26 goals
Born: Nottingham, 29 December 1870.
Died: Nottingham, August 1920
Career: Notts Mapperley FC (1889), Notts County (1890), Loughborough Town (1891), FOREST (May 1894), Leicester Fosse (May 1896), Bristol City (July 1987), Ilkeston (August 1898), Bristol City (November 1898), Thames Ironworks FC (June 1899), Millwall Athletic (August 1900), Ilkeston (July 1901). Retired in 1903 (through injury).

Albert Carnelly was a goalscoring inside-forward who leapt from Midland League football to the First Division and finished up as Forest's top-scorer in his first season with the club. He had not figured too much with County and after leaving Forest netted 10 goals in 31 games for Fosse. He then hovered from club to club, playing for Bristol City in their initial season in the Southern League and scoring four goals in their first-ever FA Cup-tie. He was with Thames Ironworks when the London club was in its final season under that name before becoming West Ham United.

CARR, Franz Alexander

Winger: 147+12 apps. 3 goals
Born: Preston, 24 September 1966
Career: Blackburn Rovers (September 1982, professional July 1984), FOREST (£100,000, August 1984), Sheffield

Wednesday (on loan, December 1989), West Ham United (on loan, March 1991), Newcastle United (£250,000, June 1991), Sheffield United (£120,000, January 1993), Leicester City (£100,000, September 1994), Aston Villa (£250,000, February 1995), Reggiana/Italy (September 1996), Bolton Wanderers (October 1997), West Bromwich Albion (February 1998), Grimsby Town (trialist), Runcorn.

Mercurial winger Franz Carr failed to make the grade at Ewood Park and in 1984 was signed by Forest. A player who loved to hug the touchline, he played over 150 games for Brian Clough, but then lost his way and eventually left the City Ground for Newcastle. Long periods in the wilderness disrupted Carr's progress after that and he struggled with his form, even during his spell in Italy. An England Youth international, he gained nine caps at Under-21 level (all during his time at the City Ground), helped Forest win the Simod Cup in 1989 and the League Cup in 1990, and during his career amassed more than 250 senior appearances at club and international level (31 goals scored).

CASH, Brian Dominick

Outside-right/midfielder: 0+7 apps no goals.
Born: Dublin, 24 November 1982
Career: FOREST (trainee, June 1998, professional December 1999).

A Republic of Ireland Youth international, and product of Forest's teenage academy, skilful wide player Brian Cash has the ability to ghost past defenders and provide quality crosses for his strikers.

CHAMBERS, Robert James

Outside-right/left: 9 apps. one goal
Born: Mullaghglass, Northern Ireland, 26 July 1908.
Died: 1977
Career: Newry Town, Distillery (1924), Bury (July 1925), FOREST (August 1931-May 1932)

Jimmy Chambers was a nippy winger, able to perform equally well on both flanks. He played in 12 full internationals (one for Ireland as a Distillery player, and 11 for Northern Ireland, eight whilst with Bury and three during his time with Forest, all in 1931 v. Scotland, England & Wales in that order). He scored seven goals in 28 League games for the Shakers before joining Forest. Unfortunately, despite his international calls, he failed to make headway at the City Ground and, with injuries affecting his game he left after just one season.

CHAPMAN, Frederick William Simmons

Right-back/centre-half: 3 apps.
Born: Nottingham, circa 1880. Died: 29 February 1934
Career: FOREST (August 1904-May 1907), Oxford City (to 1910).

A rugged defender, able to occupy a variety of positions, Fred Chapman was a handy reserve at Forest for three seasons. He made his League debut v. Small Heath in November 1904 and thereafter managed just one appearance in each of the next two campaigns. He was a member of the Forest committee.

CHAPMAN, Lee Roy
Striker: 71 apps. 27 goals
Born: Lincoln, 5 December 1959.
Career: Stoke City (junior, June 1976, professional June 1978), Plymouth Argyle (on loan, December 1978), Arsenal (£500,000, August 1982), Sunderland (£200,000, December 1983), Sheffield Wednesday (£100,000, August 1984), Niort/France (£350,000, June 1988), FOREST (£350,000, October 1988), Leeds United (£400,000, January 1990), Portsmouth (£250,000, August 1993), West Ham United (£250,000, September 1993), Southend United (on loan, January 1995), Ipswich Town (£70,000, January 1995), Leeds United (on loan, January 1996), Swansea City (free transfer/non-contract, March-May 1996).

A nomadic striker whose transfer fees amounted to almost £2.5 million, served with no less than 13 different clubs over a period of 20 years, Lee Chapman, nevertheless, drew up an excellent scoring record of 264 goals in almost 700 appearances (his Football League statistics being 197 goals in 552 games). Strong in all aspects of forward play, he was courageous, willing, determined and lethal inside thee box, especially with his head. During his 15 months with Forest, he supported Nigel Clough superbly well up front before departing to allow Nigel Jemson to come into the front-line. Capped by England at 'B' and Under-21 levels, Chapman helped Forest win both the 1989 Wembley finals of the League Cup v. Luton and Simod Cup v. Everton (scoring twice in the latter triumph) and he was in Leeds' Second Division and First Division championship-winning sides of 1990 and 1992 respectively. Married to 'Men Behaving Badly' actress Lesley Ash, Chapman now runs a high profile wine bar in Chelsea. * His father, Roy, played for Aston Villa, Lincoln City, Mansfield Port Vale and Chester (1952-70).

CHAPMAN, Robert Dennis
Defender: 407+15 apps. 23 goals
Born: Aldridge, Staffs, 18 August 1946
Career: FOREST (juniors, August 1961, professional August 1963), Notts County (August 1977), Shrewsbury Town (July 1978 Tulsa Roughneck, USA (March 1979), Shrewsbury Town (September 1980 - cs. 1981).

Sammy Chapman was originally a forward but was successfully moved back into a defensive position to solve an injury crisis. He adapted to it like a duck to water, establishing himself in the centre-half berth from where he proved to be a strong and resilient competitor, although at times a trifle ungainly in his approach to the game. The club's youngest-ever player (aged 17 years, five months) at the time of his League debut v. Stoke City in January

1964, he was certainly at his best when Forest regained their top-flight status in 1977 but then, after making well over 400 senior appearances (and helping the Reds win the Anglo-Scottish Cup and gain promotion to the First Division in 1977) he was transferred to neighbours Notts County, thus allowing Scotsman Kenny Burns moving into his shoes at the City Ground. Chapman, later became a licensee of a public house in East Leake, Leicestershire.

CHARLES, Gary Andrew
Full-back: 75+6 apps. 2 goals
Born: Newham, London, 13 April 1970
Career: FOREST (trainee, June 1985, professional November 1987), Leicester City (on loan, March 1989), Derby County (£750,000, July 1993), Aston Villa (January 1995), Benfica (£1.5 million, January 1999), West Ham United (£1.2 million, October 1999), Birmingham City (on loan, September-October 2000). Forced to retire through injury in May 2002.

A League Cup runner-up and a Zenith Data Systems Cup winner with Forest in 1992 and a League Cup winner with Aston Villa in 1996, Gary Charles also gained two full and four Under-21 caps for England (two of the latter coming as a Reds' player). A very positive right-wing-back whose strengths were his speed and crossing, he made well over 250 senior appearances at club level before retiring. He took quite sometime to establish himself in the Forest team, finally taking the number 2 shirt from Brian Laws in 1991 and playing in the FA Cup final defeat by Spurs that same year.

CHARLTON, A
Forward: 3 apps.
Born: London, circa 1876
Career: Ashtead Juniors (Middlesex), Brentford (1896), FOREST (July 1898-May 1899)
A reserve inside-forward, Charlton made his Football League debut for Forest v. Stoke in October 1898 when he deputised for Sammy Richards in a 2-1 win. However, he made just two more first-team appearances for the Reds.

CHETTLE, Stephen
Defender: 503+23 apps. 14 goals
Born: Nottingham, 27 September 1968
Career: FOREST (apprentice 1984, professional August 1986), Barnsley (free transfer, November 1999), Walsall (on loan, September 2001), Grimsby Town (free, July 2002) Burton Albion (August 2003).
Centre-half Steve Chettle spent more than 15 years with Forest. He was a first-team regular from 1987-99 and twice made more than 50 senior appearances in a season. A rock-like competitor, strong in all aspects of defensive play, Chettle was honoured with 12 England Under-21 caps and he helped Forest lift the Simod Cup in 1989, the League Cup in 1990, the ZDSC in 1992 and the First Division Championship in 1998, as well as appearing in

the 1991 FA Cup final defeat by Spurs and helping the team reach the Premiership (first time round) in 1994.

CHRISTIE, Trevor John

Striker: 20 apps. 7 goals

Born: Cresswell, Northumberland, 28 February 1959

Career: Leicester City (apprentice, September 1975, professional December 1976), Notts County (June 1979), FOREST (£175,000, July 1984), Derby County (£100,000, February 1985), Manchester City (exchange for Mark Lillis, August 1986), Walsall (£30,000, October 1986), Mansfield Town (£30,000, March 1989), Kettering Town (free transfer, July 1991), Hucknall Town (November 1992), VS Rugby (March 1992), Arnold Town (player-coach, March 1994); retired with an achilles tendon, suffered in October 1994.

Trevor Christie - a bold front-runner, strong in the air and excellent at shielding the ball - netted 147 goals in 497 League appearances in a senior career that spanned 15 years. When he joined Forest in 1984 he had already netted 71 League goals but unfortunately he never hit it off with the Reds and spent only seven months at the City Ground. He was given his League baptism as a 19-year-old by Frank McLintock at Leicester and was the Foxes' top-scorer (under Jock Wallace) in 1978-79. Christie, who helped both Derby and Walsall win promotion in 1986 and 1988 respectively, has since worked as a salesman in Mansfield.

CLARK, Frank Albert

Full-back: 155+2 apps. one goal

Born: Rowlands Gill, Highlands, County Durham, 9 September 1943

Career: Preston North End (associate schoolboy forms), Crook Town (August 1960), Newcastle United (£200, October 1962, professional November 1962), FOREST (free transfer, July 1975). Retired in July 1979 to become assistant-manager of Sunderland to July 1981; FOREST (assistant-trainer/coach, August 1981), Orient (assistant-manager October 1981, manager May 1983-July 1991, remaining at Brisbane Road as Managing-Director, initially appointed, November 1986); FOREST (manager: May 1993-December 1995).

Frank Clark, who took over from Brian Clough as Forest's manager, was replaced briefly in the hot-seat by defender Stuart Pearce before Dave Bassett arrived halfway through the 1995-96 season when the team was bottom of the Premiership.

After serving his apprenticeship as a laboratory technician and learning the game with Crook Town for whom he played in the 1961 FA Amateur Cup final and earned himself an amateur international cap for England - as well as declining offers from both PNE and Sunderland to join them professionally - Frank Clark began his career in earnest with Newcastle. A solid, crisp-tackling and totally dependable left-back, he spent 13 years at St James' Park

during which time he made 487 first-team appearances (two goals scored) before transferring to Forest in 1975. He was capped three times by his country at youth-team level (1963), represented the Football League (1970) and helped United win the Second Division title (1965), lift the Inter Cities Fairs Cup in 1969 and he also played in the 1974 FA Cup final defeat by Liverpool. Handed a controversial free transfer by Newcastle (following the resignation of manager Joe Harvey), he immediately joined Brian Clough at Forest. Settling in quickly, Clark proved to be an excellent signing and amassed a fine record with the Reds of 157 League and Cup appearances (one goal), performing in the main as partner to Viv Anderson. After assisting Forest win promotion to the top flight and lift the Anglo-Scottish Cup in 1977, and become Football League champions in 1978 (making 12 appearances) he then collected successive League Cup winners medals (1978 & 1979) and also added a European Cup winners medal to his tally (also in 1979). After retiring as a player Clark served briefly with Sunderland before returning to Forest and then, after a decent spell in charge of Orient (gaining promotion from Division Four in 1989) he took over the reins at the City Ground in May 1993, guiding the Reds to promotion from Division Two in 1994 and then earning the LMA 'Manager of the Year' award the following year. Clark, never lost his affection for Newcastle United and is deservedly recognised to this day as one of the club's best ever servants. Clark, who was also a very fine cricketer, was rewarded with a testimonial match in 1976.

* He was appointed Chief Executive of the Managers' Association in 1992.

CLARK, John Robert

Inside-right: 5 apps. 2 goals

Born: Newburn, Newcastle, 6 February, 1903. Died: Byker, Newcastle, 1977.

Career: Spencer's Welfare FC, Hawthorn Leslie FC, Newburn Grange, Newburn FC, Prudhoe Castle, Newcastle United (£130, February 1923), Liverpool (£3,000, January 1928), FOREST (July 1931), North Shields (August 1932), later becoming player-coach, September 1937).

Hefty forward Bob Clark, 6 feet tall and 14 stones in weight - was a very popular Novocastrian figure between the two wars. He spent only one season with Forest, making his debut for the club on the opening day of the 1931-32 campaign against Charlton Athletic. However, he was soon replaced in the team by a fit-again Cyril Stocks. Earlier in his career (at St James' Park) Clark played alongside the great Hughie Gallacher and he scored 16 goals in 77 outings for the Geordies, helping them win the First Division title in 1927.

CLARK, Thomas George
Left-half/inside-right: 29 apps.
Born: Trehaford, Glamorgan, 31 October 1913.
Career: Bargoed FC, Aberaman Athletic, Bolton Wanderers (1935), FOREST (October 1938-January 1940). He did not figure after the war.
Tom Clark made 21 League appearances for Bolton before joining Forest for the last full League season before WW2. He made his debut for the Reds in a thrilling 4-3 defeat by Manchester City in November 1938 and spent the first half of the 1939-40 season with the club before entering the conflict in Europe.

CLARKE, James
Left-back: 20 apps.
Born: West Bromwich, 7 December 1923
Career: FOREST (junior 1945, professional May 1947-May 1955).
Reserve full-back Jim Clarke bided his time for quite a while at the City Ground before being released by the club at the end of the 1954-55 season. Indeed, during his ten years with Forest he made only 18 League appearances, ten in 1952-53 when he deputised for Jack Hutchinson. Nevertheless, he did serve the second XI splendidly, helping them win five successive Midland League titles (1950-54 inclusive).

CLOUGH, Nigel Howard
Centre-forward: 402+10 apps. 131 goals
Born: Sunderland, 19 March 1966.
Career: Heanor Town, FOREST (professional, September 1984), Liverpool (£2.275 million, June 1993), Manchester City (£1.5 million, January 1996), FOREST (on loan, December 1996), Sheffield Wednesday (on loan, September 1997), Burton Albion (October 1998, later player-manager).
An England international, capped by his country at senior level on 14 occasions (he won his first call up v. Chile at Wembley in May 1989) Nigel Clough also played in 15 Under-21 matches (1986-88) and appeared in one 'B' game as well as representing the Football League. With Forest he was twice a League Cup winner in 1989 (two goals scored v. Luton Town) and 1990 (v. Oldham Athletic) and he also gained a winner's medal in the Simod Cup Final (v. Everton) in 1989 and the Zenith Data Systems Cup (v. Southampton) of 1992. He was, however, an FA Cup loser v. Spurs in 1991 and a League Cup loser v. Manchester United 12 months later. Forest's leading scorer four seasons running (1985-89) he topped the charts again in 1990-91 and 1992-93. During his senior career Clough netted some 150 goals in 533 competitive matches. A splendid centre-forward who held the ball up well, he gave Forest excellent service and formed a wonderful partnership up front with a variety of strikers, including Peter Davenport, Garry Birtles, Paul Wilkinson, Lee Chapman and Nigel Jemson, plus a few others. More

recently he has carried out a useful job as player-manager of Burton Albion, leading them into the Nationwide Conference (as Unibond League champions) in 2002.

CLUROE, Malcolm
Inside-forward; One app.
Born: Nottingham, 6 February 1935
Career: FOREST (amateur, July 1952, professional, November 1954-May 1955)
Reserve inside-forward Malcolm Cluroe made his only first-team appearance for Forest in a 5-1 home defeat at the hands of Luton Town in December 1954 (Division 2).

COBB, Walter William
Utility: 37 apps. 7 goals
Born: Newark, Notts, 29 September 1940
Career: Ransome & Marles, FOREST (professional, September 1959), Plymouth Argyle (October 1963), Brentford (October 1964), Lincoln City (November 1966), Boston United (July 1968 to May 1971).
Billy Cobb had the honour of scoring Forest's first goal in a major European competition, obliging against Valencia (at home) in the Inter Cities Fairs Cup in October 1961. A competent performer, he later scored 23 goals in 71 League games for Brentford and 10 in 67 for Lincoln. His best season with Forest was 1962-63 when he made 16 appearances in the First Division, donning six different numbered shirts! He was later licensee of the Sherwood Inn on Mansfield road for 20 years.

COLEMAN, John George
Inside-forward: 39 apps. 16 goals
Born: Kettering, Northants, 26 October 1881.
Died: London, 20 November 1940.
Career: Kettering Town (May 1900), Northampton Town (May 1901), Woolwich Arsenal (May 1902 with Everard Lawrence), Everton (February 1908), Sunderland (May 1910), Fulham (July 1911), FOREST (August 1914-May 1915). Served with the Footballers' Battalion during WW1 and was at one time reported missing. Returning to play briefly for Tunbridge Wells Rangers in season 1919-20, he later became a respected coach in Holland.
'Tim' Coleman, an England international (one cap gained v. Ireland in February 1907 and also twice a Football League representative when playing for Arsenal) had a very useful career that spanned some 20 years in total. He did exceedingly well in Southern League circles before establishing himself with Arsenal, for whom he scored 84 goals in 196 senior matches. He was almost 33 years of age when he joined Forest and after just one season with the Reds his playing days (at competitive level) were ended by the hostilities in Europe. He helped Arsenal win promotion from Division Two in 1904 finish runners-up and then win the Southern Professional Cup in 1904 and 1906 respectively. He netted 186 goals in 404 League games all told (45 in 94 for Fulham, including hat-tricks

in successive games v. Wolves and Stockport in 1913). He sadly died in an industrial accident at the age of 59.

COLEMAN, Sidney

Left-Back: 13 apps.
Born: circa 1865
Career: FOREST (seasons 1889-91)

Sid Coleman played alongside Guttridge during Forest's first season in the Football Alliance. A forceful, intelligent, no-nonsense full-back, he enjoyed a challenge and was thoroughly reliable

COLES, Frederick Gordon

Right-half/centre-half: 3 apps
Born: Nottingham, 1875.
Died: Nottingham 22 April 1947.
Career: Post Office FC (Nottingham), Notts County (August 1895-May 1896), FOREST (March 1900), Woolwich Arsenal (June 1900), Grimsby Town (June 1904). Retired in 1907 and later became coach to FC Gothenburg (Sweden) and also trainer/coach of the Dutch side FC Haessche Voetbal Vereeniging/ (The Hague) (seasons 1909-11).

Gordon Coles made his League debut for Forest in a 4-0 home win Sheffield United soon after joining the club - having 'disappeared' for a short time following his one season sorties with County. He never really settled in with the Reds and quickly moved to London. He appeared in 86 senior games for Arsenal and 44 for Grimsby. Coles was one of the pioneers of British coaching in Europe.

COLLIER, Graham Ronald

Midfielder: 15+4 apps. 4 goals
Born: Nottingham, 12 September 1951
Career: FOREST (apprentice August 1967, professional March 1969), Scunthorpe United (July 1972), Barnsley (August 1977), Buxton FC (briefly cs. 1978), York City (September 1978-November 1978).

Graham Collier had a very successful 10-year career, making more than 200 League appearances, including 161 for Scunthorpe. He made his senior debut for Forest v. Wolves in September 1969 (in a 3-3 draw) but was unable to establish himself in the first XI, hence his departure to the Old Showground where he made an immediate impact with the Iron.

COLLINDRIDGE, Colin

Outside-left: 156 apps. 46 goals
Born: Barnsley, 15 November 1920
Career: Barugh Green FC, Wolverhampton Wanderers (juniors), Sheffield United (professional January 1939), FOREST (August 1950), Coventry City (June 1954), Bath City (July 1956).

Owing to WW2, Yorkshireman Colin Collindridge entered League football late - he was 25 when he made his debut in the competition for Sheffield United v. Liverpool

in August 1946 - although he had appeared in 96 matches for the Blades (46 goals scored) during the hostilities and in fact had an unsuccessful trial with Forest at one stage. Signed by manager Billy Walker, he had a wonderful first season with the Reds, his 16 goals proving vital in the promotion success as champions of Division Three South. A huge favourite with the fans, he had speed, power and skill, was direct in his play and possessed a strong shot (in his left foot). He left the City Ground with his wing partner Tommy Capel for Coventry City in a double deal.

COLLINS, James

Inside-forward/winger: 52 apps. 17 goals
Born: Scotland, 1872.
Died: Rochester, Kent, 2 January 1900.
Career: Shawfields Athletic, Newcastle East End (1888), Newcastle West End (January 1891), Newcastle United (May 1892), FOREST (July 1893), Newcastle United (£20, August 1895), Sheppey United (August 1897), Chatham (July 1899 until his demise).

A mobile and dangerous forward, James Collins appeared in both inside-forward positions and on the wing during his career with Newcastle United for whom he scored 12 goals in a total of 52 first-team outings. Well known and admired on Tyneside, he had two successful seasons with Forest, netting 13 goals in 37 games in his first campaign when he partnered Tom McInnes and Horace Pike (in turn) on the left-wing. He had the pleasure of scoring a hat-trick on his debut for the Reds in a 7-1 home win over Wolves in September 1893.

COLLYMORE, Stanley Victor

Striker: 77+1 apps. 50 goals
Born: Cannock, 22 January 1971.
Career: Walsall (YTS, June 1989), Wolverhampton Wanderers (non-contract, July 1989), Stafford Rangers (July 1990), Crystal Palace (£100,000, December 1990), Southend United (£100,000, November 1992), FOREST (£2.25 million, July 1993), Liverpool (£8.5 million, June 1995), Aston Villa (£7 million, May 1997), Fulham (on loan, July 1999), Leicester City (£250,000, rising to £500,000, February 2000), Bradford City (free transfer, October 2000), Real Oviedo/Spain (free transfer, January-March 2001). Retired.

The son of a Barbadian tax officer, also called Stanley, Stan Collymore did not stay long with the Saddlers, leaving to sign for Wolves (his boyhood heroes). He failed to fit in at Molineux and switched to non-League soccer before returning to the Football League in December 1990 with Crystal Palace. After two years and 20 games for the Eagles he moved to Southend and eight months later Forest boss Frank Clark splashed out big money to bring him to the City Ground. He netted 50 goals in two seasons for the Reds, helping them gain promotion to the Premiership (1994) and a place in Europe. In the summer of 1995 he was snapped up by Liverpool and whilst at Anfield made

his England debut, winning the first of his three full caps, also playing in the 1996 FA Cup final defeat by Manchester United. In May 1997 he joined Aston Villa and that meant, over a period of four years a staggering £17.75 million had been splashed out on Collymore in three moves! In July 1999 he was loaned out to Fulham before re-entering the Premiership with Leicester, under manager Martin O'Neill, in February 2000. Eight months later, Collymore moved again, this time on a free to Valley Parade and scored with a terrific overhead kick on his debut for the Bantams v. Leeds United (1-1).

Collymore, a highly-strung striker, but an exceptionally useful one, made 61 appearances for Villa and netted 15 goals. He had his problems with each of his managers, perhaps more so with John Gregory at Villa Park and, indeed, he regularly hit the headlines (for various reasons) with most of the clubs he served. A real character, 'Stan The Man' could well have been a world-beater if he'd put his mind to it! There's no doubt that injuries and suspensions certainly interrupted his career, but nevertheless, during his prime he was an exciting, powerful striker whose great talent was not always fully exploited. He partnered some of the finest marksman around - Ian Wright at Crystal Palace, Ian Rush and Robbie Fowler at Liverpool, Emile Heskey and Tony Cottee at Leicester - and scored some spectacular goals. When he pulled the curtain down on his career his overall record was impressive: 316 appearances (clubs and country) and 125 goals.

COLEMAN, James
Full-back/wing-half: 14 apps.
Born: circa 1868
Career: FOREST (1889-90)
A steady defender, Jim Coleman appeared for Forest during their 1889-90 Football Alliance season. He came into the side halfway through the campaign and played against Derby Midland (away) in a 1st round FA Cup-tie in January 1890 as well as in 13 Alliance matches.

COMERY, Harold
Outside-left: one app.
Born: circa 1880
FOREST (August 1902-May 1904)
Reserve left-winger Harry Comery's only senior appearance for Forest was a Christmas present - deputising for Alf Spouncer against Notts County on 25 December 1903. The Magpies spoilt his day, however, by winning 1-0.

CONDREY, James F
Centre-forward: 7 apps. 2 goals
Born: Wrexham, 1887
Career: Nantwich Town, Wellington Town, FOREST (August 1911-April 1913).
Reserve centre-forward Jim Condrey was called into action for first-team duty by Forest when injury forced out

regular striker Frank Saunders during November and December 1911. Both his goals came in a 2-1 home win over Blackpool in his third outing.

CONNOR, James
Right-half: 8 apps.
Born: Birmingham, 1 April 1867.
Died: Birmingham, 1929
Career: Warwick County, Aston Villa (August 1889), Burlsem Port Vale (trialist, August 1891), Kings Heath FC (September 1891), FOREST (July 1892-May 1895).
Reserve wing-half Jim Connor played in four League games for Aston Villa and five for Forest, making his debut for the Reds in 3-1 away defeat at Burnley in November 1893, when he took over the position from Albert Smith.

COOPER, Colin Terence
Defender: 212+1 apps. 23 goals
Born: Sedgefield, 28 February 1967
Career: Middlesbrough (juniors June 1983, professional July 1984), Millwall (£300,000, July 1991), FOREST (£1.7 million, June 1993), Middlesbrough (£2.5 million, August 1998).
Capped twice by England at senior level and eight times for the Under-21s, Colin Cooper helped the Reds gain promotion to the Premiership in 1994 and four years later was a First Division championship winner when top flight status was reclaimed. He was already a very experienced defender when he moved from Millwall to the City Ground in 1993, having amassed 239 appearances for Middlesbrough and 87 for the Lions. He is a decisive tackler who has the uncanny knack of coming away with the ball after a fair and determined challenge. In January 2002, having returned to Middlesbrough, Cooper reached a milestone in his career of 600 League and Cup appearances.

COOPER, Richard Anthony
Defender/midfielder: 0+3 apps.
Born: Nottingham, 27 September 1977
Career: FOREST (trainee, October 1994, professional October 1996), York City (free transfer, March 2001).
A reserve with Forest, the versatile Richard Cooper was in excellent form for York City, an ever-present, before breaking his leg in January 2002 (v. Hull City). A player full of tenacity and commitment, it was not until the following December that he returned to first-team action.

CORMACK, Peter Barr
Midfielder: 86 apps. 20 goals
Born: Granton, Edinburgh, 17 July 1946
Career: Tynecastle Boys Club, Heart of Midlothian (groundstaff), Hibernian (August 1962), FOREST (£80,000, March 1970), Liverpool (£110,000, July 1972), Bristol City (£50,000, November 1976), Hibernian (February 1980). Retired December 1980; Partick Thistle

(manager, December 1980-May 1984); Anorthosis Famagusta/Cyprus (manager, season 1984-85), Botswana National team coach (1986), Hibernian (assistant-manager, 1987-88), Morton (manager, July 2001 to March 2002).

Hard-working and talented midfielder Peter Cormack, capped initially at amateur level, went on to appear in five Under-23 and nine full internationals for his country (five as a Forest man) as well as representing the Scottish League. Preferring to play on the left-side of the park, Cormack was brave, had stamina, stealth, a flair for the unexpected, a penchant for nipping in on the blind side and was a fine header and passer of the ball. He was a League Cup finalist with Hibs (1969) and won the European Cup (1973), two League titles (1973 & 1976) and the FA Cup (1974) with Liverpool for whom he made 177 appearances (26 goals), having earlier played in 182 competitive games for Hibs (75 goals).

After pulling out of football, Cormack purchased some karaoke equipment and toured various pubs and clubs in Edinburgh before starting up his own painting & decorating company. More recently he has joined the ranks of former players in the circuit of after-dinner speakers.

COTTAM, John Edward
Central defender: 104+4 apps. 4 goals
Born: Worksop, 5 June 1950
Career: FOREST (juniors June 1965, trainee July 1966, professional April 1968), Mansfield Town (on loan, November-December 1972), Lincoln City (on loan, March-April 1973), Chesterfield (August 1976), Chester City (July 1979-May 1982), Scarborough (July 1982, player-manager from June to October 1984), John Cottam was a positive, strong, resourceful defender who gave Forest excellent service before doing likewise with Chesterfield and Chester. He battled hard and long for a first-team place at the City Ground and eventually slotted into the middle line when Liam O'Kane switched to right-back. He retired from competitive football with 338 League appearances to his credit.

COX, Richard A
Goalkeeper: 4 apps.
Born: circa 1864
Career: FOREST (August 1890-May 1891)
Reserve goalkeeper Dick Cox played in four Football Alliance games for the Reds in 1890-91, conceding seven goals but never being on the losing side. He had Sam Widdowson and Willie Brown battling with him for a place between the posts.

COX, William
Utility forward: one app
Born: Edinburgh, 22 August 1897
Career: Edina Hearts, Clydebank (1916), Cardiff City

(August 1919), Newport County (July 1920), Vale of Leven (1921), Workington (January 1922), FOREST (September 1922-March 1924).

Bill Cox's only game for Forest was on 3 March 1923, at centre-forward, in a 4-0 home League defeat by West Bromwich Albion. Earlier in his career he had done reasonably well with Cardiff (scoring five goals in 21 Southern League appearances). Unfortunately he never really settled down with Forest

COYLE, Francis
Centre-forward: 3 apps
Born: Londonderry, Northern Ireland, 1 April 1924.
Career: Coleraine (1953), FOREST (March-August 1958). Capped by Northern Ireland as an amateur, Fay Coyle went on to represent his country in four senior internationals, gaining his last as a Forest player v. Argentina in the 1958 World Cup Finals. He never really settled into a set routine at the City Ground and after just three months with the Reds he returned to the Emerald Isle.

CRAGGS, John
Outside-right: 56 apps. 8 goals
Born: Trimdon Grange, Durham, circa 1880.
Career: Trimdon Grange FC, Sunderland (1901), Reading (1902), Sunderland (1903), FOREST (August 1904), West Stanley (August 1907).
Lively right-winger Jack Craggs made an impressive start to his Forest career, playing in seven successive League games halfway through the 1904-05 season. Following up by missing only two matches during the next campaign, he eventually lost his place in the forward-line (after injury) to Ben Shearman in October 1906, although he did manage eight outings in that promotion-winning campaign from Division Two.

CRAIG, Charles James T
Full-back: 148 apps. 2 goals
Born: Dundee, 1876.
Died: New Southgate, 12 January 1933
Career: Dundee Arnott FC, Dundee (1892), Thames Ironworks, FOREST (August 1902), Bradford Park Avenue, (August 1908), Norwich City (August 1909), Southend United (July 1910-12).
Able to occupy both full-back berths, Charlie Craig had an interesting career, starting in Scotland and finishing in Essex. Over a period of 20 years he amassed more than 250 appearances (at various levels). A stern, hard-tackling player, he partnered Jimmy Iremonger in the Forest defence for three seasons and after the emergence of Ginger Maltby he opted for a move to Yorkshire.

CRAWFORD, John
Centre-half/left-half: 13 apps.
Born: Renton, Dunbartonshire, Scotland, 23 February 1880. Died: 1934
Career: West Calder FC, Bonhill, Dumbarton (briefly), Renton (1897), Lincoln City (August 1900), FOREST (£400, February 1903-May 1905)
Jack Crawford - a 'rare worker who covered a tremendous amount of ground but tended to tire' - scored once in 85 League games for Lincoln before transferring to Forest where he acted, in the main, as reserve to the likes of Bob Norris and Sammy Timmins. He was, in fact, sold by the Imps to the Reds for financial reasons.

CRAWSHAW, Harold William Stanley
Centre-forward: 23 apps. 10 goals
Born: Prestwich near Manchester, 18 February 1912. Died: 1975.
Career: Newton Heath Locomotives FC, Ashington (August 1932), Portsmouth (February 1935), Mansfield Town (£225, August 1937), FOREST (£1,500 plus Charlie Gardner, July 1938), Oldham Athletic (guest, October-November 1943). Did not figure after WW2.
After helping Pompey win the London Combination title in 1936, all-action centre-forward Harry Crawshaw had a splendid season with Mansfield Town, scoring 25 goals in 41 Third Division North matches in 1937-38 (including a hat-trick on his debut) as a straight replacement for recently departed hot-shot Teddy Hartson. He also helped the Stags win the Notts FA County Cup. He was quickly snapped up by Forest (to take over from David 'Boy' Martin) but before he could make much headway, WW2 came along and ended his League career. He did, however score a hat-trick for the Reds' in a pre-season friendly and was their top marksman in the last pre-war season, having been the Third Division North leading scorer in 1937-38. Whilst working at Airspeeds on aircraft production in 1942, Crawshaw he recommended right-winger Peter Harris to his former club Portsmouth. Harris became an outstanding player and won three England caps.
* Crawshaw's elder brother, Richard, was an inside-forward with Manchester City during the 1920s.

CROSBY, Gary
Midfielder/winger: 196+18 apps. 25 goals
Born: Sleaford, Lincs, 8 May 1964
Career: Lincoln City (schoolboy forms, October 1979, non-contract September 1980), Ruston Sports, Lincoln United (August 1982), Lincoln City (non-contract, August 1986), Grantham (October 1987), FOREST (£20,000, December 1987), Grimsby Town (on loan, September 1993), Huddersfield Town (September 1994-May 1997), Rushdon + Diamonds (cs.1997 to September 1997), Lincoln United (July 1998 to October 1998) Burton Albion (assistant manager November 1998). A League Cup winner (v. Oldham Athletic), an FA Cup

Finalist (v. Spurs) and a Zenith Data Systems Cup winner (v. Southampton) in 1990, 1991 and 1992 respectively, Gary Crosby also played for Forest in the 1992 League Cup final defeat by Manchester United and helped them reach the Premiership two years later. A neat and tidy footballer, hard-working, he loved to hug the touchline, taking on his opponent on the outside with a fair turn of speed. Initially he and Franz Carr battled to take hold of right-wing berth at the City Ground, Crosby finally taking charge in 1989 and retaining it until 1993 when Kingsley Black and Ian Woan arrived on the scene.

CROSS, J
Right-back: 3 apps.
Born: circa 1871
Career: FOREST (season 1893-94)
A Forest reserve, Cross came into the side at the end of the 1893-94 season, making his senior debut in the United Counties League at Sheffield United, with his Football League baptism following a week later against Newton Heath. He faded quickly from the scene.

CROSSLEY, Mark Geoffrey
Goalkeeper: 390+3 apps.
Born: Barnsley, 16 June 1969
Career: FOREST (trainee, June 1985, professional July 1987), Millwall (on loan, February 1998), Middlesbrough (free transfer, July 2000), Stoke City (on loan, November 2001 and again, January-May 2003), Fulham (August 2003).
Goalkeeper Mark Crossley, six feet tall and 16 stones in weight, made almost 400 senior appearances for Forest while serving the club for 15 years. He has represented both England and Wales - capped by the former three times at Under-21 level (in 1990) and by the latter in one 'B' and six full internationals - he took over the number one position from Steve Sutton in 1990, played in the FA Cup final defeat by Spurs a year later before helping Forest reach the Zenith Data Systems Cup final in 1992 and clinch a place in the Premiership in 1994. Powerfully built, brave and an excellent shot-stopper, he was signed by Middlesbrough as cover for the giant Australian Mark Schwarzer but made only a handful of appearances at the Riverside Stadium.

CROWE, Christopher
Inside-forward: 78 apps. 5 goals
Born: Newcastle-upon-Tyne, 11 June 1939 Died: 2003
Career: Leeds United (junior, July 1954, professional June 1956), Blackburn Rovers (March 1960), Wolverhampton Wanderers (February 1962), FOREST (August 1964), Bristol City (January 1967), Walsall (September 1969), Auburn FC/Sydney, Australia (May 1970), Bath City (February-May 1971, retired).
Capped by Scotland as a schoolboy, Chris Crowe went on to represent England, gaining youth honours, four Under-

23 caps and playing in a senior international v. France in October 1962 (as a Wolves player). During his career he amassed almost 450 competitive appearances (over coming 400 in the Football League), scoring more than 100 goals. He was tutored, albeit briefly, by the great John Charles at Elland Road and wherever he played he gave a good account of himself, never resisting a challenge, competing strongly, his blond hair always to the forefront.

CURRAN, Edwin
Winger/forward: 53+2 apps. 17 goals
Born: Hemsworth, Yorkshire, 20 March 1955
Career: Doncaster Rovers (juniors, June 1971, professional July 1973), FOREST (£60,000, August 1975), Bury (on loan, October 1977), Derby County (£50,000, November 1977), Southampton (£60,000, August 1978), Sheffield Wednesday (£100,000, March 1979), Sheffield United (£100,000, August 1982), Everton (on loan, February 1982, signed permanently September 1983), Huddersfield Town (July 1985), Panionios/Greece (July 1986), Hull City (October 1986), Sunderland (November 1986), Grantham Town (non-contract, September 1987), Grimsby Town (November 1987), Chesterfield (non-contract, March-May 1988), later Goole Town (manager, November 1989).
Terry Curran had a nomadic career, helping Forest win promotion from Division Two in 1977 being one of his few highlights! One of the game's great 'rovers' he served with no fewer than 15 different clubs (14 holding major League status) and he appeared in well over 500 competitive games (432 in the Football League), scoring in excess of 80 goals.
A fine crosser of the ball, he was tricky, had pace and loved to run at defenders, not always getting the better of his opponent, indicating that at times he was quite greedy. He also had a maverick streak that could infuriate supporters and coaches alike. He showed his best form, without doubt, at Hillsborough (under Jack Charlton's management) and at one point he was on the fringe of international honours. After leaving football Curran worked as a sales assistant in Yorkshire.

CURRIE, David Norman
Forward: 4+4 apps. one goal
Born: Stockton-on-Tees, 27 November 1962
Career: Middlesbrough (professional, February 1982), Darlington (free transfer, June 1986), Barnsley (£150,000, February 1988), FOREST (£750,000, January 1990), Oldham Athletic (£460,000, August 1990), Barnsley (£250,000, September 1991), Rotherham United (on loan, October 1992), Huddersfield Town (on loan, January 1994), Carlisle United (free transfer, July 1994), Scarborough (on loan, January 1997, then month-to-month contract to May 1997).
Another soccer 'wanderer', David Currie spent only seven months with Forest, failing to establish himself in the team, at the City Ground. He later gained both Second and Third Division championship medals with Oldham in 1991 and Carlisle in 1995 respectively. During his senior career he amassed a fine record of 150 goals in 568 competitive games, with his best spells coming at his first three clubs and with Carlisle.

DAFT, Harry Butler
Outside-left: 4 apps. one goal
Born: Radcliffe-on-Trent, Notts, 5 April 1866.
Died: High Cross, Herts, 12 January 1945
Career: Notts County (1882), FOREST (1883), Newark Corinthians, Notts County (August 1888, professional, May 1891), FOREST (January 1893), Notts County (season 1893-94), Newark Corinthians (June 1894-May 1896).
Like his father (Richard) before him, Harry Daft was also a great Notts County cricketer and lacrosse player (at Trent College) as well as being a superb footballer, occupying the outside-left-position.
Capped five times by England (1889-92) he was certainly a fine, attacking winger, very fast, who was an FA Cup winner with Notts County in 1894, three years after collecting a runners-up medal. He had a brief spell with Forest as a teenager and his three separate stints with the Magpies realised a total of 137 League appearances (58 goals scored).
He made his debut for Forest against Derby County a few days after joining the club.
* Harry's father, Richard, played in 254 senior matches (many as captain) for Notts, scoring 9,788 runs at an average of 25.42. He also took 59 wickets (average 20.98) and claimed 155 catches. He topped the first-class batting averages in 1867 (with an average of 53.85) and was second to the great WG Grace in 1869, 1870, 1871 & 1873. He toured North America in 1879. His brother, Richard Parr Daft and his nephew, Charles Frederick Daft, both played County cricket for Nottinghamshire.

DARCHEVILLE, Jean-Claude
Midfielder/striker: 15+4 apps. 2 goals.
Born: Sinnamary, French Guyare, 25 July 1975
Career: Stade Rennais (1995), FOREST (on loan, July 1998-April 1999). Lorient (cs. 1999) Bordeaux (cs 2002).
Jean-Claude Darcheville was manager Dave Bassett's first signing for Forest. Hoping to follow in the footsteps of his fellow countryman, Thierry Bonalair, he faded after a bright enough start in the Premiership when he scored a cracking goal against Southampton. He struggled thereafter and left the City Ground at the end of the summer of 1999, returning to France.

DAVENPORT, Peter
Striker: 141+6 apps. 58 goals
Born: Birkenhead, 24 March 1961
Career: Cammel Laird FC, (August 1980), FOREST

(professional, January 1982), Manchester United (£570,000, March 1986), Middlesbrough (£750,000, November 1988), Sunderland (£350,000, July 1990), Airdrieonians (free transfer, June 1993), St Johnstone (August 1994) Stockport County (free transfer, March 1995), Southport (player/assistant-manager September 1995), Macclesfield Town (player-coach, August 1997, later manager, January 2000-January 2001), Congleton Town (April 2001), Bangor City (manager May 2001).

Utility forward Peter Davenport made his League debut for Forest against Liverpool in May 1982 at the rather advanced age of 21. A positive front-runner, he grafted hard and long during his four years with the club, teaming up superbly well with the likes of Ian Wallace, Gary Birtles and Trevor Christie. He scored a goal every four games (26 in 109) for Manchester United after leaving the City Ground. Signed as a replacement for Mark Hughes, he eventually moved on following Hughes' return to Old Trafford after spells in Spain and Germany. He later played in the 1992 FA Cup final for Sunderland. Capped once by England at senior level v. Republic of Ireland in 1985 (as a Forest star) he also played for his country's 'B' team. He took over from another former Manchester United player, Sammy McIlroy, as manager of the Silkmen in 2000, holding the position for barely four months. All told (playing for clubs and country) Davenport appeared in almost 550 competitive games and scored more than 130 goals. He netted three hat-tricks for Forest (all in the League).

DAVIDSON, Alan Edward
Full-back: 5 apps.
Born: Melbourne, Australia, 1 June 1960
Career: Altonc City, South Melbourne (1978), Forest (November 1984), South Melbourne (1986), Melbourne Croatia (1987 to 1992).
An Australian international full-back, physically strong with a good turn of foot, Alan Davidson failed to establish himself in Forest's League side and had no hesitation in returning to his homeland when released by the club. He made his debut v. Watford a month after signing for the Reds. Davidson won 77 caps for the Socceroos between 1980 and 1991.

DAVIES, Robert Griffith
Centre-half: 59 apps. 4 goals
Born: Blaenau Ffestiniog, North Wales, 19 October 1913. Died: Nottingham, 10 May 1978.
Career: Blaenau Ffestiniog FC (July 1932), FOREST (professional, November 1936); Blackpool & Leicester City (WW2 guest). Retired, May 1947 to become second-team coach at the City Ground, remaining in office for seven years during which time five successive Midland League titles were won (1949-50 to 1953-54 inclusive), and during that time the Reds had a run of 72 home games without defeat. In those five seasons the team played 222 matches in total and scored 592 goals. Davies

later became a respected physiotherapist, attending to both Forest players and Nottinghamshire county cricketers. He lost his job at the City ground when Allan Brown took over as manager in 1974, having given Forest 38 years' dedicated service. He then took over as physio at Walsall, quitting his position in May 1978 when he was taken ill. The club arranged a testimonial match (v. Aston Villa) but sadly he died five days later.

One of the few players to represent Forest before, during and after WW2, Bob Davies was a well built 'Policeman-like' defender. Good in the air he had an excellent first full season with Forest, appearing in 28 senior games. During the hostilities he had over 50 outings but made only six in 1946-47 before announcing his retirement.

A Welsh international trialist in 1936, he turned down the chance of winning a cap by signing as a professional for Forest, the Blaenau receiving just £55 for the deal - the takings of a friendly match against Forest in North Wales. He was kept out of the senior Welsh side by Tommy Jones and served in the RAF during the war, making over 300 parachute jumps and breaking both legs following one mishap on landing. Davies won four caps for Wales during WW2 (v. England in 1940, 1944 and 1945 and v. Scotland in 1945). He also played for a Welsh XI v. Western Command in 1942.

DAVIES, Thomas Osborne
Outside-right: 43 apps. one goal
Born: Swindon, Wiltshire, 27 March, 1882. Died: 1967
Career: Swindon Swifts, Swindon Town (August 1900), FOREST (April 1902), Reading (September 1906), Salisbury City (August 1908), Southampton (trialist, April 1909, signed permanently, August 1909, retired May 1910).
A dapper little player, willing and courageous, Tom Davies had an excellent 1903-04 season with Forest, appearing in 26 First Division matches before losing his place to Sid Sugden. He bounced back but was then found himself out in the cold once more after ex-Sunderland winger John Craggs emerged as first-choice on the right-wing. A broken leg, suffered while playing for Saints against Eastleigh in March 1910, effectively ended Davies' career at the age of 28.

DAVIS, Albert Bertram
Inside-forward: 20 apps. 7 goals
Career: Arnold St Mary's FC (July 1915), FOREST (August 1919-May 1921), Boston Town (August 1921), Reading (August 1923), Mansfield Town (season 1925-26).
Bert Davis, one of the first players signed by the club after WW1, made his Football League debut for Forest v. Hull City in October 1919. He had a decent enough first season with the Reds but faded the following year when a handful of new recruits came into the club to challenge for first-team places.

DAWSON, Andrew
Left-back: one app.
Born: Northallerton, Yorkshire, 20 October 1978
Career: FOREST (trainee, April 1994, professional October 1995), Scunthorpe United (Loan, December 1998, permanent £70,000 March 1999), Hull City (May 2003).
Never really given much of a chance at The City Ground, Andy Dawson developed into one of the finest full-backs in the Third Division with Scunthorpe. Quick in the tackle with a willingness to get forward, he made over 200 senior appearances for the Glanford
Park club, before joining Peter Taylor at Hull.

DAWSON, Kevin Edward
Defender: 9+3 apps.
Born: Northallerton, Yorkshire, 18 June 1981
Career: FOREST (trainee, June 1997, professional, June 1998), Barnet (on loan, March-April 2001), Chesterfield (July 2002).
A tough-tackling, no-nonsense central defender, Kevin Dawson, brother of Andy and Michael, never let the side down when called into action. He moved on to chesterfield where he has overcome injuries to establish himself as a regular.

DAWSON, Michael Richard
Defender: 64 apps. 6 goals.
Born: Northallerton, Yorkshire, 18 November 1983
Career: FOREST (trainee, June 1999, professional November 2000).
Also a central defender, firm with his tackle, michael - youngest of the three Dawson brothers and an England Youth and Under-21 international - developed through the youth and reserve teams to make his League debut for Forest in a 3-2 home defeat by Walsall on Easter Monday 2002. He was named in the full England squad in 2002, confirming his high rating within the club.

DEAN, Alfred
Outside-right: 7 apps.
Born: West Bromwich, 2 January 1877. Died: 1959
Career: Tantany Rangers, West Bromwich Standard, Walsall (September 1895), West Bromwich Albion (May 1896), Walsall (September 1898), FOREST (February 1901), Grimsby Town (May 1901), Bristol City (April 1902), Swindon Town (August 1905), Millwall Athletic (May 1906), Dundee (July 1907), Millwall Athletic (July 1908-May 1909); later assisted Wellington Town.
A much-travelled winger, Alf Dean, short in stature but not negligible in weight, possessed good pace and dribbling ability and on his day was regarded as one of the most dangerous forwards in the game. During his nomadic career he scored well over 100 goals in more than 300 competitive matches. His best spells came at Millwall (in the Southern League) Walsall and Bristol City.

DENNIS, George Thomas
Outside-left/left-half: 33 apps. 4 goals
Born: Moira, Leicester, 12 September 1897.
Died: Burton-on-Trent, 13 October 1969
Career: Newhall Swifts, FOREST (professional, July 1920), Luton Town (August 1924), Norwich City (May 1929), Bristol Rovers (August 1930-May 1931).
George Dennis was a labourer, working for the Public Works authority before signing professional forms for Forest. He could play equally well in two left-sided positions and could control a ball superbly when on the move. It was reported in the 1920s that he scored from 22 successive penalty kicks. He netted 42 goals in 139 League games for Luton (most of them from the spot). He made his debut for Forest on the left-wing versus Cardiff City in February 1921 and the following season helped the Reds gain promotion from Division Two.

DENNISON, Robert Smith
Centre-forward/inside-left/centre-half: 17 apps. 6 goals
Born: Ambleside, Northumberland, 6 March 1912.
Died: Gillingham, Kent 19 June 1996.
Career: Radcliffe Welfare United, Newcastle United (£10, professional, May 1929), FOREST (May 1934), Fulham (June 1935), Northampton Town (WW2 guest 1939-40, signed permanently for £450, August 1945; become assistant-coach at the County Ground, placed in charge of the colts, May 1948, then senior manager, March 1949), Middlesbrough (manager, July 1954-January 1963, also assuming secretarial duties from August 1955 until 1961), Hereford United (manager, December 1963-December 1967), Coventry City (Chief scout, December 1967, becoming assistant-manager December 1969, and thereafter employed in various other roles including a spell as caretaker-manager, March-June 1972). He retired in 1978 but later worked as a part-time scout for Coventry to 1994.
Bob Dennison came from a Scottish family of ten that settled in Northumberland. A promising youngster, he developed quickly as a play-maker with Newcastle before joining Forest for whom he made an impressive debut - starring in a 5-1 win over his former club (Newcastle) in August 1934. Unable to settle in with the Reds he moved to Craven Cottage, later making his name with Northampton as a centre-half during WW2 when he appeared in 191 regional games. As a manager he produced several star players including Mick McNeill, Alan Peacock and a certain Brian Clough (for Middlesbrough).
Dennison was involved with football at a professional level for 65 years. He took Hereford to the Southern League championship in 1965 - his only managerial success.

DENNEHY, Jeremiah
Outside-left: 41+5 apps. 4 goals
Born: Cork, 29 March 1950
Career: Cork Hibernian, FOREST (January 1973), Walsall (July 1975), Bristol Rovers (July 1978), Trowbridge Town (August 1980), Cork FC.
Miah Dennehy was a smart winger who had pace and a good technique. Capped by his country once at Under-23 level, he later added 11 full caps to his collection of international honours, while also making over 220 League appearances and scoring 32 goals. He was signed by Forest manager Dave Mackay and after a steady start he had a useful spell in the first team between August and December 1974 before being shut out by new boss Brian Clough.

DENT, John George
Centre-forward: 207 apps. 122 goals
Born: Spennymoor, 31 January 1903.
Died: West Bridgford, Notts, 6 November 1979.
Career: Spennymoor Rangers (July 1919), Tudhoe United, Durham City (August 1923-May 195), Tow Law Town (season 1925-26), Huddersfield Town (professional, June 1926), FOREST (£1,500, October 1929), Kidderminster Harriers (August 1937-May 1939). Served in the RAF during WW2, later played for the West Bridgford Cricket Club. Johnny Dent claimed five hat-tricks for Forest (four in the League, one in the FA Cup). An honest, thrustful, courageous and hard-working striker, powerfully built with strength to match, he first tasted League football with Durham City when he scored 26 goals in 47 games in the Third Division (North). He then averaged almost a goal every two games for Huddersfield (22 in 53) before becoming a superstar with Forest, having missed out on FA Cup glory with the Terriers in 1928. One of the many footballers to come from the coal-mining area in the North-east of England, he had a never-say-die attitude, and drew up an excellent understanding with his fellow marksman Tom Peacock as the obvious bludgeon-and-rapier combination rattled in more than 100 goals for the Reds during the 1930s before Dent departed.

DERRICK, John Henry
Inside/centre-forward: 147 apps. 36 goals
Born: Nottingham, 8 December 1891.
Died: 1938
Career: Christ Church FC (Nottingham), FOREST (August 1909), Aberaman (seasons 1919-21).
Jackie Derrick spent ten years with the Reds and his appearance and goalscoring records would have been considerably better if WW1 hadn't intervened. A well-built, brave and forceful inside or centre-forward (very clever at times) he competed with great determination and scored twice on his Forest debut in a 4-0 win over Everton in April 1910. He established himself in the front-line the very next season when he had to battle hard and long with Tom Marrison to earn his place as leader of the attack,

although he switched to the inside-right berth in 1911-12 to accommodate Frank Saunders. He fell on bad times just prior to his death.

DEWEY, Joseph
Outside-right/inside-forward: one app.
Born: Burton-on-Trent, 4th quarter of 1873
Career: Burton Swifts, FOREST (November 1896), Burton Swifts (December 1896)
Joe Dewey made his only senior appearance for the club in the League game away to Preston North End (away) in November 1896 when he played on the right-wing in place of Fred Forman. He was not retained.

DEXTER, Arthur
Goalkeeper: 274 apps.
Born: Nottingham, 1905.
Career: Highbury Vale Methodists, Vernon Athletic, Stapleford Brookhill FC, FOREST (April 1923, retired in May 1937).
After understudying Len Langford for almost five years, Alf Dexter grabbed his chance of regular League football with both hands and he remained Forest's first-choice 'keeper for six seasons before Percy Ashton challenged him for the number one position.
Decisive in his approach, he had a safe pair of hands and was one of the club's most consistent players during the period 1930-33, missing only a handful of League and Cup matches. Dexter, a printer by profession who continued in that line of work until 1926, chose to retire when Allan Todd was signed from Port Vale in 1937.

DICKINSON, William
Inside-forward/outside-right: 143 apps. 73 goals
Born: Wigan, 18 February 1906.
Died: 17 December 1978.
Career: Wigan junior football, Wigan Borough (August 1924), FOREST (June 1928), Rotherham United (August 1934), Southend United (May 1936), Hull City (May 1938). He did not figure after WW2.
Bill Dickinson was a regular with each of his five major clubs and all told he amassed in excess of 400 senior appearances and netted 225 goals, with his Football League record standing at 385 games and 203 goals. Thirsty for goals, he used to shoot from anywhere, any distance with either foot. He was a very consistent player, a workaholic who was still bulging the net when war broke out in 1939. He averaged a goal every two games for Forest, including a brace on his debut v. Swansea Town in August 1928. At first he found it difficult to break into the first XI owing to the presence of Johnny Dent, Clive German, Leo Loftus and Cyril Stocks but once in he stayed and formed a wonderful partnership with Dent before losing his place to Tom Peacock.

DODSON, Albert
Right-half: one app.
Born: circa 1890
Career: FOREST (season 1911-12)
Reserve wing-half Bert Dodson made just one senior appearance for Forest, lining up in place of Jack Armstrong against Bradford Park Avenue (away) in the penultimate League game of the 1911-12 season.

DOIG, Christopher Ross
Defender: 46+14 apps. one goal
Born: Dumfries, 13 February 1981.
Career: Queen of the South (associate Schoolboy forms, 1996), FOREST (trainee, June 1997, professional March 1998).
Quality central defender Chris Doig, capped 13 times by Scotland at Under-21 level after previously representing his country in both Schoolboy and Youth internationals, made his League debut north of the border for Queen of the South v. Berwick Rangers in April 1997 at the age of 16, watched by just over 1,000 spectators. Still a teenager, his first outing for Forest came as a substitute against Manchester United in the Premiership at Old Trafford on Boxing Day 1998 when the turn out was 55,216. Unfortunately he sustained a serious knee ligament injury which brought his 2001-02 season to an abrupt end and he was only on the fringe of the first team in 2002-03.

DONOVEN, Alfred Ernest
Inside-left/left-half: 3 apps.
Born: Bulwell, Notts, 20 June 1900
Career: Bulwell FC, FOREST (August 1919), Mansfield Town (free transfer, May 1922) Southend United (£500, May 1925-May 1936). Retired through injury.
A former pit lad, Dickie Donoven, who gained honours in local junior football in the Bulwell area, was certainly a player who 'got away' from Forest. Diminutive, but skilful in all aspects of the game, he spent just one season with the Reds (not doing too much) before coming to the forefront with Mansfield Town for whom he struck 87 goals in 119 Midland League matches. He then switched to Southend, where he was transformed into an exceptionally fine half-back, and over the next 11 years or so, to the end of the 1935-36 season, he scored 55 goals in 318 League games for the Shrimpers. Donoven, who stands fifth in the Stags' all-time scoring chart, could play most musical instruments. He was also a fine golfer and a very useful cricketer and tennis player.

DRABBLE, Francis
Goalkeeper: 8 apps.
Born: Southport, 8 July 1888.
Died: Staines, Middlesex, 29 July 1964
Career: Southport YMCA, Tottenham Hotspur (trialist July 1909, signed professional October 1909), FOREST (February 1911), Burnley (December 1911), Bradford

Park Avenue (July 1913); guested for Brentford, Fulham and Southport during WW1; Bolton Wanderers (July 1919), Southport (June 1921 to 1922), Queen's Park Rangers (March 1924).
Frank Drabble, a schoolteacher by profession, made only three appearances for Spurs before joining Forest where he briefly took over between the posts from Jack Smith before losing out to Jack Hanna. He later made 32 League appearances for Bradford and 29 for Bolton. Frank subsequently worked as a bookmaker and an estate agent.

DUDLEY, Walter William
Full-back: 300 apps.
Born: Seaton, Nottinghamshire, December 1882.
Career: Nottingham junior football, FOREST (August 1900-May 1914), Mansfield Mechanics FC (retired during WW1).
After signing for Forest as a teenager, Walter Dudley spent the first few years of his career playing - and learning the game - in the reserves before establishing himself in the League side in 1905 (after excelling himself on Forest's tour to Argentina). He had made his debut at left-back on 27 December 1902 v. Sheffield United - the club he supported as a youngster - but following the emergence of Ginger Maltby, he switched over to the left side and together they formed a terrific partnership, Dudley going on to top the 300 mark in appearances for Forest before leaving the club in 1914 (having gained a Second Division championship medal in 1907). A clean kicker of the ball, never hurried, he always gave a steady performance, whatever the circumstances.

DULSON, Joseph
Inside/centre-forward: one app. 2 goals
Born: Basford, Notts, 31 January 1913.
Career: Newstead Colliery FC, Accrington Stanley (trialist), FOREST (1931), Accrington Stanley, Bournemouth & Boscombe Athletic (on trial).
Joe Dulson scored twice in his only senior game for Forest v. Swansea Town on 23 April 1932 (League Division 2). After struggling at his next two clubs, he returned to Forest as a WW2 guest and netted 20 goals in 38 appearances between 1943-45.

DUNCAN
Forward: 2 apps. one goal
Born: circa 1870
Career: FOREST (1890-91)
Duncan Scored on his debut for Forest, in 5-4 home defeat by Small Heath in a Football Alliance game in February 1891 when he deputised for the injured Shaw.

DWIGHT, Royston Edward
Centre-forward/outside-right: 53 apps. 27 goals
Born: Belvedere, Kent, 9 January 1933.
Died: Woolwich, London, 9 April 2002.

Career: Hastings United, Fulham (juniors, July 1949, professional June 1950), FOREST (£6,000, July 1958), Gravesend & Northfleet (1960), Coventry City (January 1962), Millwall (January-May 1964), later Tooting & Mitcham United (manager: 1966-73) and then racing manager of the Crayford Greyhound Stadium, Essex (to 1984)

After scoring the opening goal, outside-right Roy Dwight sadly broke his leg in Forest's FA Cup final win over Luton Town in 1959. As a result he never went up to collect his medal, having watched the remainder of the game from his hospital bed with his leg in plaster. The nephew of Reg Dwight (aka Sir Elton John) he spent the first five years of his professional career languishing in Fulham's reserves before going on to play in 80 games for the Cottagers, scoring 57 goals. He took over from Billy Gray on Forest's right-wing and had a wonderful first season at the City Ground, netting 26 goals in 50 League and Cup matches before that sickening blow at Wembley. He was out of the game for two years (recovering full fitness) and never got back into Forest's first XI, leaving the club for non-League side Gravesend before his old Fulham team-mate Jimmy Hill revived his career by signing him for Coventry City early in 1962. Two years later Dwight, still as keen as ever, switched to Millwall and when he quit top-class soccer at the end of the 1963-64 season (basically through injury) he had amassed in excess of 160 senior appearances. During his time as manager of Tooting, he saw the non-League side have a terrific FA Cup run in the early 1970s. He underwent a triple heart by-pass operation in 1984, causing him to take early retirement at the age of 51.

DYSON, James Middleton
Outside/inside-right: 16 apps.
Born: Middleton near Lancaster, Lancs. 4 March 1907.
Career: Northwich Victoria (1925), Oldham Athletic (amateur, February 1928, professional, March 1928), Grimsby Town (£2,350, March 1932), FOREST (February 1938-May 1939).
A small, stylish player, Jimmy Dyson scored 39 goals in 122 games for Oldham and 38 in 139 appearances for Grimsby before joining Forest. He made his debut in a red shirt at Newcastle a few days afterwards and held his position in the side for eight games, making less of an impact the following season. Dyson was surprisingly only a regular in three of his six seasons at Blundell Park and he was sold by Oldham for financial reasons.

EARP, Martin John
Right-back: 50 apps.
Born: Sherwood, Nottingham, 1872
Career: Sherwood Foresters, FOREST (September 1889), Everton (November 1891), FOREST (April 1892), Sheffield Wednesday (August 1893), Stockport County (May 1900).
Right-back and younger brother of Teddy, (a long-serving player and committee man) Jack Earp made 34 appearances in the Football Alliance during his first spell

with Forest. He then moved to Everton with whom he made his Football League debut before returning to the club to help them clinch the Football Alliance title (1892). His Football League baptism for the Reds was against his former club from Merseyside in September 1892. He struggled to hold down a regular place in the side, however, and moved across to Sheffield Wednesday where he became a very fine defender, amassing 174 appearances and scoring eight goals for the Owls. He was an immensely popular player with colleagues and supporters alike and skippered Wednesday to FA Cup glory in 1896. A man of deep conviction and strong principle, Earp always preferred not to play on Christmas Day, yet he thoroughly enjoyed the hurly-burly of the game and loved nothing better than to lead the charge on the opposing goal. He represented the Football League v. the Irish League in 1898 and as an amateur was not dependent upon football for a living. Nevertheless he was still a very fine player.

EDDS, Gareth James
Full-back/midfielder: 12+5 apps. one goal
Born: Sydney, Australia, 3 February 1981
Career: FOREST (trainee, June 1997, professional, February 1998), Swindon Town (August 2002), Bradford City (July 2003).
A versatile player, Gareth Edds was released by manager Paul Hart after struggling to get into the first team during the 2001-02 season, making only one appearance.

EDGAR, Daniel J
Right-back/defender: 104 apps. one goal
Born: Jarrow 3 April 1910.
Died: 23 March 1991.
Career: Jarrow St Bede's FC, Walsall, Sunderland (1931), FOREST (July 1935-37)
A versatile defender and sure-kicker, Danny Edgar certainly gave a good account of himself during his two seasons with Forest, making well over 100 first-team appearances, most of them as partner to Jimmy Barrington. He made his debut for the Reds on the opening day of the 1935-36 season (v. Bury) and played in 34 League outings that campaign. An ever-present in 1936-37, he eventually lost his place during the second half of 1937-38 when Reg Trim was preferred at right-back.

EDWARDS, Christian Nicholas Howells
Defender: 46+10 apps. 3 goals
Born: Caerphilly, 23 November 1975
Career: Swansea City (trainee, April 1992, professional July 1994), FOREST (£175,000, March 1998), Bristol City (on loan, December 1998), Oxford United (on loan, February 2000), Crystal Palace (on loan, November 2001), Oxford United (on loan, January 2003). Bristol Rovers (July 2003).
A Welsh international (capped seven times at Under-21 level, twice for his country's 'B' team and once by the

seniors) Christian Edwards, 6ft 2ins tall and 12st 8lbs in weight, is a well-built defender, physically strong defender, effective in the air and brave in the tackle. Owing to the form of fellow defenders at the City Ground, he failed to get a look in during seasons 2001-03 when he was loaned out three times, twice to Oxford.

EDWARDS, John
Inside-forward: 83 apps. 22 goals
Born: Salford, 23 February 1924.
Died: Nottingham, December 1978
Career: Manchester United (on trial), Long Eaton United, FOREST (on trial April 1944, signed professional May 1944), Southampton (£10,000, June 1949), Kidderminster Harriers (on loan, July 1952), Notts County (in exchange for Alex Simpson, November 1952), King's Lynn (July 1954).
Jack Edwards somehow slipped through the net at Old Trafford before being recommended to Forest boss Billy Walker when playing in a Royal Navy side during WW2. A brainy footballer of the stylish type, described in some handbooks as a 'real box of tricks', Edwards was rather light in build but fairly tall and did pretty well in aerial battles. He scored on his League debut for Saints and made his first appearance for Forest in the local derby v. Notts County in April 1945 (FL North). Edwards sadly lost his life following a street mugging in Nottingham shortly before Christmas, 1978.

ELLIOTT, Bernard Harry
Wing-half: 10 apps.
Born: Beeston, Notts, 3 May 1925
Career: Beeston Lads' Club, FOREST (October 1942), Boston United (August 1948), Southampton (October 1949), Poole Town (July 1959-May 1960).
Bryn Elliott - a never-say-die competitor - made well over 30 appearances for Forest during WW2. Unfortunately he didn't get much of a chance at the City Ground after the hostilities, and after leaving the Reds he became a regular with Southampton for whom he made over 250 appearances. He actually made his debut for Saints in a vital promotion encounter v. Spurs at White Hart Lane. After a brief spell with Poole he became a licensee taking over a pub just a stone's throw away from the Dell.

ELLIOTT, Stephen Blair
Inside/centre-forward: 4 apps.
Born: Haltwistle, Northumberland, 15 September 1958
Career: FOREST (apprentice, April 1975, professional September 1976), Preston North End (March 1979), Luton Town (£95,000, July 1984), Walsall December 1984), Bolton Wanderers £25,000, (July 1986), Bury (September 1988), Rochdale (October 1989, Guiseley (cs.1991).
Steve Elliott had a fine career in League football, scoring 125 goals in 436 appearances, including 70 in 208 outings for PNE. He had the likes of Butlin, Withe and Woodcock

ahead of him in the chase for a place in the front-line at the City Ground and in the end was sold for a bargain fee by manager Brian Clough.

ELLIOTT, Thomas William
Inside-right/centre-forward: 28 apps. 7 goals
Born: Annfield Plain near Chester-le-Street, County Durham, 6 April 1890.
Career: West Stanley, Gainsborough Trinity (1910), South Shields (1911), Huddersfield Town (May 1912), Grimsby Town (December 1919), FOREST (July 1920), Brentford (August 1921), Durham City (season 1923-24), Crewe Alexandra (season 1924-25).
Tom Elliott made his League debut for Forest against Stoke in August 1920. He thrived on hard work, was a strong runner with a fierce right-foot shot who was perhaps surprisingly transferred to Brentford after an excellent season with the Reds. Elliott netted 50 goals in a career total of 203 League appearances.

FAIRCLOUGH, Courtney Huw
Defender: 126+8 apps. 2 goals
Born: Nottingham, 12 April 1964
Career: FOREST (apprentice, June 1980, professional October 1981), Tottenham Hotspur (for a tribunal-set fee of £385,000, June 1987), Leeds United (on loan, March 1989, signed permanently for £500,000, April 1989), Bolton Wanderers (£500,000, July 1995), Notts County (free transfer, July 1998), York City (on loan, March 1999, retired in February 2001).
Chris Fairclough worked his way through the Forest ranks to make his senior debut in a League Cup-tie in December 1981, although it was not until September 1982 that he made his bow in League football (v. Liverpool at Anfield). Described as 'an outstanding prospect' he soon replaced Scotsman Willie Young at the heart of the Reds' defence but when his contract expired at the end of the 1988-89 season (with Clough slow to offer him a new one) he quickly left the City Ground to join David Pleat's Spurs. He appeared in 70 first-class games for Spurs and then made over 240 more appearances for Leeds and 106 for Bolton. Fairclough was capped seven times by England at Under-21 level and played once for the 'B' team. He was a Second and then First Division championship winner with Leeds in 1990 and 1992 respectively. In 1997 he helped Bolton reach the Premiership as Division One champions and he was also a Charity Shield winner in 1992. Fairclough, who made almost 620 senior appearances as a professional (39 goals scored) was signed for York by his former junior team-mate at Forest, Neil Thompson.

FALCONER, Fleming
Wing-half: 2 apps.
Born: Hutchesontown, Scotland, 25 May 1899.
Career: Glasgow Eastern FC, Glasgow Ashfield, FOREST (August 1923), Providence Clamdiggers FC (July 1924), Bo'ness FC, then played in the USA with J & P Coates

(Rhode Island) and New Bedford Whalers, Bristol Rovers (March 1928 to cs. 1929).

A most astute wing-half with great stamina, Fleming Falconer failed to make his mark with Forest despite two reasonable performances in the Football League, both against Lancashire clubs, Manchester City at Maine Road in February 1924 (his debut) and Bolton Wanderers at Burnden Park. He replaced Jackie Belton each time.

FARMER, Alexander

Centre-half/left-half/inside-left: 16 apps.
Born: Lochgelly Fife, 9 October 1908
Career: Kettering Town, FOREST (August 1930), Leicester City (briefly, 1932), Yeovil & Petters United (1933), Queen's Park Rangers (July 1933-1944).
Alex Farmer could play in three positions with confidence, but preferred the centre-half slot. He struggled hard to establish himself in the Forest team but did very well with QPR for whom he scored 11 goals in 164 competitive games before and during WW2.

FARMER, Ronald James

Wing-half: 10 apps.
Born: Guernsey, Channel Islands, 6 March 1936
Career: FOREST (juniors, June 1951, professional May 1953), Coventry City (£6,000 with goalkeeper Arthur Lightning, November 1958), Notts County (£12,000, October 1967, Grantham Town (April 1969), later Coventry City (youth team coach), then an employee at Massey Ferguson.
Channel Islander Ron Farmer was a resilient wing-half who failed to establish himself in the first team with Forest but later amassed 315 senior appearances for Coventry (285 in the Football League), helping the Sky Blues rise from the Fourth to the First Division in double-quick time. At Highfield Road he formed a splendid half-back line with George Curtis and Mick Kearns and received a £10,000 pay-off when he left the Sky Blues for Meadow Lane. Farmer's brother, Bill (q.v) was a goalkeeper with Forest and Oldham Athletic, also having trials with Coventry.

FARMER, William Henry

Goalkeeper: 58 apps.
Born: Guernsey, Channel Islands, 24 November 1927.
Career: St Martin's FC (Guernsey), FOREST (May 1951), Brush Sports, Loughborough (June 1957), Oldham Athletic (£400, July 1957), Worcester City (July 1958), Coventry City (on trial, August-September 1959), Corby Town (October 1959 cs. 1962).
Bill Farmer (eight appearances) helped Forest win promotion from the Second Division in 1956-57. Vigorous, sturdy and utterly fearless, he was signed as understudy to George Walker at the City Ground, having his best run in the side in 1954-55 (34 League and Cup outings). He had a torrid time with Oldham, conceding 13 goals in five League games.

FASHANU, Justinus Soni

Striker: 35+1 apps. 4 goals
Born: Kensington, London, 19 February 1961.
Died: Shoreditch, London, 2 May 1998
Career: Norwich City (apprentice, September 1977, professional December 1978), Adelaide FC/Australia (on loan, May-July 1980), FOREST (£1 million, August 1981), Southampton (on loan, August-October 1982), Notts County (£150,000, December 1982), Brighton & Hove Albion (£115,000, June 1985), Los Angeles Heat/NASL (player-manager June 1986), Edmonton Brickmen/Canada (player-coach, July 1988), Manchester City (non-contract, October 1989), West Ham United (non-contract, November 1989), Leyton Orient (non-contract, March 1990), Southall (player-coach, March 1991), Newcastle United (non-contract, October 1991), Leatherhead (November 1991), Toronto Blizzard/NASL (briefly), Torquay United (free transfer, December 1991, appointed assistant-manager, June 1992), Airdrieonians (February 1993), FC Trelleborg/Norway (May 1993), Heart of Midlothian (July 1993-February 1994), Toronto Blizzard (March-July 1994); then to the NASL (as a coach, from August 1994).
A former Dr Barnado's Boy, Justin Fashanu, a former ABA heavyweight finalist and steel-erector, was labelled a £1 million misfit following his transfer from Carrow Road. A 6ft 1in striker he did some good work (at times) during his eighteen months at the City Ground but his scoring record was poor. However, during a varied career he netted well over 80 goals in more than 300 senior appearances with his nine English-based League clubs (40 in 103 outings for the Canaries). Honoured by England at Youth and 'B' team levels he also gained 11 Under-21 caps. Fashanu actually retired in 1986 due to injury but after lengthy treatment was persuaded to return to action and continued to play for another eight years or so. He created a sensation by becoming the first professional footballer to 'come out' declare himself to be gay, following which his career nosedived. Tragically he committed suicide after fleeing the United States where he was the subject of a police investigation.
Justin's brother John was a Tyland International striker.

FETTIS, Alan

Goalkeeper: 5+1 apps.
Born: Belfast, 1 February 1971
Career: Ards (1987), Hull City (£50,000, August 1991), West Bromwich Albion (on loan, November 1995), FOREST (£250,000, January 1996), Blackburn Rovers (£300,000 September 1987), York City (free transfer March 2000). Hull City (January 2003)
Capped by his country as a Schoolboy and Youth team player, 6ft 1in goalkeeper Alan Fettis then went on to appear in three 'B' and 25 full internationals while also accumulating an excellent record at club level. After 155 games for Hull City and three for WBA, he joined Forest

as cover for Mark Crossley. However, he never really got a look in at the City Ground - despite some impressive displays for the reserves - and after half-a-dozen outings he moved to Ewood Park where again he failed to establish himself in the first XI. But then, after dropping down the ladder, he became number one at Bootham Crescent and in 2002 passed the milestone of 100 League games for the Minstermen when he was also voted 'Clubman of the Year.' In May 1995 Fettis played as a striker for Hull v. Blackpool and scored!

FIELDING, Alec Ross

Outside/inside-right: 10 apps. one goal
Born: Trentham near Stoke-on-Trent, January 1880.
Died: 1952
Career: Stoke Priory FC, Stoke (December 1901), FOREST (April 1902), Stoke (March 1903), West Bromwich Albion (June 1908), Stoke (June 1909), Burton United (October 1909). Retired during WW1.
An ebullient forward with excellent dribbling skills and wonderful body-swerve, Ross Fielding made over 100 appearances during this three separate spell with Stoke, but never really made much headway elsewhere. When he joined West Brom he was actually out hunting with the hounds on his father's estate in North Staffordshire.

FIRTH, Robert Edwin

Outside-right: 145 apps. 15 goals
Born: Sheldon, Birmingham, 20 February 1887.
Career: Birmingham Corporation Transport, Golder's Green FC, Birmingham (professional, April 1909), Wellington Town (April 1911), FOREST (September 1911), Port Vale (June 1921), Southend United (July 1922). Retired in May 1923.
Bob Firth was working as a tram conductor when Birmingham signed him in 1909. Mainly a provider of chances, able to centre accurately on the run, his overall play was little appreciated at St Andrew's and he left with his pal Fred Banks for Wellington and in fact, they were playing colleagues together for nine years, joining Forest together in 1911. Firth made his Football League debut for the Reds on the first Saturday in October 1911 against Burnley, on the opposite wing to Banks who had made his bow in the previous match (versus Grimsby). They played together in some 50 games for Forest (42 in the League) up to 1914.

FISHER, Alfred

Full-back/half-back: 105 apps.
Born: Nottingham, circa 1888
Career: Notts Olympic, FOREST (April 1909-September 1915). Did not figure after WW1.
A willing worker, who always played a cool and effective game, Alf Fisher made his League debut for Forest at left-half against Preston in March 1910, replacing George Needham. He was called up for duty intermittently the following season before establishing himself in the right-

half berth with Joe Mercer and Needham the two other middle-line players. Fisher later moved to right-back and remained there until he went off to serve his country in WW1.

FISKE, William Archibald

Goalkeeper: 5 apps.
Born: Beccles near Lowestoft, circa 1887.
Career: Blackpool (April 1907), FOREST (August 1914). Did not feature in League football after WW1 having served his country as a soldier.
Signed as second reserve behind Harold Iremonger and Jack Powell, goalkeeper Bill Fiske made his League debut for Forest in place of the latter (injured) against Derby County at the City Ground on Christmas Day 1914, having previously played 224 times between the posts for Blackpool. He conceded 12 goals in his five outings for the club. Although a little on the short side, Fiske made up for any handicap with surprising agility and courage.

FLEMING, Gary James

Defender: 78+6 apps.
Born: Londonderry, 17 February 1967
Career: FOREST (apprentice, June 1983, professional November 1984), Manchester City (£150,000, August 1989), Notts County (on loan, March 1990), Barnsley (£85,000, March 1990, retired through injury, June 1997).
A Northern Ireland international (capped 31 times at senior level as well as winning Under-23 honours) Gary Fleming was a classy player who could play as an orthodox defender or as a sweeper. He was forced to quit the game at the age of 30 with a serious knee injury after making 271 appearances for his last club, Barnsley.

FLETCHER, S Ernest

Centre-half: one app.
Born: Nottinghamshire, circa 1892
Career: FOREST (April 1914-September 1915). He did not return to League football after serving his country during WW1.
A reserve centre-half, Ernie Fletcher made his debut for Forest against Bury on 26 September 1914 when he deputised for Joe Mercer in a 4-2 defeat.

FLOOD, Charles William

Inside-forward: 100 apps. 22 goals
Born: Newport, Isle of Wight, 18 July 1896.
Died: Beverley, 14 November 1978
Career: Army football (Royal Garrison Artillery team), Plymouth Argyle (as an amateur, season 1919-20), Hull City (July 1920), Bolton Wanderers (May 1922), FOREST (January 1923), York City (June 1926), Swindon Town (February 1927, retired August 1928). Returned to Humberside where he settled to become a prominent cricketer, playing as a wicket-keeper and attacking batsman for Hull CC whom he later coached: 1963-65. Earlier in his career Flood had played cricket for

both Notts and Devon CCC's and for Julian Kahn's XI.
A tall, lanky player at 6ft 1in and 12st 2lbs, Charlie Flood possessed an indomitable attitude that drove him at full stretch to the final whistle. Always helping out in defence while giving his full weight to the attack, he made well over 200 appearances in League and Cup football (more than 60 goals scored) for the six clubs he served.

FORD, Joseph Bertram
Outside-right or left: 104 apps. 12 goals
Born: Northwich, Cheshire, 7 May 1886
Career: Witton Albion (1903), Crewe Alexandra (1905), Manchester United (October 1907), FOREST (June 1910), Goole Town (July 1914).
A former apprentice fitter and turner, Joe Ford was a slim and sprightly winger who could perform on both flanks. He was understudy to England international George Wall at Old Trafford before joining Forest for whom he scored on his debut against Preston in a 2-0 win (September 1910). Despite the Reds' form slumping to such an extent that they took only one point from 13 games during the last third of the 1910-11 season, Ford maintained his composure and form and went on to appear in over a century of games for the club in four years before moving to Goole Town.

FORMAN, Francis
Half-back: 260 apps. 30 goals
Born: Aston-upon-Trent, Notts, 1875.
Died: West Bridgford, Notts 4 December 1961.
Career: Aston-Upon-Trent FC, Beeston Town, Derby County (March 1894), FOREST (December 1894, retired May 1905). Forest committee member: 1903-61 and also a Life Member of the club. After announcing his retirement, Forman was engaged in business as a building contractor in West Bridgford, Nottinghamshire, with his brother-in-law, and former Forest goalkeeper Jimmy Linacre.
An FA Cup winner with Forest (v. his former club Derby) in 1898, Frank Forman also played in nine full internationals for England (1898-1903). An exceptionally fine right or centre-half, rated one of the best in Britain, he was a born leader whose generalship and tactical know-how were of the highest order. A natural successor as captain when John MacPherson retired, he was calm, imaginative and unflurried in the tightest of corners and when on the attack, could slip a pass through a tightly packed defence with great precision.
* He and his brother Fred (below, q.v) played in the same Forest team together and also for England, being the last pair of brothers to do so until Jack Charlton joined Bobby on the international scene in 1965.

FORMAN, Frederick Ralph
Utility: 188 apps. 41 goals
Born: Aston-upon-Trent, Notts, 1873.
Died: Nottingham, 14 June 1910

Career: Aston-upon-Trent FC, Beeston Town, Derby County (July 1893), FOREST (July 1894, retired in May 1903). Forest Committee Member: 1903-1910.
A railway draughtsman by profession and brother of Frank (above) Fred Forman was also capped by England, winning three caps in 1899. Regarded as a player of some versatility and competency, he could perform equally well at half-back, inside-forward or outside-left and although a little lethargic at times, he still gave a good account of himself out on the park. He and his brother played together in more than 120 matches for Forest.
* Fred actually made his League debut for Forest six months before Frank, lining up against Everton in September 1894, whereas his brother made his bow in March 1895 v. Bolton Wanderers.

FORMAN, Thomas
Outside-left: 5 apps
Born: Basford, Notts, 26 October 1879.
Career: FOREST (August 1900), Manchester City (April 1902), Sutton Town, Barnsley (June 1907), Tottenham Hotspur (February 1911), Sutton Junction FC (June 1912-15). Did not play League football after WW1.
Younger brother of the two Formans (above) unfortunately Tommy never made it with Forest but after leaving the club he did very well, especially with Barnsley (16 goals in 126 League games) as well as having nine outings with Spurs. Recognised as being one of the fastest wingers in the Second Division when he first moved to Oakwell, he was a member of Barnsley's FA Cup final side in 1910 (beaten in a replay by Newcastle United).

FORREST, John Reid
Outside or inside-right: 14 apps. 3 goals
Born: Tranent near Edinburgh, East Lothian, 3 May 1908
Career: Gorgie Juniors (Edinburgh), Rosewell Rosedale FC (Midlothian), FOREST (May 1930-May 1933)
A reserve forward at the City Ground, Jack Forrest made his League debut against Second Division champions-elect Everton in February 1931 when he partnered Noah Burton on the right-wing in a 2-0 defeat at Goodison Park. He had to wait seven months, until September, for his next outing (at outside-right) and soon afterwards made ten in succession, scoring his first Forest goal in a 2-1 win in the local derby v. Notts County.

FOSTER, Colin John
Defender: 83+4 apps. 6 goals
Born: Chislehurst, Kent, 16 July 1964
Career: Leyton Orient (apprentice, July 1980, professional February 1982), FOREST (February 1987), West Ham United (September 1989), Notts County (on loan, January 1994), Watford (£100,000, March 1994), Cambridge United (free transfer, March 1997, retired June 1998).
When he chose to retire in the summer of 1998, Colin

Foster's playing record was impressive: 536 League and Cup appearances and 38 goals. He had 210 of those games with Orient before moving to Forest, playing alongside Des Walker at the heart of the Reds' defence and doing a wonderful job in 1987-88 when 3rd place was attained in the First Division. A huge defender, 6ft 4ins tall and over 14st in weight, Foster was reliable, safe and resilient, a fierce tackler who gave nothing less than 100 percent effort whatever the circumstances.

FOY, Keith Patrick
Left wing-back: 19+3 apps. one goal
Born: Dublin, 30 December 1981
Career: FOREST (trainee, April 1998, professional January 1999), Doncaster Rovers (February 2003 to June 2003).
Selected by the Republic of Ireland at Youth team level (Under-16s) winger Keith Foy later added seven Under-21 caps to his collection as he made steady progress at the City Ground. He was placed on the transfer list by manager Paul Hart at the end of the 2001-02 season after failing to oust Jim Brennan from the left-back position.

FRANCIS, Trevor John
Inside-forward: 92+1 app 37 goals
Born: Plymouth, 19 April 1954
Career: Birmingham City (apprentice, June 1969, professional May 1971), Detroit Express/NASL (on loan, May-August 1978), FOREST (£1 million charges, February 1979), Detroit Express, again (on loan, June-August 1979), Manchester City (£1.2 million, September 1981), Sampdoria/Italy (£800,000, July 1982), Atalanta/Italy (£900,000, July 1986), Glasgow Rangers (free transfer, September 1987), Queen's Park Rangers (March 1988, appointed player-manager in December 1988), Sheffield Wednesday (free transfer, February 1990, manager from June 1991 to May 1995); spent 1995-96 working for Sky TV, Birmingham City (manager, May 1996 to October 2001), Crystal Palace (manager, from November 2001-April 2003).
Trevor Francis became Britain's first £1 million footballer when he moved to Forest in 1979. He had exploded onto the League scene with 15 goals in his first 21 games for Birmingham City, including four in one match against Bolton Wanderers in February 1971 when he was still only 16 years of age. He displayed electrifying speed off the mark, intricate dribbling skills, a powerful shot and amazing self-confidence that were to be his trademarks during a long and successful playing career. His impressive total of goals for Blues would have been even better but for two serious injuries. Throughout the 1970s - after helping the second city club reach the top flight in 1972 - it seemed as though Francis alone was keeping Birmingham in the First Division, but with the team destined for the drop in 1979 he was whisked away by Brian Clough after asking to leave St Andrew's. From there he changed clubs

regularly, yet always played at top level, going to it on to amass a terrific record of more than 750 appearances (with all clubs) and scoring over 220 goals.
He was a European Cup winner with Forest in 1979 (his headed goal saw off FF Malmo in the final) and a year later collected a Super Cup prize (after Barcelona had been defeated in the annual contest) and also a League Cup runners-up medal when the Reds lost to Wolves in the final. He was a member of Sampdoria's Italian Cup winning side in 1985 and then helped Rangers win the Scottish League Cup in 1988 and Sheffield Wednesday clinch the double in 1991: League Cup glory (over Manchester United) and promotion from Division Two.
He did not have too good a time in his first spell as manager with QPR, but with Wednesday he did rather better, guiding the Owls to runners-up spot in both the FA Cup and League Cup competitions in 1993. Then, to a certain extent he did quite well with Birmingham, having the ill-luck to miss out in the Play-offs three seasons running: 1999, 2000 & 2001, and lose in the final of the Worthington Cup, beaten on penalties by Liverpool, also in 2001.
On 14 February 1979, just 24 hours after moving to Forest, Francis played for the 'A' team v. Notts County (away) in front of 40 spectators!

FRASER, Douglas Michael
Defender: 94 apps. 4 goals
Born: Busby, Renfrewshire, Scotland, 8 December 1941.
Career: Rolls Royce FC, Eaglesham Amateurs, Blantyre Celtic (1956), Aberdeen (April 1958, professional December 1959), West Bromwich Albion (£23,000, September 1963), FOREST (£35,000, January 1971), Walsall (£8,000, July 1973, player-manager at Fellows Park from January 1974-March 1977). A year after retiring from football (1978), Fraser joined the prison service, based at Nottingham gaol, turning out for the Prison officers' side in 1981-82.
A gritty performer not without style, Doug Fraser was a League Cup and FA Cup winner with WBA in 1966 & 1968 respectively and twice a League Cup runner-up in 1967 & 1970, skippering the Baggies in the latter final defeat by Manchester City. A Scottish international (two caps gained v. Holland in 1968 and Cyprus in 1969) he also toured Australia with his country in 1967 and made 325 senior appearances during his seven-and-a-half years at the Hawthorns, starting off as an attacking right-half and ending up as a very efficient right-back. Forest secured his services in an effort to bolster up their midfield and he certainly gave a good account of himself, playing in almost 100 first-class games for the club before his transfer to Walsall when Reds' manager Brian Clough had a clear-out. As manager of Walsall he kept them in a mid-table position while taking them into the 5th round of the FA Cup in 1975. At the start of his career Fraser made 88 appearances for Aberdeen.

G

FRASER, William Alexander

Goalkeeper: 2 apps.

Born: Australia, 24 February 1929.

Died: 7 March 1996

Career: Cowie FC (Scotland), Third Lanark (1947), Airdrieonians (£350 in 1949), Sunderland (£5,000, March 1954), FOREST (December 1958-May 1960).

Willie Fraser, lithe, six-feet tall and weighing 12st 6lbs, was one of the smartest goalkeepers in the First Division during his four-and-a-half years at Roker Park during which time he appeared in 127 League matches. Capped twice by Scotland (v. Wales and Northern Ireland in 1955) he was understudy to Chick Thomson at the City Ground and was perhaps unfortunate to concede no fewer than 12 goals in his two outings for the club, letting in seven on his debut against Birmingham City soon after arriving from Roker Park, and five v. Luton Town in the April (1959) before being released the following year.

FREEDMAN, Douglas Alan

Striker: 61+22 apps. 23 goals

Born: Glasgow, 21 January 1974

Career: Queen's Park Rangers (apprentice April 1990, professional May 1992), Barnet (July 1994), Crystal Palace (£800,000 September 1995), Wolverhampton Wanderers (£800,000 October 1997), FOREST (£950,000 August 1998), Crystal Palace (£600,000 October 2000).

Honoured by his country as a schoolboy, Dougie Freedman has now represented Scotland in eight Under-21, one 'B' and two senior internationals. An intelligent, hard-working striker who can turn a defender inside out with a couple of swift movements, Freedman failed to make the first team at QPR but then did very well as a marksman at Barnet (32 goals), Palace (34) and Wolves (12) before linking up with Pierre van Hooijdonk at Forest. Again he continued to find the net before returning to Selhurst Park in the autumn of 2000 when David Platt was toying with Stern John, Jack Lester and Marlon Harewood up front.

FREEMAN, David

Striker: 2+7 apps.

Born: Dublin, 25 November 1979

Career: FOREST (trainee, July 1995, professional December 1996), Port Vale (on loan September 2000) Carlisle United (September 2002) St Patrick's Athletic early 2003).

A busy little player, with a good first touch and plenty of pace, Freeman represented the Republic as a Youth team player before appearing in one Under-21 international. He struggled to get a regular run in the Forest team before his release in July 2002.

FRENCH, John William

Wing-half: 86 apps. 8 goals

Born: Stockton-on-Tees, 19 January 1925

Career: Middlesbrough (October 1943), Southend United (February 1947), FOREST (November 1952), Southend United (July 1956-May 1957).

Jack French had already scored more than 20 goals in almost 200 League and Cup games for Southend before joining Forest at the age of 27. A most conscientious player, clever and enthusiastic, he gave the Reds valuable service for three-and-half years before returning to the Shrimpers where he ended his senior career. French made his first and last League appearances for Forest against the same club, Rotherham United (in November 1952 & March 1956).

FRYER, John Leavy

Inside-forward: 25 apps. 9 goals

Born: Widnes, 23 September 1911

Career: Runcorn junior football, Everton (as an amateur 1929, professional 1930), Wrexham (July 1933), Hull City (June 1937), FOREST (June 1938-September 1939), Hull City (guest in friendly matches, 1944). Did not re-appear after WW2

Jack Fryer was a well-built attacker with progressive ideas that included plenty of hard shooting. Although he never made the first XI at Goodison Park, he found the net frequently elsewhere, amassing a League record of 57 goals in 144 appearances.

Fryer's son, Jack junior, was also registered with Forest but failed to make the grade.

FULLARTON, William M

Centre-half: 21 apps.

Born: Scotland, circa 1879

Career: Bonnybrigg Thistle (1898), Queen's Park (1900), Sunderland (August 1903), FOREST (July 1905), Plymouth Argyle (August 1906), New Brompton (September 1907).

As a reliable centre-half, strong in the tackle, Bill Fullarton gave precious little away and was a gritty performer wherever he played. He made over 40 appearances for Argyle and more than 30 for Sunderland.

GAGER, Horace Edwin

Defender: 267 apps. 11 goals

Born: West Ham, London, 25 January 1917. Died: 1984

Career: Vauxhall Motors FC, Luton Town (professional, November 1937), Glentoran (guest WW2), FOREST (February 1948-May 1955).

Like so many other footballers who became League professionals in the mid-to-late 1930s, Horace Gager lost a major part of his career to WW2. However, after doing well at Kenilworth Road, gaining a lot of experience, he soon settled in at the City Ground and showed what a fine player he was by producing some superb displays at the heart of the Forest defence. When Bob McCall dropped out of the first team in 1951, Gager who himself had played a vital role when Forest won the Third Division South title that year, was appointed captain. He went on to play senior football until he was 37 years of age, finally retiring in 1955. Many ardent Forest fans believed that Gager would have represented England had it not been for the war. Gager, who played with David 'Boy' Martin when guesting in Ireland during WW2, scored twice in 62 League games for Luton before transferring to Forest.

GALLEY, John Edward

Striker: 36+7 apps. 8 goals
Born: Clowne near Chesterfield, 7 May 1944
Career: Wolverhampton Wanderers (groundstaff, June 1959, professional May 1961), Rotherham United (£10,000, December 1964), Bristol City (£29,000, December 1967), FOREST (December 1972), Peterborough United (on loan, October 1974), Hereford United (December 1974, retired in May 1977). After quitting football Galley became a 'rep' for the Beswick Paper Group/Company (Leicester).
A very useful centre-forward with an eye for goal, John Galley found it hard to get first-team football with Wolves (owing to a dearth of excellent strikers) but after leaving Molineux he certainly made up for lost time, going on to net over 150 goals in more than 400 competitive matches. Brought in to partner Neil Martin in attack, he scored on his debut for Forest (at Fulham in December 1972) and did well for a while before injuries hindered his progress. He was eventually replaced in the Reds' attack by Barry Butlin.
* Galley is the nephew of Tom Galley who played for Wolves, Grimsby Town and England (either side of WW2).

GALLOWAY, Septimus Randolph

Centre-forward: 43 apps. 8 goals
Born: Sunderland, 22 December 1896.
Died: Mapperley, 10 April 1964
Career: Sunderland Tramways (1921), Derby County (October 1922), FOREST (November 1924), Luton Town (June 1927), Coventry City (December 1927), Tottenham Hotspur (on trial, July 1928, signed permanently August 1928), Grantham Town (September 1929).
After a good spell with Derby for whom he scored 25 goals in 66 League games, Randolph Galloway was recruited by Forest - and he continued to impress with some determined displays alongside Walker in the Reds' front-line. However, after two goals in 11 outings he drifted into the reserves but bounced back in 1925-26 and produced some of the best football of his career. Unfortunately he failed to maintain his form and struggled after leaving the City Ground, making very few appearances over the next two years.

GARA, Andrew

Inside/centre-forward: 6 apps. one goal
Born: Ireland, 1875
Career: Temple Bar Juniors (Belfast), Wigan County (August 1896), Preston North End (January 1898), FOREST (August 1902), Bristol City (November 1902).
An Irish international (2 caps won) Andy Gara played the best football of his relatively short with Preston for whom he scored 27 goals in 66 League appearances. A keen and enthusiastic forward with a powerful right-foot shot, he never really settled in at the City Ground and left after just three months.

GARDINER, A Charles

Outside-right/inside or centre-forward: 42 apps. 8 goals
Born: Perth, Scotland, 1915
Career: Cherrybank BC, Roselea FC, FOREST (professional, August 1935), Mansfield Town (July 1938-May 1939). Did not play League football after WW2.
Charlie Gardiner scored on his debut for Forest in a 5-2 defeat at West Ham at month after joining the club as a raw-boned 20-year-old. Quite quick over the ground and a straight shooter he was in and out of the side during his first season at the City Ground and although he had 16 League outings the following year he was mainly confined to the reserves, switching to Field Mill in readiness for the start of the 1938-39 campaign. He made 27 appearancses for the Stags (4 goals scored) and during WW2 guested for Forest, Leicester City, Bournemouth, Derby County and the Scottish club Greenock Morton.

GARDNER, Ross

Midfielder: 1+1 apps
Born: South Shields, 15 December 1985
Career: Newcastle United (trainee, April 2001, professional December 2002), FOREST (undisclosed fee, July 2003).
Capped by England at Youth team level, midfielder Ross Gardner did not make a first team appearances for Newcastle and moved to Forest with his colleague James Beaumont.

GAYNOR, Thomas

Centre-forward: 61+17 apps. 19 goals
Born: Limerick, 29 January 1963
Career: Limerick City, Doncaster Rovers (December 1986), FOREST (£25,000, October 1987), Newcastle United (on loan, November 1990), Millwall (March-June 1993).
Tommy Gaynor was a League Cup and Simod Cup winner with Forest in 1989. He made a name for himself with some really gutsy performances for Doncaster (scoring 8 goals in 36 games) before Brian Clough took a fancy to him, bringing him across country as cover for son Nigel and Paul Wilkinson. He remained loyal to Forest with whom he spent five-and-a-half years, scoring a goal every four games.

GEARY, George

Outside-left: 12 apps. one goal

Born: Nottinghamshire, circa 1869

Career: FOREST (September 1893), Long Eaton Rangers (July 1895), Chesterfield (August 1899-May 1902)

George Geary - a speedy, energetic, resourceful winger - scored his only goal for Forest in a 4-3 win over rivals Notts County in a United Counties League game in April 1894. He hit 12 goals in his 59 League outings for Chesterfield.

GEMMELL, Thomas

Right or left-back: 41 apps. 6 goals

Born: Glasgow, 16 October 1943

Career: Meadow Thistle (Wishaw), Coltness United, Celtic (July 1961), FOREST (£40,000, December 1971), Dundee (July 1973, retired in December 1976, then manager at Dens Park June 1977-April 1980). Albion Rovers (manager, January 1986 to December 1988 and again April 1993 to January 1994). Later a Perthshire hotelier and also a branch manager for the Sun Life Assurance Company

Long-striding, hard-tackling defender Tommy Gemmell scored a stunning goal when Celtic won the European Cup in 1967. A real old-fashioned full-back (preferring the left flank rather than the right), he spent a decade at Parkhead, during which time he appeared in 418 competitive games for the Bhoys (63 goals scored), gaining 18 full caps for Scotland in the process. Besides his European Cup triumph, Gemmell also helped Celtic win six successive League titles (1966-71 inclusive); triumph in three Scottish Cup finals (1965-67-69) and succeed in four League Cup finals (1966-69 inclusive) and he was also a runner-up in the 1970 European Cup, Scottish Cup in 1966 & 1970 and the League Cup in 1965. Later he gained a fifth League Cup winners medal with Dundee (1974). He spent 18 months with Forest, partnering fellow Scot Doug Fraser and then Peter Hindley in front of goalkeeper Jim Barron.

GEMMILL, Archibald

Midfielder: 78+2 apps. 5 goals

Born: Paisley, Scotland, 24 March 1947

Career: Drumchapel Amateurs, St Mirren (professional, 1964), Preston North End (£13,000, May 1967), Derby County (£66,000, September 1970), FOREST (September 1977), Birmingham (£150,000, August 1979), Jacksonville Teamen/NASL (March-August 1982), Wigan Athletic (September 1982), Derby County (November 1982 to May 1984), FOREST (June 1984, initially as coach, then as reserve team manager), Rotherham United (as joint-manager with John McGovern, September 1994 to 1996).

Despite standing only 5ft 5ins tall, Archie Gemmill was a real handful for any opponent. He was an all-action, dynamic and aggressive midfielder who amassed more than 650 appearances (589 in the Football League with 324 coming in two spells with Derby) and scored over 60 goals in a marvellous career that spanned some 20 years. The first substitute to be used in the Scottish League (by St Mirren v Clyde in August 1966) Gemmill was capped 43 times at senior level by his country and once by the Under-23s, was a League championship winner in 1972 and 1975 (with Derby) and in 1978 (with Forest) also celebrating a League Cup victory with the Reds in 1979. He netted one of the finest individual goals in World Cup football for Scotland against Holland in the 1978 and although his time at the City Ground was fairly short (less than two years in fact) he gave the supporters plenty to cheer about. Certainly one of the best attacking midfielders in the game during the 1970s, always eager to drive forward in support of his strikers and not at all hesitant when electing to shoot, Gemmill was a grafter to the last.

GEMMILL, Scot

Midfielder: 289+22 apps. 29 goals

Born: Paisley, 2 January 1971

Career: FOREST (juniors April 1986, apprentice June 1987, professional January 1990), Everton (£250,000, March 1999).

Son of Archie (q.v), Scot Gemmill scored twice when Forest won the Zenith Data Systems Cup in 1992. That same year he was in the Reds' beaten League Cup final side, helped the team reach the Premiership in 1994 and then return to the top flight as champions of Division One four years later. Capped 27 times by Scotland at senior level, he has also represented his country in two 'B' and four Under-21 internationals and like his father he too is an industrious and perceptive midfielder with great stamina and willpower. He established himself in the Reds' engine-room in 1992 playing alongside Roy Keane. He remained a key member of the squad for many years and injuries and suspensions apart made well over 300 appearances for the club before moving to Everton.

GEORGE, Charles Frederick

Forward: 4 apps. one goal

Born: Islington, North London, 10 October 1950

Career: Arsenal (apprentice, May 1966, professional February 1968), Derby County (July 1975), St George's FC/Australia (on loan, May 1977), Minnesota Kicks/NASL (on loan, May 11978) Southampton (record fee of £400,000, December 1978), FOREST (on loan, January 1980), Bulova FC/Hong Kong (September 1981), Bournemouth (March 1982) Derby County (March 1992), Dundee United (on trial, September 1982), Coventry City (August 1983). Retired in 1984; later ran a country pub in the New Forest, Hampshire, was a partner in a garage firm before becoming a matchday host in the hospitality area at Highbury, while also helping run Arsenal's museum.

Charlie George was a key player in the Arsenal team that won the double in 1970-71, scoring a superb winner in the FA Cup final victory over Liverpool. A Swaggering skillful stricker with a tremendous shot he also did well at Derby before injuries began to affect his carrer. He came to the City Ground with a view to a permanent transfer, but played just four games before returning to Southampton. Two of his appearances came in the European Super Cup games against Barcelona, when he scored the winner in the first leg as Forest went on to win 2-1 on aggregate. He won a singleCap for England (v. Republic of Ireland 1976) and five caps at Under-23 level.

GERMAN, Arthur Clive Johnson

Inside-right/centre-forward: 32 apps. 10 goals
Born: Ashby-de-la-Zouch, Leicestershire, 28 June 1906. Died: 1968
Career: Rawden FC, (Ashby), Corinthians (August 1924), FOREST (January 1928), Corinthians (April-September 1931). Rewarded with Life Membership of the Corinthians, 1932-33.
An amateur throughout his career, Clive German did well with Forest, averaging a goal every three games. Never overawed by the situation, he was speedy and clever with an accurate, forcible shot. He scored on his League debut for the Reds against arch-rivals Notts County in a 2-1 win at Meadow Lane in February 1928. He netted twice in 28 competitive games for the Corinthians.

GETTY, John

Outside-right: 20 apps. 3 goals
Born: Bonhill, Scotland, 23 April 1918
Career: Milngavie FC, Ashfield FC, FOREST (May 1936), Dumbarton (August 1939). Did not play competitive League football after WW2.
A well-built right-winger Jack Getty - initially signed as cover for Richard Brown and Arthur Masters - spent three seasons at the City Ground, making his League debut against Blackburn Rovers in December 1936. He had his best spell in the first team halfway through the 1938-39 season when he netted twice in 10 matches.

GIBSON, Sydney George

Outside-right: 276 apps. 55 goals
Born: Walgrave, Northants, 20 May 1899. Died: 1938
Career: Kettering Town, FOREST (May 1921), Sheffield United (£5,000, September 1928); retired in May 1932 through injury.
A quick and clever winger with a powerful right-foot shot, Syd Gibson helped Forest win promotion to the First Division in his first season with the club: 1921-22. He made his League debut for the Reds at centre-forward against West Ham at Upton Park in October 1921 but quickly reverted to his chosen wing-position and became a prominent member of the side, holding his place without a serious challenger for some six years. Many thought he

should have played at a higher level and, indeed, on occasions he looked international class. Unfortunately he became unsettled at Forest when the club refused to meet his wage demands and he eventually moved to Bramall Lane. Despite losing his confidence and being somewhat inconsistent, Gibson still managed to score 29 goals in 118 senior games for the Blades. He suffered a serious knee injury that forced him into retirement at the age of 33.

GIBSON, Thomas

Full-back/centre-forward: 192 apps. 35 goals
Born: Maxwelltown near Dumfries, Scotland, 23 October 1888.
Career: Amisfield Town FC, Maxwelltown Volunteers, Greenock Morton, FOREST (September 1907), Notts County (December 1919), Southend United (June 1923 to cs.1924).
Tommy Gibson was a solid, hard-tackling full-back who could play on either flank as well as slotting in as an emergency centre-forward. He didn't have the greatest of baptisms in the Reds' defence, being on the losing side in a 4-0 defeat at Villa Park in December 1907, but he quickly brushed that experience aside and battled hard and long in the reserves before establishing himself in the first team in 1911. After leaving the City Ground he scored five goals in his 63 League outings for County, eventually quitting League football in 1925.

GLOVER, Edward Lee,

Striker: 79+23 apps. 13 goals
Born: Kettering, Northants, 24 April 1970
Career: FOREST (apprentice June 1986, professional May 1987), Leicester City (on loan, September 1989), Barnsley (on loan, January 1990), Luton Town (on loan, September 1991), Port Vale (£200,000, August 1994), Rotherham United (£150,000, August 1996), Huddersfield Town (on loan, March 1997), Macclesfield Town (July 2000), Mansfield Town (September 2002) Burton Albion (October 2002), Corby Town (December 2002).
With Forest, Lee Glover gained a League Cup winners medal (as a non-playing substitute) in 1989, played in the 1991 FA Cup final defeat by Spurs, collected a Simod Cup winners prize 12 months later and three years after that helped the Reds clinch promotion to the Premiership in 1994. Capped by Scotland at Youth team level, he went on to play in three Under-21 internationals and during his senior career he amassed in excess of 400 League, Cup and international appearances and netted more than 80 goals.
A very capable player, he found if difficult at times to hold down a place in the first XI at the City Ground but when called into action he was totally committed and his honest endeavour was certainly appreciated by his fellow team-mates as well as the fans.
* Glover gained a BSc (Honours) degree in Sports Science (after a four-year course) and in 2001-02 he duly completed the UEFA 'B' coaching certificate.

GOODCHILD, George

Outside/inside-right: 4 apps.

Born: Wearside, circa 1870

Career: Ryhope Colliery, Sunderland (June 1894), Derby County (June 1896), FOREST (March 1897), Burton Swifts (October 1897), Jarrow FC (July 1899), South Shields Athletic (July 1901).

George Goodchild was basically a reserve with every club he served, making only 16 League appearances during his entire professional career. He made his League debut for Forest in April 1897 v. Sheffield Wednesday (away).

GORDON, Leslie William

Left-half: 2 apps.

Born: Barking, Essex, 13 July 1903.

Career: Grimsby Rovers, Sheffield United (August 1923), Crystal Palace (1925), Shirebrook, FOREST (September 1927), Shirebrook (March 1928), Brighton & Hove Albion (August 1928).

Reserve left-half Les Gordon failed to get a single first-team call up from Sheffield United or Palace and after his two outings for Forest he went on to make 18 League appearances for Brighton before drifting back into a lower grade of football.

GOUCHER, George Henry

Full-back: one app.

Born: Shirebrook, 18 May 1902.

Career: Shirebrook FC, Notts County, FOREST (August 1928), Torquay United, Shirebrook.

Another reserve team player, George Goucher made only one League appearance for County and six for Torquay either side his association with Forest, for whom he made his senior debut against Barnsley on 6 October 1928 (lost 3-1).

GOUGH, Richard Charles

Defender: 7 apps.

Born: Stockholm, Sweden, 5 April 1962

Career: Wits University/South Africa (1977), Dundee United (apprentice June 1979, professional March 1980), Tottenham Hotspur (£750,000, August 1986), Glasgow Rangers (£1.5 million, October 1987), San Jose Earthquake/NASL (May 1998), FOREST (free transfer, March 1999), Everton (free, June 1999), Northern Spirit/Australia (July 2001).

After representing South Africa at schoolboy level, Richard Gough went on to gain 61 full caps for Scotland and played five times for the Under-21 side. A well-built, highly efficient central defender, he won 19 club medals north of the border - ten in the League championship stakes, (nine with Rangers), five in the League Cup and three in the Scottish Cup. He also gained both League Cup and Scottish Cup runners-up medals with Dundee United and played for Spurs in their 1987 FA Cup final defeat by Coventry City. During an outstanding career, spanning well over 20 years, Gough accumulated in excess of 900 appearances at senior level (792 for his British

clubs) and scored over 80 goals. Twice voted Scotland's 'Footballer of the Year' in 1986 and 1989, he played for the Football League v. the Rest of the World in the centenary match at Wembley. He was well past his best when he joined Forest but still produced some solid displays at the heart of the defence.

* Gough's mother was Swedish while his father (Charlie) was also a professional footballer, with Charlton Athletics.

GRAHAM, James Arthur

Centre-forward: 34 apps. 14 goals

Born: Corby, Northamptonshire, 13 January 1911.

Died: Bath, 28 November 1987.

Career: Corby British Legion, Desborough Town, FOREST (September 1932), York City (July 1935), Hartlepools United (October 1935), Southend United (December 1935), Clapton Orient (May 1937 to cs. 1938). Making his senior debut against Fulham in December 1932 (Division 2), Jimmy Graham quickly established himself in Forest's League side and scored 13 goals in 29 League games for the club before losing his place to Johnny Dent. He later continued his career with a number of lower division clubs.

Jimmy was the brother of Dick Graham, manager of Crystal Palace, Orient, Walsall and Colchester.

GRAHAM, Thomas

Centre-half: 391 apps. 7 goals

Born: Hamsterley, County Durham, 5 March 1907.

Died: 29 March 1983

Career: Hamsterley Swifts (August 1922), Consett Celtic (1923), FOREST (on trial, signed in August 1927). Retired as a player in 1944 and soon afterwards was appointed as the club's trainer, a position he held until 1961 when he was forced to give it up due to his poor health. He remained with the Reds, working as an advisor to the youth teams while also acting as a casual scout.

No relation to Jimmy (above), Tommy Graham played no football whatsoever at school but then took up the game with Hamsterley Swifts, a pit lads team, in 1922. Developing quickly, he was invited for trials by Newcastle United but failed to impress. He then joined Forest (also on trial) but had a mishap in training and was sidelined for seven months. He came back (March 1928) and in his first match was carried off injured. However, Forest gambled on his fitness and Graham eventually came good, gaining full England internationals honours against France (lost 5-2) and Ireland (won 6-2) in May and October 1931 while also making almost 400 appearances for the Reds. A very able-bodied defender, Graham was something of a stripling when he first joined the club but became a great player and in all he spent some 40 years with Forest. He was related to ex-Forest star Harry Bulling via marriage.

GRANT, G

Left-back: one app

Born: Scotland, circa 1865

Career: Broxburn, Edinburgh St Bernard's, FOREST (August 1889-May 1890)

Full-back Grant spent just one season with Forest during which time he appeared in a single Alliance game, a 5-3 defeat away at Long Eaton Rangers in November 1889.

GRANT, Brian Patrick

Full-back: 22 apps.

Born: Coatbridge, Scotland, 10 May 1943

Career: FOREST (juniors, 1958, professional May 1960), Hartlepool United (January 1966), Bradford City (on trial), Cambridge United (c. 1968 to 1972).

A capable, workmanlike defender who was loyal to Forest for six years during which time he battled hard and long to gain first-team football. Unfortunately his debut game for the Reds was a 6-0 hammering at Everton in October 1961. He later made 35 League appearances for Hartlepool and 14 for Cambridge.

GRAY, Andrew David

Right wing-back/midfielder: 41+35 apps. one goal

Born: Harrogate, Yorkshire, 15 November 1977

Career: Leeds United (apprentice, 1993, professional July 1995), Bury (on loan, December 1997), FOREST (£175,000, September 1998), Preston North End (on loan, February 1999), Oldham Athletic (on loan, March 1999), Bradford City (July 2002).

A right-footed wing-back or midfielder, who can play on both flanks but prefers the left, Scottish Youth international Andy Gray comes from a footballing family, his father Frank and uncle Eddie both played for Leeds and represented their country (Scotland). Quick and skilful and a fine crosser of the ball, he failed to make headway at Elland Road, playing in only 28 first-class matches before his transfer to Forest. He did well at times at the City Ground but with Forest struggling to come to terms with life in the Premiership, he was one of several players who lost their way. Gray struggled with injury during the 2001-02 season and was released by manager Paul Hart at the end of that campaign.

GRAY, Francis Tierney

Left-back/midfielder: 118 apps. 8 goals

Born: Castlemilk, Glasgow, 27 October 1954

Career: Leeds United (junior May 1970, professional November 1971), FOREST (record fee of £475,000, August 1979), Leeds United (£300,000, May 1981), Sunderland (£100,000, July 1985), Darlington (player-coach, June 1989, retired as a player, May 1991, then manager, June 1991-February 1992; acted as scout for Blackburn Rovers and Sheffield Wednesday (1992-93), Harrogate Town (manager, June 1994), to Bahrain (as coach, 1995-97).

In 1980, left-back/left-sided midfielder Frankie Gray - brother to Eddie (also of Leeds United & Scotland) - played left-back for Forest in their League Cup final defeat by Wolves and was thereafter a double winner when the Reds beat the German side Hamburg SV to clinch the European Cup and then knock over Barcelona to lift the European Super Cup. After representing his country as a teenager, he went on to win 32 caps for Scotland (playing in the 1982 World Cup finals) and starred in five Under-21 internationals.

A very positive, attacking player with flair and aggression (when required) he made 405 appearances in his two spells at Elland Road (35 goals scored). He helped Sunderland win the Third Division championship in 1988 having earlier collected runners-up medals when Leeds lost in the finals of the European Cup Winners Cup in 1973 and European Cup two years later. Father of Andy Gray (above).

GRAY, Stuart

Defender/midfielder: 57+2 apps. 3 goals

Born: Withernsea near Kingston-upon-Hull, 19 April 1960.

Career: FOREST (apprentice, June 1976, professional December 1980), Bolton Wanderers (on loan, March-May 1983), Barnsley (£40,000, August 1983), Aston Villa (£150,000, November 1987), Southampton (£200,000, September 1991). Retired as a player in May 1993, Bognor Regis Town (seasons 1994-96); Southampton Coach June 1997, then manager July-October 2001), later Aston Villa (coach and assistant-manager, May 2002)

A versatile defender, able to play as a centre-half or left-back (as well as in midfield) Stuart Gray made almost 60 appearances for Forest in seven years and more than 125 for Barnsley before joining Aston Villa. He spent four years at Villa Park and amassed a further 132 appearances (15 goals scored), skippering the side on several occasions and helping them gain promotion from the Second Division in 1988. He was forced to quit first-class soccer in 1993 through injury.

GRAY, William Patrick

Outside-right/inside-forward/left-back: 224 apps. 34 goals

Born: Dinnington, County Durham, 24 May 1927.

Career: Dinnington Colliery FC, Wolverhampton Wanderers (amateur, season 1943-44), Gateshead (amateur, 1945), Leyton Orient (professional, May 1947), Chelsea (March 1949), Burnley (£16,000, August 1953), FOREST (June 1957), Millwall (player-manager, November 1963-May 1966), Brentford (manager: July 1966-September 1967), Notts County (manager, September 1967-September 1968), Fulham (coach, January 1969), Forest (groundsman 1970 onwards).

An FA Cup winner with Forest in 1959, Billy Gray gained one England 'B' cap (v. Switzerland in 1950) and during his career amassed a fine record of 506 League appearances and 73 goals. Fast and clever, he was a first-team regular at Stamford Bridge for four seasons helping Chelsea twice reach the semi-final stage of the FA Cup. A very popular player wherever he went, he moved from the wing to inside-forward and then to left-back as the years gradually caught up with him at the City Ground, always putting in some sterling performances. As a manager the influential Gray guided Millwall to runners-up spot in Division Four and then Division Three in successive seasons of 1965 and 1966. He signed Les Bradd and future Scottish international Don Mason when manager at Meadow Lane.

GREEN, Arthur William
Centre-forward: 39 apps. 16 goals
Born: Aberystwyth, 5 December 1881.
Died: Nottingham, 24 September 1966.
Career: Aberystwyth FC (August 1897), Swindon Town (briefly on trial), Aston Villa (August 1900), Ebbw Vale (September 1901), Walsall (Midland League, late 1901), Notts County (July 1902), FOREST (January 1907), Stockport County (cs. 1908 to May 1909), Brierley Hill Alliance (season 1911-12). Did not play after WW1.
Arthur Green, who helped Forest win the Second Division title in 1907, was a Welsh international, capped eight times between 1901 & 1908, his last two coming as a Forest player. A prolific marksman with Aberystwyth, Green was described by a local journalist in 1899-1900 as 'the greatest centre-forward in Wales'. Sadly he failed to impress with Aston Villa despite scoring well in the reserves, but was Notts County's leading scorer in 1902-03 with 19 goals in 30 games and was joint-top scorer in the two subsequent seasons. He gave Forest good service for a year-and-half, playing in between fellow countryman Gren Morris and Tom Marrison, and netting regularly including a spell of five goals in nine games at the start off the 1907-8 campaign.
Possessing a powerful shot, he never missed a penalty during his career (so the reference books say) but was a little inclined to selfishness. He was not the type of player to exert himself, however, and was reluctant to drop back and help out in centre-field or defence. The highlight of his international career was to score a hat-trick in a 4-4 draw with Ireland at Wrexham in 1906. A Nottinghamshire county tennis player, Green was also an expert golfer. His main job was that of representative for a window manufacturing company from which he retired in 1949.

GREEN, Harold
Half-back: 4 apps.
Born: Sedgley near Wolverhampton, 3 August 1904.
Career: Coseley Amateurs, Redditch United, Sheffield United (August 1925), FOREST (July 1927), Halifax Town (August 1928).
Able to occupy any of the three half-back positions, Harry Green was a reserve at every club he served, making only six League appearances during his entire professional career. His Forest debut was against Port Vale (away) a month after joining the club.

GREEN, John
Outside-right/inside-right/centre-forward: 14 apps. 3 goals
Born: Blackburn, circa 1897. Died: 1927
Career: Blackburn Rovers (briefly, 1915), Fleetwood, FOREST (September 1921), Luton Town (August 1923), Lancaster Town.
Jack Green was only 30 years of age when he died suddenly in 1927. Basically a reserve to Messrs Harold and Gibson at the City Ground, he had his best spells in the first team during the second half of the 1922-23 season when his three goals.

GREENWOOD, Patrick George
Defender: 19 apps.
Born: Hull, 17 October 1946
Career: Hull City (juniors, July 1961, professional October 1964), Barnsley (£12,000, November 1971), FOREST (£10,000, October 1974-January 1976, left club by mutual consent), Boston Minutemen/NASL (player-coach, May 1976), Bridlington Trinity (as a player, December 1977).
Paddy Greenwood - lithe in performance and in performance, both solid and fluent - had already amassed in excess of 250 League appearances when he moved from Oakwell to Forest. Unfortunately a broken leg sustained when playing for the Reds in February 1975 shortened his first-class career.

GRIFFITHS, Harold
Inside-left: 8 apps. one goal
Born: Aston, Birmingham, circa 1879
Career: St Andrew's FC, Reading (1901), FOREST (season 1903-04)
A reserve forward with Forest, Harry Griffiths appeared in just eight League games for the club, making his debut in a 1-0 home defeat by Blackburn Rovers in September 1903. His only goal was scored in a comprehensive 5-1 home win over Derby County in March 1904.

GRUMMITT, Peter Malcolm
Goalkeeper: 352 apps.
Born: Bourne, Lincolnshire, 19 August 1942
Career: Bourne Town (August 1957), FOREST (professional May 1960), Sheffield Wednesday (January 1970), Brighton & Hove Albion (December 1973-May 1977).
First choice 'keeper at the City Ground for almost a decade, Peter Grummitt gained three England Under-23 caps (all with Forest) and also represented the Football League. He was so impressive in the reserves that he was handed his League debut at the age of 18 against Bolton Wanderers in November 1960, being beaten by a Jim Iley own-goal before he had even touched the ball! The game ended in a 2-2 draw. He kept his place in the side until February 1968, helping Forest reach the FA Cup semi-final and finish runners-up in Division One in 1966-67. Unfortunately, after breaking his arm, he was unable to

H

regain the number one position from Alan Hill and after just two outings in 1969-70 he moved to Hillsborough. Grummitt, surely one of the Reds' finest goalkeepers who was desperately unlucky not to win a full England cap, later ran a newsagents shop in his home town of Bourne

GUINAN, Stephen Anthony

Striker: 4+5 apps. one goal
Born: Birmingham, 24 December 1975
Career: FOREST (apprentice, 1991, professional January 1993), Darlington (on loan, December 1995), Burnley (on loan, March 1997), Crewe Alexandra (on loan, March 1998), Halifax Town (on loan, October 1998), Plymouth Argyle (on loan, March 1999), Scunthorpe United (on loan, September 1999), Cambridge United (free transfer, December 1999), Plymouth Argyle (March 2000), Shrewsbury Town (March 2002), Hereford United (2002).
A tall, strong 6ft 1in, 13st 8lbs striker, Steve Guinan, was unable to get into Forest's first team (on a regular basis) and was loaned out to six different clubs in four years before leaving the City Ground for Cambridge in 1999.

GUNN, Alfred H

Centre-forward: 2 apps.
Born: West Germany, 11 July 1924
Career: FOREST (February-May 1947)
Reserve centre-forward Alf Gunn spent barely three months at the City Ground, appearing in just two away League defeats against Manchester City and Spurs following the arctic winter of 1947.

GUNN, Brynley Charles

Full-back/defender: 159+7 apps. 2 goals
Born: Kettering, Northants, 21 August 1958
Career: FOREST (apprentice, August 1974, professional August 1975), Shrewsbury Town (on loan, November-December 1985), Walsall (on loan, January 1986), Mansfield Town (on loan, March 1986), Peterborough United (free transfer, August 1986), Chesterfield (July 1989), Corby Town (June 1992, joint player manager 1993-94), Oakham United (May 1994).
Bryn Gunn helped Forest win the 1980 European Cup final, coming on as a sub for Frankie Gray. A typical specimen of the honest defender, 6ft 2ins tall and 13st 8lbs in weight, he was strong in the tackle and powerful in the air, his positional sense was second to none and his overall performances were generally first-class. He spent 13 years with Forest and was a regular from 1981-83 when occupying a variety of positions. Gunn made 131 League appearances for Posh and 91 for Chesterfield, ending his senior career with a total of 373 outings to his credit in that competition.

GUNNARSSON, Brynjar Bjorn

Midfielder: 6+4 apps.
Born: Iceland, 16 October 1975
CareerL Orgryte IS/Sweden, Stoke City (£600,000, January 2000), FOREST (free transfer, July 2003)
An Icelandic international with over 40 full caps to his credit plus eight at Under-21 and three at Youth team levels, Brynjar Gunnarsson made over 150 senior appearances for stoke City (20 goals scored) before joining Forest. He sometimes lacked consistency during his time at The Britannia Stadium, but on his day he can be a match for any other player in his position in the First Division.

GUTTRIDGE, Frank H

Utility: 20 apps. 2 goals
Born: Nottingham, 12 April 1866. Died: 1918
Career: Notts County (season 1888-89), FOREST (August 1889), Notts County (August 1894), Southampton (briefly during 1895-96)
Frank Guttridge made 18 appearances for Forest in the club's first season in the Football Alliance (1889-90) occupying three different positions, those of right-back (his best), outside-right and centre-forward. He was a fairly steady player who found it hard to bed in with the Reds after that initial campaign and thereafter played second fiddle to the likes of Earp and Scott.

HAALAND, Alf-Inge Rasdal

Defender/midfielder: 75+18 apps. 7 goals
Born: Stavanger, Norway, 23 November 1972
Career: Bryne FC (Norway), FOREST (January 1994), Leeds United (£1.6 million, July 1997), Manchester City (£2.5 million, June 2001, retired in 2003 through injury).
A Norwegian international (34 caps gained at senior level plus another 29 with the Under-21 side as well as representing his country as a Youth team player) Alfe-Inge Haaland helped Forest clinch promotion to the Premiership in 1994 after joining the club from the Norwegian outfit, Bryne FC. A versatile performer, strong and aggressive, he mixed his decisive tackling with some surging runs and had his best season at the City Ground in 1996-97 when he netted six goals to finish up as the club's joint top-scorer.
He had done extremely well at Elland Road up to 2000, but then surprisingly found himself out in the cold and after a spell in the reserves he moved to Maine Road. Sadley Knee problems eventually led to his retirement from the game.

HADLEY, Harold

Half-back: 12 apps. one goal
Born: Barrow-in-Furness, 1878. Died: 1950
Career: Colley Gate United, Halesowen (September 1895), West Bromwich Albion (February 1897), Aston Villa (February 1905), FOREST (April 1906),

Southampton (April 1907), Croydon Common (July 1908), Halesowen (February 1910), Merthyr Town (player-manager, May-August 1919, then manager until April 1922), Chesterfield (manager, April-August 1922), Aberdare (November 1927-April 1928), Merthyr Town (manager, April-November 1928 & August 1930-September 1931), Gillingham (manager, briefly mid-1930s), Bangor City (manager, July 1935-April 1936).

Harry Hadley had plenty of experience when he joined Forest. A very useful and effective wing-half, cool and calculated, he was methodical and energetic but was often criticised for giving the ball too much air when clearing downfield. He appeared in over 180 senior games for WBA, helping the Baggies win the Second Division championship in 1902. An England international (one cap gained v. Ireland in 1903) he was in charge of Merthyr Town when they entered the Football League in 1920, and despite being offered jobs at a higher level. Hadley preferred to remain in charge of a lower-division club. His brother Ben also played for WBA.

HAGUE, Eric Montague
Utility forward: 4 apps.
Born: Sheffield, 21 July 1901.
Career: Gainsborough Trinity, FOREST (August 1928), West Ham United (briefly on trial), Walsall (August 1929), Crewe Alexandra (1930).

Able to play on either wing or as a centre-forward, Eric Hague served with five different clubs in three years and never made his mark with any of them. His Forest debut was against Bradford PA (home) a month after joining the club.

HALES, Herbert
Outside-left: 3 apps.
Born: Kettering, Northants, 21 November 1908.
Died: Gainsborough, 1982
Career: Desborough Town (1925), FOREST (on trial, March 1929, signed April 1929), Northampton Town (on trial, August 1929), Peterborough & Fletton United (late 1929), Stoke City (December 1930), Preston North End (July 1931), Chesterfield (July 1933), Stockport County (December 1934), Rochdale (July 1935), Burton Town (August 1937), Kidderminster Harriers (season 1938-39). Did not figure after WW2.

Although regarded as an out-and-out left-winger, Herby Hales could also play on the right and had to wait quite some time before making his mark in League football. Fast and clever, he went on to have a more than useful career, amassing well over 160 League and FA Cup appearances and scoring some 25 goals. He signed for Forest initially as a trialist and did well to secure a permanent deal with the club. However, he never quite fitted in at the City Ground and left after just three senior outings, his first coming against Millwall at the Den shortly after arriving.

HALL, Colin Thomas
Winger: 28+10 apps. 2 goals
Born: Wolverhampton, 2 February 1948.
Career: FOREST (juniors, April 1964, professional March 1966), Bradford City (June 1970), Bristol City (July 1972), Hereford United (September 1972-May 1973).

An England Youth international winger, Colin Hall played his best football with Bradford for whom he scored seven goals in 72 senior matches. He was reserve to Joe Baker at Forest for quite a while and never really got a look in, although when he did enter the fray he showed a lot of composure and was not afraid to take on defenders and try a shot at goal.

HALL, Marcus Thomas
Defender/full-back: one app. no goals
Born: Coventry, 24 March 1976
Career: Coventry City (trainee, July 1992, professional July 1994), FOREST (August 2002), Southampton (August 2002), Stoke City (December 2002)

Signed on weekly contracts at the start of the 2002-03, Marcus Hall appeared in the opening game at Portsmouth before quickly moving on to Southampton.

He gained one 'B' and eight Under-21 caps during his ten-year association with the Highfield Road club for whom he made 157 senior appearances. A veteran of several relegation battles with the Sky Blues, he was recruited to strengthen the defence and to add more experience as well as encouraging competition.

HAMILTON, Alexander Maxwell
Goalkeeper: 7 apps.
Born: Bulwell, Nottingham, circa 1890
Career: Bestwood, FOREST (August 1911-May 1913)

Reserve goalkeeper at Forest, Alex Hamilton made only a handful of senior appearances during his two years at the club during which time he understudied the more accomplished John Hanna. He conceded two goals on his debut for the Reds against Fulham in December 1911.

HAMILTON, Thomas
Right-half: 26 apps. one goal
Born: Nottinghamshire, circa 1870
Career: FOREST (August 1891-May 1893).

Tom Hamilton scored his only goal for Forest in a 5-1 home win over Walsall Town Swifts in the Football Alliance in September 1891. He made 16 appearances in the competition that season and earned himself a championship medal in the process.

HANCOCK, J B
Outside/inside-right: 2 apps. one goal
Born: circa 1872
Career: FOREST (seasons 1894-96)

Jack Hancock scored his only goal for Forest in a United Counties League game at Sheffield United (won 6-2) in March 1895.

HANNA, A John
Goalkeeper: 101 apps.
Born: Belfast, circa 1889
Career: Linfield, FOREST (July 1911), Scunthorpe & Lindsey United (August 1919 to cs.1921).
Jack Hanna was a fine, upstanding goalkeeper, very smart with both hands and an excellent close-range shot-stopper, often using his feet to good effect. He made his first-team debut for Forest against Leeds City on the opening day of the 1911-12 season and remained first choice at the City ground for three seasons. He was capped twice by Ireland as a Forest player (v. Scotland and Wales in 1912).

HARBY, Michael John
Goalkeeper: 3 apps.
Born: Nottingham, 7 November 1948
Career: FOREST (juniors, 1964, professional July 1966-May 1968).
A reserve to Peter Grummitt, local lad Mick Harby made his Football League debut against Sunderland in March 1968, being on the wrong end of a 3-0 defeat at Roker Park.

HARDSTAFF, Joseph
Inside-right: 12 apps. one goal
Born: Kirby-in-Ashfield, 9 November 1882.
Died: Nuncargate, Notts, 2 April 1947
Career: FOREST (1904 to 06).
Joe Hardstaff was a diligent inside-forward who did far better with the small hard red ball than he did with the large leather brown one. In fact, he was known in the cricketing world as 'Hardstuff' and spent 22 years as a middle-order right-hand batsman with Notts, appearing in 340 first-class matches, scoring 17,146 runs for an average of 31.34. His highest score was 213 not out v. Sussex at Hove in 1914. He was an occasional stop-gap fast-medium bowler (58 wickets). He also appeared in five Tests for England (1907-08) and hit 311 runs for an average of 31.10. He registered 1,000 runs in a season seven times plus once overseas, his best effort coming in 1911 (1,547 runs for an average of 45.50). He later became a first-class umpire, going with the MCC to the West Indies in that capacity in 1929-30, and officiated in Test Matches until the inclusion of his son in the England side prevented this.
Joe junior was born in 1911 and he also played cricket for Notts. Hardstaff senior is the grandfather of Joseph, who was a cricketer with the Free Foresters.

HARDY, Samuel
Goalkeeper: 109 apps.
Born: Newbold Verdun, Derbyshire, 26 August 1883.
Died: Chesterfield, 24 October 1966.
Career: Newbold White Star (July 1901), Chesterfield (professional, April 1903), Liverpool (£500, October 1905), Aston Villa (May 1912), FOREST (August 1921-May 1925). Retired and became a hotelier in Chesterfield.

"One of the greatest goalkeepers I ever played in front of" said Jesse Pennington, the West Bromwich Albion and England full-back of the pre-First World War era. Sam Hardy was at times quite brilliant and during a splendid career amassed in excess of 600 appearances at club and international level.
His anticipation was so masterly, he made the art of goalkeeping look easy and would have been considered a classic player in any era. He won 21 full caps for England over a period of 14 years: 1907-21. He also starred in three Victory internationals and represented the Football League. He won First Division and Second Division championship medals with Liverpool and Forest (in 1922) respectively. In between times he also collected two FA Cup winners' medals with Aston Villa: 1913 & 1920. He joined Liverpool soon after playing superbly well despite conceding six goals for Chesterfield against the Merseysiders. He made 239 League and Cup appearances for the Anfield club and starred in 183 competitive matches for Villa before going on to play more than 100 competitive games for Forest (plus another 75 during WW1) having made over 70 for Chesterfield at the start of his career.
During WW1 Hardy served in the Royal Navy and escaped serious injury on two occasions. He also guested for Forest in the 1919 Victory Shield play-off against Everton at Goodison Park, helping the Reds lift the trophy with a 1-0 scoreline after a 0-0 draw at the City Ground.

HARDY, William Henry
Inside-right: one app.
Born: Denaby, 25 October 1915. Died: 1990.
Career: Rotherham United (May 1935), FOREST (March 1937), Gainsborough Trinity (September 1937).
Did not play League football after WW2.
After netting 11 goals in 46 League games for Rotherham, Bill Hardy made just one League appearance for Forest, deputising for Tom Peacock in a 2-1 defeat at Leicester in April 1937.

HAREWOOD, Marlon Anderson
Striker: 145+60 apps. 55 goals
Born: Hampstead, London, 25 August 1979
Career: FOREST (trainee, July 1995, professional September 1996), Ipswich Town (on loan, January 1999). West Ham United (£500,000, September 2003).
A determined striker, 6ft 1in tall, big and strong, Marlon Harewood has all the key attributes for a goal-scorer, perhaps lacking that extra bit of consistency to be a top-notch marksman. Nevertheless, he finished as Forest's second top-scorer in 2001-02 with 11 goals. The following season he was the perfect foil in attack for David Johnson, netting a total of 21 goals including four in a 6-0 win over Stoke City.

HARKES, John Andrew
Full-back/midfield: 3 apps.
Born: Kearney, New Jersey, USA, 8 March, 1967
Career: North Carolina University, Sheffield Wednesday
(£70,000, October 1990), Derby County (August 1993),
West Ham United (on loan, October 1995), Washington
DC United/NASL (1998), FOREST (January 1999),
New England Revolution (March 1999), Columbus Crew
(May 2001).
American World Cup player (and occasional skipper),
capped by his country 90 times, the versatile John Harkes
did very well with both Wednesday and West Ham,
accumulating a tally of 155 League appearances. He loved
to drive forward, possessed a powerful right-foot shot and
was always totally committed. An agonising foot injury
ruined his spell with Forest.

HARRIS, Frederick McKenzie
Outside-right/centre-forward: 48 apps. 12 goals
Born: Rothwell, Northants, 1884.
Career: Northampton Town (briefly), Kettering Town,
FOREST (January 1914), South Shields (1915), Swansea
Town (September 1919), Southend United (July 1921),
Kettering Town (May 1922).
Introduced to the Reds' attack 25 matches into the 1913-
14 season, the versatile Fred Harris quickly made his mark
by scoring on his Football League debut for Forest, in a 1-
1 draw at Huddersfield in February 1914. His presence up
front certainly boosted the Reds' strike-force and he
worked very well alongside the likes of Jack Lockton and
Jackie Derrick. In 1914-15 he started off on the right-
wing but was quickly transferred into the centre before
WW1 arrived to ruin his stay at the City Ground.

HARRIS, Leonard James
Full-back: 2 apps
Born: Nuneaton, Warwicks, 29 May 1949
Career: FOREST (juniors, July 1965, professional, June
1966-May 1971), Doncaster Rovers (on loan, September
1970).
Reserve full-back, Len Harris played in just two League
games for Forest, deputising for Peter Hindley against
Spurs (home) in April 1969 and Leeds United (also at the
City Ground) the following August. He was released by
the club at the end of the 1970-71 season.

HARRISON, Albert
Centre-half: 81 apps. 3 goals
Born: Leigh, Lancashire, 15 February 1904.
Career: West Leigh FC, Wigan Borough (1922), Atherton
Collieries, Chorley (1925), FOREST (July 1927),
Leicester City (December 1929), Dundalk (May 1931),
Drumcondra (August 1932), Wigan Athletic (July 1933).
England trialist Albert Harrison was a tall, blond defender
who toured South Africa with the FA party in 1931
(playing in one Test Match). He made his League debut

for the Reds against Port Vale in August 1927, taking over
from Gerry Morgan. His tackling and clean-kicking were
of the highest class and he never gave less than 100 percent
effort out on the field. Known throughout his career as
'Snowy', he made 33 appearances for Leicester after
leaving Forest.

HARROLD, Sidney
Outside-right or left: 52 apps. 8 goals
Born: Dudley, Worcestershire, 5 June 1895.
Career: Willenhall (1914), Stourbridge (1916),
Wednesbury Town (1918), Leicester City (February 1919),
FOREST (May 1920), Accrington Stanley (July 1922).
Sid Harrold, a 1922 promotion winner with Forest, was a
straight replacement on the Reds' left-wing for Ben
Shearman, and he certainly gave a good account of
himself, showing plenty of pace and skill while creating
several chances for his fellow forwards.
He made his Forest debut in a 2-2 draw with Stoke a
month after joining the club from Leicester and remained
at the City Ground for two seasons before losing out to
Harry Martin.

HART, Horace Alfred
Inside-right: 6 apps. one goal
Born: Nottingham, 16 August 1894
Career: Stalybridge Celtic, FOREST (August 1919-
May 1920)
Reserve forward Alf Hart played half-a-dozen games in the
Reds' first XI. After making his debut in a 2-0 win at Stoke
on January 1920, he scored his only goal in another 2-0
victory over Grimsby Town a month later. He deputised
for Albert Davis five times.

HART, Paul Anthony
Defender: 87 apps. 3 goals
Born: Golborne near Manchester, 4 May 1953.
Career: Stockport County (apprentice June 1969,
professional September 1970), Blackpool (June 1973),
Leeds United (March 1978), FOREST (May 1983),
Sheffield Wednesday (August 1985), Birmingham City
(December 1986), Notts County (player-coach, June
1987), Chesterfield (manager, November 1988 to January
1991), Grantham Town (as a player), Nottingham Forest
(coach, June 1991), Sheffield Wednesday (coach, 1994),
Leeds United (Director of Youth Coaching and also acted
as caretaker-manager for a brief spell when Howard
Wilkinson left Elland Road in September 1996),
FOREST (club coach, Youth Academy Director, then
manager from July 2001).
Paul Hart was a fine, strapping centre-half who gave
nothing away, being persistent in his efforts and strong in
defence. He made 87 League appearances for Stockport,
143 for Blackpool and 191 for Leeds before joining Forest
and after leaving the City Ground he had 52 outings for
Wednesday and 23 for the Magpies, but had the

misfortune to break his leg in his only game for Birmingham against Plymouth Argyle in December 1986 when he collided with team-mate Tommy Williams. This turned out to be his only appearance for the St Andrew's club. His brother Nigel is the former Wigan Athletic, Leicester City, Blackburn Rovers, Crewe and Bury defender, while his father Johnny Hart starred for Manchester City as an inside forward.

HARTFORD, Richard Asa
Midfielder: 3 apps.
Born: Clydebank, 24 October 1950,
Career: Drumchapel Amateurs, West Bromwich Albion (apprentice April 1966, professional, October 1967), Manchester City (£225,000, August 1974), FOREST (£450,000, July 1979), Everton (£400,000, August 1979), Manchester City (again, £350,000, October 1981), Fort Lauderdale Sun (United Soccer League/USA) (May 1984), Wolverhampton Wanderers (on trial, August 1984), Norwich City (September 1984), Norway (coach, May-June 1985), Bolton Wanderers (July 1985), Stockport County (player-manager, June 1987), Oldham Athletic (March 1989), Shrewsbury Town (coach, July 1989, manager January 1990-January 1991), Boston United (February 1991), Blackburn Rovers (coach, 1992), Stoke City (assistant-manager/coach, November 1991), Manchester City (coach/assistant-manager 1995, caretaker-boss briefly in 1996 after Alan Ball had left, then reserve team manager, 1999). Also played for West Bromwich Albion All Stars (1990s).
Asa Hartford will be remembered as a tremendous midfield player who amassed well over 900 senior appearances over a period of 24 years, 710 in the Football League, but only three for Forest (all of them wins incidentally). He made his debut for the Reds in a 1-0 away victory at Ipswich a month after joining the club from Maine Road but then left for Merseyside, having fallen out with the management at the City Ground.
Leeds signed him in a £170,000 deal in 1971, but he quickly returned to the Hawthorns after doctors diagnosed a heart problem. He was eventually sold to Manchester City for a then record fee three years later. Capped by Scotland 50 times at senior level, Hartford also represented his county as a Youth team player and played in one Under-21 and five Under-23 internationals. He appeared in three League Cup finals - for WBA against his future club Manchester City in 1970 (collecting a runners-up tankard), then for Manchester City v. Newcastle in 1976 and for Norwich City v. QPR in 1985, receiving winners' medals in these last two encounters, and having the pleasure of scoring the winning goal with a deflected shot for the Canaries. In 1986 he again visited Wembley, this time in the final of the Freight Rover Trophy with Bolton. His last League appearance was at the age of 40, for Shrewsbury away to Brentford on New Year's Day 1991.

* Hartford was christened Asa after the great American singing star, Al Jolson who was his father's favourite artist.

HARVEY, Lee Derek
Full-back/winger/midfielder: 0+3 apps.
Born: Harlow, Essex, 21 December 1966
Career: Leyton Orient (trainee, April 1983, professional December 1984), FOREST (free transfer, August 1993), Brentford (free, November 1993). Stevenage Borough (cs. 1997).
Capped by England at Youth team level, right-sided midfielder Lee Harvey appeared in 237 senior games for Orient (31 goals scored) before moving to the City Ground. He never really settled in with Forest and after just three outings as a substitute he moved back to London to sign for Brentford. He suffered a serious leg injury (v. PNE) in December 1996 (on his 30th birthday) and never regained full fitness. He was released from Griffin Park in the summer of 1997 having made 128 appearances for the Bees.

HASLEGRAVE, Sean Matthews
Midfielder: 11+2 apps. one goal
Born: Stoke-on-Trent, 7 June 1951
Career: Stoke City (juniors, June 1966, professional November 1968), FOREST (July 1976), Preston North (September 1977), Crewe Alexandra (August 1981), York City (July 1983), Torquay United (August 1987-May 1989; then on coaching staff at Plainmoor).
During his career Sean Haslegrave appeared in almost 600 competitive matches (493 in the Football League) and scored a dozen goals. He had already played 113 games in the First Division for the Potters before transferring to Forest in 1976. Unfortunately he was another player who never settled in at the City Ground and after just one full season with the Reds he departed to Deepdale. On his day - especially with Stoke - he was a tireless worker, astute, constructive and totally committed.

HASSELL, Albert Arthur
Goalkeeper: 39 apps
Born: Bristol, circa 1884
Career: Bolton Wanderers (1906), Middlesbrough (1907), FOREST (August 1909), Swindon Town (April 1911).
Having failed to appear in Bolton's first XI and made just one League appearance for Middlesbrough, goalkeeper Albert Hassell was signed by Forest as cover for Jack Smith who had not been all that impressive after taking over between the posts from Jimmy Iremonger. Hassell made his debut for the Reds in a 4-1 defeat at Villa Park in January 1910 and played in 16 League games that season and 19 the next before Smith returned to the side. At times Hassell made the most difficult shots look easy to save but occasionally his positional sense let him down badly.

HAZELDENE, John
Full-back: one app.
Born: circa 1868
Career: FOREST (seasons 1889-91).
Reserve full-back. Jack Hazeldene's debut - and indeed, his only senior game for the club - was against Bootle in the Football Alliance on 28 September 1889 when he replaced Jim Southward.

HEATHCOCK, Joseph Bert
Centre-forward: 20 apps. 14 goals
Born: Cradley Heath, 5 December 1903
Died: Cradley Heath 21 May 1990.
Career: Leamington Town, Leicester City (October 1923), FOREST (£150, June 1928), Cradley Heath (June 1930), Hereford United (September 1931).
Before joining Forest for a modest fee, centre-forward Bert Heathcock was frustrated at the lack of first-team opportunities with Leicester, having rattled in plenty of goals for the reserves during his first season at Filbert Street, including nine in a 22-0 win over Ibstock Colliery. He also scored twice in his only League game for the Foxes in a 3-0 win at Sheffield United in March 1927. He looked a fine player early on at the City Ground, netting 14 goals in 16 League outings, six coming in four matches in December 1928. but then he struggled to keep his place in the side (with Messrs Dent, German and Loftus challenging strongly) and as a result he moved into non-League football in 1930.

HENDERSON, George
Half-back: 111 apps. 6 goals
Born: Burnbank, Scotland, 1876.
Career: Coatbridge St Patrick's, Motherwell (1893), Airdrieonians (1895), Preston North End (August 1897), Swindon Town (July 1898), Millwall Athletic (August 1900), FOREST (July 1901-May 1906).
Durable and dependable, George Henderson could play in any half-back position. He joined Forest after spells with Swindon and Millwall, having developed his football in Scotland. He had just two First Division outings with PNE (v. Wolves & Aston Villa) before amassing almost 100 at senior level for Swindon and Millwall. He went straight into the Forest first XI at the start of the 1901-02 season, occupying the centre-half position initially before switching over to the left. Injuries, however, began to disrupt his game during 1903 and 1904 and after another set-back in December 1905 and subsequently losing his place to Jack Armstrong, he announced his retirement from top-class soccer at the end of that season.

HENNESEY, William Terrence
Wing-half/defender: 183 apps. 6 goals
Born: Llay, Mid-Wales, 1 September 1942.
Career: Birmingham City (juniors, June 1957, professional September 1959), FOREST (£45,000,

November 1965), Derby County (£110,000, February 1970), Tamworth (manager, April 1974), Kimberley Town (coach, 1977), Tulsa Roughnecks/NASL (assistant-coach, summer 1978), Shepshed Charterhouse (coach 1978 to October 1980), Tulsa Roughnecks/NASL (assistant-coach, November 1980, then chief coach 1981-83), Vancouver Whitecaps/NASL (assistant-coach/manager mid-1980s to Alan Hinton, ex-Wolves, Derby & Forest winger), Toronto (coach/manager), Heidelberg FC/Australia (coach/manager, 1987-88). Later moved to Melbourne where he now manages a cling-film company.
Before joining Forest, Terry Hennessey played in more than 200 senior games for Birmingham City, gaining an Inter Cities Fairs Cup runners-up medal in 1961 and a Football League Cup winners' prize in 1963. Then, after leaving the City Ground, he helped Derby County win the League championship and Texaco Cup in 1972, while also taking his tally of full international caps for Wales up to 39, having previously gained six at Under-23 level and a handful as a schoolboy. He won 15 full caps as a Forest player and skippered his country on several occasions (as he did his club sides).
A strong tackler, he was able to bring the ball out of defence and then distribute it with telling effect and throughout the 1960s he was the leading light in Birminghams' regular battles against relegation. He spent four good seasons with Forest, where he settled into the back four, although many supporters would have preferred him to have played in midfield, as he was one of the fittest players at the club and still in his twenties.
When he left the Reds he became Derby's first six-figure signing, being described by manager Brian Clough as a 'world class player'. Sadly, a spate of injuries (he underwent two cartilage operations) ruined his stay with the Rams for whom he made 63 appearances. He later became a respected coach overseas.

HESLOP, Robert
Inside-left/left-half: 99 apps. 23 goals
Born: Annfield Plain near Chester-le-Street, County Durham, 5 February 1907
Career: Pontop Villa, Annfield Plain FC, Burnley (amateur forms, February 1928), Annfield Plain, FOREST (professional, August 1928), Annfield Plain (August 1934).
Bob Heslop once scored 121 goals in a season of schoolboy football. He worked down the mine and played in the Northern Combination before joining Forest as a full-time professional at the age of 21. Blessed with speed, skill and intelligence, he did exceedingly well at the City Ground, and averaged a goal every four games, his best season coming in 1932-33 when he weighed in with 11 in 28 League matches. He moved on following the emergence of Tom Peacock.

HEWITT, Arthur Harper
Left-back: 5 apps.
Born: Beeston, Notts,10 January 1900
Career: Ilkeston Town, FOREST (September 1924), Watford (August 1925-April 1926)
Competent reserve to Percy Barratt, Arthur Hewitt made his League debut for Forest in the goalless local derby with Notts County in January 1925. He failed to make the first team at Watford.

HICKS, Thomas George
Left-back: 8 apps.
Born: Trehaford, Glamorgan, 1903
Career: Pontypridd (1921), Preston North End (July 1924), FOREST (£300, July 1927), Northampton Town (season 1928-29), Chester (June 1929).
Left-back Tom Hicks had around a dozen outings for PNE before joining Forest for the start of the 1927-28 season. Strong and aggressive, he lacked the panache required to become a regular first-team player and during his entire career accumulated just 22 League appearances.

HIGGINS, Alexander
Centre/inside-forward: 35 apps. 7 goals
Born: Kilmarnock, 4 November 1885.
Died: Newcastle upon Tyne, 15 March 1939
Career: Belle Vue Juniors, Kilmarnock (1904), Newcastle United (£250, June 1905), Hull City (WW1 guest, 1916-17), Kilmarnock (August 1919), FOREST (June 1920) Jarrow (player-manager, September 1921), Norwich City (player, November 1921), Wallsend (December 1922), FC Berne/Switzerland (trainer, 1925), Preston Colliery (player/coach/trainer, November 1926-27).
Sandy Higgins came to prominence during the 1908-09 season when he played wonderfully well for Newcastle as they raced on to win the League title. He was one of several young stars who were groomed at St James' Park during the club's Edwardian heydays. Possessing a marvellous left foot, he went on to score 41 goals in 150 appearances for the Magpies before spending a season with the Reds, and doing his bit to preserve the club's First Division status. He followed in the footsteps of his father Alex (below) as a Forest player.
Chiefly an inside-left, but able to play at centre-forward and inside-right, he was skilful, dashing and resourceful with a marked inclination towards individualism. He gained four caps for Scotland (1910-11), was an international trialist and he helped Newcastle win the FA Cup in 1910 and take the runners-up spot a year later. After WW1 he was awarded a Scottish Cup winners' medal with Kilmarnock although he never played in the final, being forced to withdraw from the team at the last minute following the death of his father. Regarded as one of the finest Scottish-born footballers in the game, Higgins served in the Durham Light infantry during WW1 and was awarded the Military Medal and a citation.

After retiring from the game he settled on Tyneside and ran a grocer's shop in Byker and was also employed as a publican in Newcastle.

HIGGINS. Alexander F
Inside-forward: 105 apps. 84 goals
Born: Ayrshire, 1865. Died: 17 April 1920
Career: Kilwinning FC, Irvine FC, Kilmarnock, Derby County (August 1888), FOREST (September 1890); retired April 1894.
After scoring 26 goals in 45 games for Derby and playing in the Rams' first-ever League encounter against Bolton Wanderers on 8 September 1888, Alex 'Sandy' Higgins - father of Alex junior (above) - had the honour of scoring Forest's first-ever goal in the Football League, in a 2-2 draw at Everton on 3 September 1892. He also scored five times for Forest in their emphatic 14-0 FA Cup win at Clapton in January 1891 and was in superb form when the Reds won the Football Alliance championship in 1891-92, hitting 26 goals in only 20 games.
One of several Scotsmen signed after the immensely disappointing 1889-90 season when the club finished second to bottom of the Football Alliance, Higgins was a natural footballer, expert in close dribbling and one whose marksmanship placed him among the most feared forwards of his day. Blessed, too, with evenness of performance, a quality well demonstrated in his Forest record of a goal every 112 minutes.
Higgins was one of the unluckiest of all international players! He scored four goals on his debut in an 8-2 win over Ireland in 1885 yet never represented his country again.

HIGHAM, Peter
Outside-right/centre-forward: 27 apps. 5 goals
Born: Wigan, 8 November 1930
Career: Wigan Athletic (August 1946), Portsmouth (amateur, July 1948, professional November 1949), Bolton Wanderers (November 1950), Preston North End (May 1952), FOREST (August 1955), Doncaster Rovers (March 1958-May 1959).
Peter Higham, a member of Forest's 1956-57 Second Division promotion-winning squad, was a strongly-built, hard-working winger or centre-forward whose career brought him 36 goals in 99 League appearances. He made his bow for Pompey in their League championship-winning season of 1949-50 but failed to get a game with Bolton. After netting 10 goals in 15 outings for PNE he joined Forest and in his second season at the City Ground hit four goals in 20 appearances to earn himself a medal. He lost his place in the side when Billy Gray was signed.

HILL, Alan
Goalkeeper: 46 apps.
Born: Barnsley, 3 November 1943
Career: Barnsley (juniors, 1959, professional April 1961), Rotherham United (June 1966), FOREST (£12,000,

March 1969); retired June 1970. Later appointed assistant-manager and chief scout at the City Ground.

Standing a fraction over six-feet tall, goalkeeper Alan Hill had already made more than 220 senior appearances while assisting Barnsley and Rotherham. Recruited by Reds' manager Matt Gillies after Peter Grummitt had been sidelined with a broken finger, he had Gordon Marshall also challenging for a first-team place but held his position until February 1970 when he too was injured at Everton. On loan Dave Hollins then took over the green jersey and with Jim Barron ready to move in at the City Ground, Hill found himself out in the cold, at which point he announced his retirement.

HILLEY, David

Inside-forward: 82+16 apps. 16 goals
Born: Glasgow, 20 December 1938
Career: Muirend Amateurs, Jordanhill FC (early 1958), Pollock Juniors (April 1958), Third Lanark (June 1958), Newcastle United (£40,000, with Stewart Mitchell, August 1962), FOREST (£25,000, December 1967), Highlands Park FC/South Africa (November 1970), Hellenic FC/South Africa (1973), Scarborough (October 1975), South Shields (July 1976), Bedlington Terriers (July 1977). Retired in May 1978.

Dave Hilley, though slightly built, was a creative player who didn't mind mixing it with more stronger and robust opponents. A Scottish schoolboy star, he went on to play in two unofficial internationals for his country as well as gaining one Under-23 cap and representing the Scottish League. He replaced Ivor Allchurch as playmaker at Newcastle and during his five years at St James' Park appeared in 209 first-class games, scoring 33 goals. Unlucky not to win a full cap, he helped the Magpies win the Second Division championship in 1965, having five years earlier collected a runners-up medal when Third Lanark lost the Scottish League Cup final. He scored on his home debut for Forest, earning them victory over Sheffield United in December 1967 and thereafter, injuries permitting, was a regular member of the side until his departure in 1970 (with Tommy Jackson and fellow Scot Doug Fraser ready to move in).

Residing on Tyneside and a former schoolteacher at Oakfield College, Newcastle (until his retirement in 1996) Hilley now writes regular features for the Sunday Post newspaper.

HINCHCLIFFE, Thomas

Inside-forward: one app.
Born: Denaby, 6 December 1913.
Died: Rushcliffe, 1978
Career: Denaby United (1930), Grimsby Town (£300, October 1933), Huddersfield Town (February 1938), Derby County (November 1938), FOREST (WW2 guest from October 1939, signed full-time, May 1946), Denaby United (August 1947).

An intelligent forward, adjudged a good prospect after his seasons in Midland League football with Denaby, Tom Hinchcliffe was a regular for Grimsby in 1937-38 before making his move to Huddersfield. Unfortunately WW2 took away seven years of his career and he played in only one League game for Forest, against Barnsley in August 1946. He appeared in almost 20 games for Forest as a guest during the conflict.

HINDLEY, Francis Charles

Centre-forward: 8 apps. 3 goals
Born: Worksop, 2 November 1914
Died: Worksup, March 2003.
Career: Netherton United, FOREST (August 1938), Brighton & Hove Albion (May 1939-May 1947)

Frank Hindley was a decidedly quick centre-forward who competed in the famous Powderhall Sprint when at his prime. He never quite fitted the bill at the City Ground and WW2 disrupted his progress at Brighton. He managed only 15 appearances for the Hove club (10 in the Football League).

Hindley's son, Peter (see below) was a player with Forest for 15 years.

HINDLEY, Peter

Right-back: 416 apps. 11 goals
Born: Worksop, 19 May 1944
Career: FOREST (juniors, 1959, professional June 1961), Coventry City (January 1974), Peterborough United (July 1976).

Son of Frank (above), Peter Hindley was a centre-forward when he first joined Forest as a 15-year-old. Switched to the defence by manager Andy Beattie where he was used as a centre-half, he found his first-team chances limited owing to the presence of Bob McKinlay. Determined to make his mark, eventually Hindley found his niche at right-back and it was from this position that he served Forest superbly well, going on to amass well over 400 senior appearances, forming a solid partnership with John Winfield. His best years came in the late 1960s/early '70s when he helped Forest reach the semi-final of the FA Cup and finish runners-up in the First Division in 1966-67 (when he was an ever-present), as well as gaining England Under-23 honours. He lost his place to Liam O'Kane and was allowed to leave the City Ground for Coventry City, later winding down his career with Peterborough for whom he made 112 League appearances.

HINTON, Alan Thomas

Outside-left: 116+6 apps. 24 goals
Born: Wednesbury, Staffs, 6 October 1942
Career: Wolverhampton Wanderers (juniors, July 1957, professional October 1959), FOREST (January 1964), Derby County (£30,000, September 1967), Dallas Tornado/NASL (March 1977), Vancouver Whitecaps/NASL (October 1977), Tulsa

Roughnecks/NASL (October 1978), Seattle Sounders/NASL (player-coach, November 1979 until January 1983), Tacoma Stars/MISL (player-coach: season 1983-84).

Alan Hinton was an England international left-winger who gained three full, seven Under-23 and two Youth caps, collecting his first two at senior level as a Forest player v. Belgium and Wales, both at Wembley in 1964 (scoring against the Belgians).

After scoring 29 goals in 78 games for Wolves, virtually all of his career highlights then came at Derby, who rescued him from relative obscurity as he drifted along at the City Ground having lost out to wing-rivals Barry Lyons and Storey-Moore. Able to cross a ball with remarkable accuracy when in full flight (keenly admired by Jimmy Greaves), Hinton possessed a stunning shot and was an expert with corners and free-kicks. When he left the City Ground for Derby some Forest committee members reckoned that the Rams would soon want their money back as Hinton was well past his sell by date. But Brian Clough and Peter Taylor had other ideas and at The Baseball Ground he produced some quite brilliant performances, being a vital member of the Rams 1968-69 Second Division championship winning side (6 goals in 226 games) and then starring in two League championship winning outfits: 1971-72 (15 goals in 38 outings) and 1974-75 (2 goals in 13 games). Hinton went on to appear in well over 300 games for Derby (83 goals). On leaving England he did exceedingly well in the States and in 1978 set a new NASL record for 'assists', his total of 30, beating the previous one, jointly held by Pele and George Best. In 1980 Hinton was voted NASL 'Coach of the Year'. When the NASL folded in 1983 he moved into the Major Indoor Soccer League with Tacoma. He quit the soccer scene in the mid-80s and now assists his wife run a real estate business in the USA.

HITCH, Alfred
Right-half: 13 apps. one goal
Born: Walsall, 1876
Died: Uxbridge, Middlesex, 1962.
Career: Walsall Unity, Walsall (April 1897), Wellington Town (January 1898), Thames Iron Works (September 1898), Grays United (1898), Queen's Park Rangers (August 1899), FOREST (July 1901), Queen's Park Rangers (July 1902), Watford (August 1906 to cs. 1908).
After failing to establish himself with Walsall, wing-half Alf Hitch scored seven goals in 61 senior games in two seasons with QPR before spending 12 months at the City Ground where, at times, he found it hard going. He returned to QPR and during the next four years took his overall appearance tally with the London club to 183 (20 goals).

HJELDE, Jon Olav
Defender: 252+22 apps 6 goals
Born: Levanger, Norway, 30 April 1972
Career: Rosenborg BK (Norway), FOREST (£600,000, August 1997, Pusan Kons/South Koren (July 2003), released May 2003)
Big, muscular centre-back Jon Hjelde - 6ft 1in tall, 13st 7lbs in weight - helped Forest regain their Premiership status in 1998 (as Second Division champions). Strong in the air and solid on the ground, he had numerous partners in Forest's back division but in 2002, after taking his senior appearance tally to past the 150 mark, he lost his place in the side.

HOCKEY, Trevor
Winger/midfielder: 80 apps. 8 goals
Born: Keighley, Yorkshire, 1 May 1943.
Died: Keighley, 1 April 1987
Career: Bradford City (amateur June 1958, professional May 1960), FOREST (£15,000, November 1961), Newcastle United (£25,000 November 1963), Birmingham City (£22,500 November 1965), Sheffield United (£35,000 January 1971), Norwich City (February 1973), Aston Villa (£38,000, June 1973), Bradford City (June 1974), Athlone Town (player-manager, March 1976), San Diego Jaws/NASL (April 1976), Las Vegas Quicksilver/NASL (March 1977), San Jose Earthquakes/NASL (June 1977), Stalybridge Celtic (manager, August 1977). Later attempted to start a soccer section at Keighley Rugby League Club; coached the British Army on the Rhine children's team and also coached soccer at Pontins Holiday camp in Filey.

Trevor Hockey was a footballing nomad whose professional career spanned close on 16 years during which time he accumulated well over 600 senior appearances whilst playing on all 92 League club grounds in that time, and having by far his best spell at St Andrew's. Initially a winger, he developed into a hard working, sometimes fiery but very effective midfielder, a player full of Yorkshire grit who always produced a 100 percent performance no matter what the circumstances or the game. His natural driving power and the ability to foster team spirit were invaluable. His job was to man mark an opponent and he often came into conflict with the authorities for his robust play. During his two years at the City Ground Hockey aided and abetted Henry Newton and Calvin Palmer (among others) in the engine-room and missed only one League game in 1962-63 (against his future club Sheffield United). He was a Second Division championship winner with Newcastle in 1965 and gained nine full caps for Wales (none with Forest) making his debut in 1972 (v. Finland) and then having the ill-luck to be sent off in his last international match (v. Poland in Katowice in 1974).

Off the field he was a larger than life personality with his thick beard and long hair. He was also the proud owner of a pink piano and once made a record entitled: 'Happy 'Cos I'm Blue' appearing on stage in a concert at Birmingham Town Hall. He died of a heart attack shortly after playing in a five-a-side tournament in his native Keighley.

HODDER, William

Centre-forward: One app. 2 goals
Born: circa 1867
Career: Notts County (1888-cs1889), FOREST (September 1889), Nolts Rangers (Late 1889) Sheffield Wednesday (cs.1890) Lincoln City (cs. 1891 to cs. 1892). Centre-forward, William Hodder - who had netted three times in 20 games for Notts County in their first season of League Football - made his senior debut for Forest in September 1889, scoring twice in a 3-1 Football Alliance away win at Walsall Town Swifts - the club's first game in this competition.

HODGE, Stephen Brian

Midfielder: 267+6 apps 66 goals
Born: Nottingham, 25 October 1962
Career: FOREST (apprentice, May 1978, professional, October 1980), Aston Villa (£450,000, August 1985), Tottenham Hotspur (£650,000, December 1986), FOREST (£575,000, August 1988), Leeds United (£900,000 July 1991), Derby County (on loan, August 1994), Queen's Park Rangers (£300,000, October 1994), Watford (free transfer, February 1995), Hong Kong football (January 1996), Leyton Orient (August 1997);
An exceptionally skilful, hard-working left-sided midfield player, Steve Hodge had a fine career that spanned some 20 years. In that time he amassed well over 500 club and international appearances and scored more than 100 goals. Capped 24 times by England (earning his first against USSR in March 1986), he also represented his country in two 'B' and eight Under-21 matches.
In his first spell with Forest Hodge played alongside the likes of Ian Bowyer and Mark Proctor, and two Dutch men, Johnny Metgod and Frans Thijssen in the midfield-zone, making over 120 League appearances, being an ever-present in 1984-85.
An FA Cup beaten finalist with Spurs in 1987, Hodge was sent-off in manager Terry Venables' first match in charge of the London club and after that his career at White Hart Lane was on the line! However, despite suffering with injuries he still produced several useful performances and netted some vitally important goals before returning to Forest in 1988 where he oiled up in the engine-room with Neil Webb and Garry Parker etc. He was twice a League Cup winner during his second spell at the City Ground (1989 & 1990), gained a Simod Cup winners prize as well (in 1989) and played in the 1991 FA Cup final defeat against his former club Spurs. In 1992 Hodge helped Leeds win the last Football League championship before the Premiership was introduced.

HODGES, Glyn Peter

Midfielder: 3+2 apps
Born: Streatham, London, 30 April 1963
Career: Wimbledon (apprentice, June 1979, professional February 1981), Newcastle United (£200,000, July 1987), Watford (£300,000, October 1987), Crystal Palace (£410,000, July 1990), Sheffield United (£450,000, January 1991), Derby County (free transfer, February 1996), Sin Tao/Hong Kong (July 1996), Hull City (August 1997), FOREST (February 1998), Scarborough (January 1999 - retired in February 1999 through injury). Later coaching staff and then caretaker-manager of Barnsley (2002-03).
Attacking/goalscoring midfielder Glyn Hodges had already amassed 588 club appearances and scored 100 goals when he joined Forest in 1998 at the age of 35. He had also represented Wales in one 'B', five Under-21 and 18 senior international matches, having earlier played for his country's youth team. A driving force in the centre of thee park, he helped Wimbledon win the Fourth Division title in 1983 and overall had an excellent career, being especially prominent with the Dons (264 games) and Sheffield United (171 outings). He was in the twilight off his career with Forest, taking part in just five matches.

HODGKINSON, Vincent Arthur

Inside-right: 9 apps. one goal
Born: Woolaton, Notts, 1 November 1906.
Died: 28 June 1990
Career: Magdala Amateurs, FOREST (August 1925), Blackpool (May-September 1927), Grantham Town, (September 1928), Loughborogh corinthias (cs.1931) Lincoln City (September-October 1933), Lysaght's Sports (North Lindsey League: July 1935-September 1939). Also played cricket for Notts (groundstaff, 1926) and Lincolnshire, starring in 44 games for the latter in the Minor Counties Competition (1936-52) taking 162 wickets.
As a footballer, Vince Hodgkinson never really made his mark, having just 10 League outings in all (9 for Forest and one for Lincoln).

HOLDER, Alan Maurice

Wing-half: 4 apps.
Born: Oxford, 10 December 1931
Career: Army football (while serving with the 6th Battalion RAOC), FOREST (amateur October 1951, professional April 1952), Lincoln City (July 1955), Tranmere Rovers (December 1956), Headington United (July 1958-June 1959).
Rose to the professional ranks at the City Ground after doing extremely well with his Army side. Reserve wing-half Alan Holder made only 17 League appearances during his entire career, his debut for the Reds coming in October 1954, away at Plymouth Argyle (Division 2).

HOLDSTOCK, Herbert
Half-back: one app.
Born: St Albans, 29 October 1879
Career: Luton Star FC (1897), Luton Town (August 1899), FOREST (July 1904-May 1905).
Reserve half-back Bert Holdstock made his only appearance for Forest on April Fool's Day 1905 against Newcastle United (away) when he and the rest of the team performed badly in a 5-1 defeat. He scored once in 13 League appearances during his five years with Luton.

HOLLAND, John Henry
Goalkeeper: 26 apps.
Born: circa 1863
Career: Notts County (season 1888-89), FOREST (August 1889-May 1891).
Jack Holland made 19 of his senior appearances for Forest in the club's first season in the Football Alliance (1889-90) before playing second fiddle to Bill Brown.
He had earlier kept goal in nine of Notts County's 22 games in their first season of the Football League.

HOLLINS, David Michael
Goalkeeper: 9 apps.
Born: Bangor, North Wales, 4 February 1938
Career: Brighton & Hove Albion (professional, November 1955), Newcastle United (£12,000, March 1961), Mansfield Town (£2,500, February 1967), FOREST (on loan, March-May 1970), Aldershot (July 1970), Portsmouth (on loan, March-April 1971), Romford (May 1971-72). Son of the former Wolves and Bangor City goalkeeper Bill Hollins and brother of John (ex-Chelsea, QPR, Arsenal midfielder), Roy (ex-Brighton & HA) and Tony (non-League) he now runs a painting & decorating business in London.
Dave Hollins thought he was an Englishman (like his father and brothers) and, in fact, he didn't appreciate that he had been born in Wales until he was selected to play for the Welsh Under-23 side. He went on to win two caps at that level and also appeared in 11 full internationals (all with Newcastle). Once he had donned the famous Red jersey Hollins was as patriotic as the next Welshman and proud of his new found nationality.
After two years National Service he got his chance in Brighton's League side in 1958 when Eric Gill's unbeaten run of 247 consecutive appearances came to an end. He was on the receiving end of a nine-goal drubbing but he quickly put that experience behind him to become a competent custodian, agile but liable to the odd slip here and there. He saved a penalty on his debut for Newcastle v. Spurs but then let in six goals in his next match. Nevertheless, he went on to produce many excellent performances for the Magpies for whom he appeared in 121 senior games before moving to Mansfield, being part of the Stags' FA Cup giant-killing side in 1968-69 and helping them win the 'Giant-Killers' Cup in 1969. He

played in the last nine League games of the 1969-70 season for Forest (following an injury to Alan Hill) and was on the winning side just once - in his final appearance at home to Ipswich Town (1-0).
After quitting football Hollins settled in Guildford where he ran a decorating business. He also played bowls for the London Welsh Club.

HOLLIS, Joshua N
Outside-right: one app. one goal
Born: circa 1872
Career: FOREST (1896-98)
Reserve winger Joe Hollis made his only first team appearance for Forest on 24 October 1896 when he deputised for Fred Forman in a 4-1 home win over Burnley, scoring to celebrate the occasion.

HOLMES, J Albert
Outside-left: 6 apps. one goal
Born: Mansfield, Notts, circa 1882
Career: FOREST (seasons 1904-07)
A reserve left-winger with Forest, Albert Holmes managed just half-a-dozen appearances in the first-team during his three years with the club, making his debut in a 1-1 draw at Blackburn in December 1905 when he deputised for Alf Spouncer. His only goal for the club was scored in a 6-2 FA Cup win over Bury in January 1906 when again he stood in for Spouncer.

HOOD, Clarence
Outside-right: 3 apps.
Born: Mansfield, Notts, 24 April 1912
Career: Bilsthorpe Colliery, FOREST (August 1934-May 1935).
Reserve to Arthur Masters, Clarence Hood made his Football League debut for Forest against Port Vale in December 1934. He was an adaptable player with good speed and strong physique.

HOOPER, William G
Outside-right: 155 apps. 25 goals
Born: Lewisham, 20 February 1884.
Died: 3 September 1952
Career: Catford Southend FC, Army football (Service Corps), Grimsby Town (August 1905), FOREST (February 1907), Notts County (August 1912), Barrow (June 1913), then Gillingham, Southport Central, Lancaster Town after service in the Army (again) during WW1. He was also a very useful club cricketer.
Bill Hooper was 'a little man with plenty of speed and dash'. A successful competitor in Grimsby area sprint handicaps while a Mariner he was difficult to contain on his day and centred and released exquisite long passes in fine fashion. He scored six goals in 32 games for Grimsby and helped Forest win the Second Division title in 1907. During his first three years at the City Ground he and Tom Marrison worked superbly well together down the

right and then he had a decent run with Lockett before losing his place to Bob Firth. He made well over 250 appearances at senior level during his career.

HORROCKS, John

Outside-left: 22 apps.

Born: Lees near Oldham, Lancs, September 1887

Career: Failsworth Juniors, Stockport County (July 1908), FOREST (August 1909), Bury (April 1911).

After an excellent season with Stockport (5 goals in 34 League and Cup games) Jack Horrocks was signed by Forest as a possible replacement for the ageing Alf Spouncer. Full of dash and resource, with neat skills, he also had Bill Palmer to contest the left-wing position with at the City Ground and during his first year with the club he made 16 League appearances. Thereafter he failed to hold his place in the side and was subsequently transferred to Bury.

HOWE, Stephen Robert

Midfielder: 11+9 apps. 2 goals

Born: Cramlington near Blyth, Northumberland, 6 November 1973

Career: FOREST (trainee, April 1989, professional December 1990), Ipswich Town (on loan, January 1997), Swindon Town (£30,000, January 1998-Havant + Waterlooville (cs. 2002),

A hard-working, strong-running central midfielder, Bobby Howe - an England Youth international - helped Forest reach the Premiership in 1994, appearing in four First Division matches. He spent almost nine years at the City Ground and at no time was he a first-team regular, his best season coming in 1995-96 when he had 11 outings (six as a substitute). He reached the personal milestone of 150 League & Cup appearances during 2002 - 135 for Swindon.

HOWELL

Goalkeeper: one app.

Born: circa 1868

Career: FOREST (1889-90)

Reserve 'keeper Howell made his only senior appearance for the club in a Football Alliance game against Bootle (away) in April 1890 when he deputised for Jack Holland.

HOWIE, Charles

Outside-right: 24 apps. 2 goals

Born: Larbert, Scotland, 25 April 1906

Career: Arthurlie, Larkhall Thistle Stenhousemuir, FOREST (October 1928), Stenhousemuir (May 1931).

A lightweight winger, a shade on the small side but surprisingly quick, Charlie Howie had one excellent season with Forest, that of 1928-29 after coming into the side after 11 games had been fulfilled. Unfortunately he lost his way the following year when Jack Scott took over on the right flank and struggled after that, returning to Scotland in 1931.

HOWLETT, Harold W A

Centre-forward/outside-left: one app.

Born: Bishop Auckland, 23 June 1910. Died: 1989

Career: Evenwood FC, Rochdale (1928), Cockfield FC (1929), Portsmouth (1931), FOREST (September 1932), Poole Town (July 1933).

Signed as cover and, indeed, as a reserve to Johnny Dent and Bob Pugh, Harry Howlett's only first-team game for Forest was against Plymouth Argyle (at home) in October 1932 when he deputised for Dent in the 1-1 draw.

HUCKERBY, Darren Carl

Striker: 11 apps. 5 goals

Born: Nottingham, 23 April 1976

Career: Notts County (briefly), Lincoln City (apprentice, June 1982, professional July 1993), Newcastle United (£400,000, November 1995), Millwall (on loan, September 1996), Coventry City (£1 million, November 1996), Leeds United (£4 million, August 1999), Manchester City (£2.25 million, December 2000), FOREST (on loan, February-May 2003).

Recruited by manager Paul Hart to boss the Forest attack at a crucial stage in the season, Darren Huckerby scored some vital goals as the Reds confirmed their place in the First Division Play-offs.

Fast, direct, with an eye for goal, Huckerby who was capped by England once at 'B' team level and four times by the Under-21's earlier in his career, broke into League football with the Imps but failed to make any impression at St James' Park. He then did well with Coventry (scoring 34 goals in 109 outings), struggled to hold down a regular place in the first team at Leeds (six goals in only 57 games, 43 as a substitute) and after helping Manchester City win the First Division championship (2002) he was frozen out at Maine Road following the arrival of his former Elland Road team-mate Robbie Fowler, plus the fact the Kevin Keegan had far too many strikers to keep happy!

HUDDLESTONE, Edward Thomas

Centre-forward: one app.

Born: Nottingham, 29 September 1935

Career: Blackpool (amateur, September 1951), FOREST (December 1956-February 1957), Ilkeston Town, Long Eaton United.

An amateur centre-forward, Ted Huddlestone was handed just one first-team game by Forest manager Billy Walker, lining up as leader of the attack in a Second Division game at Grimsby (0-0) 72 hours after joining the club. He stood in for Jim Barratt but failed to impress.

HUGHES, Edwin

Right-half: 176 apps. 6 goals

Born: Wrexham, 1886. Died: Montgomery, 17 April 1949

Career: Wrexham St Giles (Chester & District League), Wrexham Victoria (Wirral League), Wrexham (August 1903), FOREST (April 1906), Wrexham (April 1911),

Manchester City (March 1912), Aberdare Athletic (June 1920), Colwyn Bay United (1922), Llandudno Town (season 1924-25), taking over a public house after retiring and then working as an artificial stone manufacturer. He died suddenly when taking a weekend break.

Eddie Hughes helped Forest win the Second Division championship in 1907. A Welsh international (16 caps gained between 1906-14) he was 'a stylish wing-half who could feed his forwards and knew how to supply his colleagues with precise passes that produced results.' A well-built player, said to 'stand any amount of work' Hughes was an early exponent of the long throw-in. Originally reserve to Maurice Parry, he quickly established himself in the Welsh side and was a key performer in his country's red shirt for eight years and in the red of Forest for five, producing several outstanding displays. His brother Richard was capped by Wales as an amateur.

HULLETT, William Alexander

Centre-forward: 15 apps. 2 goals
Born: Liverpool, 19 November 1915.
Died: Cardiff, 6 September 1982
Career: Everton (professional, December 1935), New Brighton (January 1937), Everton (April 1937), Plymouth Argyle (October 1937), Manchester United (March 1939), Plymouth Argyle (as a guest, 1945), FOREST (guest, September 1941 and Merthyr Tydfil, April 1946), Cardiff City (February 1948), FOREST (November 1948), Merthyr Tydfil (player-manager, June 1949), Worcester City.

In the post-war boom, centre-forward Bill Hullett was close to being the biggest name in South Wales football and his memory still brings a dewy-eyed response from Merthyr fans who had the privilege of seeing him in action. He was doing pretty well with his local church team in Liverpool when Everton signed him in 1935 (as cover and a possible replacement for a certain Dixie Dean). His spell with New Brighton was fruitless however, and so was his second stint at Goodison Park, but he did well with Plymouth (hitting 20 goals in 28 games in two seasons); yet he failed to make the first team at Old Trafford. Then, after serving in the RAF during WW2 (based in Palestine & Egypt) Hullett netted a hatful of goals for Merthyr and followed up by scoring 15 in 27 League games for Cardiff. His association with Forest wasn't a happy one - unfortunately - and he had no hesitation in returning to Merthyr as player-manager. His arrival heralded the greatest period in the history of the Penydarren Park club. Indeed, the names of Hullett and Merthyr were inseparable and Hullett himself became, a legend to the Merthyr public who still relate the tales of his goalscoring exploits to this day.

HULME, Eric Martin

Goalkeeper: 6 apps.
Born: Houghton-le-Spring, County Durham, 14 January 1949
Career: Spenny___ r Uni__ l (1966), FOREST (March 1970), Lincoln___ y (c__ loan, September 1972, signed permanently for ___ _,00_, October 1972), Gainsborough Trinity (on loan, Jan__ ry 1973), Worksop Town free transfer, July 1974).

Never really able to dislodge Jim Barron from the goalkeeping slot at the City Ground, Eric Hulme was a very competent performer at reserve-team level. He had 23 outings for the Imps.

HUNT, Arthur A

Left-back: 2 apps
Born: circa 1871
Career: FOREST (May 1894-June 1896)

Arthur Hunt, a reserve full-back, made his senior debut for Forest in a United Counties League game v. Leicester Fosse on 4 April 1895, following up with his first Football League outing against Burnley in March 1896.

HUNT, Ashley Kenneth

Goalkeeper: 2 apps.
Born: Kirkby-in-Ashfield, 24 November 1921
Career: Hawley's Athletic, FOREST (professional, December 1938-March 1940). Did not re-appear after WW2.

Signed as cover for Percy Ashton and Allan Todd, goalkeeper Kenny Allen made his League debut for Forest in February 1939 against Tranmere Rovers (2-2), playing in the next Second Division game as well (a 2-0 defeat by Southampton). Unfortunately WW2 brought an end to his senior career.

HUNT, Joseph Frederick

Inside-right: one app.
Born: Belfast, circa 1910
Career: Crusaders, FOREST (March-May 1935)

Inside-forward Paddy Hunt had been associated with the Crusaders club in Northern Ireland before joining Forest at the end of the 1934-35 season. He made only one League appearance during his brief stay at the City Ground, lining up against Bradford City in May 1935, setting up one of Tom Peacock's two goals in a 2-0 victory.

HUTCHINSON, John A

Full-back: 254 apps.
Born: Heanor, Derbyshire, 1 June 1921.
Career: FOREST (junior August 1943, professional May 1945, Ilkeston Town (coach, cs. 1959).

Jack Hutchinson helped Forest win the Third Division South title in 1951 (playing in only six matches) and was also a member of the club's Second Division promotion winning side six years later. Initially a forward, he was successfully converted into a full-back and made his League debut in November 1946 - after more than 20 outings for the Reds during the latter stages of WW2. He was an excellent, intelligent defender who showed great positional sense. Never flustered, he had to battle hard and long to get first-team football owing to the presence of Geoff Thomas and Bill Whare, but he was always there, ready and willing to produce the goods when called into action. After missing out on Forest's FA Cup win in 1959 Hutchinson decided to retire.

ILEY, James

Wing-half: 103 apps. 5 goals
Born: South Kirby, Yorkshire, 15 December 1935
Career: Moorthorpe St Joseph's Boys Club, Pontefract FC, Sheffield United (juniors, March 1951, professional December 1952), Tottenham Hotspur (£16,000, August 1957), FOREST (£16,000, August 1959), Newcastle United (£17,000, September 1962), Peterborough United (player-manager, January 1969-September 1972), Cambridge United (scout, October 1972-March 1963), Barnsley (manager, April 1973), Blackburn Rovers (manager, April 1978), Luton Town (scout, October 1978), Bury (manager, July 1980-February 1984), Exeter City (manager, June 1984-April 1985), Charlton Athletic (scout), Luton Town (scout).
An England Under-23 international (one cap) and Football League representative, Jim Iley, a former colliery lad at Frickley pit before turning professional, made his League debut for Sheffield United as a 17-year-old. He quickly began to be noticed and earned a move to White Hart Lane where he won his England cap. He failed to settle in London and opted to move back north, joining Forest in 1959 when manager Billy Walker was rebuilding his team following FA Cup glory. He did well at the City Ground, especially in his first season when he appeared in 35 League games. He became the cornerstone, alongside Stan Anderson, of Newcastle's Second Division promotion-winning side in 1965. The always seemingly balding Iley was regarded as the complete player, possessing good control, versatility, tremendous shooting power (mainly right-footed), consistency and a team-man's attitude. He skippered most of the clubs he played for and during a wonderful career accumulated more than 600 appearances (545 in the Football League) and scored over 35 goals.
Iley took over as player-manager of Posh following the resignation of Norman Rigby and later had a turbulent 172 days in charge at Ewood Park. After leaving football he resided in Bolton and ran an Italian restaurant in Chorley. Iley's brother-in-law is Colin Grainger, the ex-Sheffield United and England winger.

IMLACH, James John Stewart

Outside-left: 204 apps. 48 goals
Born: Lossiemouth, Scotland, 6 January 1932.
Died: October 2001.
Career: Lossiemouth FC, Bury (October 1952), Derby County (May 1954), FOREST (July 1955), Luton Town (June 1960), Coventry City (October 1960), Crystal Palace (July 1962), Chelmsford City (February 1965), Crystal Palace (February 1966).
Stewart Imlach helped Forest win promotion to the First Division in 1957 and two years later played his part in the 2-1 FA Cup final victory over Luton Town, the club he joined in 1960. Capped by his country on four occasions, he was, in fact, the first Forest player to represent Scotland, doing so versus Hungary in May 1958 at Hampden Park, going on to play in the 1958 World Cup finals in Sweden. Fast and direct, with an eye for goal he made 423 appearances at League level for his six English clubs.

INGRAM, Alexander David

Centre-forward: 31 apps. 3 goals
Born: Edinburgh, 2 January 1945
Career: Ayr United, FOREST (December 1969), Ayr United (February 1971).
A Scottish amateur international and Scottish League representative (with Ayr), Alex Ingram was a Forest player for 14 months, during which time he produced some useful performances following his debut on Boxing Day 1969 against Arsenal. He eventually lost his place in the side after the Reds' rather disappointing start to the 1970-71 season and when Neil Martin arrived on the scene he returned to Ayr.

INNES, Robert A

Right-half: 26 apps.
Born: Lanark, Scotland, 23 July 1878
Career: Clydesdale, Royal Ordnance Factory, Gravesend United, New Brompton, Notts County (July 1901), FOREST (August 1903), Brighton & Hove Albion (May 1905), Swindon Town.
Bob Innes made his League debut for Forest against Bury a week or so after joining the club from neighbours County for whom he had appeared in more than 50 first-class matches. A good, stern tackler, who backed his forwards up well, he was a steady player rather than a spectacular one who took over the right-half slot from Sammy Timmins when he was pushed forward.

IREMONGER, Harold

Goalkeeper: 11 apps.
Born: New Basford, Notts, circa 1889.
Career: Sherwood Institute, FOREST (seasons 1912-17).
Did not re-appear after WW1.
Harold Iremonger made his League debut for Forest in April 1914 in a 2-1 defeat by Stockport County. Brother of Jimmy (below), he was always struggling to get first-

team football (owing to the presence and good form of Jack Hanna and then Jack Powell) although the Great War certainly played its part in reducing his career. He played his last game for Forest against Bradford PA in January 1917

IREMONGER, James
Full-back/occasional goalkeeper: 301 apps. 13 goals
Born: Norton, West Yorkshire, 5 March 1876.
Died: Nottingham, 25 March 1956.
Career: Wilford FC, Nottingham Jardine's Athletic, FOREST (January 1896, retired in May 1910); later coach at Notts County (1919-27). Played cricket for Nottinghamshire CCC from 1897 to 1914, scoring 16,622 runs (including 31 centuries and a top-score of 272 v. Kent in 1904) and taking 619 wickets (his best being 6-7 v. Essex in 1910). He also toured Australia with the MCC in 1911-12 and was on the coaching staff at Trent Bridge (1921-38).
England international Jim Iremonger, heftily built, was capped twice at senior level, at right-back v. Scotland at the Crystal Palace in March 1901 and at left-back v. Ireland in Belfast in March 1902. He was equally adept in both full-back positions and could use both feet - and at times he was no mug between the posts. He could be erratic at times, however, and some of his clumsy, uncontrolled lunges did prove costly to his side.
NB: His brother Albert was a trialist with Forest who made 564 League appearances for Notts County and 35 for Lincoln City, while his other brother, Harold (above), was also a Forest goalkeeper.

IRVING, Richard James
Forward: 0+1 app
Born: Halifax, Yorkshire, 10 September 1975
Career: Manchester United (trainee, August 1991, professional October 1992), FOREST (July 1995), Macclesfield Town (October 1997), Runcorn (February 1998).
An England Schoolboy and Youth international, released from Old Trafford without appearing in the first team, Richard Irving made just one substitute appearance in the Premiership for Forest, coming on in place of Bobby Howe in the 1-1 home draw with his former club Manchester United in November 1995. He later made 11 appearances for Macclesfield before leaving to join Runcorn by mutual consent.

JACKSON, Henry
Centre-forward: one app.
Born: Nottinghamshire, 1864
Career: Sneinton Wanderers (1882), Notts County (1888), FOREST (season 1889-90).
Harry Jackson - a reserve forward - made his only senior appearance for Forest on 22 March 1890, lining up in a crushing 9-0 defeat at Darwen in the Football Alliance. He was the club's eighth different centre-forward called into action that season. He failed to impress.

JACKSON, Thomas
Midfielder: 87+8 apps. 6 goals
Born: Belfast, 3 November 1946
Career: Glentoran, Everton (£10,000, February 1968), FOREST (£150,000, player-exchange deal involving Henry Newton, October 1970), Manchester United (£75,000, June 1975), Waterford (July 1978).
After 32 League games for Everton, Tommy Jackson arrived at Forest at a time when manager Matt Gillies was looking to change his midfield - and after a slow start he settled down well and went on to make almost 100 appearances for the Reds before transferring to Old Trafford. He won a total of 35 caps for Northern Ireland (19 with Forest, with his first coming against Spain in November 1970) and he also represented his country in one Under-23 international. He skippered Manchester United's second XI in his first season with the club, being unable to hold down a place in the senior side. He later managed several clubs in Ireland before becoming a self-employed upholsterer, working mainly for Bannon & Co (Belfast).

JEACOCK, Thomas W
Left-half/outside-right: 52 apps.
Born: circa 1866
Career: Mellors FC, FOREST (1890), Burton Swifts (1892), FOREST (August 1894-May 1895).
The versatile Tommy Jeacock made over 40 appearances in the Football Alliance during his first spell with Forest, being an ever-present in the left-half position in 1890-91. He later returned to the club and made his League debut on the right-wing in September 1895, in a 6-1 defeat at Everton.

JEMSON, Nigel Bradley
Striker: 58+3 apps. 20 goals
Born: Hutton, near Preston, Lancs, 10 October 1969
Career: Preston North End (trainee, August 1985, professional July 1987), FOREST (£150,000, March 1988), Bolton Wanderers (on loan, December 1988), Preston North End (on loan, March 1989), Sheffield Wednesday (£800,000, September 1991), Grimsby Town (on loan, September 1993), Notts County (£300,000, September 1994), Watford (on loan, January 1995), Rotherham United (on loan, February 1996), Oxford United (£60,000, July 1996), Bury (£100,000, February 1998), Ayr United (free transfer, July 1999), Oxford United (free transfer, January 2000), Shrewsbury Town (free transfer, July 2000 to June 2002).
Scorer of Forest's goal in their 1990 League Cup final victory over Oldham Athletic, Nigel Jemson - a real soccer journeyman - reached a career milestone of 450 League and Cup appearances in 2002 with Shrewsbury Town and he also chalked up his 120th competitive goal. He played in exactly 100 games for Oxford (33 goals). A very hard-working forward, able to occupy all three central positions equally well, he was a smart dribbler too but was criticised for holding on to the ball far too long during the early part

of his career.

NB: Jemson (as a substitute) was called into action (for Steve Hodge) during Forest's 5th round FA Cup-tie at Southampton in February 1991. As he peeled off his tracksuit top he realised he hadn't put on his playing shirt. He quickly grabbed the jersey of another sub, Ian Woan, and went on and helped his side earn a 1-1 draw.

JENAS, Jermaine Anthony
Midfielder: 33 apps. 4 goals
Born: Nottingham, 18 February 1983
Career: FOREST (trainee, June 1999, professional February 2000), Newcastle United (£5 million, February 2000).

Extremely talented midfield player who showed real class either in the centre of the park or in a wide-left role. His mature play earned a £5 million transfer to St James' Park and he soon stepped up to the full England Squad. Tall and athletic he was voted the PFA 'Young Player of the Year' in 2003'.

JENNINGS, Samuel
Inside-right/left or centre-forward: 28 apps. 17 goals
Born: Cinderhill, Nottingham, 26 December 1898.
Died: Sussex 26 August 1944.
Career: Highbury Vale Methodists, Basford United, 5th Reserve Battalion Coldstream Guards, Basford National Ordnance Factory, guested for both Notts County and Tottenham Hotspur during WW1; Norwich City (May 1919), Middlesbrough (£2,500, April 1920), Reading (initially on loan, April 1921), West Ham United (June 1924), Brighton & Hove Albion (March 1925), FOREST (May 1928), Port Vale (June 1929), Stockport County (September 1931), Burnley (January-May 1932), Wisbech Town (player, then secretary-coach, 1932-33), Olympique Marseille/France (as an instructor/coach, May 1933), Scarborough (player-coach, September 1934), player in Switzerland (season 1935-36), Glentoran (coach, June 1936), Rochdale (manager, October 1937 to September 1938).
During his career Sam Jennings scored 172 goals in 349 League games including 61 in 110 outings for Brighton, 45 in 110 for Reading and 42 in 63 for Port Vale. Unfortunately he found it hard to break into Middlesbrough's team after his big-money transfer in 1920. A tall inside or centre-forward, he made his debut for Forest in a 5-1 League defeat at home to Stoke in August 1928 but after that scored some cracking goals, including a superb hat-trick v. Swansea Town (won 5-3) before moving on following the emergence of Barry Heathcock. Later in his career while playing on the Continent Jennings met Jimmy Hogan who had a major influence on his thinking about coaching. However, he met with little success as manager of Rochdale and quit the job through ill-health. His brother William played for Luton Town and Northampton Town.

JERKAN, Nikola
Defender/midfielder: 14 apps.
Born: Split, Yugoslavia, 8 December 1964
Career: Hajduk Split, Real Oviedo/Spain (August 1991), FOREST (£1 million, July 1996), Rapid Vienna (cs 1997) RSC Charleroi (cs.1998).
The versatile Nikola Jerkan, a Croatian international, was signed by Forest after his impressive displays for his country in Euro '96. Able to play as a sweeper or defensive midfielder, he struggled to fine his form at the City Ground and departed after just a season in England. He made over 200 League appearances for the Spanish club Real Oviedo whom he served for five years.

JESS, Eoin
Midfielder/forward: 30+20 apps. 5 goals
Born: Aberdeen, 13 December 1970
Career: Glasgow Rangers (juniors, 1986), Aberdeen (professional, November 1987), Coventry City (£1.75 million, February 1996), Aberdeen (£700,000, July 1997), Bradford City (free transfer, December 2000), FOREST (in a player-exchange deal involving, Andy Gray, July 2002).
Scotland international with 14 Under-21, two 'B' and 18 senior caps to his credit, Eoin Jess was Bradford City's top-scorer in 2001-02 before transferring to Forest. Prior to that he had netted 94 goals in almost 375 games during his two spells with Aberdeen, helping them win the Scottish League Cup in 1989. A strong competitor, he possesses silky passing skills and delivers a powerful shot in his right foot. He has played as a central midfield player during his latter years.

JOHN, Stern
Striker: 56+24 apps. 20 goals
Born: Trinidad, 30 October 1976
Career: Columbus Crew/USA (1996), FOREST (£1.5 million, November 1999), Birmingham City (free transfer, February 2002).
Stern John was, to a certain extent, a victim of the small print written into his contract when he moved from the USA to the City Ground in 1999. It was revealed that Forest (his buyers) would have to pay £90,000 a goal once he had netted 15 times and he was eventually allowed to move to St Andrew's for a cut-down price. He scored eight important 'promotion' goals at the end of the 2001-02 season when his poise, pace, close control and, indeed, his overall ability added something special to the Birmingham' attack at a crucial stage of the proceedings. Capped several times by Trinidad & Tobago, John produced some excellent performances for the Reds, having his best season in 2001-02 when he netted 14 goals in 27 outings, mainly having as his partner(s) Marlon Harewood and/or Jack Lester in attack.

JOHNSON, Andrew
Midfielder: 110+18 apps. 10 goals
Born: Bristol, 2 May 1974
Career: Norwich City (trainee, June 1990, professional March 1992), FOREST (£2.3 million, July 1997), West Bromwich Albion (£200,000, September 2001).
Midfielder Andy Johnson was capped by England at Youth team level before going on to appear in eight senior internationals for Wales. He helped Forest reach the Premiership (as Division One champions) in 1998 and then did likewise with WBA (as runners-up) in 2002. An industrious box-to-box player, who loves to drive forward from centre-field, he has scored some fine goals, many of them from distance. He did well initially with Forest before having a stop-start season prior to moving to the Hawthorns for a cut-down fee. In 2002 he reached the personal milestone of 250 League appearances (30 goals).

JOHNSON, Damien Michael
Midfielder: 5+1 apps.
Born: Lisburn, Northern Ireland, 18 November 1978
Career: Blackburn Rovers (trainee, June 1995, February 1996), FOREST (on loan, January 1998), Birmingham City (March 2002).
Damien Johnson made six appearances for Forest at a crucial late stage of their 1997-98 First Division championship winning season and then he did the same with Birmingham at the end of the 2001-02 campaign when they also reached the Premiership.
An Irish international with 24 full, 11 Under-21 and a handful of Youth caps to his credit, Johnson was also a Worthington League Cup winner with Blackburn (v. Spurs) in 2002.
A talented central midfield player, totally committed, combative who never shirks a tackle, he perhaps surprisingly left Ewood Park for St Andrew's soon after Rovers lifted the League Cup.

JOHNSON, David Anthony
Striker: 90+8 apps. 36 goals
Born: Kingston, Jamaica, 15 August 1976
Career: Manchester United (trainee August 1992, professional July 1994), Bury (free transfer, July 1995), Ipswich Town (£800,000, November 1997), FOREST (£3 million, January 2001), Sheffield Wednesday (on loan, February 2002), Burnley (on loan, March 2002).
After playing for England at both Schoolboy and 'B' team levels, David Johnson went on to gain four full international caps for Jamaica. He was an FA Youth Cup winner with Manchester United in 1975 but was released from Old Trafford without making the first team. He later helped Bury win the Second Division title in 1997. A fast and lively striker he struggled early on at the City Ground but after loan spells at Hillsborough and Turf Moor he returned full of vim and vigour and had a tremendous 2002-03 season, scoring 29 times in 47 matches. Earlier,

he netted 23 goals in 115 games for Bury and 62 in 158 outings for Ipswich.

JOHNSON, Joseph
Goalkeeper: 54 apps.
Born: Tibshelf, Derbyshire, circa 1888
Career: Ripley Athletic (1904), Aston Villa (May 1905), Plymouth Argyle (August 1906), Crystal Palace (November 1907), FOREST (June 1919), Sutton Town (May 1921-April 1922).
Josh Johnson was a cool, competent goalkeeper who used his fists to good effect when clearing high crosses. He failed to make the first XI at Villa Park, had only a handful of games for Argyle but then appeared in 293 Southern League and FA Cup games for Palace. He represented the Southern League on three occasions during his time at Selhurst Park.

JOHNSON, Thomas
Inside-forward: 73 apps. 30 goals
Born: Gateshead, 21 September 1921. Died: March 1999.
Career: Gateshead (professional, September 1941), FOREST (WW2 guest, signed permanently, August 1948). Retired in May 1952
'Tucker' Johnson played his part in helping Forest win the Third Division South title in 1951. Described in some reports as being 'dashing and fearless, a damaging forward who played with gusto, proving difficult to knock off the ball'. A genuinely fine marksman.

JOHNSTON, Thomas Deans
Left-half/inside or centre-forward/outside-left: 69 apps. 26 goals
Born: Coldstream, Berwickshire, 30 December 1918. Died: 1994
Career: Coldstream Juniors, Kelso United (1935), Peterborough United (semi-professional, July 1937), FOREST (June 1942, full-time professional May 1944), Notts County (August 1948 to May 1957), Valkeakoski Harka/Finland (coach, June-August 1957), Birmingham City (coach, September 1957), Heanor Town (player-manager, July 1958), Rotherham United (manager, November 1958-July 1962), Grimsby Town (manager, July 1962-October 1964), Huddersfield Town (manager, October 1964-May 1968), York City (manager: October 1968-January 1975), Huddersfield Town (general manager, January 1975-April 1977, back to general manager April-September 1977, and finally manager once more, September 1977-August 1978).
Canny Scotsman Tommy Johnston scored almost a goal every two games for Forest during WW2 (46 in just over 100 appearances) and then after leaving the City Ground he netted 88 in 267 League outings for County. Preferring to occupy the outside-left berth, he was astute on the ball, quick over short distances and packed a fine shot. He netted 14 times in 32 Second Division matches in the first

peacetime season of 1946-47 and after moving inside he continued to hit the target on a regular basis before his transfer to Meadow Lane (following the arrival of Wally Ardron from Rotherham United). When the Magpies won the Third Division South title in 1950 he formed a brilliant partnership up front with England centre-forward Tommy Lawton.

As manager of Rotherham he took them to the first League Cup final in 1961 when they were defeated over two legs by Aston Villa. Later he had three separate spells in charge of Huddersfield Town - all at critical times during the club's history - a unique record. On each occasion he initially turned round the fortunes of the team that had been struggling at the wrong end of the League table. Between 1969 and 1975 he completely transformed York City, a team on the brink of seeking re-election, taking them, up two divisions from the Fourth to the Second on limited resources. This was and still is the highest level the Bootham Crescent club has ever reached. A shrewd strategist, Johnston's quietly-spoken, pipe-smoking image hid the fact that he was a stickler for discipline. He relied mainly on home-grown talent at Leeds Road and did a splendid job, being a good motivator and an excellent judge of players' capabilities. A qualified FA coach, Johnston's first spell in charge of the Terriers saw the team reach within two points of a Second Division promotion place, and make the semi-finals of the League Cup (1968). His second spell in charge saw him acting as general manager alongside Scottish international Bobby Collins. Unfortunately, the partnership never really worked and Huddersfield were relegated to the Fourth Division for the first time in their history.

JONES, Albert Thomas

Full-back: 16 apps.

Born: Talgarth, Breconshire, 6 February 1883.
Died: Belper, Derbyshire, 28 July 1963

Career: Builth Juniors, Burlth Town, Talgarth, Harborne Lynwood (Birmingham), Aston Villa (briefly, in July-August 1902), Swindon Town (October 1902), FOREST (September 1903), Notts County (December 1905), Norwich City (May 1907), Wellington Town (August 1908). Retired in 1910 to take over the Buck's Head (hotel) in Wellington, but made a surprise return to the game as an amateur with Swansea in 1913. He was actually capped by Wales at that level prior to WW1 before deciding to hang up his boots for good in 1915.

A full Welsh international (2 caps gained, both v. England in 1905 & 1906) Tom Jones could play in either full-back position. The son of Peace Jones (a Builth chemist) he was a dogged performer who tackled hard and fair. He made 30 League appearances for County after leaving Forest but struggled with the Canaries in the Southern League, having just six outings.

JONES, Charles

Outside-left/right-half: 111 apps. 22 goals

Born: Troedyrhiw near Merthyr Tydfil, South Wales, 12 December 1889. Died: Brentwood, Essex, April 1966

Career: Troedyrhiw, Cardiff City (August 1919), Stockport County (August 1921), Oldham Athletic (£1,000, March 1923), FOREST (£750, September 1925), Arsenal (£4,850, May 1928), Notts County (manager, May-December 1934), Crittall's Athletic (secretary-manager, August 1935-September 1939). Did not participate in football after WW2.

After helping Stockport win the Third Division North title (1922), Charlie Jones' consistent play for Oldham (56 League games, six goals) prompted Forest to sign him in 1925. At the City ground he produced brilliant form, being instrumental when playing in his first international for Wales in their victory over England at Selhurst Park in 1926. That day he caught the eye of several leading clubs yet it was two years later before he moved into the 'big league', manager Herbert Chapman signing him for Arsenal for what was then a record fee (for Forest) of almost £5,000.

Jones was very much a thinking player who tackled well and never knew when he was beaten. He was converted from a left-winger into a right-half at Highbury following the emergence of a youthful forward named Cliff Bastin. He became an integral part of the Gunners' armoury, helping them win the League championship in 1931 and 1934 and going on to appear in 188 senior games for the London club. He was capped eight times in all by Wales (appearing in four internationals against England). After his associations with Notts County (he resigned from his position there after a disagreement with the directors) and whilst he was with the Essex side Crittall's (where he coached the players wearing a pair of carpet slippers) Jones ran a successful hairdressing salon in London and also worked briefly as a hospital stoker.

JONES, Charles Wilson

Centre-forward: 7 apps. 5 goals

Born: Pentre, Broughton near Wrexham, 29 April 1914. Died: Birmingham, 9 January 1986.

Career: Brymbo Green FC (August 1930), Oswestry Town (1931), Wrexham (amateur, May 1932, professional September 1932), Birmingham (£1,500, September 1934), guested for Huddersfield Town, West Bromwich Albion & Wrexham during WW2, FOREST (September 1947), Kidderminster Harriers (July 1948), Redditch United (August 1949). Retired, May 1950 to enter the licensing trade, remaining as 'mine host' until 1979.

A consistently hard worker, one of the brainiest footballers in the game, Welsh international centre-forward Wilson Jones was only 5ft 7ins tall and weighed 10st 9lbs, but he was a game performer, 'a leader of real merit' wrote one journalist. Birmingham were willing to spend £1,500 on Jones after he had scored 33 goals in season 1933-34 for

Wrexham and he continued to hit the target during his first two years at St Andrew's before injuries and loss of form effected his overall play. He was past his best when he joined Forest but still managed to score a few goals. He helped Birmingham win the Football League (South) championship in 1946 and was capped twice by Wales (v. Northern Ireland in 1935 and France in 1939).

JONES, David Edward

Defender: 41 apps. 2 goals
Born: Gosport, Hampshire, 11 February 1952
Career: Bournemouth (apprentice, June 1968, professional January 1970), FOREST (August 1974), Norwich City (£55,000 in total, September 1975-April 1980), Wroxham (August 1980-May 1985)
Welsh international defender (eight full and four Under-23 caps gained) David Jones made 134 League appearances for Bournemouth before joining Forest and after leaving the City Ground he added a further 125 to his tally in the same competition with the Canaries. A sound, powerful footballer, he impressed with his aerial dominance and his will-to-win attitude. He will perhaps be remembered by the Welsh supporters for being the innocent party in the infamous 'handball' incident with Joe Jordan (at Anfield) which cost Wales a place in the 1978 World Cup finals.
After leaving football he worked with the Bournemouth School of Excellence before developing a printing business in the town.

JONES, Eric

Left or right-winger: 18 apps. 3 goals
Born: Ulverston near Barrow-in-Furness, Cumbria, 23 June 1931.
Career: Notts County (amateur, 1950), Preston North End (professional, January 1952), FOREST (September 1955), Doncaster Rovers (March 1958), Accrington Stanley (July 1959), Southport (July 1960), Lancaster City (August 1962).
Eric Jones made his League debut rather later in life - he was 22 years of age when (with first reserve Campbell sidelined) he deputised for England's Tom Finney in a First Division game for Preston North End against Burnley in December 1953. He was also basically a reserve team player with Forest, making only 18 senior appearances in two-and-a-half years, his first coming against Stoke City in September 1955 when he stood in for Peter Small on the left-wing.

JONES, Gary Steven

Utility player (defender/midfielder): 26+13 apps. 2 goals
Born: Chester, 10 May 1975
Career: Tranmere Rovers (trainee, June 1991, professional July 1993), FOREST (free transfer, July 2000), Tranmere Rovers (September 2002).
Before he joined Forest, the versatile Gary Jones scored 33

goals in 220 first-team outings for Tranmere, occupying a string of different positions but always looking to play an attacking role, preferably from midfield. Standing 6ft 3ins tall and weighing 14st, he is a player who can rough it with the toughest opponents around and he has always been a threat inside the penalty-area when going up for set pieces.

JONES, George William

Centre or left-half: 8 apps.
Born: Carlton, Notts, 30 November 1896.
Career: Carlton Swifts, FOREST (July 1920), Mansfield Town (May 1921-May 1922)
Although well-built and strong in the tackle, George Jones - described early in his career as a commanding centre-half - failed to establish himself in the Forest defence and played second fiddle to Messrs Parker and Armstrong for the majority of his time at the club. He made his Football League v. Bury in October 1920 and, in fact, all his eight senior outings for the Reds were in succession. He made 33 Midland League appearances in his only season with Mansfield.

JONES, Harry

Full-back: 239 apps. 10 goals
Born: Blackwell, Derbyshire, 24 May 1891.
Career: Blackwell Wesley Guild, Blackwell Colliery, FOREST (July 1911-May 1924), Sutton Town (December 1924-April 1925)
Full-back Harry Jones was in excellent form when Forest won the Second Division championship in 1922, missing only two games. The following year (May 1923) he was capped by England against France in Paris. Effective in both the right and left-back berths, he appeared in more than 120 games for Forest during WW1, helping the Reds win the Victory Shield in 1919. He retired at the end of the 1923-24 season but after a seven-month lay-off he was persuaded to return to the game by Swindon Town whom he served briefly in the Southern League, finally hanging up his boots at the age of 34.

JONES, Thomas Daniel

Inside or outside-left: 2 apps.
Born: Aberaman, Glamorgan, 1884.
Died: Porthcawl, Glamorgan, 1958
Career: Aberaman Athletic (1900), Aberdare Town (season 1903-04), FOREST (April 1904), Aberdare Town (April 1908-August 1910), Merthyr Town (secretary-manager: season 1923-24), Cardiff City (scout, until 1930).
Welsh international forward (one cap gained v. Ireland in 1908 as an Aberdare player) Tom Jones remained an amateur throughout his career and was an important pioneer of modern soccer in South Wales. He was without doubt the star forward in the Welsh valleys during the early part of the 20th century and one reporter described him as a 'brilliant runner and tricky dribbler.' He made his debut for Forest at inside-left v. Middlesbrough on the last

day of the 1903-04 season and his second outing followed a year later v. Sheffield United. He was twice a Welsh Cup runner-up (1903 & 1904) and was also capped by Wales at amateur level (1908).

Jones always had a leaning towards the administration side of the game and became secretary of the Aberdare club and also acting as a vice-President on the FAW. Jones qualified as a solicitor in 1913 and after serving in the Army during WW1, he practised in Aberdare for many years. He was secretary-manager of Merthyr Town during the 1923-24 season and later worked as a scout for Cardiff City.

* He came from a comfortable background and his father, an Aberaman grocer, was a Constable of Higher Miskin, an ancient office similar to a mayoralty but latterly merely ceremonial.

JOYCE, Christopher
Inside-forward: 10 apps.
Born: Dumbarton, Scotland, 19 April 1933
Career: Havelock FC, Vale of Leven, FOREST (September 1956), Notts County (July 1959) Nuneaton Borough (cs.1962).

During his time at Meadow Road, Chris Joyce, who was coached initially by the great Tommy Lawton, appeared in 62 League games for County, scoring 18 goals, teaming up with the late Jeff Astle, later to serve WBA and England. One reporter stated that 'his displays at times were characterised by courage and cleverness, although he did lack the killer instinct.'

JULIANS, Leonard Bruce
Centre-forward: 63 apps. 27 goals
Born: Tottenham, North London, 19 June 1933.
Died: Southend 17 December 1993.
Career: Walthamstow Avenue, Leyton Orient (professional, June 1955), Arsenal (December 1958), FOREST (June 1960), Millwall (January 1964), Detroit Cougars (cs.1967).

During his 12 years of League football, Len Julians scored 124 goals in 267 appearances including 58 in 125 games for Millwall, his marksmanship proving a significant factors in the Lions' rise from the Fourth to the Second Division in successive seasons in the mid-1960s. A fine, resolute centre-forward, not afraid to mix it with the tougher defenders, he took over from Tommy Wilson as leader of the Forest attack but after the arrival of Frank Wignall he became unsettled and eventually returned to London.

KAILE, Gordon Walter
Outside-right or left: 66 apps. 9 goals
Born: Pimperne near Wimbourne, Dorset, 7 December 1924. Died: 1988
Career: RAOC Chilwell, FOREST (May 1945), Preston North End (July 1951), Exeter City (August 1954), St Luke's College (player/coach).

Winger Gordon Kaile was signed by Forest after serving in the Army during WW2. A positive player with good pace and a strong shot, he made his League debut at home to Leeds United in October 1947 and gained a regular place in the first XI in 1949-50 when he played in 40 Third Division South matches. He was eventually replaced on the left-wing by Colin Collindridge and during his time at Deepdale deputised for Tom Finney in several matches before dropping back down the ladder.

KAMINSKY, Jason Mario George
Forward: 0+1 app
Born: Leicester, 5 December 1973
Career: FOREST (trainee, June 1990, professional July 1991, released 1993).

Jason Kaminsky failed to make the required breakthrough into top-line soccer and his only game for Forest was as a substitute v. Luton Town in April 1992 (replacing Des Walker).

KEANE, Royston Maurice
Midfielder: 154 apps. 23 goals
Born: Cork, 10 August 1971
Career: Cobh Ramblers, FOREST (June 1990), Manchester United (£3.75 million, July 1993).

Midfielder Roy Keane leads by example. Referred to as 'captain courageous' (for club and country - the Republic of Ireland) he has put his heart and soul into his performances since joining Forest back in 1990. A battler to the last, he never shirks a tackle, is totally committed and rarely accepts defeat. Contriversial at times (he's certainly suffered his fair share of sendings-off and suspensions) he has always returned to the fray just as enthusiastic as ever. With Forest, he played in the 1991 FA Cup final (beaten by Spurs) and a year later was a winner in the Zenith Data Systems Cup final and played in the League Cup final (beaten by his future club, United).

He has been a winner in 12 competitions for United: six Premiership titles, three FA Cup final triumphs and three FA Charity Shield wins. He has yet to feature in a major European final. Capped by the Republic of Ireland at schoolboy and youth team levels, he played in 58 full international matches as well as appearing in four Under-21 matches, although he was sensationally sent home from the 2002 World Cup finals in South Korea and Japan after a disagreement with coach Mick McCarthy. Keane officially announced his retirement from international football in February 2003. He has now amassed 400 plus senior appearances for United (almost 50 goals scored).

KEAR, Michael Philip
Outside-right: 26+1 apps. 5 goals
Born: Coleford near Gloucester, 27 May 1943
Career: Cinderford Town, Newport County (professional, August 1963), FOREST (December 1963), Middlesbrough (September 1967), Barnsley (on loan,

August-September 1970), Berchem Sport/Belgium (cs.1971).

Michael Kear - who had a few tricks up his sleeve - spent four years with Forest, sharing the right-wing berth initially with Storey-Moore. He then lost out completely when Chris Crowe arrived on the scene and left the club following the arrival of another outside-right, Barry Lyons. He scored seven goals in 58 League games for Middlesbrough.

KEETON, Walter William
Inside-right: 5 apps.
Born: Shirebrook near Chesterfield, 30 April 1905.
Died: 1980.
Career: Grantham Town, Sunderland, FOREST (April 1932), Sunderland (August 1933).
After scoring once in 12 League games for Sunderland, inside-right Walter Keeton was signed by Forest in an effort to boost their flagging attack. He failed to add much firepower to the front-line and after one season on Trentside returned to Roker Park.

KELLY, Bernard
Inside-forward: 3 apps.
Born: Carfin, Scotland, 21 October 1932.
Career: Dunipace FC, Law Hearts FC, Muirkirk Juniors (1951), Raith Rovers (October 1951), Leicester City (July 1958), FOREST (April 1959), Aberdeen (July 1959), Raith Rovers (August 1960).
Inside-forward Bernie Kelly scored 92 goals in 207 games during his first spell with Raith Rovers. He developed a huge reputation at Starks Park and his efforts were duly honoured in 1957 with appearances for both the Scottish 'B' team and the Scottish League XI. He was soon on the goal trail again with Leicester but failed to settle off the pitch and a brief stay with Forest did nothing to ameliorate his home-sickness. Never quite recapturing his old scoring form after returning to Scotland, he now lives in Canada where he works for a solar-heating company.

KELLY, Noel
Inside-forward: 52 apps. 12 goals
Born: Dublin, 28 December 1921. Died: 1991
Career: Dublin Bohemians (amateur), Shamrock Rovers, Glentoran, Arsenal (£650, September 1947), Crystal Palace (£8,000, March 1950), FOREST (£2,500, August 1951), Tranmere Rovers (£1,500, July 1955, later player-manager at Prenton Park: September 1955-October 1957); then Ellesmere Port Town (player-manager, 1957-58), Holyhead Town (manager, 1958-60).
A linotype operator before he signed as a full-time professional with the Gunners in 1947, Noel Kelly made only one League appearance for Arsenal (v. Everton in February 1950) although he was named in the squad for that season's FA Cup final (v. Liverpool).
An Irish international, capped once against Luxembourg

in a World Cup qualifier in 1954, he also represented the League of Ireland. An efficient inside-forward with a good first touch and neat passing ideas, Kelly did well as partner to Fred Scott in his first season at the City Ground. He scored five goals in 42 League games for Palace and six in 52 outings for Tranmere. After his footballing days had ended he ran a sports outfitters' shop in Bromborough. His son, John, signed as a pro for Tranmere Rovers in 1979 and went on to make over 500 senior appearances over the next 13 years while also assisting PNE, Chester City, Walsall, Huddersfield Town, Swindon Town and Oldham Athletic.

KENDAL, Stephen James
Midfielder: one app.
Born: Birtley, County Durham, 4 August 1961
Career: FOREST (apprentice, July 1977, professional August 1979), Chesterfield (December 1982), Torquay United (non-contract, October 1986), Gretna (player-manager, January 1988).
After battling without success to gain a regular place in Forest's first XI, Steve Kendal became a firm favourite at Saltergate and made over 130 senior appearances for the Spireites before joining Torquay in 1986.

KENT, Thomas
Outside-right: 2 apps
Born: Nottingham, circa 1874
Career: Carrington FC, FOREST (season 1898-99).
Reserve right-winger with Forest, Tommy Kent played in the last two League games of the 1898-99 season (v. Derby County and West Bromwich Albion) when several players were given their chance to show what they could do at senior level. He failed to impress and was not retained.

KERR, Neil
Centre-forward/outside-right: one app.
Born: Bowling, Dunbartonshire, 13 April 1871.
Died: 1901
Career: Cowlairs FC, Glasgow Rangers (May 1890), Liverpool (June 1894), FOREST (August 1895-May 1896), Falkirk (August 1896-1900).
A reserve forward with Forest, Neil Kerr appeared just once in the Reds' first team, lining up against Everton in a 6-2 defeat on 7 September 1895. He was seemingly always ill and quickly faded from the scene! Earlier in his career he had been an ever-present for Rangers in the first-ever season of Scottish League football (1890-91) when he lined up with several great names. He also scored three goals in 12 games for Liverpool.

KILFORD, Ian Anthony
Midfielder: 0+1 app.
Born: Bristol, 6 October 1973
Career: FOREST (trainee, July 1989, professional April 1991), Wigan Athletic (on loan, December 1993, signed

permanently, July 1994), Bury (August 2002) Scunthorpe United (November 2002).

A Third Division championship and Auto-Windscreen Shield winner with Wigan in 1997 and 1999 respectively, Ian Kilford made 271 first-team appearances for the Latics before his release in the summer of 2002. A stylish midfielder, he never really got a chance with Forest and his only game in a red shirt was as a sub in a 4-3 defeat at the hands of Bolton Wanderers in September 1993.

KING, Marlon Francis
Striker: 6+1 apps. one goal
Dulwich, 26 April 1980
Career: Barnet (trainee, June 1996, professional September 1998), Gillingham (£255,000, June 2000), FOREST (£950,000, October 2003).

A well-built, strong-limbed 6ft 1in striker, signed as a straight replacement for Marlon Harewood (sold to Norwich City), Marlon King took quite some time to settle in at Forest and, in fact, he didn't open his goal account for the Reds until his ** match, tucking home a penalty to beat West Bromwich Albion in a 3rd round FA Cup-tie in January 2004. Prior to moving to The City Ground, he had netted well over 50 goals for his two previous clubs.

KIRRAGE, Frank Bernard
Outside or inside-right: one app.
Born: Bromley, Kent, 3 March 1893.
Career: FOREST (September 1917), Ilkeston United (August 1920).

Signed by Forest during WW1, reserve forward Frank Kirrage played his first game for Forest on the right-wing in a Midland Section (Principal Tournament) fixture against Birmingham in November 1917 and had to wait until September 1919 before appearing in his only Football League game for the club against Stockport County when he took the inside-right berth.

KNIGHT, Frank
Left-half: 53 apps. one goal
Born: Hucknall, Notts, 26 October 1921.
Died: 18 December 1993
Career: Hucknall Town, Mansfield Town (July 1939), FOREST (non-contract, May 1943, then full-time professional after WW2, retired in May 1950)

Another wartime signing by Forest, Frank Knight was a solid defensive wing-half who gave precious little away and was totally dependable. He handed over his shirt to Jack Burkitt who switched from the right-half berth. Before moving to the City Ground, Knight had played a few reserve-team matches for the Stags.

KNIGHT, Peter Robert
Outside-right: 4+1 apps
Born: Ilford, Essex, 26 December 1937
Career: Southend United (professional June 1958), FOREST (August 1959), Oxford United (July 1960), Reading (November 1964), Guildford City (cs.1966).

Right-winger Peter Knight - after failing to make Southend United's first XI and having just a handful of outings with Forest - made things work for him at the Manor Ground, going on to score 12 goals in 106 League and Cup games for Oxford when he played in front of Ron Atkinson and his brother Graham. Of average height and possessing a jaunty run, Knight made his Forest debut as a second-half substitute (for Tommy Wilson) against Wolverhampton Wanderers in the FA Charity Shield in August 1959, following up his with League bow v. Manchester City soon afterwards.

LANGFORD, John William
Outside-left: 4 apps.
Born: Kirkby-in-Ashfield, Leicestershire, 4 August 1937.
Career: Leicester City (amateur), FOREST (professional, August 1955), Notts County (August 1958 to cs. 1959), Spalding United, Ilkeston Town.

John Langford spent three years with Forest during which time he acted, in the main, as a permanent reserve to Stewart Imlach. His four senior outings all came in October 1955, against Leeds United, Fulham, Rotherham and Barnsley. He had 16 League outings with County.

LANGFORD, Leonard
Goalkeeper: 144 apps.
Born: Alfreton, Derbyshire 30 May 1899.
Died: Stockport, 26 December 1973
Career: Coldstream Guards (aged 15, WW1), Attercliffe Victory FC, Rossington Main Colliery, FOREST (November 1924), Manchester City (June 1930), Manchester United (June 1934-June 1937).

Len Langford won the Household Brigade middle-weight boxing title in 1921. He was also a decent wicket-keeper, playing in the Lancashire League for many years.

As a goalkeeper he totalled 263 League appearances, 112 coming with Manchester City before he handed over his jersey to Frank Swift, having played in the 1933 FA Cup final defeat by Everton. Earlier, as Forest's number one, he produced several outstanding performances, being safe and re-assuring to his defenders, regularly dictating his penalty area with authority. After six years at the City Ground he handed over his gloves to Arthur Dexter. He later shared the senior goalkeeping duties at Old Trafford with England international Jack Hacking.

LANGHAM, Francis
Centre-half: 2 apps.
Born: Circa 1890
Career: South Nottingham, FOREST (1911), South

Nottingham (1912), Rushden.
Reserve centre-half, Frank Langham deputised for Joe Mercer in two League games for Forest (v. Blackpool and Stockport County) both towards the end of the 1911-12 season.

LANGLEY, Ronald
Outside-right: 5 apps. one goal
Born: Basford, Notts, 8 March 1912.
Career: Quarry Road Old Boys, FOREST (seasons 1931-33).
During his two seasons with Forest, Ron Langley got very few opportunities in the first team, stepping into the front-line for five successive League outings during the months of November and December 1932 before Billy Simpson reclaimed the left-wing position, having switched inside to accommodate Langley.

LAWS, Brian
Full-back/midfield: 191+18 apps. 5 goals
Born: Wallsend, 14 October 1961
Career: Burnley (apprentice, April 1977, professional October 1979), Huddersfield Town (August 1983), Middlesbrough (March 1985), FOREST (July 1988), Grimsby Town (player-manager, December 1994), Darlington (non-contract, November 1996), Scunthorpe United (non-contract, January 1997, taking over as team manager, February 1997).
A League Cup winner with Forest in 1989 & 1990 and a Simod Cup winner, also in 1989, right-back Brian Laws also played (as a substitute) in both the 1991 FA Cup and 1992 League Cup final defeats by Spurs and Manchester United respectively. He then helped Forest gain promotion to the Premiership in 1994. During a fine playing career he amassed in excess of 630 League and Cup appearances (38 goals), played once for England 'B' and in 1982 was a Third Division championship winner with his first club, Burnley. One of the finest and safest full-backs in the game, never flashy, he tackled well, was smart in recovery and was most consistent. As a manager he guided Scunthorpe into the Second Division (via the play-offs) in 1999.

LAWS, Joseph Minto
Outside-left: 8 apps. one goal
Born: Cornsay, County Durham, 6 July 1897.
Died: Euxton, Chorley, 26 December 1952.
Career: Spennymoor United (after WW1), Grimsby Town (May 1921), Worksop (August 1923), York City (1924), FOREST (September 1926), Southport (August 1927), Macclesfield (July 1929), Ashton National FC (October 1930), Macclesfield (1931), Chorley (1932-33).
After representing the North Eastern League in 1920-21 and scoring five goals in 55 senior games for Grimsby Town as well as having a brief association with York City, Joe Laws made his Forest debut on 2 October 1926 against Manchester City, starring in a 3-3 draw. Reputed

to be the fastest and cleverest winger in the lower Divisions at the time of his arrival at the City Ground, he was only 5ft 3ins tall - making him one of the smallest players ever to don a Forest shirt. Unfortunately he took a few knocks early in his career with the Reds and struggled after that. He later scored 11 goals in 81 League games for Southport.

LAWTON, James Allsop
Utility: 3 apps.
Born: Ripley, Yorkshire, 27 September 1893
Career: Ilkeston United, FOREST (August 1919-May 1921), Ripley Town.
Initially a reserve defender, Jim Lawton spent two seasons with Forest. He made his League debut at centre-half in a 4-0 defeat at Wolves in November 1919, then, in the very next match he played as an emergency centre-forward in a 0-0 home draw with South Shields.

LAY, Peter John
Left-back: one app.
Born: Stratford, London, 4 December 1931
Career: RAF Watnall, FOREST (professional April 1953), Queen's Park Rangers (July 1956, King's Lynn (cs.1957).
A reserve left-back, Peter Lay's only senior game for Forest was against Bristol Rovers (away) in a Second Division game in April 1955 when he deputised Jack Hutchinson, allowing Geoff Thomas to switch to the number 2 slot. He made only one League appearance for QPR, scoring against Crystal Palace.

LEE, George Thomas
Outside-left: 80 apps. 20 goals
Born: York, 4 June 1919. Died: Norwich, 2 April 1991.
Career: Acomb FC, Scarborough (1935), York City (juniors, June 1936, professional July 1937), FOREST (£7,500, August 1947), West Bromwich Albion (£12,000, July 1949), Lockheed Leamington (June 1958) Vauxhall Motors (January 1959), West Bromwich Albion (trainer/coach, June 1959), Norwich City (trainer/coach, May 1963-May 1987).
A powerful, fast raiding left-winger with a cannonball shot, George Lee gave Forest two years excellent service before entering the top-flight with WBA. He was a huge success with the Black Country club, helping the Baggies win the FA Cup and finish runners-up to Wolves in the League championship in 1954. Nicknamed 'Ada' by the fans at the Hawthorns, he scored 65 goals in 295 senior outings for Albion before moving into non-League football in 1958.
* Lee made his first and last appearance for Forest in the League against the same club, Bury, on 23 August 1947 and 7 May 1949.

LEE, Jason Benedict
Striker: 49+45 apps. 15 goals
Born: Forest Gate, London, 5 September 1971
Career: Charlton Athletic (trainee, August 1987, professional May 1989), Stockport County (on loan, February 1991), Lincoln City (£35,000, March 1991), Southend United (August 1993), FOREST (£200,000, March 1994), Charlton Athletic (on loan, February 1997), Grimsby Town (in loan, March 1997), Watford (£200,000, June 1997), Chesterfield (£250,000, August 1998), Peterborough United (£50,000, January 2000), Falkirk (August 2003).
Jason Lee, 6ft 3ins tall and 13st 8lbs in weight, was a useful target man who perhaps did his best work in the lower Divisions, scoring 22 goals in 93 League games for Lincoln.
He helped Forest gain promotion to the Premiership in 1994 and was a Second Division championship winner with Watford in 1998. All told he netted 75 goals in 383 senior appearances at club level. Looking awkward at times, almost half of his 94 appearances for Forest came as a substitute. Lee became nationally famous after his hairstyle was featured regularly on the television programme (Fantasy Football League).

LE FLEM, Richard Peter
Outside-left: 151 apps. 20 goals
Born: Bradford-on-Avon, 12 July 1942
Career: Guernsey football, FOREST (professional May 1960), Wolverhampton Wanderers (January 1964), Middlesbrough (February 1965), Leyton Orient (March 1966 to cs. 1967).
An orthodox outside-left, fast and energetic, 'Flip' Le Flem was capped by England at Under-23 level during his three-and-a-half years at the City Ground. He was signed by Wolves to replace ex-Forest star Alan Hinton but he never really settled at Molineux, nor at either of his other two League clubs, making less than 50 appearances in that competition after leaving the Reds.

LEMOINE, Harold M
Goalkeeper: 9 apps.
Born: Shepherd's Bush, London, circa 1890
Career: Shepherd's Bush FC, Clapton, Southend United, FOREST (May 1912), Woking. (August 1914). Did not play competitive football after WW1.
Signed as cover for Jack Hanna, Harold Lemoine was called into the first team by Forest nine times during his two seasons with the club, making his debut in a 1-1 home draw with Bury in December 1913.

LEMON, Arthur
Forward: 24 apps. one goal
Born: Neath, Glamorgan, 25 January 1931
Career: Neath Old Boys FC, FOREST (February 1951, retired through injury, May 1955).

Versatile forward Arthur Lemon's footballing career was cut short through injury. He was playing well for Forest before damaging his leg early in the 1954-55 season. He battled in vain for eight months before announcing his retirement from top-class soccer.

LENNOX, William
Outside-right: 9 apps. one goal
Born: Holytown, County Durham, May 1901.
Died: 1976
Career: Shildon Colliery FC, FOREST (May 1928), Washington Colliery FC (September 1930).
A League debutant for Forest in January 1929 v. Bradford Park Avenue, right-winger Billy Lennox never really got much of a chance in the first team owing to the continued form of first Charles Howie and then Jack Scott.

LESSONS, G Frederick
Centre-forward; 34 apps. 8 goals
Born; Stockport, Cheshire, 1885
Career: Notts Jardine, FOREST (April 1904), Northampton Town (cs. 1907).
A useful centre-forward, who could shoot powerfully with either foot, Fred Lessons had one particularly good season with Forest, scoring three goals in 16 League games in 1904-05 when he played alongside Grenville Morris.

LESTER, Jack William
Striker/midfielder: 77+26 apps. 24 goals
Born: Sheffield, Yorkshire, 8 October 1975
Career: Grimsby Town (juniors, June 1992, professional July 1994), Doncaster Rovers (on loan, September 1996), FOREST (£300,000, January 2000) Sheffield United (July 2003).
An England Schoolboy international, Jack Lester scored 25 goals in 167 first-class games for Grimsby Town before joining Forest after a loan spell with Doncaster. He also helped the Mariners win the Auto-Windscreen Shield at Wembley in 1998. A trier to the last, he runs his heart out for the team, a never-say-die competitor, who always seeks to get in a shot at the target.

LEVERTON, Ronald
Inside-forward: 105 apps. 36 goals
Born: Worksop, 8 May 1926.
Died: 19 August 2003.
Career: FOREST (juniors, July 1942, professional October 1943), Notts County (October 1953), Walsall (July 1956-May 1957).
Ron 'Tot' Leverton helped Forest win the Third Division South title in 1950-51. An influential part of the new look Forest team that took to the field immediately after the hostilities had ended in 1945, he went on to serve the club superbly well until moving to nearby Meadow Lane in 1953. At times he showed a masterly technique, was a splendid passer of the ball who could shoot hard and

straight given the chance. He netted five times in 45 League outings for the Magpies and twice in 17 for the Saddlers.

LIGHTENING, Arthur Douglas

Goalkeeper: 5 apps.
Born: South Africa, 1 August 1936.
Died: Durban, South Africa, October 2001
Career: Queen's Park FC (South Africa), FOREST (December 1956), Coventry City (November 1958), Middlesbrough (August 1962-May 1963), Durban City (1963-66).

Arthur Lightening understudied Harold Nicholson and Chick Thomson at the City Ground and therefore his opportunities of first-team football were limited. He later appeared in 150 League games for Coventry City, helping them win promotion from the Fourth Division in 1959 after taking over from veteran Jim Sanders (ex-WBA). On his day he was a sure-handler of the ball, cool under pressure and commanded his area with authority, but was prone to the odd slip here and there which proved costly.

LINACRE, James Henry

Goalkeeper: 335 apps.
Born: Aston-upon-Trent, Derbyshire, 1881.
Died: Nottingham, 11 May 1957
Career: Aston-upon-Trent FC, Draycott Mills, Derby County (December 1898), FOREST (August 1899, retired through injury in May 1909).

Harry Linacre was capped twice by England in 1905 v. Wales and Scotland and he also represented the Football League. In 1907 he helped Forest win the Second Division title. A six-footer, he was recommended to the Reds by his brother-in-law Frank Forman, and following an initial breaking-in season, he made the goalkeeping position his own in 1900-01, going on to amass over 300 League appearances. A huge favourite with the Trent Bridge faithful, he was alert, courageous and above all very consistent, performing brilliantly during Forest's South American tour in 1905.

LINDLEY, Tinsley

Centre/inside-forward: 32 apps. 17 goals
Born: Nottingham, 17 October 1865.
Died: 31 March 1940
Career: Cambridge University (Caius College: Blue 1885-86-87, captain 1888), Corinthians (1885-94), Casuals, Notts County, Crusaders, Swifts (London), FOREST (between August 1883-April 1892), also one game for Preston North End (February 1892). He played county cricket for Nottinghamshire in 1888 and for Cambridge University without getting a blue. He also played rugby for Old Leysians and Notts RUFC and was a dedicated Forest committee man who was later made a Life Member of the club.
Called to the bar in 1889, he practised on the Midland circuit and was a law lecturer at Nottingham University. He was awarded the OBE in 1918 for his work as Chief Officer of the Nottingham Special Constabulary. He later became a County Court judge.

A Victorian 'larger than life' figure and a Cambridge Blue, Tinsley Lindley was perhaps one of the finest amateur footballers of his time. An out and out striker, he made a scoring debut for England in a 6-1 win over Ireland in Belfast in 1886 and then notched further goals in each of his next eight internationals, including a hat-trick in a 7-0 victory over the Irish in 1887. He went on to earn 13 full caps and scored a total of 15 goals. During the 11-year period from 1881-92 it was not always certain as to which club he was officially attached, and being an amateur he tended to play (if available) for anyone who required his services. Something of a character, Lindley refused to wear a traditional pair of football boots, claiming they lessened his tremendous speed and therefore he used to play in ordinary walking shoes instead. How he coped in the muddy and slippery winter conditions is anyone's guess! They certainly did the trick, for it is believed that he scored perhaps 200 goals in all games during a wonderful career.

LINLEY, Edward A

Inside or outside-left: 31 apps. 5 goals
Born: East Retford 26 September 1894.
Career: Worksop Town (1919), Birmingham (£800 plus Tom Pike, December 1920), FOREST (July 1926), Sutton Town (June 1927), Mansfield Town (February 1928).

A Division Two championship winner with Birmingham in 1920-21, the balding, knock-kneed Ted Linley was not an obvious choice as a professional footballer. Appearances can be deceptive, however, and he showed himself a guileful performer for several years, mainly at St Andrew's where he fought off the challenges of a host of players who were bought in to replace him. He had only short spells at Forest and Mansfield after scoring 11 goals in 118 games for Birmingham.

LISHMAN, Douglas John

Inside/centre-forward: 38 apps. 22 goals
Born: Erdington, Birmingham, 14 September 1923.
Died: December 1994
Career: Paget Rangers, Walsall (August 1946), Arsenal (£10,500, May 1948), FOREST (£8,000, March 1956-May 1957). Later managed the family's furniture shop business in Stoke-on-Trent. During WW2 he took part in the Walcheren Island (Holland) landing.

Doug Lishman, a dynamic personality with intuitive skill and deadly shot, helped Forest gain promotion to the First Division in 1957, having earlier given Arsenal great service, scoring 137 goals in 244 senior games and helping them win the League championship in 1953 and was named as reserve for the 1950 FA Cup final v. Liverpool.

He suffered a broken leg in December 1950 but recovered well and netted eight hat-tricks (including three in consecutive home matches) in his tally of goals for the Gunners. His career realised a haul of 173 goals in 323 League games.

LLOYD, Clifford John
Left-half: 4 apps.
Born: Swansea, 1902.
Career: Swansea Town (professional, 1926), FOREST (June 1930), Southend United (briefly in season 1931-32), Crystal Palace (August 1932).
Short, stocky wing-half Cliff Lloyd spent only a short time with Forest, appearing in just four senior matches, his first against Bury in December 1930 when he took over from Bill Farmer. He played in more than 40 games for the Swans and 14 for Palace, but failing to establish himself with the Shrimpers.

LLOYD, Laurence Valentine
Defender: 213+1 apps. 13 goals
Born: Bristol, 6 October 1948
Career: Bristol Rovers (juniors, August 1965, professional July 1967), Liverpool (£60,000, April 1969), Coventry City (£240,000, August 1974), FOREST (£60,000, October 1976), Wigan Athletic (player-manager/coach, March 1981, retiring as a player, March 1983), Notts County (manager, July 1983-October 1984). Later became a publican in Nottingham
With Forest, 6ft 2in centre-half Larry Lloyd was an Anglo-Scottish and Second Division promotion winner in 1977. He followed up with a League championship and League Cup double in 1978, added a second League Cup winners prize to his tally in 1979, gained successive European Cup winners medals in 1979 & 1980 and then earned himself a Super Cup winners' prize, also in 1980. A tremendous and majestic defender, strong in the air and on the ground, he made 43 appearances for Bristol Rovers, 54 for Coventry and over 50 for Wigan. Lloyd helped Liverpool complete the League Championship and UEFA Cup double in 1972-73 when he was an ever-present and had the pleasure of scoring against the German outfit Borussia Monchengladbach in the final of the latter competition. He won three England caps whilst at Anfield and added a fourth to his collection as a Forest player. He also played in eight Under-23 internationals as well as gaining Youth honours as a teenager.
As a manager he guided Wigan to promotion from Division Four in 1982. Lloyd worked as a football pundit for a local radio for a while.

LOCKETT, Henry
Left-half/inside-right: 23 apps. 5 goals
Born: Market Drayton, 27 December 1887
Career: Wilmslow (1904), Crewe Alexandra (1905), Whitchurch (1908), Bolton Wanderers (August 1909),

FOREST (August 1910), Exeter City (August 1911), Chesterfield (July 1913), Stalybridge Celtic (May 1921-July 1923).
Harry Lockett was an efficient footballer, as keen as mustard who gave a good account of himself for every club he served. He had a very useful half-season with Forest before injury and a loss of form saw him slip into the reserves. He played in 16 games for Bolton, 74 for Exeter and in more than 70 for Stalybridge Celtic but failed to make the first XI at Chesterfield.

LOCKTON, John H
Inside-left: 22 apps. 3 goals
Born: Peckham, London, 22 May 1892. Died: 1972
Career: London University, FOREST (January 1914-May 1915), Crystal Palace (season 1919-20).
An amateur inside-forward, Jack Lockton spent a season-and-a-half with Forest, having one decent run of 11 successive League outings between mid-February and mid-April 1914, scoring his first goal in a 3-1 home win over Birmingham. He failed to make a first-team appearance for Palace.

LOCKYER, Thomas W
Goalkeeper: one app.
Born: Hucknall, Notts, circa 1876
Career: Hucknall St John's FC, FOREST (seasons 1899-1901)
Reserve goalkeeper Tom Lockyer deputised for Dan Allsopp when appearing in his only League game for Forest against Preston North End on the opening day of the 1899-1900 season (won 3-1).

LOFTUS, Joseph Leo
Inside-left: 56 apps. 18 goals
Born: Ferryhill near Bishop Auckland, County Durham, 24 January 1906. Died: 1992
Career: Willington (1924), South Shields (August 1926), FOREST (October 1929), Bristol City (August 1932), Gillingham (May 1935), Burton Town (September 1936), Barrow (October 1936-May 1938).
Joe Loftus was a brave, robust forward who feared no-one. He gave as good as he got in every game he played and during his career he netted almost 100 goals (at various levels) including 29 in 93 competitive games for Bristol City, six in 30 for South Shields and ten in 28 for Barrow. His best season with Forest was his first (six goals in 24 League outings) when he partnered Noah Burton on the left-wing.

LOUGHLAN, Anthony John
Midfielder/winger: 2 apps. one goal
Born: Croydon, Surrey, 19 January 1970
Career: Leicester City (apprentice, June 1986), Leicester United (1988), FOREST (August 1989), Kettering Town (July 1993), Lincoln City (non-contract October 1993-May 1994).

Wide midfielder Tony Loughlan scored in the first minute of his League debut for Forest against Wimbledon in March 1991. After than splendid start, however, he failed to establish himself in the side and was released after recovering from a long spell on the injury list. He proved a useful acquisition for the Imps, netting twice in 12 outings before being given a free transfer.

LOUIS-JEAN, Matthieu
Full-back: 174+8 apps. 3 goals
Born: Mont St Aignan, France, 22 February 1976
Career: Le Havre (July 1993), FOREST (September 1998)
Right-sided wing-back Matthieu Louis-Jean (who can also play on the left if required) made 78 appearances in the French First Division with Le Havre before joining Forest. An Under-21 international who reads the game well, he made 20 first-team appearances during his first season of Premiership football with the Reds and 32 the following season (after relegation). He lost his place in the side under manager David Platt and thereafter struggled with a groin injury before coming back into the frame under new boss Paul Hart.

LOVE, John Thomson,
Inside-forward: 60 apps. 20 goals
Born: Edinburgh, 18 March 1924
Career: Leith Athletic (August 1941), Hibernian (1945), Leith Athletic (1947), Albion Rovers (January 1948), FOREST (£7,000, February 1949), Llanelli (player-manager, June 1952), Walsall (as a player March 1955, then player-assistant-manager March 1955, manager September 1955 to December 1957), Wrexham (manager December 1957-October 1959).
John Love was a strong, well-built inside-forward who helped Albion Rovers take the runners-up spot in the Scottish B Division in 1948 and three years later played in four games when Forest won the League Division South title in 1950-51 (scoring one goal). He had done well the previous season when he netted 11 goals in 37 League games, partnering Fred Scott on the right wing for the majority of the time.
He scored 11 goals in his 40 League outings for Walsall. He surprisingly dropped out of top-line soccer to join Llanelli in 1952 before returning with Walsall after almost three years in South Wales. He became Major Frank Buckley's assistant at Fellows Park, taking the hot seat when Buckley resigned in 1955. Love gained the DFC after being wounded by shrapnel during the crossing of the Rhine in 1944. He served as a flight lieutenant with Bomber Command and was then a glider pilot.

LOWE, Henry Charles
Half-back: 9 apps.
Born: Whitwell, Derbyshire, 20 March 1886.
Died: Worksop, 25 October 1958
Career: Whitwell St Lawrence FC, Gainsborough Trinity

(June 1907), Liverpool (April 1911), FOREST (WW1 guest, then signed March 1920-May 1921), Mansfield Town (May 1923), Newark Town (to 1930).
After playing in more than 120 first-team games for Liverpool, Harry Lowe - who was rather small for a centre-half (he stood less than 5ft 9ins tall) - made almost a century of appearances as a guest for Forest during WW1, helping them win the Victory Shield in 1919. A wonderfully consistent footballer, able to play anywhere in the half-back line, he skippered Liverpool on many occasions but sadly missed the 1914 FA Cup final through injury. In 1920 a journalist in a Nottingham football annual spoke of his 'admirable powers of imparting steadiness and solidarity to his wing, both in attack and defence, feeding and supporting his forwards well.' He was well into his forties when he finally hung up his boots after spending several years with Newark Town.

LYALL, Charles Thomas
Inside-right: one app.
Born: Eckington, Derbyshire, 14 September 1899
Career: FOREST (May 1919), Eckington Red Rose (December 1919), FOREST (September 1920), Eckington Works FC (August 1921), Chesterfield (season 1922-23)
Tom Lyall had two spells with Forest and at no time did he ever look like establishing himself as a regular in the first XI. His only senior outing was against Coventry City (home) in the last League game of the 1920-21 season on 7 May when he was selected in place of Jack Spaven in what was realistically a meaningless fixture.

LYALL, George
Midfielder/forward: 126+10 apps. 29 goals
Born: Wick, Scotland, 4 May 1947
Career: Kingskettle Amateurs (Fife) (1962), Raith Rovers (professional, June 1964), Preston North End (£8,000, March 1966), FOREST (£40,000, May 1972), Hull City (£17,500, November 1975). Retired through injury, January 1978, but joined Scarborough in March 1978; Goole Town (June 1979, appointed player-manager February 1980), Grantham Town (player, February 1981), Bridlington Town (August 1981), North Ferriby United (October 1981-May 1982). Later settled in South Humberside.
A workaholic, George Lyall was a typical Scottish craftsman whose excellent scoring record with Raith Rovers quickly attracted the attention of English clubs. Preston were the first to offer him terms - and he repaid some of the fee involved by helping the Deepdale club win the Third Division title in 1971. He scored 16 goals in 105 League outings for North End and then did exceedingly well with Forest, linking up smartly with the likes of Paul Richardson and Martin O'Neill, and also Ian Bowyer (among others) before notching five in his 42 outings for Hull City.

LYMAN, Colin Chadd
Outside-left: 27 apps. 10 goals
Born: Northampton, 9 March 1914.
Died: Cambridge, 9 May 1986.
Career: Rushden Town (1932-33), Southend United (September 1933), Northampton Town (March 1934, professional November 1934), Tottenham Hotspur (£3,000, June 1937), WW2 guest for Aldershot, Chesterfield, Coventry City, Derby County, Leicester City, Northampton, Nottingham Forest, Notts County and Port Vale; signed for Port Vale on a permanent basis (May 1946), FOREST (October 1946), Notts County (August 1947), Long Eaton Town (player-manager, July 1948-May 1950).
Left-winger Colin Lyman failed to make an impression with Southend before signing for Northampton. He did well with the Cobblers (30 goals in 92 games) and in June 1937 was transferred to Spurs with whom he remained until May 1946. He guested for a number of clubs during WW2 and also starred in several representative matches for the RAF and the FA. He scored 20 goals in 87 first-team appearances during his time at White Hart Lane. He had a pretty good season with Forest, producing some good skills down the flank before moving on following the arrival of George Lee from York City who ironically was later to join Lyman's former club, West Brom.

LYNAS, Ralph John Langtrey
Inside-left: 22 apps. 2 goals
Born: Belfast, 29 February 1904.
Career: Cliftonville (1921), FOREST (July 1925), Ards (May 1927-29)
Irishman Paddy Lynas made his League debut for Forest in the 0-0 draw with Darlington in August 1925. It was thought that he would fill the problem inside-left berth (seven different players had been utilised there in 1924-25). He struggled to settle down at first but later had two decent runs in the senior side when he scored two goals - the winner v. Clapton Orient and a second in a 4-0 win over Hull City, both at home.

LYNE, Neil George Francis
Winger: 0+1 app.
Born: Leicester, 4 April 1970
Career: Leicester United (June 1986), FOREST (professional, August 1989), Walsall (on loan, March 1990), Shrewsbury Town (on loan, March 1991, signed on a permanent basis, July 1991), Cambridge United (January 1993), Chesterfield (on loan, September 1993, and again, March 1994), Hereford United (July 1994), Northampton Town (non-contract, August-October 1996).
Reserve Neil Lyne's only senior appearance for Forest was as a sub versus Burnley at Turf Moor in a League Cup game in October 1990 when he came on for Steve Hodge in a 1-0 win. He later scored 17 goals in 70 League games for Shrewsbury and two in 63 for Hereford.

LYONS, Barry
Winger: 237+2 apps. 33 goals
Born: Shirebrook near Chesterfield, 14 March 1945
Career: Shirebrook Miners' Welfare FC, Rotherham United (juniors, June 1961, professional September 1962), FOREST (£45,000, November 1966), York City (on loan, August 1973, signed for £15,000, September 1973), Darlington (July 1976, then player-coach at Feethams, June 1977-July 1978), York City (Youth team coach, August 1978, caretaker-manager March 1980-December 1981, then coach, again, until July 1982).
For his four major clubs, right-winger Barry Lyons netted well over 80 goals in 575 senior appearances, with 72 coming in a 510 League games. He played in 132 games for Rotherham, just over 100 for Darlington and 98 for York, playing his part in the Minstermen's drive towards the Second Division in the mid-1970s. In his first season with Forest he helped the Reds reach the semi-final stage of the FA Cup and finish runners-up in Division One; the following year he played in the Fairs Cup competition and in 1967 he also won international recognition, lining up for England in an Under-23 match v. Italy. At the City Ground he was greatly influenced by Tommy Cavanagh who changed him from an attacking winger into a midfield defensive player-cum-winger, a role he occupied for the remainder of his career. He turned down a £50,000 move to Sheffield Wednesday in March 1971. He is now a very keen and active golfer playing off a handicap of 9 at the Easingwold course near Rotherham

LYTHGOE, John
Centre-forward/inside or outside-left: 63 apps. 13 goals
Born: Dixon Fold near Bolton, Lancashire, 3 April 1892.
Died: Little Hulton near Bolton, June 1969.
Career: Walkden Central, Bury (November 1913), FOREST (August 1919), Newport County (cs. 1921), Norwich City (June 1922), Eccles (November 1923), Crewe Alexandra (1924-25), Margate (August 1925).
During WW1 Jack Lythgoe was in the Machine Gun Corps and the Tank Regiment. A very powerful all-action forward with an excellent scoring reputation as shown by his initial 69 goals for Bury, he gave Forest splendid service for two years before having no luck during a brief spell at Maine Road. Advancing years caught up with him at Norwich and after that it was all down hill.

LYTTLE, Desmond
Right-back: 220+9 apps. 3 goals
Born: Wolverhampton, 24 September 1971
Career: Leicester City (trainee, July 1987, professional January 1990), Worcester City (August 1991), Swansea City (£12,500, July 1992), FOREST (£375,000, July 1993), Port Vale (on loan, November 1998), Watford (free transfer, July 1999), West Bromwich Albion (free transfer, March 2000 to May 2003). After taking over the right-back berth from Gary Charles, Des Lyttle twice helped

Forest gain promotion to the Premiership, in 1994 and 1998, the latter as champions of Division One. A fine, attacking full-back whose crosses were sometimes perfection for the likes of Stan Collymore and Kevin Campbell among others, he was later first choice at the Hawthorns until losing his pace in the Baggies' team, to the Slovakian international Igor Balis. In 2003 Lyttle was fast approaching the milestone of 400 senior appearances at club level.

McARTHUR, Barry

Centre-forward: 9+1 apps. 4 goals
Born: Nottingham, 4 May 1947
Career: FOREST (juniors, June 1963, professional May 1965), Barrow (July 1969), York City (December 1969-March 1970); Matloch Town.

Despite a good strike-record with Forest, Barry McArthur never quite fitted the bill and in fact during his career he only appeared in 16 League games (4 goals). He netted on his full League debut for Forest in a 2-0 win over Leicester City in December 1965. He had taken his bow as a sub versus Leeds United at Elland Road three months earlier.

McCAFFREY, James

Winger: 9+2 apps.
Born: Luton, 12 October 1951
Career: FOREST (apprentice, November 1967, professional March 1969), Mansfield Town (July 1972), Huddersfield Town (January 1977), Portsmouth (February 1978), Northampton Town (December 1978-May 1980). Later ran a newsagents' business in Northamptonshire.

An England Youth international, Jim McCaffrey never really stood much of a chance of regular first-team football with Forest due to the abundance of other players occupying or able to play in an identical role. After leaving the City Ground, he did very well at Field Mill, scoring 21 goals in 178 League games for Mansfield. He also had a decent stint with the Cobblers (six goals in 57 League outings).

McCALL, Robert Henry

Left-back/right-half/centre-forward: 172 apps. one goal
Born: Worksop, 29 December 1915. Died: 1992
Career: Worksop Town (1932), FOREST (May 1935, retired in 1952, then groundsman and later 'A' team coach at the City Ground), Worksop Town (manager, July 1953-54).

A versatile footballer in every sense of the word, Bob McCall would, and could, play in any position to get a game! He was a great competitor who actually started out as a forward before choosing to settle in the half-back line while occasionally slotting in at full-back. He represented Forest before, during and after WW2, making almost 160 appearances for the Reds between 1939 and 1946. He skippered the team, more so in peacetime football (after 1945) and it was not until the 1949-50 season that he lost

his place in the first XI to Jack Hutchinson. Unfortunately he did not make an appearance when Forest won the Third Division South title a year later. On his retirement - having played in his last competitive League game at centre-forward against Brentford in September 1951 - McCall was immediately appointed groundsman at the City ground while also taking over as coach of Forest's 'A' team. He later had a spell as manager of his former club Worksop Town.

McCALLUM, Cornelius Joseph

Inside or outside-right: 42 apps. 15 goals
Born: Bonhill, Scotland, 3 July 1868.
Died: 5 November 1921.
Career: Renton (1886), Celtic (May 1888), Blackburn Rovers (February 1890), Celtic (January 1891), FOREST (August 1892), Notts County (July 1894), Heanor Town (season 1896-97).

A penetrative and especially fast winger Jock McCallum could cut inside his full-back and shoot powerfully at goal, and during an excellent career he found at the net at regular intervals. He played his best football north of the border (with Celtic) although he certainly gave good service to Forest, averaging a goal every three games. He made his debut for the Reds in the club's first-ever game in the Football League v. Everton in September 1892 and his last outing was against West Bromwich Albion in March 1894. All told he scored 19 goals in 33 games for Celtic.

McCANN, Daniel

Inside-right/centre-forward: one app.
Born: Hurlford, Scotland, 1889
Career: Dundee (March 1908), Celtic (May 1910), Dundee Hibernians (May 1911), FOREST (September 1911), Hurlford Athletic (October 1911).

Dan McCann was recruited from Dundee Hibernians, initially as cover for Messrs Derrick, Saunders and Morris, anticipating that he might take over the from one of them in the long run. Unfortunately he never settled in Nottingham and left the City Ground after barely a month, his only League game coming against Grimsby Town (h) on 30 September 1911. He played in seven games for Celtic.

McCANN, James

Forward: 2+4 apps one goal
Born: Dundee, 20 May 1954
Career: FOREST (apprentice, June 1970, professional May 1972-May 1977), Stockport County (on loan, October 1975), Halifax Town (on loan, October 1976), Corby Town.

Reserve forward Jim McCann was released by Forest at the end of the 1976-77 season having failed to gain a regular place in the first XI. He made just five League appearances for Stockport and two for Halifax.

McCRACKEN, James Peter

Left-back/left-half: 133 apps.

Born: Glasgow, 1867. Died: circa 1930

Career: Springburn FC (Glasgow), Third Lanark (1886), Sunderland Albion (cs.1890), FOREST (August 1892), Middlesbrough (May 1899), Chesterfield (season 1900-01). Peter McCracken, a tough-tackling, resolute and self-confident defender, quit League football in 1903 with almost 250 appearances under his belt (north and south of the border). He had done reasonably well in Scotland and also with Sunderland Albion before joining Forest for their first season in the Football League. He made his debut for the Reds in their opening match v. Everton, occupying the left-half position alongside fellow half-backs Hamilton and Smith. He missed only one game in that 1892-93 campaign and after overcoming injury problems he did very well after that, accumulating more than 130 senior appearances while playing in all three middle-line positions. He played in Middlesbrough's first-ever League game v. Lincoln City in September 1899 and during his season with the Teeside club he also occupied the right-back position.

McCURDY, William

Right-back: 11 apps.

Born: Bridgton, Glasgow, Scotland, 4 September 1876

Career: Vale of Clyde FC, Luton Town (June 1900), FOREST (February 1901), New Brompton (May 1902), Tottenham Hotspur (May 1904), New Brompton (July 1905), Luton Town (August 1906). Retired May 1910.

Scottish-born full-back Bill McCurdy was in much demand when he decided to leave Vale of Clyde with both Partick Thistle and Clyde keen to sign him. He chose to play in England instead and during his time south of the border amassed a pretty useful appearance record although he never really bedded in with Forest. He made his League debut for the Reds against Everton (away) in March 1901 when he took over from Teddy Peers in a 4-1 defeat.

McDIARMID, George

Right or left-back/right-half: 3 apps.

Born: Garterage near Glasgow, Scotland, 1880. Died: 1946

Career: Cambuslang, FOREST (August 1900), Airdrieonians (December 1901), Grimsby Town (June 1903), Glossop (September 1905), Clyde (July 1907), Grimsby Town (October 1907-May 1908).

Outside football George McDiarmid was a highly successful sprinter and therefore added speed to his other qualities as a wholehearted competitor on the soccer field. Remarkably he was only on the losing side on four occasions during his 18 months with Airdrie whom he helped win the Scottish Second Division championship in 1903. He failed to settle with Forest but had a pretty good first spell with Grimsby, making 64 League appearances and adding a few more to his tally when he returned to the Mariners.

McDONALD, Joseph

Right or left-back: 124 apps.

Born: Blantyre near Glasgow, Scotland, 10 February 1929. Died: Australia, 7 September 2003.

Career: Bellshill Athletic, Falkirk (December 1951), Sunderland (£5,500, March 1954), FOREST (£5,000, July 1958), Wisbech Town (July 1961), Ramsgate (player-manager, seasons 1963-65), Yeovil Town (manager June 1965-May 1967).

Joe McDonald, who took over from Geoff Thomas at left-back in the Forest side, played in the 1959 FA Cup win over Luton Town, completely blotting out the threat of his former Roker Park team-mate and Irish international right-winger Billy Bingham. A good positional player, crisp and solid in the tackle, McDonald, who commanded surprisingly moderate fees for such a classy player, was capped twice by Scotland at senior level and he also represented Great Britain against the Rest of Europe in 1955, to celebrate the 75th anniversary of the Irish FA. He made 137 League appearances for Sunderland before his move to the City Ground.

McGLINCHEY, Charles

Outside-left: one app.

Born: Coatbridge, Scotland, 1942

Career: Belshill Athletic, FOREST (August 1961), Ramsgate (August 1962).

Reserve left-winger Charlie McGlinchey made just one senior appearance for Forest - taking over from the injured Dick Le Flem in the home League Cup-tie with Gillingham in September 1961.

McGOVERN, John Prescott

Midfielder: 330-+5 apps. 11 goals

Born: Montrose, Scotland, 28 October 1949

Career: Hartlepool United (apprentice, July 1965, professional May 1967), Derby County (£7,500, September 1968), Leeds United (£125,000, August 1974), FOREST (£60,000, February 1975), Bolton Wanderers (player-manager, June 1982-January 1985, retiring as a player in 1984), Horwich RMI (manager, 1985-86); lived in Tenerife before becoming manager of Chorley (February 1990), Plymouth Argyle (assistant-manager to Peter Shilton, March 1992), Rotherham United (joint manager with Archie Gemmill September 1994 to September 1996).

As a grafting midfielder - and influential captain with Forest - John McGovern gained a League Championship medal in 1978, was twice a European Cup winner in 1979 & 1980, helped the Reds lift the European Super Cup in the latter year and collected winners and runners-up medals in the League Cup finals of 1979 and 1980 respectively. He was also a key member of the team that gained promotion to the top flight (as Second Division runners-up) and won the Anglo-Scottish Cup in 1977. McGovern was introduced to League football by Brian

Clough at Hartlepool. He followed his manager to Derby, Leeds (where he quickly fell from favour after Clough sensationally left Elland Road) and then Forest. He starred for the Rams when they rose from Division Two and then went on to lift the First Division title in 1972 while also gaining two Under-23 caps for Scotland. He was on the verge of the full international side and almost made it into the 1978 World Cup finals squad, but missed out at the death. During his career McGovern appeared in more than 670 competitive matches and scored almost 40 goals. He was dismissed as manager of Bolton, victim of a bout of internal politics at Burnden Park and he didn't have too much luck with his former team-mate Archie Gemmill at Rotherham either.

McGREGOR, Paul Anthony

Midfielder/striker: 7+30 apps. 4 goals
Born: Liverpool, 17 December 1974.
Career: FOREST (trainee, June 1990, professional December 1991), Carlisle United (two loan spells, September and November 1998), Preston North End (free transfer, March 1999), Plymouth Argyle (free transfer, July 1999), Northampton Town (free transfer, July 2001 to May 2003).
An attack-minded winger-cum-striker with quick feet, Paul McGregor promised so much in 1995-96 but then virtually became a permanent substitute for Forest, although he was frustrated by a lengthy knee injury that required surgery. As an Argyle player, he scored 24 goals in 90 first-team appearances during his two seasons at Home Park. He formed his own pop group - Merc - which earned him a few plaudits.

MACHIN, Prestwood Uriah

Right-back: one app.
Born: Nottingham, 1 July 1892.
Career: Halifax Place Missionaries FC, FOREST (May 1911), Notts County (season 1912-13)
Uriah Machin was a reserve right-back who made his only League appearance for Forest against Fulham in April 1912 when he stood in for Tom Gibson, allowing Walter Dudley to switch to the left.

McINALLY, James Edward

Full-back: 41 apps.
Born: Glasgow, Scotland, 19 February 1964
Career: Celtic Boys Club, Celtic (junior 1980, professional, June 1982), FOREST (June 1984), Coventry City (January 1986), Dundee United (May 1986).
Jim McInally was a skilful full-back whose interceptions and anticipation qualities were of the highest quality. He had an excellent run in Forest's first team between December 1984 and August 1985 before being dogged by injury, eventually being replaced in the side by Gary Fleming. He made only five League appearances for Coventry before returning to Scotland.

McINNES, Thomas

Outside-right or left/inside-forward: 195 apps. 57 goals
Born: Glasgow, 29 August 1870. Died: December 1937
Career: Dalmuir Thistle, Cowlairs, Newcastle East End, Clyde (1888), FOREST (June 1892), Third Lanark (December 1898), Lincoln City (September 1900-May 1903).
A Scottish international winger (one cap gained v. Ireland in 1889) Tom McInnes also represented Glasgow in an Inter-City match and played for the Anglo Scots v. the Home Scots in an international trial. Regarded as one of the best left-wingers of his day, he was an FA Cup winner with Forest in 1898 when he had an excellent game against Derby County. Switched from the left-wing to the right by Forest (to accommodate Alf Spouncer) he didn't like the move at all and with his efficiency being reduced considerably, he duly returned to Scotland. He went on to score 20 goals in 79 games for Lincoln, being among the most distinguished of the Imps' early players. A pen-picture of McInnes stated that he was 'tricky, a fine shot and plays the combination game to a nicety.'

McINTOSH, James William

Winger: 54+7 apps. 3 goals
Born: Forfar, Angus, 19 August 1950
Career: Arbroath Victoria, Montrose (March 1970), FOREST (£15,000, September 1970), Chesterfield (on loan, January 1976), Hull City (£5,000, March 1976), Dundee United (July 1977), Montrose (November 1977).
Looked upon as a direct outside-left at Forest, where he had the unenviable task of competing with Scottish international John Robertson, Jim McIntosh still managed almost 60 first-class appearances for the Reds during his five-and-a-half years at the City Ground. At times he looked international-class, showing some clever touches and a fair amount of skill without realising his full potential!

McKAY, Thomas Galloway

Inside-forward: 4 apps
Born: Possilpark, Glasgow, 16 July 1910.
Died: Southport, 16 October 1988
Career: Lyon Street Church (Glasgow), FOREST (June 1930), Queen of the South (June 1933), Southport (July 1936), Wigan Athletic (season 1939-40). Did not play after WW2.
Reserve inside-forward Tom McKay was handed just four League outings by Forest during his three years with the club. He made his debut in a 4-3 home win over Charlton Athletic in April 1931 when he deputised for Cyril Stocks, helping set up two of the goals. After leaving the Reds he scored five goals in 68 League games for Southport leading up to WW2.

McKENNAN, Hughbert

Centre-forward: one app.
Born: Airdrie, Scotland, 8 February 1905.
Died: Airdrie, Scotland, 1962

Career: Airdrie Merchants FC, FOREST (May 1927), St Johnstone (August 1928). Played his only League game for Forest against Stoke City in April 1928

McKENZIE, Duncan
Forward: 117+7 apps. 46 goals
Born: Grimsby, 10 June 1950
Career: FOREST (juniors, July 1965, apprentice July 1967, professional June 1968), Mansfield Town (on loan, March 1970 and again, February 1973), Leeds United (£240,000, August 1974), RSC Anderlecht Belgium (£200,000, June 1976), Everton (£200,000, December 1976), Chelsea (£165,000, September 1978), Blackburn Rovers (£80,000, March 1979-May 1981), Tulsa Roughnecks/NASL (player-exchange deal involving Viv Busby, June 1981), Chicago Sting/NASL (May 1982), Bulova/Hong Kong (June 1983). Later employed by Everton as Football in the Community officer.
Scorer of 112 goals in 330 League games for his six clubs, Duncan McKenzie made his League debut for Forest against Sunderland at the start of the 1969-70 season. A player blessed with heaps of natural skill, he had flair and huge reserves of energy although often doubtful commitment. He formed a fine strike-force with Graham Collier in the second XI but took quite a while before he established himself as a marksman in the first team. After two loan spells at Field Mill he returned to the City Ground full of confidence and topped the Second Division scoring charts in 1973-74 with 28 League and Cup goals. He was placed on England's bench for the Home International tournament that season but was not called into action.
McKenzie, who once wrote a column for the Today newspaper (early 1990s), now lives in Newton-le-Willows (Merseyside) where he owns a delicatessen. He is also an accomplished after dinner speaker.

McKINLAY, Robert
Centre-half: 683+3 apps. 10 goals
Born: Lochgelly, Fife, Scotland, 10 October 1932.
Died: August 2002
Career: Bowhill Rovers, FOREST (professional October 1949, retired May 1970 to join the club's backroom staff, later having a spell as chief trainer/coach before leaving to join the prison service, working at Lowdham Grange.
Bob McKinlay was an ever-present for Forest a record eight times, performing superbly well when promotion was gained to the First Division in 1957 and the FA Cup lifted two years later. Earlier, he had helped the Reds' second XI win the Midland League four seasons running: 1951-54.
Between April 1959 and October 1965 he made 291 consecutive appearances for the Reds (265 in the First Division) a club record.
Recommended to Forest by his uncle, Billy McKinlay, who played for Forest between the wars (q.v), Bobby was

originally an outside-right and it was only after he switched to centre-half that he revealed his true potential. He went on to establish a club appearance record that still remains intact today. A fearless yet cultured defender (opponents feared his skill, never his tactics) he was rewarded for his dedication and commitment to the club, with a testimonial against Celtic in 1965 and four years later he received a long service medal from the football League to mark his 20 years as a player at the City Ground.
* McKinlay was the nephew of the former Forest player, Billy McKinlay (q.v).

McKINLAY, William Hodge
Right-right: 357 apps. 13 goals
Born: Dysart near Bathgate, Scotland, 23 August 1904.
Died: Glasgow, February 1976
Career: Lochgelly United, Bathgate FC (1925), FOREST (£757, July 1927, retired in May 1937), FOREST (scout, based in Glasgow: 1937-48).
Standing only 5ft 6ins tall, Billy McKinlay - uncle to Bobby McKinlay (above) - established himself as a quality right-half after taking over that position in an emergency. He was signed by Forest in the face of strong competition from Glasgow Rangers and spent ten years at the City Ground, making well over 350 senior appearances. Replacing Jackie Belton in the first team, he had two back-to-back ever-present campaigns (1932-34) and was loved by the Forest supporters who admired his unflagging work-rate and commitment. A player with a telling tackle he was always prepared to drive forward with the ball to aid his half-backs and even his front men. He made his last appearance for the Reds on Good Friday 1937.
McKinlay was instrumental in sending his nephew Bob to Forest!

McKINNON, Raymond
Defender/midfielder: 6+1 apps. one goal
Born: Dundee, Scotland, 5 August 1970
Career: Dundee United (1988), FOREST (July 1992), Aberdeen (August 1993), Dundee United (November 1995), Luton Town (August 1998), Livingston (September 1999), Raith Rovers (August 2000), East Fife (November 2000), Montrose (November 2001), Raith Rovers (January 2003). Although he spent a season in the Football League with Forest when he struggled with injury, Ray McKinnon - generally endowed with any amount of grit and endurance - was happy playing in his home country and during an excellent career north of the border he amassed well over 250 senior appearances.

McKNIGHT, James
Inside-forward: 11 apps. one goal
Born: Belfast, 1889
Career: Glentoran (1908), Preston North End (August 1911), Glentoran (October 1912), FOREST (May 1913), Belfast Celtic (June 1914).
An Irish international (2 caps won) Jim McKnight entered

the Football League with Preston in season 1911-12. He made 12 senior appearances and scored two goals for the Deepdale club before returning to Ireland. He returned for a second spell in England with Forest but never really asserted himself despite battling hard to hold down a regular first-team place.

McLACHAN, Edwin Rolland

Inside or outside-right: 8 apps. 2 goals
Born: Glasgow, 24 September 1903.
Died: Leicester, 16 March 1970
Career: Queen's Park (June 1921), Clyde (amateur, June 1922), Third Lanark (July 1924), Vale of Leven (August 1925), Leicester City (as an amateur, January 1927), FOREST (May 1927), Mansfield Town (May 1928), Northampton Town (July 1930), Mansfield Town (free transfer, July 1931-May 1932).

A renowned winger in Scotland, Ted McLachan was an amateur international trialist on several occasions before his job brought him down to Leicester. He failed to make his mark at Filbert Street, struggled to settle in at the City Ground (after turning down a professional contract), did very little in his two spells with Mansfield and played in 11 games for Northampton. He scored on his senior debut for Forest in a 2-0 win at Reading in October 1927 (when he deputised for Cyril Stocks). A member of the Stags' 'Egg & Milk' FA Cup team of 1928-29, McLachan became secretary to the Leicestershire Senior League in the mid-1930s and served as chairman of the Leicestershire County FA from 1963 until his death at the age of 66.

McLAREN, Hugh

Inside-right/outside-left: 33 apps. 15 goals
Born: Hamilton near Motherwell, Scotland, 24 June 1926.
Died: Derby, 8 December 1965
Career: Bothwell FC, Bellshill, Kilmarnock (professional, August 1945), Derby County (£7,000, October 1949), FOREST (January 1954), Walsall (July 1955-May 1956), Burton Albion (July 1956), Gresley Rovers (July 1957-May 1959). Left-winger Hugh McLaren scored 56 goals in 131 League and Cup games for Derby County before joining Forest. He replaced Frank Broome at the Baseball Ground and instantly achieved an ambition by partnering his idol and Scottish international Billy Steel in the Rams front-line. Speedy, with fine close ball control, McLaren did over-elaborate at times (much to the annoyance of his colleagues and supporters) and he could also be somewhat erratic, but nevertheless developed a fine scoring record for a wide-man although occasionally he lined up at inside-right. Unfortunately he his stay at the City Ground was a relatively short one (just 18 months) but during that time he showed the odd touches of magic while netting on average a goal every two games.

McMILLAN, Stuart Thomas

Inside or outside-right: 13 apps.
Born: Leicester, 17 September 1896.
Died: Ashbourne, Derbyshire, 27 September 1963
Career: Derby County (professional December 1914), Chelsea (July 1919), Gillingham (March 1921), Wolverhampton Wanderers (June 1922), Bradford City (May 1924), FOREST (June 1927), Clapton Orient (August 1928-May 1930). He then became a licensee of the Nag's Head pub at Mickleover while scouting for Derby in his spare time. He was subsequently appointed Derby County's football advisor in 1942, then manager January 1946-November 1953. He also played cricket for Derbyshire CCC.

Stuart McMillan's League career realised 14 goals in 169 appearances made over a period of 16 years either side of WW1. As a manager he guided Derby County to FA Cup glory over Charlton in 1946 - some 31 years after playing once in the Ram's Second Division championship winning side of 1914-15. The son of Johnny McMillan (ex-Leicester Fosse and Derby and former boss of Gillingham) he moved around as an honest run-of-the-mill footballer and gave a good account of himself practically everywhere he went, although he never played for Chelsea's first team. He joined his father at Gillingham, was relegated to the Third Division North with Wolves and went down into the same division with Bradford City in 1927. He was unable to find a regular place in the Forest side and after just over a dozen senior outings he went down to London to sign for Orient, retiring as a player in 1930. As Derby's manager - besides his Wembley triumph - he twice broke the British transfer record - paying £15,000 for Billy Steel from Morton and £24,500 for Johnny Morris from Manchester United. He guided the Rams to fourth and third spots in the First Division in 1948 and 1949 respectively and took them to the FA Cup semi-final (1948). However, following relegation in 1953 and with the team struggling near the bottom of the Second Division he left the Baseball Ground to run the Station Hotel in Ashbourne, Derbyshire. As a cricketer McMillan was a right-hand batsman and right-arm medium fast bowler. He played in four County matches and averaged just 7.5 at the crease.

McNAUGHTON, Gibson Norrie

Left-half/inside-left: 82 apps. 13 goals
Born: Broughty Ferry near Dundee, Scotland, 30 July 1911.
Died: West Bridgford, 16 September 1991.
Career: Dundee Violet, Clyde, Dundee, Dunfermline Athletic, FOREST (July 1936), Notts County (August 1939). Ilkeston Town January 1948, player-manager cs. 1949 to cs. 1950).

Gibson McNaughton was an experienced player when he joined Forest at the age of 25. having chalked up well over 200 appearances at various levels north of the border. On his day he was one of the most effective footballers in the game and during his three years at the City Ground he produced some excellent performances, having by far his best season in 1937-38 when, for the majority of the time, he linked up splendidly down the left with Messrs Brown and Pugh. He failed to get a senior game with County.

McNAUGHTON, John

Right or left-back: 11 apps.
Born: Perth, Scotland, 19 January 1912.
Died: Almondbank, Scotland, 27 June 1986.
Career: Perth Roselea, FOREST (professional July 1934), Brighton & Hove Albion (seasons 1936-39). Did not play competitive football after WW2.
Basically a reserve full-back during his two seasons with Forest, John McNaughton made his League debut in a 5-1 win over Newcastle United a month after joining the club as a professional. Thereafter he had to battle hard and long for a place in the first team owing to the ongoing form of Jimmy Barrington, Harry Smith and Jack Burton. He had only six League outings with Brighton.

McPHAIL, Stephen

Midfielder: 15+1 apps.
Born: Westminster, 9 December 1979
Career: Leeds United (trainee, April 1995, professional December 1996), Millwall (on loan, March-April 2002), FOREST (September 2003)
A Republic of Ireland international (capped at Youth, Under-21 and senior levels) Stephen McPhail, who has a trusty left-foot, made almost 100 first-class appearances for Leeds United during his eight years or so at Elland Road, collecting an FA Youth Cup winner's medal in 1997.

MacPHERSON, John

Centre-half: 291 apps. 34 goals
Born: Motherwell, Scotland, 28 February 1867.
Died: Canada, circa 1935.
Career: Cambuslang, Heart of Midlothian, FOREST (professional May 1891), Heart of Midlothian (May 1892), FOREST (September 1892), Motherwell (August 1902), Cambuslang. Subsequently emigrated to Canada and lived and worked in Regina, Saskatchewan.
Scottish international centre-half Jock MacPherson gained one full cap for his country, lining up against England in 1891. He also represented the East of Scotland FA and scored in Forest's 3-1 FA Cup final win over Derby County in 1898. Six years earlier, in 1891-92, he had appeared in 19 of the 22 games when the Reds won the Football Alliance championship. He was a Scottish Cup winner with Hearts in 1891.
MacPherson had superb judgement in all aspects of defensive play and this cancelled out any lack of speed. He was a fine captain for both Hearts and Forest.

McURICH

Inside-right: one app.
Born: circa 1865
Career: FOREST (season 1889-90).
McUrich appeared in just one competitive game for Forest, lining up in place of the injured Fred Burton in a Football Alliance game against Grimsby Town on 21 September 1889.

MABBOTT

Inside-right: one app.
Born: circa 1867
Career: FOREST (season 1889-90).
Mabbott made his only first-team appearance for Forest in a 9-0 Football Alliance defeat against Darwen on 21 September 1889.

MALTBY, George Henry

Left-back: 232 apps. 3 goals
Born: Long Eaton, Notts, 1887
Career: Notts Rangers, FOREST (May 1906), Doncaster Rovers (August 1914)
'Ginger' Maltby, a tough and sturdy character, being 'resourceful and plucky and quick to recover' helped Forest win the Second Division title in 1907. Spotted playing with Notts Rangers, despite his tender years, he walked straight into the Forest team and surprised everyone with his all-round performances. He formed an excellent partnership with right-back Walter Dudley who was extremely influential in nurturing the young Maltby along. He lost his place to Tom Gibson in 1913 and moved to Doncaster at the end of that season.

MANNINI, Moreno

Defender: 8+1 apps.
Born: Imola, Italy, 15 August 1962
Career: Imola FC, Forli (1981-82), Como (cs. 1982), Sampdoria (cs.1984), FOREST (August 1999; retired in January 2000 through injury).
After 15 years and more than 500 appearances in Italy's Serie A & B and domestic cup competitions, veteran international defender Moreno Mannini (10 caps won) joined Forest for the 1999-2000 campaign, fulfilling his wish to play in England. Unfortunately he struggled with injury during his early weeks with the Reds and halfway through the season announced his retirement, returning to Italy.

MARRIOTT, Andrew

Goalkeeper: 13 apps.
Born: Sutton-in-Ashfield, 11 October 1970
Career: Arsenal (trainee, June 1987, professional October 1988), FOREST (£50,000, June 1989), West Bromwich Albion (on loan, September 1989), Blackburn Rovers (on loan, December 1989), Colchester United (on loan, March 1990), Burnley (on loan, August-November 1991),

Wrexham (£200,000, October 1993), Sunderland (£200,000, August 1998), Wigan Athletic (on loan, January 2001), Barnsley (free transfer, March 2001). Birmingham City (March 2003).

In 1992 goalkeeper Andy Marriott was between the posts for Forest when they won the Zenith Data Systems Cup and lost in the final of the League Cup (to Manchester United). Unfortunately he never really got much of a chance after that owing to the form of Mark Crossley and he was sold to Wrexham for £200,000. He made over 260 appearances for the Racecourse Ground club and helped them win the Welsh Cup in 1995. Capped by England at Schoolboy, Youth and Under-21 levels, Marriott later added five full Welsh international caps to his collection. He also helped Burnley win the Fourth Division title in 1992 (making 15 appearances).

MARRISON, Thomas

Inside-right/centre-forward: 174 apps. 38 goals

Born: Rotherham, January 1885.

Career: Sheffield Wednesday (February 1902), Rotherham Town (1905), FOREST (£500, November 1906), Oldham Athletic (£200, June 1911), Bristol City (£150, May 1912-May 1913).

Tom Marrison - who could score goals as well as make them - was a member of Forest's Second Division championship winning side of 1907. He was a very effective player, capable of roughing it with the toughest defenders in the game, he possessed a strong right-foot shot, was useful in the air and above all had a terrific engine which kept on going for 90 minutes! He failed to make much headway at Sheffield or Rotherham, but after scoring on his League debut for Forest (in a 2-1 win at Blackpool) he never looked back and gave the Reds' supporters plenty to cheer about over the next five years or so. After leaving the City ground he never really made much of an impact at Boundary Park or indeed at Ashton Gate.

MARSDEN, Harold

Right-back: 14 apps.

Born: Bentley, Yorkshire, 1902.

Career: Bentley Colliery, Doncaster Rovers (as an amateur, season 1923-24), Wombwell, FOREST (May 1925), Brighton & Hove Albion (August 1929), Gillingham (season 1934-35), York City (1935).

Harry Marsden had worked as a cinematograph operator for two years after leaving school. He didn't figure at all with Doncaster and after a year with Wombwell he joined Forest, making his League debut in a 4-0 defeat at Wolves in February 1926. He fought hard and long to get into the side on a regular basis but with no luck owing to the impressive form of Bill Thompson and duly left for Brighton where he became an outstanding performer, amassing well over 170 senior appearances for the Seagulls over a period of five years at Hove.

MARSDEN, John W

Right-back: one app.

Born: circa 1887

Career: Stanton Hill Victoria, FOREST (August 1908-May 1910).

Jack Marsden spent two seasons as a reserve full-back with Forest, making just one League appearance, on Christmas Day 1909, in a 2-2 draw away at Tottenham. He replaced Walter Dudley (injured).

MARSHALL, Gordon

Goalkeeper: 7 apps.

Born: Farnham, Surrey, 2 July 1939

Career: Heart of Midlothian (July 1956), Newcastle United (£18,500, June 1963), FOREST (£17,500, October 1968), Hibernian (£2,500, April 1969), Celtic (free transfer, July 1971), Aberdeen (January 1972), Arbroath (June 1972-July 1975), Newtongrange Star (player-coach, August 1975), Arbroath (November 1975), Newtongrange Star (player-coach, February 1980-May 1981). He later ran a newsagents and barber's shop in Edinburgh, close to the capital's famous Princes Street thoroughfare.

Born in deepest England, when his father was serving in the Army stationed at Aldershot, Gordon Marshall was raised in Lothian and was picked up by Hearts as a teenager. A tall, commanding goalkeeper, brave and consistent, he made a big name for himself at Tynecastle, appearing in 338 first-class matches, earning a League championship medal in 1959-60, and three League Cup winners' medals in 1959, 1960 and 1963 besides winning an England Under-23 cap.

Snapped up by Newcastle, he went on to add 187 appearances to his tally with the Magpies, helping them win the Second Division title in 1965.

Marshall made 177 League appearances for Newcastle before joining Forest as cover for Peter Grummitt. Unfortunately he never really settled down in Nottingham and after just seven games for the Reds he moved to Easter Road, later playing in one European Cup game for Celtic (his only outing for the Scottish club).

Marshall comes from a sporting family: his eldest son, also named Gordon, played in goal for Celtic while his younger offspring Scott was a defender with Arsenal and a member of Scotland's Youth World Cup squad in 1989. Additionally his daughter appeared for the British basketball team.

MARSHALL, William Henry

Left-half/inside-forward: 19 apps. 3 goals

Born: Hucknall, Notts, 16 February 1905.

Died: Linby, Notts 9 March 1959

Career: Hucknall Primitives, Bromley's Athletic, Bromley United, FOREST (February 1924), Southport (August 1926), Wolverhampton Wanderers (£1,500, March 1928), Port Vale (£1,000, March 1930) Tottenham

Hotspur (£1,200, March 1932), Kidderminster Harriers (July 1933), Brierley Hill Alliance (August 1934), Rochdale (August 1935), Linfield (June 1938, retired during season 1939-40).

A strongly-built, forceful player, able to occupy a wing-half or inside-forward position, Harry Marshall played his best football after leaving Forest where he had huffed and puffed but never really set the house on fire. He went on to score 68 goals in 257 League games while serving with Southport, Wolves, Port Vale, Spurs and Rochdale, actually playing in more than 100 competitive games for the latter club. * Marshall's brother, Bob, played for Manchester City and Sunderland.

MARTIN, David Kirker

Inside or centre-forward: 86 apps. 48 goals
Born: Belfast, Northern Ireland, 1 February 1914.
Died: Belfast, Northern Ireland, 9 January 1991
Career: Cliftonville (1929), Royal Ulster Rifles, Cliftonville, Belfast Celtic (£5, professional, August 1932), Wolverhampton Wanderers (£5,000, December 1934), FOREST (£7,000, August 1936), Notts County (November 1938), Glentoran (initially WW2 guest, 1943-45, signed 1945-47).

'Boy' or 'Davy Boy' Martin, a former orphanage lad and prize boxer, came to the fore when leading the Royal Ulster Rifles and Army teams while serving as a drummer before being engaged by Belfast Celtic in 1932 for a fee of just £5. He was capped by Ireland against Wales, Scotland and England in 1933 and immediately set the football world talking with his all-action style and red-hot shooting. He went on to gain nine full caps for his country and after played superbly well for Wolves (18 goals in 27 outings) he did even better with Forest, averaging more than a goal every two games, following on with 26 more goals in only 26 League games in his one season at Meadow Lane. Despite his enormous talent, Martin was a temperamental player and was often in trouble with referees and indeed his manager! In the summer of 1936 Forest manager Harry Wightman paid what was then a club record fee to secure the services of Martin. He quickly repaid some of that money by beating Enoch West's long-standing record of goals in a season by notching 31 in 38 games in his first campaign at the City Ground.

He lost his way in 1937-38 and played only seven times the following year before moving across the River Trent.

MARTIN, Frederick H

Forward: 7 apps
Born: Nottingham, 13 December 1925
Career: Cinderford Colliery, FOREST (professional October 1944-May 1949).

Freddy Martin had a short-lived career as a striker who never really made his mark in Forest's first XI despite a lot of encouragement. His League debut for the Reds was against Cardiff City (h) in October 1947 (lost 2-1).

MARTIN, Henry

Outside-left: 114 apps. 13 goals
Born: Selston, Notts, 5 December 1891. Died: 1974
Career: Sutton Junction (1909), Sunderland (January 1912), FOREST (WW1 guest 1915-19, then signed May 1922), Rochdale (June 1925, trainer June 1929, then caretaker-manager, July-August 1930), Mansfield Town (trainer-coach November 1933, manager, December 1933-March 1935), Swindon Town (trainer, June 1935, remaining on the staff at the County Ground until 1955).

Left-winger Harry Martin won one full England cap - against Ireland at Middlesbrough in February 1914, having earlier helped Sunderland win the First Division championship and finish runners-up (to Aston Villa) in the FA Cup in season 1912-13. He also played for the Football League XI on three occasions and gained two unofficial caps for his country in Victory internationals. As a WW1 guest (50 games played in total) he helped Forest win the Victory Shield in 1919. Unusually tall for an outside-left, he had a great, raking stride that made him a daunting adversary for any defender. He could centre brilliantly when going at full speed down the wing. A penalty king, he had gone off injured in a League game with Bolton on Boxing Day 1924 when Forest (1-0 down at the time) were awarded a penalty. Skipper Bob Wallace raced to the dressing room, dragged Martin back onto the pitch and, hobbling on one leg, he struck home the equaliser from the spot! He scored 23 goals in 211 League games during his ten years at Roker Park. After retiring, he was brought back by Rochdale to make one appearence in 1930-31.

MARTIN, James

Outside-left: one app
Born: Glasgow, Scotland, 3 March 1937
Career: Ballieston, FOREST (June 1958-May 1959)
Jim Martin spent one season at Forest, acting as reserve to Stewart Imlach. His only senior game was a League fixture against Leeds United on 22 April 1959 (lost 3-0).

MARTIN, Neil

Striker: 135+4 apps. 34 goals
Born: Tranent near Alloa, Clackmannanshire, 20 October 1940
Career: Tranent Juniors, Alloa Athletic (1959), Queen of the South (£2,000, 1961), Hibernian (£6,000, July 1963), Sunderland (£50,000, October 1965), Coventry City (£90,000, February 1968), FOREST (£65,000, February 1971), Brighton & Hove Albion (July 1975), Crystal Palace (March 1976), St Patrick's Athletic (October 1976), Al-Arabi Sporting Club/Kuwait (player-coach/assistant-manager, 1978), Walsall (youth team coach, then joint-manager with Alan Buckley, July 1981, sole manager later that season to June 1982).

Capped three times by Scotland at senior level, striker Neil Martin also represented his country in one Under-23 international and played twice for the Scottish League side whilst at Easter Road. He netted 78 goals in Scottish football (40 coming in 1964-65 for Hibs) and then, after leaving Easter Road for Sunderland, he claimed a further 115 goals in 337 League games. Very good in the air, mobile enough to elude defenders on the ground, he spent four years with Forest during which time he linked up well initially with Peter Cormack and Ian Storey-Moore and then with Duncan McKenzie and to a certain extent with Alan Buckley, John Galley and George Lyall, and finally with Garry Birtles.

MARTIN, Thomas
Goalkeeper: 6 apps.
Born: circa 1875
Career: FOREST (seasons 1896-98)
A reserve goalkeeper with Forest, Tom Martin had Dan Allsopp barring his way between the posts but when called into action he always gave a good performance, playing particularly well on his League debut v. Preston in April 1897 (0-0) and in a 3-1 home victory over the reigning double winners Aston Villa in March 1898.

MARTIN, Thomas
Wing-half/inside-forward: 50 apps. 4 goals
Born: Glasgow, 21 December 1924
Career: Shettleston Juniors, Heart of Midlothian (1942), Stirling Albion (October 1949), Doncaster Rovers (July 1950), FOREST (£15,000, November 1952), Hull City (£7,000, June 1955), Rothes (player-coach, September 1957-59).
Wing-half Tom Martin was a record signing by Forest in 1952. Something of a two-footed player, capable of outstanding performances, whether at wing-half or inside-forward, he was a true Scottish stylist. Perhaps a touch of inconsistency caused his failure to win international recognition. He made well over 200 senior appearances during his career (150 in the Football League).

MARTINDALE, Harling Richardson
Inside-right: one app.
Born: Beeston, Notts, 10 September 1899.
Career: North Staffordshire Regiment, FOREST (season 1919-20).
An amateur who was registered with Forest for the first post WW1 League season, 'Army Officer' Martindale made just one senior appearance for the Reds, lining up against Wolves at Molineux in November 1919 (lost 4-0).

MASON, William
Outside-right: 24 apps. 6 goals
Born: circa 1870
Career: FOREST (July 1890), Burton Swifts (February 1892-94)
Bill Mason helped Forest win the Football Alliance title in 1891-92, appearing in 19 of the 22 games. He was described as being a 'smart, compact winger with a fine turn of speed.' He scored twice in 17 League games for Burton.

MASTERS, Arthur
Outside-right: 117 apps. 26 goals
Born: Coppull near Chorley, Lancs, 17 August 1910.
Died: July 1998
Career: Horwich RMI (Lancashire Combination), FOREST (March 1933), Port Vale (June 1937 in exchange for Allan Todd). Left Vale Park in May 1939 and did not play competitive League football after WW2.
Arthur Masters was a clever, right-sided forward who had showed good pace and delivered excellent crosses while also packing a fine shot in his right foot. He made his League debut for Forest against Lincoln City in April 1933 and after doing pretty well at the City Ground (having taken over the outside-right slot from Bill Dickinson) he went on to score 15 goals in 72 games for the Valiants. During a League fixture against Crewe in January 1938, he was knocked out twice and after recovering had no recollection of having played in that game!

MATTSSON, Jesper Bo
Defender: 5+1 apps.
Born: Visby, Sweden, 18 April 1968
Career: Gefle IF (1991) BK Hacken (1994) Halmstads BK (1995), FOREST (£500,000, December 1998, retired May 2001).
Signed by manager Ron Atkinson after making well over 100 senior appearances for Halmstads BK, tall, dominant centre-back Jesper Mattson, a Swedish international (one cap gained) was thrown straight into the first team on his arrival at the City Ground (v. Leicester City) hoping that he would shore up and stabilize the defence. He played in the next match v. Blackburn Rovers but was then sidelined for some considerable time after sustaining rib and lung injuries, returning as a substitute in that 8-1 home drubbing by Manchester United (February).

MATRECANO, Salvatore
Defender: 13 apps.
Born: Napoli, Italy, 5 October 1970
Career: Ercolanese (1986), V Lamezia (cs. 1988), Audax Ravag (1988), Turris (cs.1990), Foggia (cs.1991), Parma (cs.1992), Napoli (cs.1994), Udinese (November 1995), Perugia (August 1996), FOREST (£1.2 million, August 1999 to May 2001). With almost 250 League appearances in Italian football under his belt, rugged defender Salvatore Matrecano was hoping to show his worth in season 1999-2000 but, despite showing a lot of confidence, he never recovered from cruciate ligament trouble and he left the club in the summer of 2001 (out of contract).

MAWSON, Joseph Spence
Inside/centre-forward: 4 apps. one goal
Born: Brandon, County Durham, 26 October 1905.
Died: Stoke-on-Trent, 10 September 1959.
Career: Brandon Colliery FC, Crook Town (1921), Washington Colliery, Durham City, Stoke City (January

1929), FOREST (September 1933), Stockport County (September 1935), Linfield (December 1935), Crewe Alexandra (August 1936-May 1937).

Joe Mawson played his best football with Stoke City when he appeared (late on) in the same forward-line as Stanley Matthews. Initially a miner, brought up on the Durham coalfield, he developed his football with Crook Town. Stoke kept a watchful eye on his progress and duly signed him as a professional halfway through the 1928-29 season. Within a month he scored on his debut but then languished in the reserves before re-establishing himself in the first team, becoming the club's top-scorer in 1931-32 and 1932-33 and helping Stoke win the Second Division championship in the latter campaign. He netted 50 goals in 93 appearances during his time at the Victoria Ground before transferring to Forest where he was basically in the twilight of his career, managing only four senior games for the Reds and netting one goal, in a 3-0 FA Cup win over Manchester United in January 1935.

MAY, Edward H

Inside-forward/outside-right or left: 9 apps. 5 goals

Born: Nottingham circa 1865

Career: Notts Rangers, Burslem Port Vale (July 1886), Notts County (March 1887), Burslem Port Vale (guest, September 1887), FOREST (August 1890-May 1892), Burton Swifts (seasons 1892-93 & 1895-96).

A versatile footballer, Teddy May played for Notts County in their first season of League football (scoring 3 goals in 11 games). He was never a regular performer with Forest although he did grab four goals in a 7-0 Football Alliance victory over Bootle in October 1890.

MEE, George Edwin

Inside-forward: 12 apps. one goal

Born: Blackpool, 20 May 1923. Died: 1974

Career: Aston Villa, FOREST (guest May 1940, signed as a full-time professional, May 1945), Blackpool (May 1947).

George Mee, who was the son of the former Notts County, Blackpool, Burnley, Mansfield Town, Accrington Stanley and Rochdale outside-left of the same name, played in ten WW2 games as a guest for Forest. Like his father before him, he had a massive frame and loved to rough it with the hefty half-backs who opposed him, never shirking a tackle, always giving a good account of himself.

* His uncle was Bertie Mee, the former Derby County and Mansfield Town player who managed Arsenal to the double in 1970-71.

MELTON, Stephen

Defender/midfielder: 3+1 apps.

Born: Lincoln, 3 October 1978

Career: FOREST (trainee, October 1993, professional October 1995), Stoke City (free transfer, February 2000), Brighton & Hove Albion (August 2000), Hull City (Loan November 2002 permanent December 2002).

With his chances rather limited at the City Ground, hard-working utility player Steve Melton languished in the reserves for long periods before finally departing on a free transfer to Midland rivals Stoke City. He later helped Brighton win the Third Division championship (2001).

MERCER, Joseph Powell

Centre-half: 158 apps. 6 goals

Born: Ellesmere Port, Cheshire, 21 July 1890.

Died: Ellesmere Port, 20 May 1927.

Career: Burnell's Ironworks FC, Ellesmere Port Town, FOREST (May 1910), Ellesmere Port (June 1915), Tranmere Rovers (August 1921).

Joe Mercer was an attacking centre-half with a tremendous engine. He was registered with Forest for five years. He was a wonderful footballer who produced some exhilarating displays at the heart of the defence. He made his League debut for the Reds against Tottenham Hotspur in October 1910 and played his last game for the club in April 1915 against another North London club, Arsenal.

MERINO, Carlos Alberto

Midfielder: 4+8 apps.

Born: Bilbao, Spain, 15 March 1980

Career: CF Urdaneta, FOREST (September 1997), Athletic Bilbao (July 2000), Burgos (cs. 2001).

Only 5ft 8ins tall, and barely 10st in weight, busy midfielder Carlos Merino never really sparkled during his three disappointing years at the City Ground. Signed as a promising teenager, he struggled to hold down a first-team place and left in the summer of 2000 after rejecting a new contract. He made his debut in the Football League v. Barnsley on 1 October 1999 (as a substitute in a 3-0 victory). His full debut followed in the 1-1 draw with Bolton at the end of that month.

METGOD, Johannes Antonius Bernardus

Midfielder: 136+3 apps. 17 goals

Born: Amsterdam, Netherlands, 27 February 1958

Career: DWS Amsterdam, Haarlem, AZ 67 Alkmaar (cs. 1976), Real Madrid (July 1982), FOREST (£300,000, August 1984), Tottenham Hotspur (£250,000, July 1987), Feyenoord (£180,000, May 1988 to cs. 1994). Later worked as Youth Development Officer and then as first team coach (from 2001-02) at Feyenoord.

Johnny Metgod, a 6ft 4in tall Dutch international midfielder, was capped 19 times by his country. As a Spurs player he also represented the Football League v. the Irish League in 1987 and in his first season with Real Madrid collected a Spanish Cup runners-up medal. A strongly-built, upright player, confident on the ball, he certainly gave Forest good value for money during his three seasons at the City Ground. He only played in 12 League games for Spurs.

MIDDLETON, John

Goalkeeper: 112 apps.

Born: Skegness, 24 December 1956

Career: FOREST (apprentice, June 1973, professional November 1974), Derby County (£25,000 plus Archie Gemmill, September 1977; retired with a shoulder injury in May 1980).

Goalkeeper John Middleton helped Forest gain promotion to the top flight and win the Anglo-Scottish Cup in 1977; he then made five appearances when the First Division title was achieved the following year. An England Youth international (1975), he went on to gain three Under-21 caps and after leaving Forest he added 80 League and Cup appearances to his tally with the Rams. A more than useful, well-built 'keeper with a safe pair of hands, Middleton left Forest after Peter Shilton's arrival - and he replaced Colin Boulton at the Baseball Ground

MILLER, Andrew H

Forward: 5 apps.

Born: Bo'ness, Scotland, 24 March 1905.

Career: Croy Celtic, Celtic (August 1920), Dumbarton Harp (on loan), FOREST (May 1924), Bo'ness FC (October 1924), Camelon Juniors, Montrose (October 1930). A utility forward with Forest, Archie Miller never really made much headway at the City Ground, appearing in only a handful of first-team games, while occupying three different positions. He made his Football League debut at inside-left on 30 August 1924 in a 2-0 home defeat by Arsenal. He also played on both the right and left wings before returning to Scotland.

MILLS, Gary Roland

Midfielder/winger: 142+30 apps. 14 goals

Born: Northampton, 11 November 1961

Career: FOREST (apprentice, June 1977, professional November 1978), Seattle Sounders/NASL (on loan, March 1982), Derby County (on loan, October 1982), Seattle Sounders (on loan April, 1983), Notts County (August 1987), Leicester City (exchange deal involving Phil Turner, March 1989), Notts County (September 1994),Grantham Town (player-manager, September 1996), Gresley Rovers (August 1998) King's Lynn (player-manager, October 1998). Boston United (November 2000). Tamworth (player-manager January 2001), Coventry City (coach, season 2002-03).

As a teenager the versatile and dependable Gary Mills played for Forest in the 1980 European Cup success over SV Hamburg and he also gained two England Under-23 caps to add to his Youth honours whilst at the City Ground, having represented his country at both soccer and rugby as a schoolboy. Best described as an attacking midfielder, he later fell foul, however, of the Football League's attempts to tighten up on the regulations regarding loan and transfer deals with various NASL clubs and a combination of such difficulties and severe injury

problems kept him out of action in this country for quite some time. By the time he eventually moved to Meadow Lane, he had been edged out of the picture by a new generation of talent unearthed by Brian Clough, but continued to do the business for the Magpies and then later with Leicester before ending his senior career back with Notts County whom he helped win the Anglo Italian Cup in 1995.

All told Mills made 566 League and Cup appearances, with exactly 200 coming in the League for Leicester. His father, Roly, was a Northampton Town stalwart (305 League appearances: 1951-64).

MILLS, Joseph

Wing-half/inside-right: 45 apps.

Born: Cresswell near Ashington, Northumberland, 10 April 1895. Died: 1938

Career: Red Row FC, Whitwell St Lawrence FC, FOREST (July 1917), Luton Town (March 1924), Bentley Colliery FC (season 1925-26).

Joe Mills made 24 appearances for Forest during the last two seasons of WW1. He then started off the 1919-20 League season at right-half (making his debut in this competition against Rotherham County (away). Strong and efficient, he held his position until injury forced him out of action in February 1920. He failed to regain his place in the side after that, although he did have a few outings here and there before his transfer to Luton in 1924.

MOCHAN, Dennis

Full-back: 103 apps.

Born: Falkirk, Scotland, 12 December 1935

Career: East Fife, Raith Rovers, FOREST (June 1962), Colchester United (September 1966-May 1970).

A strong, well-equipped full-back, Dennis Mochan took over the number 3 shirt from Billy Gray in February 1963, making his debut in the Football League v. Leicester City at the City Ground (lost 2-0). He held his position (injury and illness apart) with confidence until December 1965 when another injury ended a run of 56 consecutive League appearances. He had 116 League outings for Colchester after leaving Forest.

MOORE, Alan

Right-winger: 104 apps. 39 goals

Born: Hebburn near Gateshead, 7 March 1927

Career: Sunderland (professional, May 1946), Spennymoor United (July 1948), Chesterfield (December 1948), Hull City (July 1951), FOREST (January 1952), Coventry City (December 1954), Swindon Town (July 1957), Rochdale (November 1958), Wisbech Town (June 1959); subsequently coached at Cambridge University for two seasons: 1967-68 & 1968-69.

Alan Moore, one of ten brothers, eight of whom were footballers, had an excellent career that spanned 13 years during which time he amassed in excess of 275 senior appearances and netted over 60 goals. Fast and direct, with a liking for cutting inside to get in a shot at goal, he possessed a full repertoire of tricks and took over from Fred Scott on the right-wing in the Reds' attack (Scott moving inside). He made his League debut for the Reds in the 3-2 local derby win over Notts County in January 1962 and retained the number 7 position virtually unchallenged until halfway through the 1954-55 campaign when he moved to Coventry, being replaced by Peter Small.

MOORE, Ian Ronald
Midfielder/striker: 4+14 apps.
Born: Birkenhead, 26 August 1976.
Career: Tranmere Rovers (apprentice, July 1992, professional July 1994), Bradford City (on loan, September 1996), FOREST (£1 million, March 1993), West Ham United (on loan, September 1997), Stockport County (£800,000, July 1998), Burnley (£1 million, January 2000).
After representing his country at Youth team level, Ian Moore gained seven England Under-21 caps and scored 13 goals in 66 first-class games for Tranmere Rovers before transferring to Forest in 1996. He helped the Reds gain promotion to the Premiership in 1998 but generally failed to make his mark at the City Ground. Nevertheless, a very consistent performer, a fetcher and carrier later in his career, he reached the personal milestone of 300 senior appearances during the 2002-03 season with Burnley.

MORGAN, Francis Gerald
Right-half/centre-half: 219 apps. 6 goals
Born: Belfast: 25 July 1899. Died: 1959
Career: Cliftonville (1916), Linfield (1919), FOREST (November 1922), Luton Town (August 1929), Grantham Town (season 1930-31), Cork (1931-32), Ballymena (1933-34).
International defender Gerry Morgan had a fine career. Capped eight times by Northern Ireland (his first v. England at the Hawthorns in October 1922 - just before he joined Forest and his last six as a Reds' player) he accumulated well over 400 appearances in almost 20 years of first-class football, half of them coming in Irish League and Cup competitions. Signed by Forest as a replacement for Jack Armstrong, he was quickly moved to centre-half following an injury to Fred Parker. He made his debut for the Reds at right-half in a 1-0 home win over Burnley in November 1922 and, in fact, played in four different positions before finally bedding down as the heart of the defence where he remained until Albert Harrison came on the scene in 1927. Rated one of the finest centre-halves in the country during the mid-1920s, Morgan was a superb header of the ball and tackled hard but fair. He struck up a fine understanding in the middle of the Forest defence with Jackie Belton and Bob Wallace.

MORGAN, Westley Nathan
Defender: 22+2 apps. 2 goal
Born: Nottingham, 21 January 1984
Career: Dunkirk (Central Midlands League side), FOREST (professional, July 2002), Kidderminster Harriers (on loan, March-April 2003).
Young 6ft 2in, 14st tough-tackling defender Wes Morgan was handed his League baptism against Scunthorpe United whilst on loan to Kidderminster Harriers in March 2003. He returned to The City Ground a more experienced player for the start of the next season and duly made his mark in Forest's defence following the departure of Ricardo Scimeca to Leicester City.

MORGAN-OWEN, Morgan Maddox
Wing-half/inside-left/centre-half: one app.
Born: Cardiff, 20 February 1877.
Died: Willington Hall, Derbyshire, 14 August 1950.
Career: Corinthians (1898-1913), London Casuals (1903-13), FOREST (April 1901), London Welsh, Rhyl, Glossop (between August 1903-May 1905), Oswestry and Corinthians Under Arms FC (1915). He served with the Essex Regiment during WW1 and skippered the Army side in various inter-war matches. He was also gassed and severely wounded in Gallipoli, but was demobilised as a lieutenant-colonel and gained the DSO for his actions during the battle of Cambrai. He also received the Territorial Decoration. Morgan-Owen was a schoolmaster at Forest School, Walthamstow until 1909 and Repton School, Derby to his retirement in 1937. Oddly enough he actually played in Shrewsbury School's first public match against Repton in 1894. President of the Corinthians from 1921, he was also vice-President pf the English Amateur FA. He remained active in public life as a magistrate and councillor until his death.
Described by Norman Creek, the Corinthians' historian of the 1930s, as 'the greatest Corinthian of the Edwardian period' Morgan-Owen scored two goals in 12 caps for Wales at senior level (1897-1907) as well as representing his country as an amateur, acting as captain on a number of occasions. He played in only one League game for Forest, lining up against Blackburn Rovers (home) on 8 April 1901 (as stand-in for Jack Calvey). He was also a soccer pioneer, and during the pre WW1 years toured with a selected team to such countries as France, Holland, Germany, Austria, Switzerland, USA, Canada and Brazil. He actually appeared in his last game of football in 1918 (aged 41).
In 1906 Morgan-Owen wrote: '...to be successful a half-back must always be cool and collected and the possessor of great patience and endurance.' He was certainly that

MORLEY, William
Wing-half: 301 apps. 10 goals
Born: Nottingham, 30 July 1925. Died: 1978
Career: Mapperley Celtic, FOREST (August 1945-May

1959), Wisbech Town (August 1959).

Bill Morley - a dour yet determined tackler - played for Forest in their 1951 League Division South championship-winning side and six years later was again in the team when promotion to the First Division was achieved. Initially regarded as a front-line player in any position, he made his Football League debut in January 1947 (v. Newport County away) and was a regular three years later, becoming a vital cog in the side, producing some exquisite all-round performances. He lost his place to former Busby Babe Jeff Whitefoot.

MORRIS, Arthur Grenville
Centre-forward/inside-left: 457 apps. 217 goals
Born: Builth, Wales, 13 April 1877.
Died: West Bridgford, Notts, 27 November 1959.
Career: Builth Town (August 1892), Aberystwyth Town (July 1893), Bury (briefly), Swindon Town (August 1897), FOREST (£200, December 1898, retired May 1913)
Welsh international Gren Morris - who became known as 'The Prince of Inside-lefts' after switching from the centre-forward berth - was Forest's top-scorer in seven out of ten seasons he spent with the club. He also netted five League hat-tricks for the Reds, helping them win the Second Division title in 1907. Scorer of nine goals in 21 outings for his country (16 caps coming as a Forest player - his first at the age of 18 when he played alongside the great Billy Meredith v. Ireland in February 1896), Morris, who was an apprentice engineer at Green's foundry in Aberystwyth and then a clerk in the drawing office at the GWR works at Swindon before becoming a professional, scored over 100 goals in only 75 games playing local football. A remarkably fit man, 'The Immortal Gren' (as he was also dubbed) was allowed to train on his own away from the club. A man of outstanding, personal charm and never known to retaliate, it is also said that he never committed a foul tackle. His biggest disappointment as a Forest player was losing in the 1900 FA Cup semi-final to Bury. Curiously he had been at Gigg Lane for a short time during his teenage years - and he actually played his first and last League games for Forest against the Shakers.

Morris was also a fine lawn tennis player. On his retirement from football he attempted to reclaim amateur status to participate in major tennis tournaments, having won a title in 1911, but was banned from doing so and duly turned to coaching instead, taking charge of the youngsters at the Nottinghamshire LTA in 1926 in addition to maintaining his business as a coal-merchant. He was 82 years of age when he died in 1959.

MORRIS, Ernest
Centre-forward: 4 apps
Born: Stocksbridge near Rotherham, 11 May 1921
Career: South Yorkshire junior football, FOREST (August 1947), York City (June 1948), Grantham Town (August 1949), Halifax Town (November 1950-April 1951).

Another leader of the attack who had only a brief spell in League football, Ernie Morris was never able to come to grips with the stern challenges the game presented.

MORRIS, Hugh
Outside-right/inside-left: 23 apps. one goal
Born: Giffnock, Scotland, 19 November 1900.
Career: Clyde (1918), Manchester City (July 1922), FOREST (August 1924), Notts County (April 1925), Southend United (December 1925), Newport County (July 1929 to cs. 1930).
After making 61 senior appearances in two seasons with Manchester City, Hugh Morris arrived at the City Ground confident of doing well with Forest - although he certainly didn't have the greatest of starts when his first four games all ended in defeats. He remained with the Reds for just a year, his only goal coming in a 3-2 home defeat at the hands of Sheffield United in February 1923. He did splendidly with Southend for whom he netted 14 goals in 117 League outings, grabbing another five in 22 outings with Newport.

MORRISON, Robert Crosson
Inside-forward: one app.
Born: Chapelhall near Glasgow, Scotland, 16 February 1933
Career: Glasgow Rangers (1951), FOREST (June 1958), Workington (July 1959-May 1961).
Although Bob Morrison spent eight years at Ibrox Park, playing with and against some of the great Scottish internationals and helping Rangers win three League championships, he never really hit the headlines north of the border. He certainly never fitted in with Forest, appearing in only one League game for the Reds, lining up at inside-right in a 5-1 defeat by Wolves on the opening day of the 1958-59 season. He went on to score 20 goals in his 53 League outings for Workington.

MORTON, Robert
Outside-left: 36 apps. 4 goals
Born: Widdrington, Northumberland, 3 March 1906.
Died: Widdrington, April 1990.
Career: Ashington (1922), Bedlington United, Barnsley (1927), FOREST (July 1928), Newark Town (August 1930), Bradford Park Avenue (1931), Port Vale (May 1932-May 1935), Throckley Welfare (seasons 1935-37).
When in possession outside-left Bob Morton was clever to the point of being cheeky. Unfortunately he didn't do too well at League level with either Ashington or Barnsley but did reasonably well with Forest, and after leaving the City Ground he scored 20 goals in 102 senior appearances for Port Vale. He had a disappointing start to his career with the Reds, being on the losing end of a 5-1 scoreline against Stoke City (home) when making his debut in August 1928. He played in the next three games but was then out of the side until returning in late November, holding his place until virtually the end of the season. In 1929-30 he

was in and out of the first XI with Noah Burton occupying the left-wing position most of the time.

MUNRO, John Scott

Left-back: 99 apps.

Born: Scone, Perthshire, Scotland, 18 August 1914.

Career: Burnside Rangers, Dundee Violet, Dundee, Hibernian, Heart of Midlothian, FOREST (September 1936-March 1940). Did not figure after WW2.

Jock Munro occupied every defensive position during his playing career but played as left-back with Forest from where he produced some fine performances. He got into the side, on a regular basis, during the 1937-38 season when he partnered Reg Trim. He played right through until March 1940 before entering the services.

MURRAY, James R

Right-back: 2 apps.

Born: circa 1871

Career: FOREST (season 1893-94)

Jimmy Murray was a sturdy full-back who played in two United Counties League games for Forest v. Notts County and Sheffield Wednesday in April 1894 when he was called in as changes were being made (through injury) to the Reds' rearguard.

MURRAY, Patrick

Outside-right/inside-forward: 29 apps. 2 goals

Born: Currie, near Edinburgh, 18 March 1874.

Died: 25 December Edinburgh, 1925.

Career: Royal Albert FC (October 1895), Hibernian, Darwen (1896), East Stirlingshire (September 1897), Preston North End (May 1898), East Stirlingshire (June 1900), Wishaw Thistle (January 1900), Royal Albert (October 1900), FOREST (December 1900), Celtic (November 1902), Portsmouth (1903), East Stirlingshire (November 1904), Royal Albert (March 1905).

Pat Murray had a fine career, especially north of the border. He scored once in his five League games for struggling Darwen, netted nine times in 51 outings for Preston and later served with Portsmouth in the Southern League. A bouncy Scot, full of vim and vigour, he continued playing football right up until 1910. His debut for Forest was against Aston Villa (away) in December 1900 and he scored his first goal for the Reds in a 4-1 reverse at Everton in March 1901. After leaving the Reds he struck three goals in 16 games for Celtic.

MURRAY, R

Centre-forward/outside-left: 2 apps.

Born: circa 1872

Career: FOREST (August 1894-May 1896)

Murray was a reserve utility forward with Forest during the mid-1890s. His two senior outings came in the space of ten weeks during the first half of the 1894-95 campaign. He took over from Tommy Rose in the League

encounter with Preston North End in October and then lined up on the left-wing as deputy for Jim McIntosh v. Sheffield Wednesday in mid-December. He didn't play League football after leaving Forest.

MURRAY, Richard

Centre-half: one app.

Born: circa 1880.

Career: FOREST (July 1899-March 1901).

Reserve centre-half, Dick Murray's only first-team outing for Forest was in the League game v. Liverpool (away) in April 1900 when he deputised for Jack MacPherson in a 1-0 defeat.

NEEDHAM, David William

Defender: 112+6 apps. 13 goals

Born: Leicester, 21 May 1949

Career: Notts County (apprentice, June 1964, professional July 1966), Queen's Park Rangers (June 1977), FOREST (December 1977, retired in May 1982). Later ran his own business in Leicester.

Dave Needham helped the Reds win the First Division title in 1978 the League Cup at Wembley a year later but was seemingly at fault for the only goal of the game when Wolves beat Forest 1-0 to lift the League Cup in 1980. Nevertheless, he was a strong defender, precise in the tackle who covered the ground well, always encouraging his fellow team-mates.

He made 429 League appearances for the Magpies (32 goals scored) whom he helped win the Fourth Division title in 1971 and then claim the runners-up spot in Division Three two years later.

NEEDHAM, George

Centre-half/left-half: 289 apps. 11 goals

Born: Shepshed, Leicestershire, 1883.

Career: Shepshed Albion, FOREST (May 1905-May 1919). Did not feature after WW1.

George 'Tag' Needham, 6ft 2ins tall, was a wholehearted defender who gained a Second Division championship medal with Forest in 1907. A firm favourite with the fans, he never gave less than 100 percent effort out on the park despite a slight disability in his left arm. He seemed to know no fear, committing himself to situations where some players wouldn't dream of venturing! He moved from centre-half to left-half to accommodate Joe Mercer. Appointed captain just before the outbreak of WW1, Needham, so consistent, did not miss a single first-team match between September 1911 and April 1915 (total: 158).

NELIS, Patrick

Centre-forward/inside-left: 60 apps. 13 goals

Born: Londonderry, Northern Ireland, 5 October 1898.

Died: Londonderry 22 April 1970

Career: Londonderry Distillery, Accrington Stanley (October 1921), FOREST (March 1922), Wigan

Borough (May 1925), Coleraine (seasons 1926-32)
An Irish international (one cap gained v. England in 1923)
Pat Nelis was a member of Forest's 1922 promotion-
winning squad. He was an intelligent forward with good
pace and a strong right-foot shot, he scored twice on his
League debut for the Reds in a 4-1 home win over
Bradford Park Avenue in March 1922. Earlier he notched
14 goals in only 11 League games for Accrington and after
leaving Forest found the net once in 15 outings for Wigan
before returning to the Emerald Isle where he continued
to play until well into the 1930s.

NEVE, Edwin
Outside-left: 37 apps. 3 goals
Born: Prescot, Lancs, 3 May 1885.
Died: August 1920
Career: St Helens Recreational, Hull City (May 1906),
Derby County (June 1912), FOREST (August 1914),
Chesterfield (April 1916). Did not play competitive
League football after WW1.
Described in a Midlands soccer annual in 1913 as being a
'speedy outside-left' some reports thought him far too slow
and casual to become a star in League football.
Nevertheless Ted Neve gave a good account of himself all
down the line, scoring 12 goals in 102 games for Hull and
once in 49 outings for Derby. WW1 disrupted his stay
with Chesterfield, although he did have a few Regional
games for the Spireites during the hostilities.

NEWBIGGING, Alexander
Goalkeeper/centre-forward/inside-right: 7 apps.
Born: Larkhall, Scotland, 27 December 1879.
Career: Paisley Abercorn, Larkhall United, Queen's Park
Ranger's (October 1900), FOREST (September 1901),
Reading (August 1905), Glasgow Rangers (cs. 1906),
Reading (cs. 1908), Coventry City (September 1909),
Inverness Thistle (season 1910-11).
Alex Newbigging was an amazing footballer. As a
youngster he played on the wing, at centre-forward, in
defence and as an occasional goalkeeper. He joined QPR
as an out-and-out striker and played for the London club
in both the Southern League and FA Cup. On joining
Forest he went back to keeping goal - and did well, making
his Football League debut for the Reds in that position in
a 1-1 draw with Stoke on 5 October 1901. In the next
game he played a blinder in a 4-0 win over Everton. After
that he dropped into the reserves and played the odd game
in the forward-line, returning to League action at inside-
right in a 2-1 home win over Sunderland in mid-February
1902. He remained with Forest for the next three years
during which time he acted, in the main, as reserve to
regular goalkeeper Linacre. He had eight outings between
the posts for Coventry.

NEWBIGGING, Henry
Inside-left: 9 apps. one goal
Born: Douglas, Lanarkshire, 25 May 1893.
Died: circa 1950
Career: Paisley Abercorn, FOREST (September 1919),
Stockport County (June 1920-May 1921).
Signed shortly after the resumption of League football
following WW1, Harry Newbigging didn't really fit the
bill at Forest, although he did score his only goal on his
debut in a 2-2 draw at Barnsley. He later obliged with one
more goal in 15 League games for Stockport.

NEWTON, Henry Albert
Left-back/wing-half: 315 apps. 19 goals
Born: Nottingham, 18 February 1944.
Career: FOREST (juniors, January 1960, professional
June 1961), Everton (£150,000 plus Tommy Jackson,
October 1970), Derby County (£100,000, September
1973), Walsall (May 1977). He retired in May 1978 with
arthritis. In 1984, when running a sub-Post Office in
Derby, he underwent a hip operation.
A tremendous competitor, Henry Newton, after filling in
at left-back (a position he didn't really enjoy) eventually
took over Jeff Whitefoot's number 4 shirt in the Forest
engine-room. Regarded as a no-nonsense performer,
supremely confident with the ball, hard working, and a
player who never shirked a tackle, he put in many fine
displays and was generally one of the stars of the side.
Indeed, Forest's overall performances were decidedly
below par when he was not on the pitch wearing a red
shirt. After making his Forest League debut in the East
Midlands derby with Leicester City in October 1963, he
went on to win four England Under-23 caps, was on the
verge of being selected for the 1970 World Cup finals in
Mexico and he also represented the Football League. He
was eventually transferred to the reigning League
champions Everton in 1970. He moved next to Derby in
1973, being Brian Clough's last signing before he
sensationally quit the Rams to take charge of Brighton.
Newton appeared in 83 competitive games for Everton,
156 for the Rams and 21 for Walsall, his last club.

NIBLO, Thomas Bruce
Right or left-winger/inside or centre-forward: 47 apps. 9 goals
Born: Dunfermline, 24 September 1877.
Died: Walker, Newcastle-upon-Tyne, July 1933
Career: Cadzow Oak FC (1893), Hamilton Academical
(1894), Linthouse (August 1896), Newcastle United
(£900, April 1898), Middlesbrough (on loan, season
1899-1900), Aston Villa (January 1902), FOREST (May
1904), Watford (May 1906), Newcastle United (July
1907), Hebburn Argyle (player-manager, August 1908),
Aberdeen (player, December 1908), Raith Rovers (August
1909), Cardiff City (£10, December 1910), Blyth
Spartans (February 1911), Fulham (WW1 guest, 1915-
16), Crystal Palace (WW1 guest), Isle of Wight football

O

(1919-20). He later returned to Tyneside where he became a publican.

A rare and stylish ball dribbler, Scottish international Tommy Niblo (one cap gained after appearing in a trial match) had a brilliant leftfoot. He displayed his versatility by appearing in all five forward-line positions during a fine career that spanned 27 years (at least). One contemporary report noted he was 'a genuine worker, who is smart in seizing opportunities.' As with many footballers Niblo's only downfall was perhaps his inconsistency and the tendency to take on far too many opponents when setting off on one of his mazy runs. Nevertheless he was good enough to play for his country (as an Aston Villa player) and all told amassed in excess of 200 appearances at senior level. Signed to replace Sid Sugden (who was switched to the right-wing) he made his League debut for Forest at centre-forward in a 3-2 defeat at Wolves in September 1904.

NICHOLSON, George Henry

Goalkeeper: 78 apps.

Born: Carlisle, 25 January 1932

Career: Carlisle United (amateur), Grimsby Town (August 1952), FOREST (on trial July 1955, signed on a free transfer, August 1955), Accrington Stanley (free, March 1958), Leyton Orient (March 1959), Bristol City (July 1960), Poole Town (July 1961).

Harry Nicholson was a well proportioned goalkeeper who helped Forest gain promotion to the First Division in 1957. He had been a reserve-team player with Grimsby for most of his three years at Blundell Park (making only 17 appearances for the Mariners) and went on to enjoy his best spell in League football at the City Ground, adding only half-a-dozen further appearances with his other three clubs (4 with Orient).

NORRIS, Robert

Left-half: 148 apps. 7 goals

Born: Preston, Lancs, 1875.

Career: South Shore, Blackpool (June 1896), FOREST (May 1898), Doncaster Rovers (August 1904-May 1906). Bob Norris played in Blackpool's first-ever Football League game against Lincoln City (away) on 5 September 1896 (Division 2). He was an ever-present that season and missed only seven games in 1897-98 before his transfer to Forest. He spent six years with the Reds, amassing almost 150 first-team appearances, following his debut in the second game of the 1898-99 season away to Sheffield Wednesday. A forceful, intelligent, no-nonsense half-back he gave very little away and although not the greatest passer of the ball, he certainly knew how to kick it...'clearing his lines with alacrity' said one reporter.

*Norris' son, Eric, was on Forest's books and so was his grandson in later years.

NORTH, Thomas Williamson

Inside-forward: 3 apps.

Born: Barrow-on-Soar, Leicestershire, 31 October 1913.

Died: 1996

Career: Banbury Spencer (Birmingham League), FOREST (August 1943-May 1947).

Tommy North made his senior debut for Forest at the age of 32 versus Watford in the FA Cup competition January 1946, having already scored 12 goals in 45 regional WW2 matches. He had proved a useful and nimble forward in the Birmingham League, but was a shade too old to make the grade in League football, despite his noble efforts.

OAKES, John

Centre-half: 2 apps.

Born: Winsford, Cheshire, 13 September 1905.

Died: Perth, Australia, 20 March 1992

Career: Cargo Fleet & Cochrane FC (May 1928), Chilton Colliery, FOREST (August 1928), Newark Town (May 1930), Clapton Orient (on trial, September 1930), Crook Town (October 1930), Southend United (March 1931), Crook Town (July 1932), Spennymoor United (February 1933), Middlesbrough Police FC (briefly in 1933), Aldershot Town (August 1934), Charlton Athletic (£1,144, March 1936); served in RAF during WW2, also guesting for Brentford, Clapton Orient, Crystal Palace, Millwall and Tottenham Hotspur; Plymouth Argyle (free transfer, July 1947-June 1948), Snowdown Colliery (manager, May 1949-February 1953), Gravesend & Northfleet (trainer, July 1953); Coached in Sweden until 1959. Later worked in a paper mill at Northfleet (1974-75) and thereafter lived in the USA before moving to Australia. Where he died at the age of 86.

An extremely strong and sturdy centre-half, John Oakes was 42 years, seven months and 21 days old when he played his 234th and final League game for Plymouth Argyle v. Bradford Park Avenue in May 1948, Pilgrims' boss Jack Tresadern having shocked the football world when he signed him from Charlton. Almost 19 years earlier (September 1929) he had made his Football League debut for Forest v. Millwall (away).

Capped by England v. South Africa in an unofficial Test Match in 1939 and v. Wales in a Wartime international in 1940, Oakes was a Football League (South) Cup winner with Charlton v. Chelsea in April 1944 and at the age of 40 he gained an FA Cup runners-up medal in 1946 when the Addicks lost to Derby County at Wembley.

Oakes, whose career saw him accumulate well over 400 club appearances, was Aldershot's leading marksman with 15 goals in 1934-35 (he hit 19 in 61 outings for the Shots all told).

OAKTON, Albert Eric

Outside-right/outside-left: 7 apps. one goal

Born: Kiveton Park, Sheffield, 28 December 1906.

Died: Sheffield, 5 August 1981

Career: Kiveton Park, Grimsby Town (November 1924), Rotherham United (July 1926), Worksop Town (May 1927), Sheffield United (briefly in 1928), Scunthorpe & Lindsey United (cs. 1930), Bristol Rovers (May 1931), Chelsea (May 1932), FOREST (June 1937 to August 1939). Did not play after WW2.

Scorer of 28 goals in 112 League and Cup games for Chelsea prior to joining Forest, Eric Oakton was certainly past his best when he signed, yet he still possessed some neat touches and an aggressive style. Very promising as a youngster, fast and direct, he took in three major clubs before he had turned 20.

O'DONNELL, Francis Joseph

Centre-forward/inside-left: 10 apps. 5 goals
Born: Buckhaven, Fife, Scotland, 31 August 1911.
Died: Macclesfield 4 September 1952
Career: Wellesley Juniors, Celtic (September 1930), Preston North End (£5,000 including his brother Hugh, May 1935), Blackpool (£8,000 plus two players, November 1937), Aston Villa (£10,500, November 1938), FOREST (January 1946), Buxton Town (player, June 1947, then player-manager and manager until his death in 1952).

A dashing, lively, well built striker, Frank O'Donnell was capped six times by Scotland (1937-38) before joining Forest. He netted a total of 72 goals in 161 games in the Football League either side of WW2 and played for PNE in the 1937 FA Cup final defeat by Sunderland, scoring in every round of that season's competition. He was well past his sell by date when he joined Forest but still averaged a goal every two games, obliging with a strike on his debut for the club in a Second Division match at Barnsley in August 1946 (lost 3-2). O'Donnell scored 58 goals in 83 senior games for Celtic.

O'HARE, John

Inside or centre-forward/latterly right-half: 122+11 apps. 20 goals
Born: Dumbarton, Scotland, 24 September 1946
Career: Sunderland (juniors, August 1961, amateur 1962, professional October 1963), Derby County (£22,000, August 1967), Leeds United (£50,000, August 1974), FOREST (£60,000 plus another player, February 1975), Dallas Tornado (on loan, April 1977 & May 1978), Belper Town (May 1980); retired in 1981, Carriage & Wagon FC (1982), Ockbrook FC (manager, 1983) then Stanton FC (March 1988), having by now entered the licensing trade in Derby after which he took employment with a combustion firm. He later worked as a stock-controller for a Derby-based car dealer.

An Anglo-Scottish Cup winner and then a League Cup winner with Forest in 1977 and 1979 respectively, John O'Hare also helped the Reds gain promotion to the First Division in 1977 (as runners-up), grab the League title in 1978 (making 10 appearances) and, albeit as a substitute,

lift the European Cup for a second time in 1980.

He had a fine career, scoring plenty of goals - well over 125 in all competitions, including 94 in 406 games in the Football League alone, helping Derby win the Second and First Division championships in 1969 and 1972 respectively. Neither stylish nor fast, O'Hare was still extremely effective. A first-rate team-man, always willing to take a target role, being rugged and so unselfish, he was capped 15 times by Scotland between 1970-72 and he also represented his country in three Under-23 internationals. Brian Clough, who had coached O'Hare when he was a young striker at Sunderland, regarded him as "absolutely essential to his style" and Alan Hinton, a former playing colleague, said: "Anyone in defence or midfield knew that 'Solly' would be available. You only had to glance up to find him and if he was given the ball, it was his. It wouldn't fizz back past you and put the defence under pressure."

O'KANE, William James

Defender: 220+14 apps. one goal
Born: Londonderry, Northern Ireland, 17 June 1948
Career: Derry City (July 1964), FOREST (£10,000, December 1968, retired in May 1977); joined Forest's coaching staff and was later appointed reserve-team coach at the City Ground, attaining first-team duties soon afterwards, a position he still retains, making him the club's longest serving member of staff (35 years).

Liam O'Kane was injured when making his League debut for Forest on the last day of the 1968-69 season (v. Leeds United). He battled hard and long throughout that summer to regain full fitness and after replacing Terry Hennessey in the centre-half position, he made 108 first-class appearances over the next three seasons before injury struck again. He then switched to right-back when taking over from Peter Hindley in March 1973 and went on to make 234 senior appearances for the Reds before another sequence of irritating injuries put paid to his career. O'Kane, a cultured defender, won 20 caps for Northern Ireland.

OLSEN, Benjamin Robert

Full-back/midfielder: 14+4 apps. 2 goals
Born: Harrisburg, USA, 3 May 1977
Career: Washington DC United (December 1997), FOREST (on loan, October 2000-March 2001).

After appearing for his country in the Sydney Olympics (narrowly missing out on a bronze medal) Ben Olsen joined Forest on an extended loan period. He did well as an effervescent wide-right midfield player who could also slot in at full-back (if required). A broken ankle, suffered in March, ended his days at the City Ground. He was capped by the USA at senior level, having earlier played in a handful of Under-23 internationals.

O'NEIL, Brian

Defender/midfielder: 4+1 apps.

Born: Paisley, Scotland, 6 September 1972

Career: Celtic Boys Club, Celtic (November 1989), FOREST (on loan, March 1997), Aberdeen (July 1997), Wolfsburg/Germany (July 1998), Derby County (November 2000). Preston North End (January 2003).

A versatile performer, able to play in defence or midfield, Brian O'Neil made 155 senior appearances for Celtic (10 goals scored) during his six years at Parkhead. A fine passer of the ball, he has represented his country in six full, seven Under-21, Youth and Schoolboy international.

O'NEILL, Martin Hugh Michael,

Midfielder: 348+23 apps. 62 goals

Born: Kilrea near Coleraine, Northern Ireland, 1 March 1952.

Career: St Columbus School/Londonderry (Gaelic football); St Malachy's College/Belfast (Gaelic football); Distillery (professional, August 1969), FOREST (£25,000, October 1971), Norwich City (£250,000, February 1981), Manchester City (£275,000, June 1981), Norwich City (£150,000, January 1982), Notts County (free transfer, August 1983, retired as a player through injury, May 1985); then out of football for two years; Grantham Town (manager, July 1987), Shepshed Charterhouse (manager, July-October 1989), Wycombe Wanderers (manager, February 1990-June 1995), Norwich City (manager, June 1995-December 1995), Leicester City (manager, December 1995-June 2000), Celtic (manager, July 2000 to date).

As a 19-year-old Martin O'Neill won the 1971 Irish Cup with Distillery (who defeated Derry City 3-0 in the final) and then played against Barcelona in the European Cup. Then, after moving to the City Ground, he added many more medals to his collection as the Reds triumphed in the following competitions: the Anglo-Scottish Cup in 1977, a League championship medal in 1978, successive League Cup winners' prizes in 1978 & 1979, European Cup and European Super Cup medals after wins over SV Hamburg and CF Barcelona respectively, both in 1980. He also helped the Reds win promotion to the First Division in 1977 and gained a runners-up medal in the League Cup final of 1980 when Forest lost to Wolves. He later assisted Norwich in gaining promotion from Division Two in 1982 before his playing career was halted following a serious leg injury suffered while playing for Forest's rivals, Notts County, in February 1985 (v. Shrewsbury Town).

As a manager he took Wycombe to glory in the FA Trophy in 1991 and 1993, and gain promotion to the Football League as GM Vauxhall Conference champions in 1993, quickly leading the Chairboys into Division Two (via the play-offs) in 1994.

He then lifted Leicester City back into the Premiership (via the play-offs) in 1996, took the Foxes to victory in the League Cup finals of 1997 (v. Middlesbrough) and 2000 (v. Tranmere Rovers) and then in his first season with Celtic, he led the Bhoys to the Scottish treble (in 2000-01), seeing them retain the League title the following year with a record 103 points and reach the final of the Scottish Cup (beaten by Rangers). He also took the Parkhead side into both the European Champions League and UEFA Cup competitions.

Despite a clash of personalities with manager Brian Clough, Martin O'Neill (who was dropped for the 1979 European Cup final v. FF Malmo) developed into a world-class midfielder with Forest. Linking up superbly well with Archie Gemmill, he gave some stunning performances in the engine-room with his strong, purposeful running and determination. He was a vital cog in the Forest mechanism as well as doing the business for his country, scoring 19 goals in 64 full internationals for Northern Ireland, his first cap coming against USSR in 1972 and his last versus Finland in 1985. In fact, he was Forest's most-capped player with 36 until that total was bettered by Stuart Pearce in 1991-92. He skippered the Irish in the 1982 World Cup finals in Spain. O'Neill, who was awarded the MBE in 1982 (for services to football, as a player) appeared in 657 competitive games as a professional (at club and international level) with 428 coming in the Football League alone. He netted a total of 125 goals (65 in the League). As a manager (to the end of the 2002-03 season) O'Neill had seen his charges participate in over 780 first-class matches, seeing Celtic lose in the final of the UEFA Cup (to FC Porto) in Seville in May 2003.

ORGILL, Harold

Goalkeeper: 7 apps.

Born: Hucknall, Notts, 1 October 1920. Died: 1980

Career: Basford FC (Notts), FOREST (March 1947, professional April 1947), Notts County (June 1947-May 1948).

An emergency signing by Forest, goalkeeper Harry Orgill played in seven League games when Reg Savage was out of action during the latter stages of the 1946-47 season. He had only two senior outings during his season with the Magpies.

ORME, Joseph Henry

Goalkeeper: 11 apps.

Born: Staveley, Derbyshire, 8 November 1884.

Died: Nottingham, June 1935.

Career: North Wingfield Red Rose, Chesterfield Town (cs. 1909), Pinxton Colliery, Watford (July 1911), Millwall (may 1913), FOREST (September 1918 to cs. 1921), Heanor.

A reserve with Forest for two seasons, goalkeeper Joe Orme made his League debut in the 1-1 draw with Tottenham Hotspur in November 1919, replacing the injured Josh Johnson. His best run in the first team came early in the 1920-21 season when he played in six successive Division One matches including home and away fixtures against Notts County.

P

ORR, Anderson
Half-back: 45 apps.
Born: Glasgow, Scotland, 19 December 1923.
Career: WW2 football, Third Lanark (July 1946), FOREST (August 1951-May 1955).
Alan Orr spent four years at the City Ground having previously done exceedingly well in the Scottish League. A hard-working wing-half, he went straight into the first team at the start of the 1951-52 season and made 24 League appearances during that campaign, the majority in the right-half position. With Horace Gager, Bill Morley, Jack Burkitt and then Jack French the main challengers for the middle-line places, he spent most of 1952-53 and half of the following season in the reserves before replacing French. Orr eventually left the Reds in 1955 when manager Billy Walker settled for a midfield trio of Morley, Bob McKinlay and Burkitt.

ORLYGSSON, Thorvaldur
Midfielder: 37+8 apps. 4 goals
Born: Akureyri, Iceland, 2 August 1966
Career: KA Akureyri/Iceland (May 1986), FOREST (£175,000, December 1989), Stoke City, (free transfer, August 1993), Oldham Athletic (£180,000, December 1995; retired, June 1999).
Icelandic international Toddy Orlygsson could play wide right or in central midfield. Combative and strong in his running, he grafted hard and long and generally gave an honest performance for every club he served. After leaving Forest he scored 19 goals in 110 games for the Potters and netted once in 88 outings for the Latics before retiring in 1999 through injury. He was capped 41 times by his country.

OSCROFT
Outside-left: one app. one goal
Born: circa 1870
Career: FOREST (season 1891-92)
Oscroft, a reserve winger, played once for Forest's first XI, scoring in a 2-1 Alliance League win away at Small Heath in April 1892

OSVOLD, Kjetil
Midfielder/winger: 5+2 apps.
Born: Aalesund, Norway, 5 June 1961
Career: IK Start (1981), Lillestrom SK (1985); FOREST (£100,000, March 1987), Leicester City (on loan, December 1987), FC Djurgaarden/Sweden (£70,000, April 1988), PAOK Thessalonika (April 1989), Lillestron SK (1990 to 1992).
Forest boss Brian Clough, despite spending big money, gave the blond Norwegian international left-sided midfielder Kjetil Osvold few first-team opportunities. In fact 'Ossie' made only 11 League appearances in the Football League - seven with Forest and four with Leicester City - before returning to Scandinavia. He scored the winning goal for Norway v. Argentina in 1986 when his career was at its peak.

OTTEWELL, Sidney
Inside-forward: 32 apps. 2 goals
Born: Horsley, Derbyshire, 23 October 1919.
Career: Holbrook Miners' Welfare, Chesterfield (November 1936), guested for Fulham, Bradford City, Blackpool, Birmingham, Chester and Tottenham Hotspur during WW2 when free from RAF duties; Birmingham City (June 1947), Luton Town (December 1947), FOREST (July 1948), Mansfield Town (January 1950), Scunthorpe United (March 1952), Spalding United (as player-manager, 1954), Lockheed Leamington (manager, 1960-January 1969).
After being recommended to Chesterfield by a Detective Sergeant in the Police Force, Sid Ottewell had a successful career at Saltergate, netting 12 goals in 42 League games, having made his debut at the age of 17. He helped the Stags finish runners-up in Division Three North in 1951. Unfortunately he failed to make his mark at St Andrew's and had a moderate time with the Hatters. Despite his powerhouse shooting he only managed two goals in more than 30 outings for Forest before joining Scunthorpe United in their second season of League football.

OYEN, Davy
Leftback: 4+5 apps.
Born: Bilzen, Belgium 17 July 1975.
Career: R C Eenk (1993), Sint Truiden (cs. 1994), RC Genk (cs. 1995), PSV Eindhoven (cs. 1998), RSC Anderlecht (cs. 1999) Nottingham Forest (February 2003).
Davy Oyen was a pre-transfer deadline signing from Anderlecht - brought in by manager Paul Hart to strengthen the possibilities on the left side of the defence. Earlier in his career he had won three caps for Belgium.

PAGE, Walter
One app.
Career: FOREST (season 1904-05)
Page made his only appearance for Forest v. Wolves on 31 December 1904.

PALMER, Calvin Ian
Utility: 106 apps. 14 goals
Born: Skegness, 21 October 1940
Career: Skegness Town, FOREST (March 1958), Stoke City (£35,000, September 1963), Sunderland (£70,000, February 1968), Cape Town FC/South Africa (summer, 1970), Crewe Alexandra (October 1971-January 1972).
Calvin Palmer made close on 350 senior appearances for his four English clubs (298 in the Football League, 165 of them with Stoke City for whom he played in the 1964 League Cup final defeat by Leicester City.
Able to play in a variety of positions, including those of full-back, right-half, centre-half (in an emergency), in midfield and as a forward, he was a grafter to the last and made his League debut for Forest against Arsenal in April 1959 (on the right-wing in a 1-1 draw). He established himself in the first team at the City Ground from

November 1960 and was a very consistent performer up to his departure (following injury) to the Victoria Ground in 1963.

Palmer now lives in Skegness.

PALMER, Carlton Lloyd

Defender/midfielder: 14+2 apps. one goal

Born: Rowley Regis, West Midlands, 5 December 1965

Career: West Bromwich Albion (apprentice July 1983, professional, October 1984), Sheffield Wednesday (£750,000 plus Colin West, February 1989), Leeds United (£2.6 million, June 1994), Southampton (£1 million, September 1997), FOREST (£1.1 million, January 1999), Coventry City (£500,000, September 1999), Watford (on loan, September 2000), Sheffield Wednesday two loan spells: February 2001 & September 2001), Stockport County (player-manager, November 2001 to September 2003).

Capped 18 times by England at senior level, the tall, lanky, long-striding Carlton Palmer also represented his country in five 'B' and four Under-21 internationals, and in 2002 he reached the personal milestone of 700 club and international appearances of which 285 came with Sheffield Wednesday. He did very well with WBA but wanted a bigger stage and moved to Hillsborough where he spent five-and-a-half years, two of them under manager Ron Atkinson who later signed him for Forest. In fact, Big Ron always admitted he made a huge mistake by not signing Palmer for Manchester United when he had the chance in 1985-86. Totally committed, aggressive, always on the surge, Palmer gave a good account of himself in the red shirt of Forest but was quickly lured away soon after the team had dropped out of the Premiership at the end of the 1998-99 campaign. He took on a difficult job at Stockport as the Edgeley Park club was already doomed to relegation from Division One when he moved into the hot seat in 2001.

PALMER, A W

Inside/centre-forward: 2 apps

Born: circa 1867

Career: FOREST (season 1889-90)

A reserve forward who had just two outings for Forest in the Football Alliance, making his debut as leader of the attack in a 4-0 defeat at Grimsby on 21 September 1889

PALMER, William

Outside-left: 16 apps. one goal

Born: Barnsley, 1888

Career: Barnsley (July 1907), Mexborough Town (March 1908), FOREST (May 1909), Rotherham County (May 1910), Bristol Rovers (August 1912), Everton (July 1913), Bristol Rovers (August 1919), Gillingham (May 1922), Doncaster Rovers (June 1923 to cs. 1924).

An efficient left-winger, with good pace, Bill Palmer made his debut for Forest in September 1909 in the local derby

with Notts County (won 2-1). He had Alf Spouncer and Jack Horrocks to contest the position with early on and then, after the emergence of Bill Vaughan in March he was placed in the reserves. He made a total of 116 League appearances in a varied career (18 goals scored).

PARKER, Frederick

Centre-half: 167 apps. 3 goals

Born: Maryhill, Glasgow, 27 March 1891

Career: Manchester City (May 1914), FOREST (August 1919), Southport (August 1926).

Standing 6ft 2ins tall, well built with powerful thighs, Fred Parker came into the Forest side to play in between Joe Mills and Jack Armstrong in the half-back line when League football resumed after WW1. A fine figure of a man, strong in the tackle, he gave everything he had out on the pitch and made 40 appearances for the Reds when promotion was gained from the Second Division in 1922. Parker began to struggle with his fitness during the 1923-24 campaign and after being replaced by Gerry Morgan he eventually left the club to sign for Southport at the age of 35.

PARKER, Garry Stuart

Midfielder: 146+5 apps.29 goals

Born: Oxford, 7 September 1965

Career: Luton Town (apprentice, June 1981, professional May 1983), Hull City (£72,000, February 1986), FOREST (£260,000, March 1988), Aston Villa (£650,000, November 1991), Leicester City (£300,000, February 1995). Retired in June 1999 to join the coaching staff at Filbert Street.

Twice a League Cup winner in 1989 and 1990, Garry Parker also played in the FA Cup final defeat by Spurs in 1991 and scored twice in Forest's 4-3 Simod Cup final victory over Everton at Wembley in 1989. He was a Worthington Cup winner with Aston Villa in 1994 and Leicester in 1997, also helping the Foxes reach the Premiership (via the play-offs) in 1996. Regarded as one of the finest right-sided midfield players in the country during the early 1990s, Parker - who took six months to gain a regular place in the Forest side, eventually taking over from Brian Rice to link up with Neil Webb and Steve Hodge - was honoured by England as a Youth team level before adding one 'B' and six Under-21 caps to his collection.

PARKER, John

Inside-right/centre-forward: 5 apps.

Born: Stoke-on-Trent, 1895.

Career: Shrewsbury Town, FOREST (February 1920), Tranmere Rovers (August 1920), Shrewsbury Town (November 1920), Bristol Rovers (August 1922), Stalybridge Celtic (October 1923), New Brighton (1927), Rhyl (1929-30).

A big, strong bustling player, Jack Parker's forceful methods made him a handful for most defenders, although at times he was rather cumbersome especially on heavy grounds. He made his League debut for Forest against Grimsby Town in February 1920 (won 2-0) and later in his career he scored six goals in 27 League games for Bristol Rovers and eight in 38 for New Brighton. He ha scored prolifically for Shrewsbury in the Birmingham League prior to this.

PARKER, Robert Norris
Centre-forward/inside-left: 51 apps. 12 goals
Born: Maryhill near Glasgow, Scotland, 27 March 1891. Died: 1950
Career: Jordan Hill, Glasgow Rangers (1909), Everton (November 1913), FOREST (May 1921-May 1923)
Bob Parker played for Forest in their 1922 Second Division promotion winning campaign directly after a terrific eight-year spell at Goodison Park. Indeed, he immediately solved the scoring problem at Everton, netting 55 goals in 65 games for the Merseysiders in his first two seasons, equalling the club record and topping the First Division charts in 1914-15 when the Toffees won the League championship. After returning to action following WW1 (he managed only 7 goals in seven games during the hostilities) he went on to register a total of 71 in 92 first-class games overall before transferring to Forest. And remember, all this was when the offside rule was different to what it is today - there had to be three men (not two) behind the ball in those days! Parker made his League debut for Forest in a 4-1 defeat at Crystal Palace in August 1921 and scored his first goal for the Reds 48 hours later in a 3-2 home win over Hull City.
It was said of Parker that he was 'a dandy of a player who likes to score goals in two and threes, not singles.' He hit seven hat-tricks for Everton.

PARKINSON, Robert
Centre-forward/outside-right: 2 apps.
Born: Preston, 27 April 1873
Career: Preston Ramblers, Preston Athletic, Fleetwood Rangers, Rotherham Town, (December 1894), Luton Town (May 1893), Blackpool (August 1896), Warmley (June 1897), FOREST (October 1898), Newton Heath (November, 1899), Watford (November 1900), Swindon Town (cs. 1901).
Mainly a centre-forward, Bob Parkinson never really made much of an impact with any of his clubs. His best form was shown with Newton Heath (scoring seven goals in 15 League games) and he who played in Blackpool's first-ever Football League game v. Lincoln City in September 1896.

PARR, Joseph
Outside-right: one app.
Born: circa 1873
Career: FOREST (season 1894-95)
A reserve right-winger, Joe Parr made his only appearance for Forest in the United Counties League game v. Leicester

Fosse on 21 April 1895 when he deputised for Horace Pike in a 3-0 win.

PARR, John Barry
Goalkeeper: one app.
Born: Weston-Super-Mare, 23 November 1942
Career: Ransome & Marles FC, FOREST (November 1962, released May 1965).
John Parr was second choice goalkeeper at the City Ground (behind Peter Grummitt) when called up for his Football League debut against Ipswich Town in November 1963. He did well in a 3-1 victory, but thereafter was confined to the reserves before leaving the club in 1965.

PASCOLO, Marco
Goalkeeper: 6 apps.
Born: Sion, Switzerland, 9 May 1966
Career: FC Sion (1985), Neuchatel Xamax (1989), Servette (1991), Cagliari /Italy (September 1996), FOREST (July 1997-May 1998), FC Zunich (1999), Servelte (May 2002). Experienced international goalkeeper Marco Pascolo (54 full caps to his credit and more than 250 appearances under his belt in Swiss League and Cup football) was 6ft 2ins tall and weighed in at 14st 4lbs. He spent just the one season at the City Ground (signed initially as competition and cover for big Dave Beasant and Mark Crossley). Injuries meant that he was pushed into early action but he was then injured himself and on regaining full fitness found his way barred by Beasant. He returned to play in Switzerland after being refused a new contract.

PATRICK, Roy
Full-back: 59 apps.
Born: Overseal, Derbyshire, 4 December 1935
Career: Derby County (juniors, June 1951, professional February 1952), FOREST (May 1959), Southampton (June 1961), Exeter City (March 1963), Burton Albion (August 1965-May 1966)
Roy Patrick made his Football League debut for Derby County v. Sunderland in September 1952 at the age of 16 years, 277 days and was the Rams' youngest post-war player until Steve Powell's debut in 1971. Strong in the tackle and positionally sound, he made exactly 50 senior appearances during his time at the Baseball Ground and was recruited by Forest immediately after the FA Cup triumph over Luton. He was introduced into the Reds' first XI in place of Bill Whare for the third game of the new season v. Blackburn Rovers and had 23 League outings in 1959-60 and 34 the following year before transferring to the Dell, later assisting Exeter City and then Burton Albion before a back injury forced him to retire in 1966. At that point he took employment at the Rolls Royce factory (in Derby) before moving to Scotland.

PEACOCK, Dennis

Goalkeeper: 24 apps.

Born: Lincoln, 19 April 1953

Career: FOREST (apprentice, June 1969, professional April 1971), Walsall (on loan, March 1973), Doncaster Rovers (July 1975), Bolton Wanderers (March 1980), Doncaster Rovers (August 1982), Burnley (on loan, September 1985). Retired from League football in May 1986.

During a splendid career, goalkeeper Dennis Peacock amassed a total of 387 League appearances, 329 for Doncaster. Powerfully built, with a safe pair of hands, over the years he pulled off some stunning saves and although he wasn't a regular in the first XI with Forest, he gained a lot of experience and know-how from watching and training with the likes of Peter Grummitt, Alan Hill, Dave Hollins and Jim Barron.

PEACOCK, Thomas

Inside-left: 120 apps. 62 goals

Born: Morton, Derbyshire, 14 September 1912.

Career: Chesterfield (as an amateur during season 1930-31), Bath City (1932) Melton Mowbray FC, FOREST (professional, August 1933-May 1946). Did not play after WW2.

Tom Peacock - a schoolteacher by profession - scored four goals in a League game for Forest on four separate occasions: twice v. Port Vale in 1933 & 1935 and versus Barnsley and Doncaster Rovers, both in 1935. He also netted a hat-trick v. Fulham in 1936 and another treble in an FA Cup-tie v. QPR in 1934.

Tall and confident, he was Forest's leading marksman in seasons 1934-36 when he formed an excellent strike-force with Johnny Dent. A thinker he was dangerous anywhere within sight of the framework of the goal and often tried a shot from well outside the penalty-area. He would have played many more games for Forest had not injury affected his routine during the 1936-38 campaigns when, in fact, he made only 16 senior appearances and netted six goals. WW2 effectively ended his footballing career although he did manage to net seven times in 17 Regional games, making his last appearance for the Reds against Derby County in October 1945. He also guested for several other clubs during the hostilities when free from his duties in the RAF, attaining the rank of flight-sergeant. On his return to Civvy Street he went back to teaching and later became headmaster at St Edmund's Primary School, Mansfield Woodhouse, Notts.

PEARCE, Stuart

Left-back: 522 apps. 88 goals

Born: Hammersmith, 24 April 1962

Career: Wealdstone, Coventry City (£25,000, October 1983), FOREST (£200,000, June 1985), Newcastle United (free transfer, July 1997), West Ham United (free transfer, August 1998), Manchester City (free transfer, July 2001, retired in May 2002, aged 40).

What a bargain buy Stuart Pearce turned out to be! Signed for just £200,000 by Brian Clough, he spent 12 years at the City Ground and during that time amassed well over 500 senior appearances, scoring almost 90 goals - a phenomenal return for a full-back. Just mention the nickname 'Psycho' and everyone knew who he was!

A living embodiment of power, passion, pride, presence and pure commitment, Pearce earned the reputation as one of the fiercest tacklers in the game. A wonderful competitor whose defensive qualities were second to none, his leadership A1, Pearce has certainly been one of Forest's greatest-ever players.

With a cracking left-footer from outside the area, he scored Forest's goal in their 2-1 FA Cup final defeat by Spurs in 1991. He was twice a League Cup winner with the Reds (in 1989 and 1990), and he also collected winners' medals for victories in the Simod Cup and Zenith Data Systems Cup finals of 1989 and 1992 respectively, and he helped Forest gain promotion to the Premiership in 1994. Honoured once by England at Under-21 level, he went on to appear in 78 full internationals (76 with Forest - the club's most capped player) including games in both the World Cup finals and European Championships. That missed penalty in the World Cup semi-final showdown with Germany in Turin in 1990, didn't affect him unduly. Indeed, like the true professional, he bounced back (as ever) and belted in his next spot-kick without blinking an eye-lid. A tremendous competitor, a true leader, he brought the curtain down on a truly wonderful career by helping Manchester City regain their Premiership status in 2002. By that time he had played in no fewer than 900 matches for his five senior clubs and for England, scoring over 100 goals in the process.

PEERS, Edward John

Right-back/centre-half: 66 apps.

Born: Hednesford, May 1876.

Career: Hednesford Rovers, West Bromwich Albion (reserves, June 1895), Walsall (May 1896), FOREST (August 1899), Burton United (October 1901), Swindon Town (season 1903-04), Coventry City (briefly, August-October 1904)

Ted Peers, no relation to the famous Welsh international goalkeeper of the same name, was a resilient, hard-tackling full-back, who scored twice in 73 League games for Walsall before joining Forest. He made his senior debut for the Reds against Preston North End in September 1899 and held the right-back berth comfortably before the emergence of Jack White, thus allowing Jimmy Iremonger to switch over from the left.

PEPLOW, Stephen Thomas

Winger: 5 apps.

Born: Liverpool, 8 January 1949

Career: Liverpool (apprentice, June 1964, professional January 1966), Swindon Town (on loan, March 1970, signed permanently May 1970), FOREST (free transfer, July 1973), Mansfield Town (on loan, December 1973), Tranmere Rovers (£6,000, January 1974-May 1981).

Frozen out at Anfield with only two League games under his belt, Steve Peplow scored 11 goals in his 40 outings with Swindon and that sort of form prompted manager Allan Brown to sign him for Forest. Unfortunately he struggled to get going at the City Ground and after a loan spell at Field Mill, he signed for Tranmere for whom he went on to do great things, making 248 League appearances and netting 44 goals, helping the Birkenhead club gain promotion to Division Three in 1976.

PETRACHI, Gianluca

Midfielder: 12+3 apps.
Born: Lecce, Italy, 14 January 1969
Career: Lecce (1986), Nola FC (cs. 1988), Taranto (cs. 1989), Arezzo (November 1990), Fidelis Andria (cs. 1991), Venezia (cs. 1993), Torino (cs. 1994), Palermo (October 1994), Cremonese (cs. 1996), Ancona, 1996), Perugia (August 1998), FOREST (£1.2 million, August 1999), Perugia (August 2000), Taranto

Signed with his colleague, Salvatore Matrecano from Italian Serie A side Perugia where he had spent a season, the experienced 29-year-old Gianluca Petrachi (with 280 Serie A and B games under his belt) had good pace and a combative approach, playing as a right-sided midfielder. However, after getting injured in mid-September 1999, he rarely figured after that and was released at the end of the season, rejoining Perugia.

PHILLIPS, David Owen

Right-back/midfielder: 146+13 apps. 5 goals
Born: Wegberg, Germany, 29 July 1963
Career: Plymouth Argyle (apprentice, July 1979, professional August 1981), Manchester City (£65,000, August 1984. Coventry City (£150,000 plus Perry Suckling, June 1986), Norwich City (£525,000, June 1989), FOREST (August 1993), Huddersfield Town (free transfer, August 1997), Lincoln City (free transfer, March 1999), Stevenage Borough (June 2000).

Although born in Germany (where his Caerphilly-born father was stationed in the RAF) David Phillips was a Welshman who was capped five times as a Youth player and on four occasions by the Under-21's, before going on to appear in 62 full internationals. He helped Manchester City gain promotion to the First Division and later assisted Forest in reaching the Premiership in 1994. A right-sided midfielder with a powerful shot (he scored some stunning goals in his time) Phillips could also do a fine job in the right-back position and if required, could be an efficient man-marker. He first made a name for himself when Argyle reached the 1984 FA Cup semi-final (beaten by Watford). He helped Coventry win the FA Cup in 1987 and was signed by Norwich to replace Mike Phelan (sold to Manchester United). He did well at

Carrow Road (186 outings) and during his six years at the City Ground, he became a firm favourite with the fans, initially as partner to Lars Bohinen, Scot Gemmill and Steve Stone in the engine-room and later aiding and abetting Chris Bart-Williams among others. When he quit top-line football in 2000, Phillips had amassed a fine record of 718 club appearances and 71 goals. His League stats were impressive too - 593 games and 62 goals.

PIKE, Horace

Outside right or left/inside-left: 180 apps. 56 goals
Born: Keyworth, 1870
Career: Keyworth, FOREST (1885), Loughborough (August 1897)

The youngest of three brothers all of whom played for Forest, Horace Pike was in excellent form in 1891-92 when Forest won the Football Alliance title. He scored 8 goals in 21 games playing mainly on the left-wing. Fast and clever with a strong shot, he made his senior debut for the Reds in a 2nd round FA Cup replay v. Chatham in February 1889 (2-2). He scored his first goal for the club five days later when Forest lost to the Kent side 3-2 in a second replay at the Oval. He lined up at inside-left in the Reds' first-ever Football League game v. Everton in September 1892, holding his place in the side until January 1896.

PLACKETT, Henry

Utility: 15 apps. one goal
Born: Nottingham, circa 1867
Career: FOREST (seasons: 1888-90)

Harry Plackett was one of the game's earliest utility players. He occupied five different positions in his first full season with Forest (1889-90), lining up at right-half, centre-half, outside-right, centre-forward and inside-left. He made his senior debut in the club's first-ever game in the Football Alliance v. Walsall Town Swifts (away) on 7 September 1889 (won 3-1).

PLACKETT, Leonard

Outside-left: 10 apps. 4 goals
Born: Nottingham, circa 1864
Career: FOREST (season 1889-90)

Podgy left-winger Len Plackett played alongside and with his brother Harry in nine Alliance games in 1889-90, making his senior debut for the club in that opening fixture against Walsall TS.

PLATT, David Andrew

Born: Oldham, 10 June 1966
Career: Chadderton, Manchester United July 1984), Crewe Alexandra (free transfer, January 1985), Aston Villa (£200,000, February 1988), Bari (£5.5 million, July 1991), Juventus (£6.5 million, June 1992), Sampdoria (£5.25 million, August 1993), Arsenal (£4.75 million, July 1995), Sampdoria (free-transfer, player/coach/manager,

August-November 1998), Nottingham (player-manager, August 1999-June 2001). Appointed England Under-21 manager/coach, July, 2001.

David Platt became Britain's most expensive footballer of all time in terms of total transfer fees (£22.2 million) when he joined Arsenal from Sampdoria in 1995. (He has, of course, since lost that distinction). He had earlier moved from Villa Park to Bari to Juventus to Sampdoria for a combined total of £17.25 million.

An attacking midfielder with flare, drive and an excellent scoring record Platt was released by Manchester United in 1985 without ever appearing in a first-team game. He was steadily nurtured at Gresty Road, and claimed 60 goals in 152 games for the Alex before making a name for himself in a big way, first with Aston Villa, next in Italy and finally with Arsenal.

Platt then returned to Sampdoria for a brief but unsuccessful spell as coach, returning to the Football League in 1998 to take charge of relegated Nottingham Forest (in succession to Ron Atkinson).

He helped Villa win promotion to the First Division in his first season with the club but the lure of the Italian lira meant that he was a certainty to play in Italy's Serie A and he spent four excellent seasons over there during which time he played in more than 120 matches and scored over 30 times.

Having netted 27 times in 62 international appearances for England, Platt is now in eighth position in the list of his country's top 10 marksmen of all-time. He scored his country's only goal in Euro' 92. He also represented England in three 'B' and three Under-21 matches and gained both a Premiership and FA Cup winners' medal with the Gunners in 1997-98. When the curtain came down on the 2000-01 season, Platt moved on, having failed to get Forest back into the Premiership (they finished 14th and 11th in Division one in successive seasons with him in charge). His overall record as a professional footballer was superb - 585 appearances and 201 goals. As boss of England's Under-21 side, Platt is now hoping to help develop younger players who will form the basis of the full international side in years to come.
* Platt is now a racehorse owner and has already seen his horses win major races.

PLATTS, Lawrence

Goalkeeper: 8 apps.
Born: Worksop, 31 October 1921.
Career: FOREST (juniors 1941, professional October 1943), Chesterfield (July 1951), Burton Albion (August 1952), Stockport County (February 1953).

WW2 interrupted goalkeeper Larry Platts' early career and he never really made his mark in the game, although he did make almost 60 appearances for Forest during the hostilities. After leaving the City Ground he had 11 League outings for Chesterfield and 28 for Stockport.

PLEAT, David John

Winger: 6 apps. one goal
Born: Nottingham, 15 January 1945
Career: FOREST (apprentice, June 1960, professional January 1962), Luton Town (£8,000, August 1964), Shrewsbury Town (1967), Exeter City (July 1968) Peterborough United (July 1970), Nuneaton Borough (player-manager, July 1971), Luton Town (reserve team coach, July 1972, chief coach, December 1977, then manager from January 1978 to May 1986), Tottenham Hotspur (manager, June 1986-October 1987), Leicester City (manager, October 1987-January 1991), Luton Town (manager, July 1991-May 1995), Sheffield Wednesday (manager, June 1995-November 1997). He subsequently returned to White Hart Lane (January 1998) as Spurs' Director of Football and after that twice acted as caretaker-manager of the London club - for a four-week period during September & October 1998 and for a short while in March & April 2001, just prior to Glenn Hoddle's arrival. David Pleat was a very useful teenage winger who represented England at Schoolboy level before joining Forest. He added a cluster of Youth caps to his collection - and had half-a-dozen first-team outings with Forest, scoring on his League debut against Cardiff City in February 1962 - before moving to Kenilworth Road. Three years and 70 League games later he was transferred to Shrewsbury and after spells with Exeter (68 League outings) and Peterborough (29 appearances) he entered management for the first time with non-League side Nuneaton Borough. Pleat guided Luton to the Second Division championship in 1982 and Spurs to the FA Cup final five years later (beaten 3-2 by Coventry City).

PLUMMER, Calvin Anthony

Winger/forward: 21+3 apps. 6 goals
Born: Nottingham, 14 February 1963
Career: FOREST (apprentice, June 1979, professional February 1981), Chesterfield (December 1982), Derby County (August 1983), Barnsley (March 1984), FOREST (December 1986) Reipas Lahti/Finland (1987), FOREST (October 1987), Plymouth Argyle (September 1988), Chesterfield (July 1989), Gainsborough Trinity (September 1991), Shepshed Albion, Corby Town, Nuneaton Borough, Birstall United (Leicester Senior League). Calvin Plummer, another of soccer's many nomads, scored 34 goals in a total of 223 League appearances made over a period of eight years (1982-90). A busy, powerful footballer, who used both feet effectively, he made his debut for Forest against Brighton (away) in February 1982 but failed to hold down his position in the first XI owing to the presence of so many different types of players including Peter Ward, Jurgen Rober and Ian Wallace - and when he returned to the City Ground (following an injury to Franz Carr) he still had to battle for his place in the starting line-up depending on the formation chosen by manager Brian Clough.

PONTE, Raimondo
Midfielder: 24+8 apps. 7 goals
Born: Windisch, Switzerland, 4 April 1954
Career: Grasshoppers/Switzerland (August 1975), FOREST (August 1980-May 1981), Bastia France (July 1981), Grasshoppers (cs. 1982),FC Baden (coach 1988-1991 and again 1993-94), FC Zurich (coach (March 1995-April 2000), Luzern (coach July 2001), Carrarese/Italy (coach cs. 2002).
Swiss international Raimondo Ponte spent just one season at The City Ground. Manager Brian Clough thought the 26-year-old would add a new dimension to the Reds' style of play. However, one feels he was never really suited to the English game and despite some useful performances he spent only eight months with Forest before moving to the French club, FC Bastia.

POOLE, Harold
Centre-forward: one app.
Born: Bulwell, Notts, circa 1890
Career: Newstead Rangers, FOREST (July 1911), Coventry City (August 1912), Sutton Town (August 1913). Did not figure after WW1.
Reserve centre-forward Harry Poole failed to make much headway with Forest, his only League appearance coming in the 2-0 home defeat by Barnsley in April 1912 (being the third different player in the No 9 position in successive matches). He didn't do much either with Coventry (just two outings).

PORFIRIO, Hugo Cardoso
Winger/forward: 3+6 apps. one goal
Born: Lisbon, Portugal, 28 September 1973
Career: Sporting Lisbon (1992), UD Leiria (on loan, 1995), West Ham United (on loan, September 1996), Racing Santarder (cs. 1997) Benfica (cs. 1998), FOREST (on loan, January 1999). Diminutive Portuguese international (2 caps)Hugo Porfirio scored four goals in 27 games for West Ham during his first spell in English soccer. A very skilful and creative player, who could be used as a direct winger or through the middle, he struggled at Forest with injury and returned to Benfica after four-and-a-half months at the City Ground.

PORTER, William Carr
Centre-half: 14 apps.
Born: Sunderland, 24 January 1908
Career: Hylton Colliery, Nottingham University, FOREST (seasons 1931-34)
A rugged, well-built defender, Bill Porter acted as first reserve to Messrs Graham and Smith and then Pugh during his three years at the City Ground. He also figured in one game at inside-left, having made his Football League debut at centre-half v. Stoke City on Christmas Day 1931 (when he played in between McKinlay and Graham).

POWELL, Alfred Frank
Inside-left: one app.
Born: Nottingham, circa 1881
Career: FOREST (seasons 1904-06)
Forest reserve, Alf Powell made just one League appearance for the Reds during his two years at the club, taking over the inside-left berth in a 3-2 home defeat by Sunderland in October 1904 when injuries caused changes to be made in the forward-line.

POWELL, John
Goalkeeper: 25 apps.
Born: Burlsem, Stoke-on-Trent, 3 June 1892.
Died: Chesterton, Staffs, 7 February 1961.
Career: Port Vale (cs. 1911), Walsall (March 1914), FOREST (season 1914-15).Port Vale (August 1916-May 1918). A reserve goalkeeper with both Port Vale and Walsall (no League games for either club) he took over between the posts at the City Ground from Harry Iremonger but had Bill Fiske challenging him for a first-team place when WW1 broke out. He did not figure in competitive football after the hostilities.

PRICE, Ernest Clifford
Inside-forward: 21 apps. 6 goals
Born: Market Bosworth, 13 June 1900.
Career: Coalville Swifts, Leicester City (amateur, January 1917), Coalville Swifts (on loan, November 1919), Leicester City (professional, October 1920), Halifax Town (June 1922), Southampton (December 1923), FOREST (July 1926), Loughborough Corinthians (October 1928), Nuneaton Town, Gresley Rovers, Snibston United. Retired in 1936.
Cliff Price scored 33 goals for Leicester during WW1 and a year after making a scoring League debut (v. Spurs) he turned professional at Filbert Street. He was a studious contributor to the attacks of both Saints and Forest, linking up well (for a time) with Noah Burton at the City Ground. * Cliff was the uncle of Fred Price who also played for Leicester City and Southampton, Wolves and Chesterfield.

PRITTY, George Joseph
Wing-half: 54 apps. one goal
Born: Aston, Birmingham, 4 March 1915. Died: 1996.
Career: HB Metro Old Boys FC, Aston Villa (May 1933), FOREST (December 1938). Retired in May 1948.
A hardy, resolute wing-half, George Pritty made only four first-team appearances for Villa, acting as reserve to Bob Iverson. Despite WW2, he fared much better with Forest, and had 21 League outing in his first season at the City Ground. After service in the forces, he returned to have another useful campaign in 1946-47 (26 League games). He lost his place to Noel Simpson in September 1947. Pritty was sent-off in April 1939 and it was more than 30 years before another Forest player was dismissed in a League game.

Q

PROCTOR, Mark Gerard

Midfielder: 72+4 apps. 9 goals

Born: Middlesbrough, 30 January 1961

Career: Middlesbrough (apprentice, June 1977, professional September 1978), FOREST (£440,000, August 1981), Sunderland (£115,000, March 1983), Sheffield Wednesday (£275,000, September 1987), Middlesbrough (£300,000, March 1989), Tranmere Rovers (free transfer, March 1993), South Shields (May 1994), Hartlepools United (non-contract, March-May 1997).

An England Youth and Under-21 international (4 caps gained in the latter category) Mark Proctor was a tireless, hard-working midfielder who amassed a fine record during his 20-year career. He played in a total of 598 club appearances (59 goal scored). With Forest, he partnered Ian Bowyer and John McGovern in the engine-room and produced some excellent displays before transferring to Roker Park.

PROUDLOCK, Adam David

Striker: 3 apps.

Born: Telford, Shropshire, 9 May 1981.

Career: Wolverhampton Wanderers (trainee, July 1997, professional July 19990, Clyde (on loan, August 2000), FOREST (on loan, March 2002), Tranmere Rovers (on loan, October 2002), Sheffield Wednesday (on loan, December 2002 permanent September 2003).

An England youth international, Adam Proudlock was brought in on loan by Forest manager Paul Hart in an effort to boost the strike-force following Stern John's departure to Birmingham City. He failed to produce the goods and quickly returned to Molineux.

PRUTTON, David Thomas

Midfielder: 153+2 apps. 7 goals

Born: Hull, 12 September 1981

Career: FOREST (trainee, August 1997, professional October 1998), Southampton (£2.5 million, January 2003).

After gaining Youth caps for England, Dave Prutton was then upgraded to the under 21's (under ex-Forest player-manager David Platt) and became a regular in the side, going on to appear in 14 internationals. A near-ever present in the Reds' side in three successive seasons, 2000-03, he performed with great stability and commitment and although he was drafted into a more defensive position, Prutton was most at home in midfield and got better by the game hence his big-money transfer to Southampton just prior to the transfer-window closing in January 2003.

PUGH, Robert Archibald Lewis

Inside-left/left-half: 265 apps. 19 goals

Born: Symonds Yat, Wye Valley, 16 September 1909.

Died: Newport, January 1986.

Career: Symonds Yat FC, Chepstow, Hereford United (1926), Newport County (as an amateur September 1926, professional December 1927), Bury (August 1929), FOREST (£200, January 1931-August 1938). Did not play after WW2. Later worked in the Royal Ordnance Factory (Nottingham) and continued his connection with Forest by becoming a scout.

A giant defender, Jack Pugh toured Canada with the Welsh FA in 1929 and on his return quickly moved from Newport to Bury. He would have gained full international honours but on checking his personal documents more thoroughly it was found that he had been born a few miles the wrong side of the Welsh border. Described as: '...tall, sometimes leisurely but always clever and an artist with the ball, especially when there is mud around' Pugh was a skilful and robust, a clever player who went into every game aiming to enjoy it. He was part of a powerful Forest half-back line with Billy McKinlay and Tommy Graham. He made a total of 342 League appearances all told (42 goals scored). He was forced to retire in 1938 after failing to recover from a serious leg injury suffered when playing for Forest against West Ham in March of that year.

QUANTRILL, Albert Edward

Outside right or left: 14 apps. 2 goals

Born: Punjab, India, 22 January 1897.

Died: Trefriw, 19 April 1968.

Career: Boston Swifts, Derby County (November 1914), Preston North End (June 1921), Chorley (August 1924), Bradford Park Avenue (September 1924), FOREST (May 1930, retired May 1932). Later became a successful insurance broker,

An England international winger (4 caps gained, 1920-21) Alf Quantrill netted 72 goals in 342 League games during a career that spanned well over 20 years. His best days came at Bradford for whom he struck over 60 goals in almost 200 competitive matches. Son-in-law of the great Steve Bloomer, he was generally regarded as an outside-left, though he also appeared on the right-wing. He had speed, a useful shot and required little space in which to take on and beat an opponent.

QUASHIE, Nigel Francis

Midfielder: 45+8 apps. 3 goals

Born: Peckham, London, 20 July 1978

Career: Queen's Park Rangers (trainee, July 1994, professional August 1995), FOREST (£2.5 million, August 1998), Portsmouth (£200,000+, August 2000).

Capped four times by England at Under-21 level, Nigel Quashie has also represented his country's Youth and 'B' teams. The talented, six-foot tall midfielder, whose first touch, vision and tackling can be of the highest quality at times, made over 60 appearances for QPR before his big-money move to Forest in 1998. He lost his way during the 2001-02 season with Pompey, collecting far too many yellow cards, but bounced back in style the following year as the Fratton Park club surged into the Premiership.

R

QUIGLEY, John

Inside-forward: 270 apps. 58 goals

Born: Glasgow, 28 June 1935

Career: Glasgow Ashfield (Glasgow), FOREST (July 1957), Huddersfield Town (February 1965), Bristol City (October 1966), Mansfield Town (£3,000, July 1968, then assistant player-manager/trainer-coach, until in November 1971). Later coached in the Middle East for two years to 1974.

Johnny Quigley had a fine career in League football, netting 64 goals in 474 League games, his best years coming at the City Ground. He made his senior debut for the Reds against Spurs (away) at the start of the 1957-58 season and was a regular in the side for some six years (injuries apart) before being replaced in the forward-line by John Barnwell. Quigley was the first Forest player to score a post-war First Division hat-trick (v. Manchester City in November 1958) and it was his FA Cup semi-final goal (v. Aston Villa) that sent the Reds through to Wembley at the end of that season where they went on to beat Luton Town to lift the trophy. He then gained an FA Charity Shield runners-up prize with the Reds (1959) and later skippered Mansfield Town, leading then in two excellent FA Cup runs and to victory in the Giant Killers Cup final in 1969.

RACE, Harold

Inside-left/centre-forward: 124 apps. 30 goals

Born: Evenwood, County Durham, 7 January 1906.

Died: 1941

Career: Raby United, Liverpool (October 1927), Manchester City (£3,000, July 1930), FOREST (June 1933), Shrewsbury Town (May 1937), Hartlepools United (August 1938 until his death).

Harry Race scored 18 goals in 43 games for Liverpool and three in 11 for Manchester City before joining Forest. A local reporter described him as 'the hardest worker and most consistent member of the attack and, on sticky grounds, the brains and driving force of the line.' Another verdict was that the 'forward-line always languished without him, Harry was a schemer who makes openings for others.' He made his League debut for Forest against Brentford in August 1933. He was killed during WW2.

RADFORD, Arthur

Inside or outside-left or right: 5 apps.

Born: Nottingham, circa 1876

Career: FOREST (seasons 1897-99), Gainsborough Trinity (to 1902).

Arthur Radford was a versatile forward whose League debut for Forest was against Bury in April 1898 when he replaced Alf Spouncer and set up one of his side's goals in the 2-2 draw. After leaving Forest, he scored 23 goals in 64 League games for Trinity.

RADNALL, Charles H

Goalkeeper: one app.

Born: Arnold, 1881

Career: FOREST (seasons 1905-07).

Reserve goalkeeper Charlie Radnall made his one and only League appearance for Forest against Lincoln City in April 1907 when he deputised for Harry Linacre in a 3-1 win.

RANSFORD, Herbert

Inside-left: 4 apps. one goal

Born: Blackwell, Derbyshire, 25 September 1901.

Career: South Normanton, FOREST (May 1922), Alfreton (August 1924).

Bert Ransford spent two seasons with Forest, playing regularly in the reserves. He made his League debut against the previous season's beaten FA Cup finalists, West Ham United, (away) in December 1923 when he was selected ahead of Noah Burton to take the place of the injured Jack Spaven.

RAWSON, Colin

Wing-half: 2 apps. one goal

Born: Langwith, Derbyshire, 12 November 1926.

Career: Shirebrook FC, Welbeck Colliery, FOREST (September 1944), Peterborough United (August 1947), Rotherham United (July 1948), Sheffield United (March 1953), Millwall (October 1955), Torquay United (July 1959), Taunton Town (1962).

After failing to gain a place in Forest's first team, wing-half Colin Rawson went on to make well over 450 appearances at senior level (427 in the Football League, including 159 for Millwall and 111 for Rotherham) before dropping down to a lower level in 1961.

A clever, stylish performer, he was a Third Division North championship winner with Rotherham in 1950-51. He added guile and class to both the Millwall and Millers' half-back lines and he skippered the Lions for four seasons before moving to Devon, quickly helping Torquay gain promotion to the Third Division in 1960. Rawson was one of the few players to appear in all six Divisions of the Football League (1,4, 3 South and 3 North).

RAWSON, Kenneth

Centre-half/inside-left: 6 apps.

Born: Nottingham, 31 March 1921

Career: FOREST (August 1944-May 1950)

After starting his career as an inside-left (he played there for Forest during the latter stages of WW2) Ken Rawson found himself acting as reserve to Horace Gager at the City Ground after the hostilities were over. He got very few first-team opportunities owing to the form of Gager (and his defensive colleagues) and after a long spell in the second XI he left the club in 1950 with only six senior games under his belt, having made his Football League debut against Plymouth Argyle (away) in December 1947.

RAYNOR, Paul James
Forward/midfielder: 4 apps.
Born: Nottingham, 29 April 1966
Career: FOREST (apprentice, June 1982, professional April 1984), Bristol Rovers (on loan, March 1985), Huddersfield Town (free transfer, August 1985), Swansea City (free transfer, March 1987), Wrexham (on loan, October 1988), Cambridge United (free transfer, March 1992), Preston North End (£36,000, July 1993), Cambridge United (free transfer, September 1995), Guang Deong FC/China (free transfer, August 1997), Leyton Orient (non-contract, February-May 1998). Stevenage Borough (cs. 1998), Kettering Town (September 1998), Ilkeston, Boston United (February 2000).
A two-footed midfielder, Paul Raynor never got a chance at the City Ground but after leaving the Reds his career blossomed and when he quit League football in 1998 his overall appearance tally (in first-class competitions) stood at more than 550 (65 goals scored). He gained two Welsh Cup winners' medals with Swansea (in 1989 & 1991).

REED, Ebor
Centre-half/left-half: 5 apps.
Born: Spennymoor, 30 November 1899.
Died: Durham, 14 November 1971.
Career: Spennymoor United, Newcastle United (August 1922), Cardiff City (August 1925), FOREST (July 1926), Rotherham United (May 1927), Derry City (1929-30).
Due to the wealth of half-backs Forest had to choose from, Ebor Reed, a strong tackler, found the chances of first-team football limited until he joined Rotherham in 1927. He failed to get a game with Newcastle, made only six appearances for Cardiff and five with Forest.

REES, Ronald Raymond
Outside-left and right: 88+13 apps. 13 goals.
Born: Ystradgynlais near Swansea, 4 April 1944.
Career: Coventry City (apprentice, July 1960, professional May 1962), West Bromwich Albion (£65,000, March 1968), FOREST (£60,000, February 1969), Swansea Town (£26,000, February 1972). Retired in May 1975 at which time he chose to work in the administration department at Cardiff City before taking full-time employment with a large car manufacturer in Bridgend. In 1989-90 he came out of retirement to appear with his son for Bishopston in the Swansea Senior League.
Welsh international left-winger Ronnie Rees won 39 full caps between 1965-72, plus seven at Under-23 level. He represented Merthyr Schools before signing apprentice forms for Coventry. He was transferred to WBA (as a replacement for Clive Clark) after scoring over 40 goals in 230 League outings for the Sky Blues, helping them win the Third Division & Second Division championships in 1964 & 1967 respectively. A player with a direct style, he took over on Forest's left flank from the injured Storey-

Moore and when Moore returned to full fitness, Rees was switched to the right. He continued to do well and it came as a bit of a surprise when he left the club (after more than 100 games), unable to hold his place in the front-line owing to the presence of Barry Lyons and indeed Storey-Moore.
A record fee (for Swansea) took him from the City Ground to the Vetch Field before injury problems forced him into retirement. Rees is now living in Bishopston, near Swansea.

REID, Andrew Matthew
Striker/winger: 85+25 apps. 14 goals
Born: Dublin, 29 July 1982
Career: FOREST (apprentice, July 1998, professional August 1999).
Already capped by the Republic of Ireland at Youth and under-21 levels (14 games for the latter) Andrew Reid is an excellent crosser of the ball, reminiscent of John Robertson in his hey-day. He is confident on the ball and looks set for bigger and better things in the game, Reid gained his first full cap for the Republic of Ireland v. Canada in 2003.

REID, Robert T
Inside-right: 10 apps. one goal
Born: Larkhall, Glasgow, circa 1890
Career: Larkhall FC, FOREST (July 1912-May 1915). Did not play competitive football after WW1.
Basically a reserve at Forest for three seasons, Bob Reid scored his only goal for the club in a 5-3 win at Burnley in January 1913 when he partnered four-goal hero Tommy Gibson in the Reds' attack. He had made his League debut against Fulham the previous month.

RICE, Brian
Midfielder: 106+12 apps. 13 goals
Born: Bellshill, Scotland, 11 October 1963
Career: Hibernian (junior 1979, professional October 1980), FOREST (August 1985), Grimsby Town (on loan, October 1986), West Bromwich Albion (on loan, January 1989), Stoke City (on loan, February 1991), Falkirk (August 1991), Dunfermline Athletic (October 1995), Clyde (August 1997), Morton (March-cs.2000).
Scottish Youth and Under-21 international Brian Rice made his First Division debut for Forest against Liverpool at Anfield in September 1985. He had gained a lot of experience north of the border with Hibs for whom he made his first senior appearance as a substitute against Motherwell in September 1980 at the age of 16. A strong-running player, who preferred to man the left-hand side of the pitch, Rice went on to amass a total of 116 appearances in the Football League (nine goals scored) before returning to Scotland with Falkirk.

RICHARDS, Charles Henry
Inside-right: 82 apps. 26 goals
Born Burton-on-Trent, Staffs, August 1875.
Career: Gresley Rovers, Notts County (summer, 1894), Nottingham Forest (January 1896), Grimsby Town (January 1899), Leicester Fosse (July 1901), Manchester United (August 1902), Doncaster Rovers (March 1903).
Sammy Richards was an FA Cup winner with Forest in 1898 and a Second Division championship winner with Grimsby in 1901. One pen-picture stated that he was '...hardly a rip-roaring character but invaluable for his foraging and ability to fit into a side'. He certainly had an eye for goal and during his career netted 68 times in almost 200 League games for his five major clubs. He was capped once by England v. Ireland in March in 1898, playing in front of his Forest team-mate Frank Forman. Richards wrote his name in the history books by scoring the first League goal under the club's new title of Manchester United in a 1-0 win at Gainsborough Trinity in 1902.

RICHARDS, Stanley
Left-back/right-half: 3 apps.
Born: Beeston, Notts, 15 April 1916.
Career: Beeston St John's (1933), FOREST (July 1937-May 1943). Did not play senior football after WW2.
A reserve at the City Ground, Stan Richards was called up for League action just twice, making his bow in the competition at right-back against Blackburn Rovers (away) in April 1938 and then having his last game v. Tranmere Rovers (home) in February 1939 (at left-back). He remained a registered player with the club until 1943.

RICHARDSON, James George
Right-half: one app.
Born: West Bromwich, circa 1875. Died: circa 1950
Career: All Saints Methodists, Churchill Swifts, West Bromwich Albion (September 1892), FOREST (August 1897-May 1899).
A reserve with WBA (no first-team outings) and also with Forest, Jim Richardson made just one League appearance for the Reds - in a 4-0 defeat at Sunderland in April 1898 when he became the fourth different player to occupy the right-half position in successive matches.

RICHARDSON, Paul
Midfielder: 224+24 apps. 21 goals
Born: Shirebrook, Notts, 25 October 1949
Career: FOREST (apprentice August 1965, professional August 1967), Chester (October 1976), Stoke City (£50,000, June 1977), Sheffield United (£25,000, August 11981), Blackpool (on loan, January 1983), Swindon Town (July 1983), Swansea City (non-contract, September-December 1984). Retired from first-class football in January 1985; became manager of Gloucester City (1985-87) and then Fairford FC, while also working for British Telecom.

Tall and stylish midfielder Paul Richardson had an excellent career in top-class football, making 437 League appearances and scoring 32 goals. An England Youth international, he made his First Division debut for Forest as a substitute in a 2-1 defeat in front of 26,724 fans at Southampton in September 1967 and played his last game 16-and-a-half years later for Swansea v. Plymouth Argyle before a crowd of 3,124 at the Vetch Field (December 1984). In between times, after giving Forest supreme service for some 11 years, he scored the vital goal (against Notts County) on the last day of the 1978-79 season to clinch promotion to the First Division for Stoke City. He actually played in a variety of positions early in his career including those of left-back, both inside-forward berths and left-half. He finally gained a regular place in the side in 1970 and formed a fine engine-room link with Peter Cormack and then Martin O'Neill. Unfortunately he did not figure in Brian Clough's plans and was subsequently signed by Alan Ball for Stoke, perhaps playing the best football of his career at the Victoria Ground.

RIDLEY, James
Outside-left: 4 apps. one goal
Born: Wallsend-on-Tyne, circa 1882.
Career: Byker East End, Willington Athletic, Newcastle United (£50, February 1907), FOREST (£150, February 1911), Wallsend FC (September 1919).
Jim Ridley made only 17 first-class appearances for Newcastle in a four-year stay at St James' Park, helping the Geordies win the First Division title in 1909 (five games). He also collected four successive North Eastern League championship-winning medals with United. A smart dribbler he was also very fast over the ground and once won the famous Morpeth Handicap as well as taking prizes in other sprinting events. He was reserve to Jack Ford during his time with Forest and scored his only goal for the club in a 3-2 defeat at Arsenal a week after making his League debut v. Sunderland (February 1911).

RILEY, David Sydney
Midfielder/forward: 8+5 apps. 2 goals
Born: Northampton, 8 December 1960
Career: Keyworth United, FOREST (January 1984), Darlington (on loan, February 1987), Peterborough United (on loan, July 1987), Port Vale (£20,000, October 1987), Peterborough United (on loan March 1990, signed permanently for £40,000), thereafter with Kettering Town (May 1992), Ponsonby FC/New Zealand (1993), Boston United (1993), King's Lynn.
After leaving the City Ground, having failed to gain a regular first-team place, David Riley went on to score 36 goals in 172 League games before drifting into a lower grade of football in 1992. A shade on the small side, he was not afraid of the bigger and stronger opponents who challenged him and he gave as good as he got in most of the games he played in.

RITCHIE, Archibald
Full-back: 205 apps.
Born: Kirkcaldy, Fife, 12 April 1872.
Died: Nottingham, 18 January, 1932
Career: Aberdour FC (Fife), East Stirling, FOREST (August 1891, retired in May 1899 through injury)
Capped once by Scotland (v. Wales in 1891), Archie Ritchie played for Forest when they won the FA Cup in 1898 - although he nearly missed the final with Derby after suffering a bad injury in the semi-final v. Southampton. Thankfully he recovered to play a fine game against the Rams. With Forest he formed a superb full-back partnership with Adam Scott and, indeed, they were perhaps the smallest players occupying those two defensive positions in the game at that time - Ritchie was 5ft 6ins tall and Scott 5ft 5ins. Ritchie was a rock-like performer, also a fine positional player, who kicked long and true and rarely did he commit a foul within shooting distance of the goal! He appeared in 17 games in season 1891-92 when Forest won the championship of the Football Alliance. After his playing days were over, he became a respected crown green bowler and won many pairs competitions with another ex-Forest star, Bob Norris. He later became a licensee in Nottingham.

RITCHIE, Samuel Joseph
Half-back: 7 apps.
Born: Northern Ireland, circa 1890
Career: Glentoran (1910) FOREST (April 1913), Belfast Celtic (August 1914).
Signed as cover for the efficient half-back trio of Armstrong, Mercer and Needham, Sam Ritchie started the 1913-14 season in Forest's first XI, making his debut at centre-half (in place of Mercer) in a 3-1 home defeat by Leicester Fosse. When Mercer returned, however, Ritchie dropped back into the reserves and was only called into action on six more occasions, playing his last game for the Reds at right-half against Blackpool in February 1914.

ROBER, Hans Jurgen
Wide-midfielder: 21+1 apps. 4 goals
Born: Gernrobe, West Germany, 25 December 1953
Career: Werder Bremen (1974), Bayern Munich (cs 1980), Calgary Boomers / NASL (April 1981) FOREST (December 1981), Bayer Leverkusen (July 1982 to cs. 1986), Rot Weics Essen (coach), Vfb Stuttgart (coach, December 1993-April 1995), Herthe BSC Berlin (coach cs. 1996-February 2002), Vfi Wolfsburg (coach March 2003). Midfielder Jurgen Rober spent just the one season with Forest, starting 21 League games in the right-wing position. His first goal in English football earned the Reds a 2-0 League Cup win over Tranmere Rovers at the City Ground in December 1981 and his first League goal secured a 1-0 win at Coventry in March 1982. He later netted at Elland Road and Goodison Park before returning to his homeland.

ROBERTS, Edward Thomas
Inside-right/centre-forward: 7 apps.
Born: circa 1880
Career: FOREST (seasons 1901-03)
Tom Roberts was registered with Forest for two seasons and during that time he made just seven League appearances, lining up for his debut against Small Heath (away) in April 1902 (1-1 draw).

ROBERTS, Griffith Orthin
Goalkeeper: 11 apps.
Born: Blaenau Ffestiniog, North Wales, 2 October 1910
Career: Blaenau Ffestiniog, FOREST (May 1946-May 1947), Blaenau Ffestiniog.
Forest's reserve goalkeeper for a season, Griff Roberts replaced Savage early on in the campaign and made seven successive League appearances during one spell. He made his debut in a 5-2 defeat at Southampton on 14 September 1946 and later conceded another four goals at Birmingham before returning to his former club in North Wales.

ROBERTS, Samuel Grenville
Inside-right: 6 apps.
Born: Blackwell, Derbyshire, 16 August 1919. Deceased.
Career: Huthwaite Swifts, Huthwaite Colliery Welfare, FOREST (March 1937-May 1939). He did not figure in top-grade football after the hostilities.
Reserve inside-forward Grenville Roberts spent the last two and a bit pre-WW2 seasons at the City Ground, making just half-a-dozen first-team appearances, partnering Arthur Betts on the right-wing in the last five (during September & October 1938. He made his debut in a 1-0 home win over Luton Town a month after joining the club.

ROBERTSON, Gregor
Defender: 11+5 apps.
Born: Edinburgh, 19 January 1984
Career: Forest (apprentice, April 2000, professional January 2002).
Developed through the ranks at The City Ground, Greg Robertson made his first team debut during the 2003-04 season.

ROBERTSON, John Neilson
Outside-left: 499+15 apps. 95 goals
Born: Uddingston near Motherwell, 20 January 1953
Career: FOREST (juniors, May 1968, professional May 1970), Derby County (June 1983), FOREST (August 1985-May 1986), Corby Town. Thereafter he was a licensee and worked as a sales associate with the Save & Prosper Group before returning to football under former Forest team-mate Martin O'Neill at Wycombe Wanderers (as chief scout), then with O'Neill at Leicester City (as assistant-manager/coach) and next in the same capacity at Celtic.

Twice a European Cup winner with Forest in 1979 & 1980 (his goal beat SV Hamburg in the latter final), left-winger John Robertson also won a League Championship medal in 1978, collected two League Cup winners medals in 1978 & 1979 - he scored a vital penalty in a 1-0 replay victory over Liverpool at Old Trafford in the former - and helped the Reds gain promotion from Division Two in 1977. He was also a winner with Forest in the Anglo-Scottish and Super Cup competitions of 1977 and 1980 and in the latter year played in the losing League Cup final v. Wolves. He continued to reap in the awards as a coach and assistant-manager, especially north of the border with Celtic.

Capped 28 times by Scotland, having earlier represented his country in one 'B' and two Under-21 internationals, Robertson was a touchline player who loved to get to the bye-line before crossing the ball, delivering it high or low, depending on the circumstances.

Although on the small side and seemingly rather slow, while often looking a pound or two overweight, he was nevertheless a fine winger who could turn the course of a game with one flash of brilliance. With his simple jink-and-feint style, he continually deceived his marking full-back and although coaches tried to back up when Robertson was on the march, he still managed to find a way through a packed defence by cutting inside. It was he who unlocked a tight Hamburg back-division to set up Trevor Francis' winning goal in the 1979 Europe Cup final.

ROBERTSON, Peter
Centre-half: 7 apps.
Born: Dundee, 1881
Career: Providence FC (Scotland), Dundee, FOREST (seasons 1904-06), Dundee.
After some useful displays north of the border, defender Peter Robertson found it tough going in the English League and, in fact, managed only seven senior appearances for the Reds during his two years with the club. He started off at the heart of the defence in 1904-05 but was then injured and after regaining full fitness he struggled with his form and as a result failed to get back into the side.

ROBERTSON, Thomas
Wing-half: one app.
Born: Torrance near Glasgow, Scotland, circa 1870
Career: Renton Union FC, Queen's Park (Glasgow), FOREST (September 1892-January 1893), Queen's Park (Glasgow).
An amateur throughout his career, Tom Robertson's only League appearance for Forest came in November 1892 when he deputised at right-half for Billy Smith in a 1-0 defeat at Sunderland. He spent just five months with the Reds.

ROBINS, Robert Walter Vivian
Outside-right: 2 apps.
Born: Stafford, 3 June 1906. Died: 1968
Career: FOREST (two seasons: September 1929-May 1931), Brewood.
An amateur whose only senior outings for Forest came 12 months apart, Walter Robins made his League debut on the right-wing against Barnsley in December 1929 (in place of Fred Scott) and then lined up in the same position against Reading the following year.

ROBINSON, George Henry
Right-half/centre-half: 92 apps. one goal
Born: Basford, Notts, 1877.
Died: March 1945.
Career: Nottingham Jardine's Athletic, Newark, FOREST (May 1898), Bradford City (June 1903-May 1915); played once as a guest for Bradford City during the hostilities and later served as the club's trainer until June 1922.
George Robinson was a splendid defender, a timely tackler and powerful header of the ball whose size (6ft 2ins) gave him a distinct advantage over the majority of opposing forwards. He made his first appearance for Forest against Bolton in April 1899 (when he replaced Bob Norris) and his last against Stoke in February 1903.
Robinson played in Bradford Citys' first-ever League game, away to Grimsby in September 1903, and in his 12-year career at Valley Parade he scored 19 goals in 377 appearances, setting a then new club record of 343 outings in the Football League (which was to stand until 1972). He also had a run of 69 appearances in succession. Robinson captained the Bantams to the Second Division title in 1908 and when they won the FA Cup three years later, being one of only two Englishmen in the side that defeated the favourites Newcastle United after a replay. He received two benefit matches at Valley Parade, in April 1909 (jointly with Jimmy Millar) v. Leicester Fosse and in March 1914 v. Everton.

ROCHE, Barry Christopher
Goalkeeper: 2+1 app. no goals
Born: Dublin, 8 April 1982.
Career: FOREST (trainee, June 1998, professional June 1999)
Tall, commanding Republic of Ireland Youth international goalkeeper Barry Roche saved a penalty on his League debut for Forest after coming on as a substitute to replace red-card victim Dave Beasant in a 3-2 win at Crystal Palace in August 2000. He made his full debut soon afterwards in a 1-0 win over Sheffield Wednesday but was then confined to reserve-team football, until the final game of the 2002-03 season when he replaced Darren Ward between the Sticks.

ROE, Thomas William
Forward: 9 apps. 4 goals
Born: Evenwood, Co. Durham, 8 December 1900.
Died: Durham Wood, December 1972.
Career: Esperley Rovers, Willington Athletic, Durham City (1922), Northfleet (season 1924-25), Tottenham Hotspur (July 1925), FOREST (May 1927), Luton Town (August 1928), Walsall (May 1929), Coventry City (May 1930).
Utility forward Tommy Roe didn't have much success with a lot of the clubs he served, playing his best football with Walsall (8 goals in 41 League games). He made his League debut for Forest in a 2-0 defeat at Fulham in September 1927.

ROGERS, Alan
Midfielder: 152+3 apps. 20 goals
Born: Liverpool, 3 January 1977
Career: Tranmere Rovers (trainee, June 1993, professional July 1995), FOREST (£2 million, July 1997), Leicester City (£300,000, November 2001).
Pacy left-sided midfielder Alan Rogers helped Forest gain a place in the Premiership in 1998 as First Division champions. An England Under-21 international (three caps gained) he made 59 appearances for Tranmere before his big-money move to the City Ground in 1997. His trademark bustling runs, made from deep, often caused problems for defenders and his crossing and shooting ability also made it difficult for the opposition. He suffered his fair share of injuries during his last season with Forest and his first at Filbert Street. He actually tore an anterior cruciate ligament at Gillingham in November 2000. As a result he was sidelined for five months as the Reds battled in vain to keep in touch with the play-off hopefuls.

RONALD, Peter Mann
Centre-forward/right-half: 4 apps.
Born: Wallsend-on-Tyne, 15 November 1899
Career: Hebburn Argyle, Watford (August 1920), FOREST (May 1921), West Stanley (August 1923).
Signed by Forest as cover for the three main strikers, Spaven, Parker and Tinsley, Peter Ronald managed just four League outings for the Reds in two seasons at the City Ground. His debut was against Hull City (away) in early September and his last outing was against Cardiff City at Ninian Park in April 1923 when he actually played at right-half in place of the injured Jackie Belton.

RORKE
Inside-right: 2 apps. one goal
Born: circa 1869
Career: FOREST (season 1891-92)
Reserve inside-forward Rorke scored on his Football Alliance debut for Forest in a 5-1 win at Bootle in September 1891.

ROSARIO, Robert Michael
Striker: 28+2 apps.3 goals
Born: Hammersmith, London, 4 March 1966
Career: Hillingdon Borough (August 1983), Norwich City (December 1983), Wolverhampton Wanderers (on loan, December 1985), Coventry City (March 1991), FOREST (March to November 1995).
Striker Robert Rosario - a 6ft 3in tall and almost 14st in weight - was an England Youth international who went on to gain four Under-21 caps. He netted 18 goals in 126 League games for Norwich and eight in 59 for Coventry before moving to the City Ground. He immediately helped Forest gain promotion from the First Division (1993-94) when he aided and abetted Stan Collymore up front. Strong and powerful both in the air and on the ground, where he shielded the ball well, Rosario was plagued by a cruciate ligament injury in his right knee during his second term with the Reds and was forced to hang up his boots at the age of 29. He subsequently made a come-back in the US-A league with Charleston Battery.

ROSE, Thomas
Centre-forward: 40 apps. 16 goals
Born: Ockbrook, Notts, circa 1872
Career: FOREST (seasons 1894-96)
Tommy Rose had a good strike record with Forest. He made his League debut on 7 April 1894 v. Newton Heath when the Reds were struggling for a centre-forward (they had already used six different players in the position during that season). The following year he was first choice and held his place until the arrival of Dave Smellie.

ROTHERY, Harry
Outside-left: 4 apps.
Born: Yorkshire, circa 1880
Career: Mexborough Town, Sheffield United (1905), FOREST (April 1906-May 1908)
A reserve with both Sheffield United and Forest, left-winger Harry Rothery spent two seasons at the City Ground during which time he made just four senior appearances, all at the start of the 1906-07 season (in place of the injured Alf Spouncer). His Football League debut was against Grimsby Town (away) on 1 September (lost 3-1).

ROWAN, A
Forward: 3 apps. one goal
Born: circa 1869
Career: FOREST (season 1890-91)
A reserve forward, Rowan played for Forest in the 1890-91 Football Alliance season, scoring his only goal for the club in a 6-3 defeat at Birmingham St George's in February when he deputised for Alex Higgins.

ROWAN, Frederick
Outside-right/inside-right: 2 apps.
Born: Southwick, Wearside, circa 1888
Career: Sunderland Royal Rovers, FOREST (August

1908-May 1910), Silksworth FC, (Wearside).

Fred Rowan spent two seasons with Forest, acting in the main as first choice cover for the striking trio of Tom Marrison, Gren Morris and Enoch West. He made his League debut in September 1909 against Liverpool (at home), replacing Marrison in a 4-1 defeat.

ROWLAND, John Douglas

Winger/centre-forward: 31 apps. 3 goals

Born: Riddings, Derbyshire, 7 April 1941

Career: Riddings FC, Ironville Amateurs, FOREST (August 1960, professional April 1961), Port Vale (£6,000, August 1962), Mansfield Town (£6,500, September 1966), Tranmere Rovers (July 1968-May 1969); later with South Shields (between 1971-73).

A fast winger (who could also fill the centre-forward berth) John Rowland possessed a powerful right-foot shot and gained England Youth honours as a teenager. He had two divided seasons with Forest when he contested the right-wing position with first Tony Barton and Billy Gray and then with Barton, Billy Cobb and Trevor Hockey. He went on to score 43 goals in 166 senior games for Port Vale, being the Valiants' leading marksman in 1965-66.

ROWLANDS, Alfred Stanley

Centre-forward: one app.

Born: Coedway near Welshpool, 12 November 1889. Died: Barnstaple, Devon, 7 October 1974

Career: Welshpool, Wellington Town (July 1909), Birkenhead North End (October 1909), South Liverpool (August 1910), Liverpool (December 1910), FOREST (on trial, March-April 1911), South Liverpool (August 1911), Wrexham (June 1912), Tranmere Rovers (season 1913-14), Reading (May 1914), Crewe Alexandra (1918-22), Wrexham (June 1922), Oswestry Town (August 1923), South Molton (player-coach September 1924, retired in May 1926).

A much-travelled, robust, with excellent shot, centre-forward Stan Rowlands' only game for Forest was as a trialist against Sheffield Wednesday (home) in April 1911 when he deputised for Tom Marrison.

He went on to bigger things after leaving the Reds, gaining a full Welsh cap (v. England at Cardiff) in 1914 as a Tranmere player, earning his place after scoring 32 goals for the Birkenhead club when they won the Lancashire Combination title. In fact, despite the gulf between that level of soccer and international football, he was far from outclassed in a 2-0 defeat. Earlier he got injured playing for Liverpool reserves and was released as being 'unsound.' He did well during his second spell at Wrexham. Having served in France during WW1, he spent three years with Crewe, helping them bed into the Football League in 1921. A tailor by profession, Rowlands weighed anchor as coach of South Molton before retiring at the age of 36.

ROY, Bryan Edward Steven

Forward: 93+17 apps. 28 goals

Born: Amsterdam, Holland, 12 February 1970

Career: Ajax Amsterdam (1987), Foggia/Italy (cs. 1992), FOREST (£2.5 million, August 1994), Herthe BSC Berlin (May 1997) NAC Brede (December 2000 to cs. 2001).

Flying Dutchman Bryan Roy arrived at Forest an experienced footballer with over 30 international caps under his belt (he went on to gain a total of 32, scoring 9 goals in the process). He was a record signing by manager Frank Clark, who said at the time: "There is no doubt about Bryan being a world class player and the fact that he has agreed to join us is a remarkable coup on our part." He was so right. Fast, tricky, two-footed with great balance, Roy set Forest alight immediately. His penetrative runs deep into the heart off the opposing defence were breathtaking at times, and he certainly created plenty of space and openings galore for Stan Collymore. He got bogged down on heavy pitches at times but nevertheless he gave the Forest supporters plenty to cheer about during his three seasons at the City Ground.

RUSSELL, David Kennedy

Half-back: 43 apps. 5 goals

Born: Shotts, Lanarkshire, 6 April 1864.

Died: January 1918

Career: Shotts Juniors, Broxburn (1885), Heart of Midlothian (1886), Preston North End (August 1887), FOREST (August 1890), Heart of Midlothian (April 1892), Ardwick (September 1892), Heart of Midlothian (July 1893-May 1895), Notts County (September-December 1895), Heart of Midlothian (January 1896), Celtic (July 1896), Preston North End (August 1898), Celtic (July 1899), Broxburn (May 1903).

David Russell made 23 senior appearances for PNE when they completed the League and FA Cup double in season 1888-89. A beaten Cup finalist (v. WBA) in 1888, he followed up with a second League championship prize with the 'Lillywhites' in 1890. He gained winners' medals with Hearts in the League (1895) and Cup (1896) and did likewise with Celtic, in the League (1898) and Cup (1900). He was also a Cup finalist with the 'Bhoys' (1901) and all told scored 12 goals in his 84 senior appearances for the Glasgow club. In between times (1891-92) he appeared in 13 games and helped Forest win the Football Alliance title.

A Scottish international, six caps gained (1895-1901), Russell also represented the Scottish League and the East of Scotland FA v. the Edinburgh Association. A marvellous defender, Russell's best position was undoubtedly centre-half, where he spent the bulk of his career. His immaculate distribution, speed and spoiling powers, abetted by a good physique, proved an ideal amalgam.

RYALLS, Joseph
Outside-right: 9 apps.
Born: Sheffield, early 1881.
Career: Montrose Works (Sheffield), Sheffield Wednesday (August 1902), Barnsley (May 1905), Fulham (briefly in 1906), Rotherham Town(cs. 1906), Brentford (cs.1908), FOREST (September 1909), Brentford (cs. 1910), Chesterfield Town (cs. 1911).
During his 12 years in competitive football, Joe Ryalls managed only 27 League appearances, his best return coming with Barnsley (17 games). He made just two appearances for the Owls, was a permanent reserve with Fulham, struggled at Rotherham and after leaving the City Ground did likewise at Brentford. He made his League debut for the Reds v. Bolton Wanderers in October 1909 and his last outing was against Chelsea in March 1910. He replaced Bill Hooper in each of his nine senior outings for Forest.

SAUNDERS, Dean
Born: Swansea, 21 June 1964
Career: Swansea City (apprentice June 1980, professional June 1982), Cardiff City (on loan, March 1985), Brighton & Hove Albion (free transfer, August 1985), Oxford United (£60,000, March 1987), Derby County (£1 million, October 1988), Liverpool (£2.9 million, July 1991), Aston Villa (£2.3 million, September 1992), Galatasary (£2.35 million, July 1995), Nottingham Forest (£1.5 million, July 1996), Sheffield United (free transfer, December 1997), Benfica (£500,000, December 1998), Bradford City (free transfer, August 1999). Retired, July 2001.
One of the game's most prolific marksmen, Dean Saunders struck his first goal in League football for Swansea against Oldham Athletic in March 1984. He continued to find the back of the net on a regular basis over the next 17 years! A positive, all-action, unselfish centre-forward who simply knew where the goal was, he scored some cracking goals. His playing record was superb - 805 appearances and 276 goals. Saunders holds the Welsh international record for being the most capped outfield player with 75 outings for his country. Surprisingly he only gained three winners' medals, the first with Liverpool in the FA Cup final of 1992, his second with Aston Villa when they lifted the League Cup in 1994 (he scored twice in the 3-1 win over Manchester United at Wembley) and his third with Forest when they were declared First Division champions in 1998.
His best performances on the whole came with Derby (131 appearances and 57 goals) and Villa (144 outings and 49 goals) but wherever he played he gave his all and during his time at the City Ground, the Forest fans certainly enjoyed what they saw from a top-class striker, who helped the Reds win the First Division, although he left halfway through that campaign for Bradford.

SAUNDERS. Frank Vincent
Centre-forward: 28 apps. 7 goals
Born: Coventry, 1888
Career: Wednesbury Old Athletic (1907), Coventry City (August 1910), FOREST (July 1911), Huddersfield Town (August 1912, retired in January 1913).
A willing, strong and brave centre-forward, Frank Saunders made his League debut for Forest against Leeds City in September 1911. He had an excellent season with the club, averaging a goal every four games before being transferred (perhaps surprisingly) to Huddersfield Town. Unfortunately he did not make the first team at Leeds Road, being forced to retire through injury suffered in training.

SAUNDERS, Glyn
Full-back: 4 apps.
Born: Nottingham, 15 June 1956
Career: FOREST (apprentice, June 1972, professional June 1974). Released by the club at the end of the 1976-77 season.
Glyn Saunders spent five years at the City Ground, during which time he managed just a handful of senior appearances, making his League debut against Fulham at Craven Cottage in August 1976 when he stood in for Viv Anderson.

SAVAGE, Reginald
Goalkeeper: 25 apps.
Born: Eccles, Lancashire, 5 July 1912.
Career: Stalybridge Celtic, Leeds United (February 1931), Queen of the South (July 1939), FOREST (December 1945), Accrington Stanley (August 1947-April 1948).
Goalkeeper Reg Savage had made 79 League appearances for Leeds United and a handful for Queen of the South before joining Forest halfway through the transitional season of 1945-46. Just the right size and build for the last line of defence he had 20 outings for the Reds during the second half of that 1945-46 campaign and made another 20 in the Second Division in the first peacetime season after WW2 before Harry Walker arrived from Portsmouth to take over the number one position.

SAXTON, A George
Outside-right: one app.
Born: Nottingham, circa 1878
Career: FOREST (August 1900-May 1902)
Reserve right-winger George Saxton played in just one League game for Forest during his two years with the club - taking over from the injured Fred Forman at Sunderland in October 1901 (lost 4-0).

SAXTON, Frederick
Outside-right: one app.
Born: Mansfield, Notts, 1916
Career: Sutton-in-Ashfield FC, FOREST (August 1934-

April 1936)

Reserve winger, Fred Saxton's only first-team outing for the Reds was in the League game against Blackpool in September 1934 when he deputised for Arthur Masters.

SAXTON, John

Right-half: 12 apps.

Born: Kimberley, Notts, 18 November 1902.

Died: Bentley, 15 October 1964.

Career: Bentley Colliery, FOREST (July 1924), Southport (August 1927) Scunthorpe & Lindsey (cs. 1928) United, Bentley Colliery (1929).

Jack Saxton made his League debut for Forest in September 1925 against Blackpool. He had two more outings immediately after that but then had to wait a year before getting back into the first team - owing to the excellent and consistent form of Jackie Belton.

He went on to make 35 League appearances for Southport after leaving the City Ground.

SCIMECA, Ricardo

Utility: 162+4apps. 8 goals

Born: Leamington Spa, Warwickshire, 13 June 1975

Career: Aston Villa (trainee, June 1991, professional July 1993), FOREST (£3 million, July 1999), Leicester City (July 2003). Ricardo Scimeca is a very competent, hard-working footballer, able to occupy a variety of positions including those of right and left-back, sweeper, centre-half and central midfield. As his game developed he represented England in one 'B' and nine Under-21 internationals and made 97 first-class appearances for Villa (scoring 2 goals) before transferring to Forest for a huge fee. Appointed captain by Forest manager Paul Hart during the 2001-02 campaign, he is strong in the tackle, effective when pushing forward and totally committed.

SCOTT, Adam

Left-back: 265 apps. 5 goals

Born: Dumfries, Scotland, circa 1867

Career: Coatbridge Albion, FOREST (August 1890, retired May 1900).

One of the smallest defenders in the game during the 1890s (he was only 5ft 5ins tall) Adam Scott formed a splendid full-back partnership with Archie Ritchie and his FA Cup winning medal gained with Forest in 1898 was due reward for his loyalty and contribution to the club. As keen as mustard, he was a tenacious tackler, and was a regular in the Forest side for over six years, helping them win the championship of thee Football Alliance in 1891-92 (missing only three games out of a total of 22). He was eventually replaced in the side by Jimmy Iremonger.

SCOTT, Frederick Hind

Right-winger: 322 apps. 46 goals

Born: Fatfield, County Durham, 6 October 1916.

Died: 1995

Career: Fatfield FC, Bolton Wanderers (January 1935), Bradford Park Avenue (May 1936), York City (February 1937), FOREST (September 1946-May 1957).

Freddie Scott played his 322nd and last game for Forest on 15 September 1956 against Rotherham United (Division 2). He remained a registered player until the end of that campaign. A diminutive winger, Scott was an excellent ball-player who could breeze past a defender with ease before delivering a pin-point cross. He was the only bright spark in an average Forest side during the late 1940s and when Wally Ardron arrived at the club, Scott's contribution was ever greater, as he set up chances galore for the centre-forward. He helped Forest win the Third Division South Championship in 1951 (being an ever-present in the side). He failed to get a League game with either Bolton or Bradford PA but made 76 for York City (16 goals). His left-wing colleague at Bootham Crescent was George Lee who joined Forest in September 1947 to be re-united with Scott. And, in fact, they played in the same Reds' forward-line on more than 60 occasions before Lee departed in 1949 for West Brom.

SCOTT, John

Outside-right/inside-right: 54 apps. 5 goals

Born: Sunderland, 5 February 1908.

Career: Seaham Harbour, Sunderland (July 1924, professional, July 1925), Darlington (August 1926), Crystal Palace (October-December 1928), Kettering Town (January 1929), FOREST (September 1929), Northampton Town (August 1931), Exeter City (August 1932), Hartlepools United (cs. 1936), Blyth Spartans (August 1938).

Jack Scott, although on the small side, was a very dangerous forward - and coolness under pressure was another of his assets. Unable to get a game with either Sunderland or Palace he moved down the ladder to gain experience with Kettering. He made his debut for Forest against Bradford Park Avenue in October 1929 and appeared in 25 League games in his first season, following on with 17 in 1930-31 before losing his place and eventually transferring to Northampton. He later played a major part in Exeter City's promotion bid in 1932-33. Scott scored 21 goals in 139 games for the Grecians and 20 in 70 League outings for Hartlepools, having earlier failed to find the net in 22 outings with the Cobblers.

SCOTT, James

Centre-forward: one app.

Born: circa 1902

Career: FOREST (season 1925-26).

A reserve centre-forward with Forest, Jim Scott made only one League appearance for the Reds, lining up against Swansea Town in February 1926 when he became the sixth player to lead the attack that season.

SEGERS, Johannes
Goalkeeper: 67 apps.
Born: Eindhoven, Holland, 30 October 1961
Career: PSV Eindhoven (November 1977, professional October 1978), FOREST (£50,000, August 1984), Stoke City (on loan, February 1987), Sheffield United (on loan, November 1987), Dunfermline Athletic (on loan, March 1988), Wimbledon (£180,000, September 1988), Wolverhampton Wanderers (free transfer, August 1996), Tottenham Hotspur (free transfer, August 1998, later appointed goalkeeping coach at White Hart Lane).
Hans Segers did well between the posts for Forest, after taking over from Steve Sutton 12 weeks into the 1984-85 season. A year later (September 1985) he was injured at West Ham, lost his place (to Sutton) and never really regained prime position. He went on to appear in 322 senior games for the Dons and when he retired in 2000, he had accumulated in some 600 League and Cup appearances for his eight club, including PSV.

SERELLA, David Edward
Centre-half: 73+3 apps.
Born: Kings Lynn, 24 September 1952
Career: FOREST (apprentice, July 1968, professional August 1970), Walsall (on loan, November 1974, signed permanently December 1974), Blackpool (August 1982), Altrincham (July 1984), Chorley.
Dave Serella was a distinctive centre-half, craggy with heavy moustache, who seemingly was always in the thick of the action, often leaving the pitch with a blood-stained shirt after yet another head or facial injury! He took over the right-half slot at the City Ground in March 1972 and had his best period with the Reds the following season when he formed a fine defensive pairing with Sammy Chapman. He made over 300 appearances for Walsall, helping them gain promotion in 1980.

SEVERN, William
Goalkeeper: 3 apps.
Born: circa 1872
Career: FOREST (season 1894-95)
Reserve goalkeeper Bill Severn deputised for Dan Allsopp in each of his three games for Forest in 1894-95, making his League debut against Preston North End in the October.

SHARRATT, Harold
Goalkeeper: one app.
Born: Wigan, 16 December 1929. Died: 19 August 2002.
Career: Wigan Athletic, Yorkshire Amateurs, Blackpool (May 1952-October 1953), Bishop Auckland, Oldham Athletic (March 1956), Bishop Auckland, FOREST (January 1958), Bishop Auckland (April 1958).
England amateur international Harold Sharratt remained an unpaid footballer throughout his career during which time he made over 200 appearances for Bishop Auckland.

He started out as a centre-half with Wigan but quickly took over between the posts and became a fine custodian, brave and reliable. In October 1951 he appeared for the North v. the South in the annual amateur international trial match and a year later made his debut in the Football League, for Blackpool against Tottenham Hotspur (Division 1). Further honours came his way - for the FA XI (v. the Royal Navy) and the UAU before winning his first England amateur cap v. Wales in 1953. He won three successive FA Amateur Cup medals with the Bishops (1955-56-57) and he also figured in the team that lost to Crook Town in the 1954 final. In the summer of 1955 he toured the Caribbean with the FA party. Sharratt's, only first-team outing for Forest was against Portsmouth in February 1958 when he deputised for Chick Thomson. He worked as a schoolteacher in Leeds in the 1950s.

SHAW, Arthur Frederick
Inside-forward/outside-right: 149 apps. 27 goals
Born: Basford, Notts, 1 August 1869
Career: Notts County (July 1887), FOREST (August 1889), Loughborough Town (May 1897).
Arthur Shaw gave Forest eight years splendid service. Said to have been 'a quick and straight shooter' he helped the Reds win the Football Alliance title in 1891-92 when he appeared in 20 games and scored two goals.

SHEARMAN, Benjamin W
Outside-left: 32 apps. one goal
Born: Lincoln, June 1884. Died: October 1958
Career: Worksop Town, Rotherham Town (seasons 1907-09), Bristol City (August 1909), West Bromwich Albion (£100, June 1911), FOREST (£250, July 1919), Gainsborough Trinity (August 1920), Norton Woodseats (trainer/coach, 1922-38).
Ben Shearman was an elusive left-winger, quick off the mark who delivered strikingly accurate deep crosses, whether hit high or low from the touchline. He gained an FA Cup runners-up medal with WBA in 1912. He also represented the Football League on two occasions (1911) and during his career played in over 250 senior matches, 143 for WBA.
He spent just the one season with Forest before moving on, his place being taken by Syd Harrold. His only goal for the Reds was scored against Coventry City.

SHEARMAN, William J
Inside or outside-right: 120 apps. 45 goals
Born: Keswick, Cumbria, circa 1894
Career: Braithwaite FC (Keswick), FOREST (April 1902-May 1909).
Bill Shearman - a clever, enterprising and honest footballer - helped Forest win the Second Division title in 1907, netting eight goals in 23 appearances. He scored on his League debut in a 2-1 defeat at Sheffield Wednesday in October 1903 and retained the inside-right position

(sometimes moving to the centre-forward slot) through to September 1905 when Enoch West arrived at the club. After that he switched to the right-wing while also slipping into other front-line positions when required. Shearman was an excellent clubman who continued to attend Forest home games long after hanging up his boots.

SHEPPERSON.

Inside-right: one app.
Born: circa 1867
Career: FOREST (1889-90)

Predominently a reserve-team player, Shepperson made his only senior appearance for Forest in the Football Alliance game v. Bootle in April 1890.

SHERIDAN, John

Midfielder: 1 app.
Born: Stretford, Manchester, 1 October 1964
Career: Manchester City (juniors), Leeds United (professional, February 1982), FOREST (£650,000, August 1989), Sheffield Wednesday (£500,000, November 1989), Birmingham City (on loan, February 1996), Bolton Wanderers (£180,000, November 1996), Doncaster Rovers (July 1998), Oldham Athletic (October 1998).

Midfielder John Sheridan - one of the game's finest passers of a ball - spent barely three months at the City Ground, making only one senior appearance for the Reds against Huddersfield Town in a 2nd round, 1st leg, League Cup fixture in September 1989. Earlier he had made 267 appearances for Leeds and after leaving Forest he amassed a further 244 for the Owls, 36 for Bolton and around 150 for Oldham. A former Youth international, Sheridan has been capped 34 times by the Republic of Ireland at senior level, once by the 'B' team and twice each by the Under-21s and Under-23s. He was a League Cup winner with Wednesday in 1991 (scoring the only goal of the final v. Manchester United) and a First Division championship with Bolton in 1997.

SHERINGHAM, Edward Paul

Striker: 62 apps. 23 goals
Born: Highams Park, London, 2 April 1966
Career: Millwall (apprentice, June 1982, professional January 1984), Aldershot (on loan, February 1985), FOREST (£2 million, July 1991), Tottenham Hotspur (£2.1 million, August 1992), Manchester United (£3.5 million, July 1997), Tottenham Hotspur (free transfer, July 2001) Portsmouth (June 2003).

Once a goalscorer, always a goalscorer - and that simply sums up Teddy Sheringham. He started bulging nets as a schoolboy, continued via Millwall's junior sides, through the reserves and into the first team. He became the Lions' record marksman with 111 goals in 262 senior appearances before transferring to Forest in 1991.

He continued to score regularly for the Reds who then

sold him for a small profit to Spurs. And still the goals flowed - 98 coming from head and both feet in 197 competitive games for the London club before he was sold to Manchester United in 1997. In fact, he was the Premiership's top marksman in 1992-93 with 22 goals. He finished up as leading scorer in four of his five seasons during his first spell at White Hart Lane. During his time at Old Trafford Sheringham was adored by the fans as he rattled in 46 goals in 153 first-class matches, including a crucial equaliser in the European Champions League final against Bayern Munich in 1999 which eventually set United up for the treble (Premiership & FA Cup being the other two prizes).

Sheringham gained a Second Division championship medal with Millwall in 1988 and a Zenith Data Systems Cup winners' medal and League Cup runners-up prize with Forest, both in 1992. And besides his treble success with United in 1999, he was also a member of two other Premiership-winning sides in 2000 & 2001.

He was honoured by his country (England) at Youth team level and has since added one Under-21 and 51 senior caps to his tally. He was also voted FWA and PFA Player of the Year for 2000-01. During the course of the 2002-03 campaign Sheringham reached the milestones of 550 League appearances, 300 Premiership appearances, 750 club appearances and 300 goals (including 225 in all League games, 120 of them in the Premiership).

SHERRATT, Brian

Goalkeeper: one app.
Born: Stoke-on-Trent, 29 March 1944
Career: Stoke City (juniors, June 1959, professional April 1961), Oxford United (August 1965), FOREST (on loan, October 1968), Barnsley (June 1969), Colchester United (August 1970-April 1971).

Brought in as cover for Peter Grummitt (injured) Brian Sherratt's only League outing for Forest was in the 4-2 defeat by Newcastle United at Meadow Lane in October 1968. He made 44 League appearances for Oxford and 15 for Barnsley.

SHIPPERLEY, Neil Jason

Striker: 13+8 apps. one goal
Born: Chatham, Kent, 30 October 1974
Career: Chelsea (apprentice, August 1990, professional September 1992), Watford on loan, December 1994), Southampton (£1.,25 million, January 1995), Crystal Palace (£1 million, October 1996), FOREST (£1.5 million, September 1998), Barnsley (£700,000, July 1998), Wimbledon (£750,000, July 2001). Crystal Palace (July 2003).

An England Under-21 international striker (7 caps gained) Neil Shipperley was a misfit at the City Ground, although injuries didn't help his cause. Big and powerful, he had already scored 50 goals while serving with Chelsea, Watford, Southampton and Palace, and on renewing his

acquaintances with Dave Bassett he simply failed to produce the goods and departed within the year for a reduced fee. He was actually sold by Palace against the wishes of manager Terry Venables. He topped the 100-goal mark in 2002-03 while playing for the Dons.

SHILTON, Peter Leslie,
Goalkeeper: 272 apps.
Born: Leicester, 18 September 1949
Career: Leicester City (apprentice, June 1965, professional, September 1966), Stoke City (£325,000, November 1974), Nottingham Forest (£270,000, September 1977), Southampton (£300,000, August 1982), Derby County (£90,000, July 1987), Plymouth Argyle (player-manager, March 1992-December 1994), Wimbledon (non-contract, January-February 1995), Bolton Wanderers (non-contract, March 1995), Coventry City (July 1995), West Ham United (January 1996), Leyton Orient (November 1996-May 1997).
England's most capped footballer with 125 appearances for his country, with a record 17 World Cup finals appearances, Peter Shilton was rated among the world's best goalkeepers during the 1980s. He was, without doubt, the complete last line of defence. Not a stylish 'keeper, far from it, he simply kept shots out whether by hand, foot or body, regularly and bravely diving at players' feet to avert danger inside the area. He had splendid positional sense and was commanding in the air, courageous and above all, added confidence to his defence. In December 1996, Shilton became the first player in history to appear in 1,000 Football League games when he kept goal for Leyton Orient against Brighton & Hove Albion.
He went on to make over 1,375 senior appearances in competitive football (clubs and country). His final League tally was 1,005 and he scored one goal - in a 5-1 win at Southampton (his future club) in October 1967.
Besides his senior international appearances, Shilton also played three Under-23 games and as a teenager collected a handful of Youth caps. A Division Two championship winner with Leicester (1971), he helped Forest win the Football League title in 1978, the League Cup in 1970, two European Cups (in 1979 & 1980), the Super Cup (also in 1979) and the FA Charity Shield (1978). Voted PFA 'Footballer of the Year' in 1978, Shilton received the PFA Merit Award in 1990, having been awarded the MBE in 1986, with the CBE following later.
As Plymouth's manager, he failed to prevent the cash-strapped Devon club from dropping into the Third Division having survived a crisis board meeting in February 1993 when chairman Dan McCauley criticised him for spending far too much money.

SHREWSBURY, Thomas P
Right-half: 4 apps.
Born: Derbyshire, circa 1870
Career: Heanor, FOREST (August 1894), Darwen (August 1895), Woolwich Arsenal (July 1896-May 1900). Basically a reserve-team player with each of his three major clubs, Tom Shrewsbury made his League debut for Forest v. Everton in September 1894. He played his last senior game for Arsenal against his former club Darwen and, in fact, he appeared in 122 matches for the Gunners (only three in the League and three in the FA Cup).

SHUFFLEBOTTOM, Frank
Full-back: 2 apps.
Born: Chesterfield, 9 October 1917.
Career: Margate, Ipswich Town (October 1936), FOREST (June 1939), Bradford City (October 1946; retired in May 1949 to become trainer at Valley Parade).
WW2 severely disrupted Frank Shufflebottom's progress in League football. He made only two appearances for Ipswich in Division 3 South (50 outings all told, most of them in the old Southern League) before the hostilities arrived and after leaving Forest he made 56 appearances for Bradford. He also played in a dozen or so wartime games for the Reds.

SILENZI, Andrea
Forward: 8+12 apps. 2 goals
Born: Rome, Italy, 10 February 1966
Career: Lodigiani (1984), Arezzo (cs.1987), Reggiana (cs. 1988), Napoli: (cs. 1990, Torino (cs. 1991), FOREST £1.8 million, 1995), Venezia (on loan October 1996) Reggiana (November 1997), Rewennc (October 1998), Torino (cs. 1999), Ravenna (cs.2000).
An Italian international (capped once in 1994 when with Torino) Andrea Silenzi (6ft 3ins tall) was a huge disappointment during his stay at the City Ground, especially in his second season when he appeared in only two matches, one as a substitute. He was recruited to add height to the attack, but with the 'play ball to feet' policy clearly being used to the full, this was obviously no use to the big Italian who actually went back home to try and get some games under his belt with Venezia before leaving Forest for good. He made his League debut for the Reds as a substitute against Coventry City (away) in September 1995.

SIMCOE, Kenneth Edward
Centre-forward: 2 apps. one goal
Born: Nottingham, 14 February 1937
Career: Central YMCA, FOREST (juniors, July 1953, professional December 1956), Coventry City (May 1959), Notts County (July 1960), Heasor Town (cs. 1961). Reserve centre-forward Ken Simcoe scored two goals in 12 League games during a short career. He made his Forest debut in the 2-0 home win over Portsmouth on 1 February 1958 and netted his only goal for the Reds in his second outing, a 3-2 defeat by WBA a week later.

SIMMS, Willard
Centre or inside-forward: 3 apps.
Born: circa 1890
Career: FOREST (August 1913-May 1915).
Did not figure after WW1.
A reserve forward at the City Ground during the two seasons leading up to the Great War, Will Simms played in three League matches for Forest, making his debut as at as leader of the attack against Glossop in a 3-0 defeat in mid-December 1913. He played in the next game v. Stockport (2-2) and later occupied the inside-left berth in the 1-1 draw with Bury (January 1914).

SIMPSON, Noel Harold
Wing-half: 50 apps. 3 goals
Born: Mansfield, Notts, 23 December 1922.
Died: Nottingham, 21 November 1987
Career: FOREST (March 1943), Notts County (WW2 guest, season 1943-44), Coventry City (£8,000, August 1948), Exeter City (February 1957, retired in May 1988).
Noel Simpson was a cultured player, perhaps more of a ball-winner than playmaker. He always performed with great consistency and if it hadn't been for the conflict of WW2 he would have certainly made more of an impact at the City Ground. He made his debut for Forest in wartime football (v. Leicester City in March 1943) and later appeared in 270 first-class games for Coventry City and 33 for Exeter. His first and last League appearances for Forest were against the same team - Luton Town - in September 1946 and May 1948. He sadly died from a heart attack, suffered while playing golf in 1987.

SIMPSON, William
Outside-left: 245 apps. 39 goals
Born: Jarrow near South Shields, 26 January 1907.
Now Deceased.
Career: Howden British Legion FC, Sheffield Wednesday (briefly in 1928), Barrow (season 1929-30) Washington Colliery Welfare, FOREST (April 1930), Barrow (August 1936). Did not re-appear after WW2.
Billy Simpson, 5ft 8ins tall and weighing 11st 7lbs, was a plucky winger, full of tricks, who regularly terrorised defenders with his all-purpose and aggressive displays. After failing to gain a contract with Sheffield Wednesday and having little joy with Barrow, he made his first appearance for Forest in a League game v. Cardiff City a few days after joining the club, in April 1930, taking over from Noah Burton. He held the left-wing position (injuries apart) until March 1936 when Roy Brown took over his duties. He returned to Holker Street at the end of that season.
* Simpson's father, George, was an FA Cup winner with Sheffield Wednesday in 1907 and he also played for West Bromwich Albion.

SLATER, Herbert
Centre-forward: 2 apps.
Born: Warwick, circa 1885
Career: Atherstone Town, Stourbridge, Aston Villa (September 1909), FOREST (August 1910-12).
Bert Slater was a reserve centre-forward who failed to get a game with Aston Villa and only managed two League outings with Forest, the first against Preston North and the second v. Notts County, both at the start of the 1910-11 season. He was not retained for the following campaign.

SMALL, Peter Victor
Right or left-winger: 94 apps. 21 goals
Born: Horsham, Sussex, 23 October 1924
Career: Horsham Town, Luton Town (August 1947), Leicester City (£6,000, February 1950), FOREST (September 1954), Brighton & Hove Albion (July 1957-May 1958).
Peter Small was a strong, compact winger, plucky at times who often cut inside to try a shot at goal. Nicknamed the 'Horsham Flier' he proved to be a key member of Forest's Second Division promotion winning side of 1957 (netting 4 goals in 24 appearances) having earlier helped the Foxes gain a place in the top-flight in 1954.

SMALLEY, Mark Anthony
Defender/midfielder: 3+2 apps.
Born: Newark-on-Trent, Notts, 2 January 1965
Career: FOREST (apprentice, June 1981, professional January 1983), Birmingham City (on loan, March 1986), Bristol Rovers (on loan, August 1986), Leyton Orient (February 1987), Mansfield Town (on loan, November 1989, signed for £15,000 January 1990), Maidstone United (May 1991-May 1992), Kettering Town (August 1992), Erith & Belvedere FC (January 1993), Sutton Town (player-coach, July 1993), Ilkeston Town (briefly in 1993), Shepshed Charterhouse (player-coach, July 1994), Hucknall Town (February 1995).
An England Youth international, Mark Smalley was a constructive footballer who looked promising during his stay at the City Ground, but failed to make the required breakthrough. Later on he amassed 64 League appearances for Orient, 49 for Mansfield and 34 for Maidstone before slipping down the footballing ladder in 1993.
* Smalley holds the record of being the first Bristol Rovers player to score a goal on their 'loaned' Twerton Park ground in August 1986, in a friendly against their landlords Bath City.

SMELLIE, Richard David
Centre-forward: 17 apps. 3 goals
Born: Scotland, circa 1861
Career: Pollockshields Athletic, Albion Rovers, FOREST (August 1894), Newcastle United (July 1896-May 1897).
Described as being 'a cool-headed and determined

goalscorer and a study athlete' Dick Smellie had done well in Scotland before trying his luck with Forest. He made his debut v. Small Heath in November 1895 and netted his first goals for the Reds v. Sheffield United a fortnight later. He had one excellent season with Newcastle (scoring 15 goals in 27 games) before surprisingly leaving the Magpies.

SMELT, Lee Adrian

Goalkeeper: one app.

Born: Edmonton, London, 13 March 1958

Career: Colchester United (juniors, June 1973, professional July 1975), Gravesend & Northfleet, FOREST (June 1980), Peterborough United (on loan, August 1981), Halifax Town (transfer, October 1981), Cardiff City (August 1984), Exeter City (on loan, March 1985 to June 1986). He later lived and worked in Cambridge.

Reserve goalkeeper Lee Smelt - stepping in for Peter Shilton - made his one and only appearance for Forest in the League game against West Bromwich Albion at the Hawthorns in March 1981 (lost 2-1). After leaving the City Ground he made 119 League appearances for Halifax, 37 for Cardiff and 13 for Exeter.

SMITH, Albert W

Wing-half: 66 apps. one goal

Born: Nottingham, 23 July 1869. Died: April 1921.

Career: FOREST (April 1888), Notts County (December 1889), FOREST (October 1890), Blackburn Rovers (November 1891), FOREST (January 1892, retired February 1894).

An amateur throughout his career, Albert Smith was a most serviceable, all-round footballer who preferred the half-back position. He came to the fore during his second spell with the Reds after assisting arch-rivals County (playing in just four League matches for the Magpies). He returned to Trentside for a third time to give many more outstanding displays, always driving his forwards on with great enthusiasm, being plucky and indefatigable. He appeared in eight (out of 22 games) when Forest won the Football Alliance championship in 1891-92, proving a decisive re-signing in the January after seven League outings for Blackburn. An England international, he won three full caps, lining up against Wales and Scotland in March and April 1891, and Ireland in February 1893 (being on the winning side each time).

SMITH, Ernest Edward

Inside/centre-forward: 2 apps. one goal

Born: Shirebrook near Chesterfield, 13 January 1912.

Career: Sutton Junction FC, Burnley (April 1931), FOREST (August 1934), Rotherham United (June 1935), Plymouth Argyle (November 1938, retired in May 1946).

Reserve inside-forward Ernie Smith's two League appearances for Forest were against the same club (Bury)

in September 1934 (away) and February 1935 (home). He later scored 44 goals in 107 League games for Rotherham but WW2 ruined his time with the Pilgrims for whom he scored five goals in 13 appearances, plus 13 in 27 Regional matches during the war.

SMITH, George

Inside-forward: 14 apps. one goal

Born: circa 1865

Career: FOREST (season 1889-90)

George Smith made his senior debut for Forest on 21 September 1889 in a Football Alliance game against Grimsby. It wasn't the happiest of baptisms as the Reds lost 4-0. but he returned to the action later in the season and occupied all three central forward positions as the team struggled to score goals.

SMITH, Henry Stanley

Full-back/wing-half/centre-half: 170 apps. one goal

Born: Newburn, Northumberland, 11 October 1908.

Died: Newcastle upon Tyne, 13 June 1993

Career: Throckley Welfare FC (Tyneside League), FOREST (professional, January 1929), Darlington (August 1937), Bristol Rovers (August 1938-May 1947).

During his career Harry Smith filled every defensive position available, being equally at ease in both the right-back and centre-half berths, producing his best form in the former. Naturally strong, he possessed a good turn of speed, kicked precisely with both feet and was a capable header of the ball, too. He made his League debut for Forest v. Chelsea in December 1929, deputising for Billy Thompson at right-back, and became a regular in the side the following season, although he occupied a variety of positions. He finally bedded himself in at centre-half in 1931-32 before reverting to full-back. He moved to Darlington after struggling to hold down his place in the side following the emergence of several new players.

SMITH, Horace

Wing-half: one app.

Born: Stourbridge, Worcs. 5 July 1908.

Career: Stourbridge, Coventry City (August 1930), Merthyr Town (June 1931), Stoke City (July 1935), FOREST (August 1936), Shrewsbury Town (June 1937), Revo Athletic (cs. 1939). Retired during WW2.

Reserve wing-half Horace Smith appeared in only six League games throughout his career - five for Coventry and one for Forest, the latter against his former club (Coventry) in September 1936 (a 1-1 draw) when he deputised for Bob Pugh.

SMITH, John

Inside-right: one app.

Born: circa 1870

Career: FOREST (seasons 1892-94)

Reserve inside-forward John Smith played in one senior

game for Forest, making his League debut against West Bromwich Albion (away) on the last day of the 1892-93 season, helping his side earn a point from a 2-2 draw.

SMITH, John
Inside right/centre-forward: 4 apps. one goal.
Born: Wardley, County Durham, 15 September 1886.
Died: Killed in action in 1916.
Career: Hebburn Argyle, Hull City (June 1905), Sheffield United (November 1910), FOREST (£450, March 1911), Nelson (August 1911), York City (August 1912), Hebburn Argyle (January 1913).
Jack Smith was a great figure in Hull City's early League campaigns, a prolific and noted marksman who headed the Second Division list in 1907-08 with 30 goals - gaining representative honours with the Football League (v. the Scottish League) for his efforts.
He went on to net a total of 91 goals in 156 senior appearances for the Tigers, managed six goals in 13 outings for the Blades and one in four for Forest, for whom he made his debut against Oldham Athletic (away) a couple of days after joining the club.

SMITH, John William
Goalkeeper: 28 apps.
Born: Beeston, Notts, circa 1880
Career: Long Eaton St Helen's, Derby County (November 1903), Newark Town (August 1906), FOREST (July 1909), Newark Town (1911).
After ten senior appearances for Derby, reserve goalkeeper Jack Smith joined Newark Town only to rejoin the Football League as a second-team player with Forest in the summer of 1909. He remained at the club for two seasons, making his debut for the Reds against Woolwich Arsenal (away) in the October, retaining his position for 15 games until Albert Hassall was signed from Middlesbrough to take over the number one slot. Thereafter Smith played second fiddle before returning for another decent run in the side halfway through the 1910-11 season. He moved on when Jack Hanna was recruited from Linfield Athletic.

SMITH, William
Right-half/inside-forward/outside-right: 97 apps.18 goals
Born: Sawley near Ripon, 10 November 1871.
Died: Nottingham, 27 September 1907
Career: Long Eaton Rangers (August 1887), Notts County (July 1889), Long Eaton Rangers (1890), FOREST (July 1890), Long Eaton Rangers (May 1894), Notts County (July 1896) Loughborough Town (August 1897), Lincoln City (July 1898), Burton Swifts (August 1899-1901).
The versatile William 'Tich' Smith scored almost 30 goals in more than 200 competitive matches (17 in a total of 122 League games) during a career that spanned 14 years (1887-1901). He appeared in 16 games when Forest won the Football Alliance title in 1891-92 (4 goals scored) and

gave the club excellent service for four seasons as a sturdy wing-half who was described as a 'most serviceable player all round, a trier to the finish of the game.' He was something of a celebrity by the time he joined Lincoln, having experienced first-class football with County and Forest while also gaining representative honours with England, capped against Canada in an unofficial international in 1892, and also playing for the Alliance XI against the Football League in 1891. He sadly died at the early age of 35.

SONNER, Daniel James
Midfielder: 12+5 apps.
Born: Wigan, 9 January 1972
Career: Wigan Athletic (apprentice, April 1988), Burnley (professional, August 1990), Bury (on loan, November-December 1992), Preussen Koln/Germany (June 1993), FC Erzgebirge Aue/Germany (August 1995), Ipswich Town (June 1996), Sheffield Wednesday (£75,000, October 1998), Birmingham City (free transfer, August 2000), Wolverhampton Wanderers (trialist, July 2002), Walsall (August 2002), FOREST (free, July 2003).
Capped four times as an Under-21 player and on seven occasions at senior level by Northern Ireland, the versatile Danny Sonner is a good midfield battler who prior to joining Forest amassed over 250 club appearances during his professional career. He enjoys a challenge and never gives less than 100 per-cent effort out on the park.

SOUTHWARD, John
Left-back: 9 apps.
Born: Bulwell, Notts, circa 1867
Career: Bulwell Forest, FOREST (September 1889-May 1891)
For two seasons full-back Jack Southward had to fight for a place in the Forest first team because of the good form shown by Messrs Guttridge and Coleman in 1888-89 and then Coleman and Scott after that. He managed a total of nine senior appearances, making his debut in the Reds' first-ever Alliance League game v. Walsall Town Swifts in September 1889 when he partnered Guttridge. One newspaper article indicated that Southward weighed over 14 stone at one time during his career. he was clearly a well-bult defender who as stated never really got much of a chance with Forest.

SPAVEN, John Richard
Inside-right: 170 apps. 50 goals
Born: Scarborough, 22 November 1891.
Died: 29 August 1971
Career: Goole Town (1915), Scunthorpe & Lindsey United (August 1919), FOREST (February 1920), Grantham (September 1926).
Jack Spaven top-scored for Forest three seasons running - 1920-23 - grabbing 18 goals in the League when the team gained promotion to the top flight in 1922. He started playing serious football with Goole Town while working

on the local dockyard. After serving with the Royal Horse Artillery in France during WW1 (when he was awarded the Military Medal) he had a brief spell with Scunthorpe before joining Forest. He was a very strong player, able to shoot with both feet, and this encouraged the Forest fans to shout 'Shoot Spav' whenever he was in range of the goal. After hanging up his boots, he became a publican in Grantham, and later moved back to Nottingham where he became landlord of the Lord Nelson on Carlton Street (1931). He retired as a licensee in 1954.

SPENCER, Frederick
Inside-forward/outside-right: 45 apps. 19 goals
Born: Nottingham, circa 1873
Career: FOREST (April 1895), Notts County (August 1900-September 1901).
A natural, incisive forward, easy moving with an explosive shot, Fred Spencer made his League debut for Forest in the same game as Dick Smellie against Small Heath in November 1895 when the team was struggling for firepower up front. That was his only outing during that season; he made eight more appearances in the League in 1986-97 (five goals scored, four in three matches) and was selected more often over the next two years before moving to neighbours Notts County in 1900.

SPOUNCER, William Alfred
Outside-left: 338 apps. 51 goals
Born: Gainsborough, Lincolnshire, 1 July 1877.
Died: Southend-on-Sea, 31 August 1962
Career: Gainsborough Trinity (August 1893), Sheffield United (July 1894), Gainsborough Trinity (June 1896), FOREST (£125, May 1897-June 1910). Later coached in Europe, including a spell with Barcelona.
Alf Spouncer, the son of a retail chemist, made his debut for Forest against his former club, Gainsborough, in a pre-season friendly in August 1897, quickly settling into the side on the left-wing. An England international (one cap gained v. Wales in 1900), he helped Forest lift the FA Cup in 1898 and the Second Division championship in 1907. He served Forest for 13 years, linking up with Gren Morris on the left hand side superbly well and accumulating a fine record of goals and appearances for the Reds. Smart, skilful in manoeuvre, he had the capability of crossing a ball with fine accuracy and would always try a shot at goal if the chance was there.
After retiring from football (on his return from Europe) Spouncer went to live and work in London (employed by a flour-making company). During WW1 he served in the Black Watch, and when he died at the age of 85 (in 1962) Forest had lost the last surviving member of their 1898 Cup-winning team.

STAINWRIGHT, David Peter
Centre-forward: 4+3 apps. one goal
Born: Nottingham, 13 June 1948
Career: FOREST (apprentice, June 1963, professional August 1965), Doncaster Rovers (July 1968), York City (July 1969, Heaner Town (cs. 1970).
A reserve centre-forward with Forest, Dave Stainwright scored on his full League debut against Tottenham Hotspur in a 4-3 defeat at White Hart Lane in April 1966, having earlier made his bow in the competition as a substitute against Newcastle United at the end of January. He had one League outing with Doncaster and just eight with York.

STANLEY, Frederick
Right-half: one app.
Born: Burton-on-Trent, Staffs, December 1884.
Career: Burton United (August 1905), FOREST (September 1907-April 1909).
Fred Stanley spent two seasons as a reserve wing-half with Forest, his only League game coming on Christmas Day 1907 when he took over the right-half slot from Edwin Hughes in a 4-0 defeat at Villa Park.

STANWAY, Reginald Edward
Right-half: one app.
Born: circa 1890
Career: FOREST (May 1910-June 1912)
Reserve half-back, Reg Stanway made his only first-team appearance for the Reds in a League game against Fulham, in April 1912 when he stood in for Jack Armstrong in the 1-1 draw at the City Ground.

STAPLETON, Lawrence
Outside-left: 10 apps.
Born: Nottingham, 19 May 1893.
Career: Basford United, FOREST (August 1919), Heanor Town (August 1921-22)
A useful left-winger with a good turn of foot, Lol Stapleton had to fight for a first-team place at the City Ground with Bill Shearman and Syd Harrold and then found his way blocked by the emergence of John Lythgoe and George Dennis. As a result he slipped away to join Heanor Town. He made his League debut (with inside-right Horace Hart) in the 2-0 win at Stoke in January 1920.

STARBUCK, Philip Michael
Forward/midfielder: 12+39 apps. 2 goals
Born: Nottingham, 24 November 1968
Career: FOREST (apprentice, April 1985, professional August 1986), Birmingham City (on loan, March 1988), Hereford United (on loan, February 1990), Blackburn Rovers (on loan, September 1990), Huddersfield Town (£100,000, August 1991), Sheffield United (£150,000, October 1994), Bristol City (on loan, September 1995), Oldham Athletic

(August 1997), Plymouth Argyle (March 1998), Cambridge City (June 1998). Hucknall Town (November 2001).

There's no doubting that Phil Starbuck played his best football with Huddersfield Town, for whom he scored 47 goals in 177 League and Cup games during a three-year stay with the Yorkshire club. During his career he found the net 54 times in 306 competitive games. He seemed unable to hold down a regular place in the first XI with Forest and in fact three-quarters of his senior appearances for the Reds came as a substitute. He scored on his League debut at Newcastle in December 1986 and his only other goal for the Club was claimed against Liverpool at the City Ground on New Year's Day 1987, earning his side a point from a 1-1 draw.

STENSAAS, Stale
Full-back: 6+1 apps.
Born: Trondheim, Norway, 7 July 1971
Career: Rosenborg BK, (1992), Glasgow Rangers (£1.75 million, July 1997), FOREST (on loan, January 1999), Rosenborg BK (June 2000).

An all-action player, aggressive when required, Stale Stensaas was secured on loan by Forest to help bolster up a leaky defence. He helped Rangers win the Scottish Premier League title in 1998.

STEVENSON, James
Inside-right: 6 apps. one goal
Born: Scotland, circa 1878
Career: Abington FC, Leith Athletic, Greenock Morton, FOREST (September 1902), New Brompton (February 1903).
Jim Stevenson was a well-built Scottish-born inside-forward who had done reasonably well north of the border before trying his luck with Forest. Unfortunately he seemed out of his depth in the Football League and after just half-a-dozen games dropped into the Southern League. He scored his only goal for the Reds v. Bolton Wanderers (away) in November 1902, having made his League debut a month earlier v. Everton on Merseyside.

STEWART, Alexander
Half-back/inside-left: 118 apps. 2 goals
Born: Greenock, Scotland, 1869.
Career: Glenalmond FC, Rosebury FC, Greenock Morton (1887), Burnley (August 1889), Everton (December 1892), FOREST (July 1893), Notts County (March 1897), Bedminster (July 1898), Northampton Town (July 1899), Burnley (August 1901), Leicester Fosse (player-trainer, August 1902-May 1905).
Alec Stewart was a player with a neat and polished style, a valuable member of the side, who made well over 250 senior appearances (211 in the Football League) in a career that spanned 16 years. He made his debut for Forest against the FA Cup holders Wolves on the opening day of the 1893-94 season, playing splendidly in a comprehensive 7-1 victory. Able to occupy both wing-half positions, he formed a fine relationship across the centre of

the park with Messrs MacPherson and McCracken and later with Frank Forman before moving to nearby Meadow Lane in 1897. He was a Lancashire Cup winner with Burnley (1890).

STEWART, Michael James
Midfielder: 12+3 apps. 2 goals
Born: Edinburgh, 25 February 1981
Career: Manchester United (apprentice June 1997, professional March 1998), FOREST (season loan deal, August 2003-May 2004).
Capped by Scotland at full, Under-21 and schoolboy levels, midfielder Michael Stewart learnt his trade with the likes of David Beckham, Nicky Butt, Roy Keane, Paul Scholes and Sebastian Veron and others at Old Trafford, and although he appeared in only 14 competitive games for the Reds, he is a quality player with a lot of class.

STOCKS, Cyril William
Outside or inside-right: 257 apps. 79 goals
Born: Pinxton, Derbyshire, 3 May 1905.
Career: South Normanton Amateurs, South Normanton Colliery, FOREST (July 1923), Grantham Town (August 1934).
A League debutant against the FA Cup holders Newcastle United in October 1924, the frail-looking Cyril Stocks quickly established himself in the Forest front-line, eventually taking over the inside-right berth when Jack Spaven moved to Grantham. He linked up wonderfully well with wing partner Syd Gibson, but injuries regularly interrupted his time at the City Ground although he remained with the club until 1934. Stocks scored three League hat-tricks for Forest v. Reading and Oldham in 1930 and v. Notts County two years later.

STONE, Stephen Brian
Midfielder: 224+5 apps. 27 goals
Born: Gateshead, 20 August 1971.
Career: FOREST (YTS, June 1987, professional, May 1989), Aston Villa ((£5.5 million, March 1999), Portsmouth (on loan, October 2002, signed permanently, December 2002).
First spotted by Forest as a 13-year-old, sturdy, energetic and forceful midfielder Steve Stone went on to appear in well over 200 first-class games for the club, winning nine England caps and a First Division championship medal in 1998, having earlier helped Forest gain promotion to the top flight in 1994 despite struggling with a knee problem for quite a while. After transferring to Villa Park he then suffered a back injury but did come on as a sub in the 2000 FA Cup final defeat by Chelsea. He linked up with his former Villa team-mate Paul Merson at Fratton Park, and duly helped Pompey reach the Premiership (2003).

STOKER, Lewis
Right-half: 12 apps.
Born: Wheatley Hill, County Durham 31 March 1910.
Died: Birmingham, May 1979.
Career: Brandon Juniors, Esh Winning Juniors, Bearpark FC, West Stanley, Birmingham (on trial, June 1930, professional September 1930), FOREST (May 1938). Retired during WW2,
Besides making almost 250 appearances for Blues, wing-half Lewis Stoker gained three full England Caps and represented the Football League during his time at St Andrew's.
An excellent feeder of the attack, a marvellously gifted and effective footballer, he loved to drive forward (given the chance) from centre-field and whenever possible tried a shot at goal, sometimes from fully 35-40 yards. After retiring from the game he worked as a charge-hand at Wimbush's bakery, just a short walk from St Andrew's. His younger brother Bob Stoker played for Bolton Wanderers and Huddersfield during the 1930s.

STOREY-MOORE, Ian
Winger: 271+1 apps. 118 goals
Born: Ipswich, 17 January 1945
Career: FOREST (amateur, February 1961, professional, May 1962), Manchester United (£200,000, March 1972, retired from top-line football on medical advice in December 1973); later served with Burton Albion (as player-manager from September 1974), Chicago Sting (making 14 appearances in 1975), Shepshed Charterhouse (also as player-manager 1976-77) and played briefly in South Africa. He was also a fully qualified FA coach. In the late 1980s he became a turf accountant with a betting office near to the City Ground, Nottingham as well as working in the licensing trade and featuring regularly on local radio
The first player with a double-barrelled name to join Manchester United, winger Ian Storey-Moore had finished up as top-scorer for Forest in four seasons running from 1968 before moving to Old Trafford - a month after a transfer deal with Derby County had fallen through (which resulted in the Rams receiving a £5,000 fine and a fierce reprimand from the FA). Fast and direct with a powerful shot (in both feet) the well-built figure of Storey-Moore certainly gave Forest an added dimension, for he could make goals as well as score them, being one of the game's finest wingmen. Unfortunately after joining United, a medical examination revealed that Moore (as he wanted to be called) had a severely damaged ankle and it was this injury that forced him to quit big-time football at the age of 28. Capped once by England at senior level (v. Holland in 1970), he played in two Under-23 internationals and twice represented the Football League. He played for Forest in the 1967 FA Cup semi-final.

STUBBS, Philip Eric Gordon
Outside-right or left: 22 apps. 6 goals.
Born: Chester, 10 September 1912
Career: Nantwich Bolton Wanderers (January 1934), Wrexham (September 1934), FOREST (July 1935), Leicester City (November 1936), Wrexham (WW2 guest), Chester (December 1945-May 1946).
A natural winger, Eric Stubbs was signed as cover for Arthur Masters and Billy Simpson by Forest - and, in fact, took over from the former at the start of the 1935-36 season following his transfer from Wrexham. He scored six goals in his 20 League games that season before dropping into the reserves and then a subsequent move to Filbert Street. He scored 15 goals in 78 outings for the Foxes.

STURTON, Thomas William
Left-half: one app.
Born: Basford, Notts, 25 September 1908
Career: FOREST (August 1926-May 1928).
A reserve for two seasons at the City Ground, Bill Sturton played his only senior game for Forest in a 2-2 home League draw with Leeds United on 21 January 1928. He replaced the sidelined Bob Wallace.

SUDDICK, James
Outside-right/inside-forward: 14 apps. 4 goals
Born: Middlesbrough, August 1873.
Career: Middlesbrough junior football, Aston Villa (July 1897), FOREST (August 1898), Thornaby (August 1900), Middlesbrough (season 1903-04), Thornaby.
Reserve inside-forward Jimmy Suddick failed to make an impact at Villa Park and appeared spasmodically for Forest after a decent run in the first team between late October and Boxing Day 1898 when he made ten consecutive appearances, scoring three goals.

SUMMERBEE, Nicholas John
Winger: 18 apps. 2 goals
Born: Altrincham, Cheshire, 26 August 1971
Career: Swindon Town (apprentice, July 1987, professional July 1989), Manchester City (£1.5 million, June 1994), Sunderland (£1 million, November 1997), Bolton Wanderers (free transfer, January 2001), FOREST (free transfer, November 2001), Leicester City (free transfer, August 2002), Bradford City (September 2003).
Capped by England once at 'B' and on three occasions at Under-21 level, Nicky Summerbee, like his father (Mike) before him, was a direct, fast-raiding outside-right.
Skilful, he loved to hug the touchline and take on his opponent down the outside before getting to the bye-line and sending over an inviting cross. He made 135 first-class appearances for Swindon, 156 for Manchester City, 108 for Sunderland and 15 for Bolton before joining Forest. He was released by Reds' manager Paul Hart after failing to recover from a groin strain. Earlier Summerbee had helped Sunderland reach the Premiership in 1999.

SUNLEY, David

Forward: one app.

Born: Skelton near Saltburn, 6 February 1952

Career: Sheffield Wednesday (apprentice, June 1968, professional January 1970), FOREST (on loan, October 1975), Hull City (£7,500, January 1976), Lincoln City (July 1978), Stockport County (March 1980-May 1982); then with Tsuen Wan FC/Hong Kong, Stafford Rangers, Burton Albion, Stocksbridge Works FC, Sheffield Club FC. Neat and progressive in style, and scorer of 45 goals in 324 League appearances during his career, David Sunley spent a month on loan with Forest, having just the one outing, in the disappointing 0-0 draw with Fulham. He scored on his debut for the Imps but had the ill-luck to play in one of Lincoln's worst-ever post-war teams.

SUGDEN, Sidney H

Centre-forward/outside-right: 49 apps. 14 goals

Born: Battersea, London, 1880

Career: Ilford, West Ham United (October 1902), FOREST (January 1903), Queen's Park Rangers (August 1905), Brentford (May 1909), Southend United (1910).

Positive, free-running, hard-shooting centre or wing-forward Sid Sugden made his Forest League debut v. Derby County the same month he joined the Reds from West Ham. He certainly put himself about a bit during his time at the City Ground, having an excellent 1903-04 season which saw him score 13 goals to finish up as the team's leading marksman in the Football League. He went on to net 21 goals in 69 first-class matches for QPR.

SURTEES, John W

Inside-forward: 98 apps. 23 goals

Born: Percy Main, County Durham, 2 July 1911

Career: Willington Juniors, Percy Main FC, Middlesbrough (December 1931), Portsmouth (March 1932), Bournemouth & Boscombe Athletic (1933), Northampton Town (briefly in 1933), Sheffield Wednesday (December 1934), FOREST (March 1936-September 1939). Did not figure after WW2.

Jack Surtees was an FA Cup winner in 1935 with Wednesday, the club he scored eight goals for in 50 games. Prior to that he had struggled to gain first-team football at Middlesbrough, Pompey and Northampton, but had netted four times in 20 League outings for Bournemouth. A well built forward and honest worker, he did very well with Forest, making his debut for the Reds against Newcastle United in October 1936. He went on to average a goal every four games during the next three-and-half years before WW2 arrived and ruined his career. He did not re-appear in League football after the hostilities.

SUTTON, Stephen John

Goalkeeper: 257 apps.

Born: Hartington, Derbyshire, 16 April 1961

Career: FOREST (apprentice, June 1977, professional April 1979), Mansfield Town (on loan, March 1981), Derby County (on loan, January 1985), Coventry City (on loan, February 1991), Luton Town (on loan, November 1991), Derby County (£300,000, March 1992), Reading (on loan, January 1996), Birmingham City (free transfer, August 1996, released June 1997), Grantham (August 1998).

Initially understudy to Peter Shilton, and then to a certain extent the Dutch duo of Hans Van Breukelen and Hans Segers, Steve Sutton finally gained a regular place in the Forest goal in season 1985-86 and he went on to serve the club supremely well, appearing in more than 250 first-class matches, gaining two League Cup winners' medals in 1989 & 1990 and a Simod Cup winners' prize, also in 1989.

A fine shot-stopper, he made in total 378 senior appearances over a period of 18 years, following his League debut for Forest v. Norwich City in October 1980.

SWAIN, Kenneth

Full-back: 138 apps.

Born: Birkenhead, 28 January 1952.

Career: Wycombe Wanderers (April 1973), Chelsea (professional August 1973), West Bromwich Albion (on loan, November 1978), Aston Villa (£100,000, December 1978), FOREST (October 1982), Portsmouth (July 1985), West Bromwich Albion (on loan, February-March 1988), Crewe Alexandra (August 1988-May 1989, then player/coach & assistant-manager under Dario Gradi), Wigan Athletic (manager, season 1993-94), Grimsby Town (reserve team coach/assistant-manager, 1995, then caretaker-manager October 1996-May 1997). Scouted for several clubs after that. He qualified in handicrafts and PE at college and played alongside Dennis Mortimer (ex-Coventry & Aston Villa) for Kirkby Boys.

Although a striker during his early days, Kenny Swain developed into a fine orthodox full-back, sound in the tackle with splendid positional sense, a steady nerve and excellent technique. He was a valuable member of Villa's League Championship, European Cup and Super Cup winning sides of 1981 and 1982 and in his four years with the club made 179 senior appearances. He took over from Viv Anderson for a while at Forest before switching over to the left-back berth, retaining the number 3 shirt until Stuart Pearce arrived in 1985. Swain helped Pompey win promotion from Division Two in 1987 and Crewe from Division Four two years later. During his playing days he amassed in excess of 500 League and Cup appearances.

TAYLOR, Gareth Keith

Striker: 18+2 apps. 2 goals

Born: Weston-super-Mare, 23 February 1973

Career: Southampton (trainee), Bristol Rovers (professional, July 1991), Crystal Palace (£750,000, September 1995), Sheffield United (£400,000, player-exchange deal involving Carl Veart & Steve Tuttle, March

1996), Manchester City (£400,000, November 1998), Port Vale (on loan, November 2000), Queen's Park Rangers (on loan, March 2000), Burnley (free transfer, February 2002), FOREST (£500,000, September 2003).

Gareth Taylor, 6ft 2in tall and 13st 8lbs in weight, had not really established himself as a goalscorer before moving to Forest early in the 2003-04 season. Indeed, he had netted almost 100 times since making his League debut in 1991. Capped seven times by Wales at Under-21 level and on 12 occasions by the seniors, he is a courageous, hardworking player who does his fair share in as an aide in defence when required. He settled in quickly at The City Ground.

TAYLOR, Joseph

Inside-right/centre-forward: 2 apps.

Born: Nottingham, 13 April 1905.

Career: Lenton United, FOREST (October 1925), Ilkeston United (July 1927), Blackpool (May 1928), Oldham Athletic (May1929-June 1931), Yeovil & Petters United (June 1934), Nuneaton Town (July 1935-May 1937).

A direct type of forward, Joe Taylor was mostly a reserve with every club he served, making a total of 18 League appearances throughout his career (8 goals scored). His career with the Latics was ended by injury (suffered against Burnley on Easter Monday, 1931). Taylor officially retired at the end of that season but three years he was persuaded to come back into the game by Yeovil. He made his debut for Forest in a 4-0 defeat away to Wolves in February 1926.

TAYLOR, William

Right-back/inside-forward: 13+11 apps. one goal

Born: Edinburgh, 31 July 1939.

Died: 30 November 1981

Career: Bonnyrigg Rose FC, Leyton Orient (professional, August 1959), FOREST (£4,000, October 1963), Lincoln City (May 1969; retired in May 1971); Fulham (coach, June 1971), Manchester City (coach, May 1976), Oldham Athletic (coach, July 1979 until his death). He also served as England coach from October 1974-November 1981.

Bill Taylor was a slightly built but very skilful footballer who made 27 appearances for Orient before joining Forest. He failed to make much of an impression at the City Ground, netting once in 24 outings over a period of six years. He made his debut in a 3-2 win over Bolton Wanderers at Burnden Park in February 1964 and scored his only goal for the Reds in a 3-0 home League win over Chelsea in September 1967. After leaving Forest he netted six times in 79 League games for the Imps. On retiring Taylor took up coaching, developing into one of the most respected in the country. Indeed, at the time of his sudden death he had been an England coach for seven years.

TEBBUTT, Thomas

Goalkeeper: one app.

Born: circa 1870

Career: FOREST (seasons 1894-96).

Reserve goalkeeper Tom Tebbutt played his only game for Forest on 5 October 1895 against Derby County when he took over from the injured Dan Allsopp. It was a game he would never forget as the Reds crashed to a 5-2 defeat.

TERRY, John George

Defender: 5+1 apps.

Born: Barking, Essex, 7 December 1980

Career: Chelsea (apprentice, June 1997, professional March 1998), FOREST (on loan, March-May 2000).

John Terry's meteoric rise to the top (in a matter of two years) continued apace despite some adverse publicity following off-field incidents during the 2001-02 season. A giant at the back for Chelsea, he quickly collected nine England Under-21 caps, got into the senior squad, and raced to the 100 appearance mark in senior competition. He was voted 'Player of the Year' at Stamford Bridge in 2002, having played in half-a-dozen games for Forest at the end of the 1999-2000 season when he was still a fledgling waiting to take flight! He made his 2003 full international debut v. Serbia in June.

THIJSSEN, Fransiscus Johannes

Midfielder: 19 apps. 3 goals

Born: Malden, Netherlands, 23 January 1952

Career: NEC Brede (1971), Twente Enschede (cs.1973) Ipswich Town (February 1979), Vancouver Whitecaps (May 1982) FOREST (October 1983), Vancouver Whitecaps (May 1984), Fortune Sittard (October 1984) Groningen (cs 1987), Vitesse Arnha (cs. 1988 to cs. 1991), Malmo FF (coach 1997-1998), De Graafschap (coach, briefly, 1999), Fortune Sittard (coach, December 2000 to June 2001).An exceptionally talented midfielder who teamed up splendidly at Portman Road with fellow countryman Arnold Muhren, Frans Thijssen always seemed to have time on the ball and he created goals aplenty for his strikers with every club he served. He scored three goals in 14 international appearances for Holland between 1975-81 and helped Ipswich Town win the UEFA Cup in 1981 (under manager Bobby Robson). He hit 10 goals in 125 games during his four-and-a-half years at Portman Road. As a Forest player he showed plenty of skill but was perhaps coming to the end of a distinguished career and in fact he spent only seven months at the City Ground. He made his debut for the Reds against neighbours Notts County in October 1983 (won 3-1) and netted his first goal for the club a fortnight later in the 1-1 draw with Sunderland.

THOMAS, Geoffrey Robert

Midfielder: 20+7 apps. 5 goals

Born: Manchester, 5 August 1964

Career: Littleborough FC, Rochdale (professional, August 1982), Crewe Alexandra (free transfer, March 1984), Crystal Palace (£50,000, June 1987), Wolverhampton Wanderers (£800,000, June 1993), FOREST (free transfer, July 1997), Barnsley (free transfer, July 1999), Notts County (free transfer, March 2001), Crewe Alexandra (free transfer, August 2001) Retired May 2002.

A widely travelled player, Geoff Thomas had already chalked up more than 450 appearances at club level, and had represented England in three 'B' and nine full internationals before he joined Forest in 1997. A 6ft 1in. driving force from midfield, always keen to get forward, he helped the Reds win the First Division title in 1998, having earlier gained a Zenith Data Systems Cup winning medal with Palace in 1991. He was plagued by injuries at Molineux and later during his second spell at Gresty Road and when he quit top-class football at the end of the 2001-02 season his overall appearance tally stood at 559 (77 goals scored).

THOMAS, Gerald Shannon

Full-back: 431 apps. one goal

Born: Derby, 21 February 1926.

Career: FOREST (Juniors, June 1941, professional September 1943-May 1960); Bourne Town (player-manager, June 1960-62). Later owned a greengrocer's shop in Woodthorpe.

As partner to Bill Whare, Geoff Thomas was a vital member of the Forest team that won the Third Division South title in 1951 and likewise six years later when promotion was gained to the top flight. He started out as a wing-half but moved to right-back when peacetime football resumed in 1946, later switching to the opposite flank. Unfortunately Thomas was desperately unlucky with injuries, sometimes finding it mighty difficult to get back into the first team after being sidelined for a length of time as Forest were blessed with two other fine full-backs in Jack Hutchinson and of course, Whare. He lost his place in the side to Joe McDonald and therefore missed the 1959 FA Cup final win over Luton, although he travelled to Wembley as one of the reserves. Thomas played his last game in April 1960, thus bringing the curtain down on an excellent career at the City Ground. Besides his 431 senior appearances, Thomas also played in 67 wartime games for Forest: 1944-46.

THOMPSON, Frederick

Right/left-half: 17 apps.

Born: Sheffield, 1870

Career: Sheffield Hastings, Sheffield Wednesday (July 1890), Lincoln City (October 1890). The Wednesday/Sheffield (July 1890), FOREST (August 1891-May 1893).

After featuring prominently in 16 Football Alliance games the previous season (when Forest won the title), Fred Thompson made his one and only League appearance for the club in the home First Division fixture with Stoke on 10 September 1892. He was not retained for the following campaign.

THOMPSON, John

Defender: 55+4 apps. 4 goals

Born: Dublin, 12 October 1981.

Career: River Valley Rangers, Home Farm, FOREST (professional, July 1999).

A tall, commanding, unflappable 6ft 1in defender, John Thompson made his League debut for Forest in the right-back position against Sheffield United in January 2002 before being moved into the centre-half spot. A serious knee injury sidelined him for the last two months of that campaign.

He scored his first goal for Forest in the 1-1 home draw with Walsall on New Year's Day 2003. He gained his first full cap for the Republic of Ireland v. Canada in 2003.

THOMPSON, Norman

Inside-left: 12 apps. 3 goals

Born: Forest Hall, 5 September 1900.

Career: Newcastle United (briefly, 1919), Seaton Delaval, Backworth FC, South Shields (July 1922), Middlesbrough (July 1925), Barnsley (January 1926), West Stanley, FOREST (March 1928), West Stanley (May 1929), Carlisle United (August 1931), West Stanley.

Rejected as a teenager by Newcastle, inside-forward Norman Thompson then spent a couple of seasons in non-League football before joining South Shields for some Third Division North action. He scored seven goals in 43 games for the North-East club but failed to make much of an impact at Middlesbrough or indeed at Barnsley. Another stint at a lower level preceded his move to Forest where he played well at times but failed to hold down a regular place in the side. He made his League debut for the Reds against Stoke City a month after joining the club.

THOMPSON, Sidney

Inside-forward: 22 apps. 8 goals

Bedlington, 14 July 1928

Career: Bedlington Terriers, FOREST (September 1947), Scunthorpe United (August 1955-May 1956).

A neat and tidy reserve inside-forward, Sid Thompson spent eight seasons at the City Ground, averaging just three appearances in each one. He had to wait until September 1952 before making his League debut, but he did do well in the reserves, helping the Reds win three successive Midland League titles: 1952-54. He failed to make the first team at Scunthorpe.

THOMPSON, William Potter
Right-back/outside-right: 389 apps. 5 goals
Born: Derby, 17 September 1899.
Career: Rolls Royce FC (1915), FOREST (May 1922), Burton Town (August 1935)
Capped by England at schoolboy level in 1914, Bill Thompson developed into a wonderful full-back. During the Great War, he worked as a draughtsman at the Rolls Royce factory in Derby and enhanced his ability as a defender by playing for the works football team. He actually joined Forest as a right-winger (as cover for Harry Bulling and Harry Jones) but made the switch to right-back with telling effect, retaining that position for eleven years and making almost 390 senior appearances for the Reds in First and Second Division soccer, while also playing in two Test Matches for England v. South Africa in 1929. A keen motorist and cricketer (he loved batting), Thompson was also a very useful snooker player, once registering a break of 110.

THOMSON, Charles Richard
Goalkeeper: 136 apps.
Born: Perth, Scotland, 2 March 1930
Career: Blairgown'e Clyde (1949), Chelsea (October 1952), FOREST (August 1957-May 1961).
After helping Chelsea win the First Division championship in 1955, four years later goalkeeper Chick Thomson gained an FA Cup winners medal with Forest after an inspired display against plucky Luton Town at Wembley. Sound and reliable, he took over from Harry Nicholson between the posts at the City Ground and was eventually replaced by Peter Grummitt. His debut for the Reds was in a Division One game against Preston North End (h) in August 1957 (won 2-1). Thomson's father played professionally in the Scottish League.

THORNHILL, J F
Goalkeeper: 3 apps.
Born: circa 1870
Career: FOREST (1892-94).
Reserve to goalkeeper Bill Brown, Thornhill played in just three League games for Forest during his two seasons with the club, making his debut in a 1-0 defeat at Preston on 17 September 1892.

THORNLEY, John Fern Walter
Right-half/centre-half: 15 apps.
Born: circa 1872
Career: FOREST (July 1896), Gainsborough Trinity (August 1899-May 1902). An honest worker just falling short of being an exceptionally fine player, Jack Thornley spent three years with Forest before going on to make almost 100 first-class appearances for Trinity (88 in the Football League). He made his senior debut for the Reds at centre-half in place of the injured Jack MacPherson against Sheffield Wednesday in January 1898 (won 1-0).

TILER, Carl
Defender: 84+3 apps. one goal
Born: Sheffield, 11 February 1970.
Career: Barnsley (YTS June 1986, professional February 1988), FOREST (£1.4 million, May 1991), Swindon Town (on loan, November 1994), Aston Villa (£750,000, October 1995), Sheffield United (£650,000, March 1997), Everton (£500,000, November 1997), Charlton Athletic (£700,000, September 1998), Birmingham City (on loan, February 2001), Portsmouth (£250,000, March 2001 to cs. 2003).
A strong, tall, dominant defender, Carl Tiler - who gained 13 England Under-21 caps - spent four-and-a-half years with Forest, during which time he helped the Reds win promotion to the First Division (1994). He struggled to hold down a first-team place during the last two seasons at the City Ground. Tiler suffered a hamstring injury on his debut for Villa and was out of action for a year before returning to score his only Villa goal against his former club, Forest. More injury problems followed before he helped Charlton reach the Premiership in 1998.

TILFORD, Arthur
Left-half: 8 apps.
Born: Ilkeston, Derbyshire, 14 May 1903.
Died: Ilkeston, 10 April 1993.
Career: Trowell St Helens, FOREST (May 1924), Blackpool (May 1926), Coventry City (May 1929), Fulham (February 1932), Southampton (on loan, February 1933), Walsall (June 1934). Did not play after WW2. Arthur Tilford was a reserve left-half who made his League debut against Sunderland in the left-half position in March 1925 (when Morgan was an absentee from the middle-line).
He helped Fulham gain promotion to the Second Division after leaving Forest and his switch to the Dell came about due to some sad personal circumstances. He had just suffered a family bereavement with the death of his young son and a temporary move to Southampton was suggested to help him recover from his loss, being allowed to continue training at Craven Cottage.

TIMMINS, Samuel
Half-back: 138 apps. 5 goals
Born: West Bromwich, June 1879.
Died: August 1956
Career: Dudley Sports, Burnt Tree FC, Dudley Town (May 1899), Walsall (1899), FOREST (March 1901), West Bromwich Albion (£50, August 1906, retired through injury in May 1911)
The versatile Sammy Timmins, short and stocky, was a self-conscious footballer with a high regard for discipline, and could occupy any of the three half-back positions. A tenacious tackler he loved to get involved in the action and suffered plenty of injuries. After appearing in 116 senior games for the Baggies, injury eventually forced him to

retire. He was licensee of the Hop Pole pub on Carter's Green, West Bromwich (1911-29).

TINSLEY, Walter Edward
Inside-left: 64 apps. 13 goals
Born: Ironville, Derbyshire, 10 June 1891.
Died: Ripley, Derbyshire, 7 March 1966.
Career: Alfreton, Sutton Town, Sunderland (March 1912), Exeter City (August-October 1913), Middlesbrough (November 1913), FOREST (WW1 guest, August 1915-April 1919, signed permanently, August 1921), Reading (April 1924-May 1926).
Walter Tinsley was in Forest's 1922 Second Division promotion winning side, having previously scored 56 goals in almost 130 games for the Reds as a WW1 guest from Middlesbrough. He played at centre-forward in the first game of the 1919 Victory Shield against Everton (0-0) but missed the return fixture which the Reds won 1-0 to lift the trophy at the City Ground. A very composed footballer with two excellent feet and a fine shot, he amassed well over 285 senior appearances and netted more than 80 goals during his career his record with Middlesbrough being 46 goals in 86 outings. Tinsley made his Football League debut for Forest against Crystal Palace (away) in August 1921 (lost 4-1).

TODD, Allan
Goalkeeper: 21 apps
Born: Kinross, circa 1912.
Career: Wellesley FC, Leith Athletic, Cowdenbeath, Port Vale (October 1932), FOREST (June 1937, in an exchange deal involving Arthur Masters), Darlington (August 1939). Did not appear in League football after WW2.
A daring goalkeeper, Allan Todd made 83 appearances for Port Vale before joining Forest as cover for Percy Ashton. He made 14 of his 21 senior appearances for the Reds in the last full League season before WW2 (1938-39).

TODD, Colin
Defender: 47 apps.
Born: Chester-le-Street, County Durham, 12 December 1948.
Career: Sunderland (apprentice July 1964, professional December 1966), Derby County (£180,000, February 1971), Everton (£333,000, September 1978), Birmingham City (£300,000, September 1979), FOREST (£70,000, August 1982), Oxford United (February 1984), Vancouver Whitecaps/NASL (May 1984), Luton Town (October 1984). Retired in May 1985; Whitley Bay (manager), Middlesbrough (Youth team coach, May 1986, assistant-manager to Bruce Rioch, May 1986, then manager, March 1990-June 1991); Bradford City (assistant-manager, January 1992), Bolton Wanderers (assistant-manager, May 1992, joint-manager, June 1995 with Roy McFarland, then manager, November 1996-September 1999). Swindon Town (manager May-

November 2000), Derby County (manager August-December, 2001). Thereafter did some local scouting for a handful of clubs.
As a player, Colin Todd helped Sunderland win the FA Youth Cup in 1967. He then gained two League championship medals with Derby (in 1972 & 1975), helped the Rams lift the Texaco Cup (also in 1972), was a member of Birmingham's promotion-winning side (from Division Two) in 1980 and was voted the PFA 'Footballer of the Year' in 1975. As a manager he guided Bolton into and out of the Premiership in 1997 and 1998 respectively. He also won 27 full and 14 Under-23 caps for England, having earlier represented his country at Youth team level. He played three times for the Football League.
Todd was one of the finest defenders in the Football League during the 1970s, certainly one of Sunderland's best-ever local finds. Always elegant, poised, scrupulously fair and a brilliant reader of the game, he was a classy player. Indeed, that was what inspired Brian Clough to pay what was then a record fee for a defender when he signed Todd for Derby. Todd always looked comfortable on the ball and in an exceptionally fine career he made over 800 senior appearances, chalking up his 500th game in the Football League (out of a total of 641) in October 1979. He is also the oldest player ever to appear in a League game for Oxford United - aged 35 years, four months (in 1984).

TOLLEY, Oliver
Outside-right/centre-forward: 14 apps. 2 goals
Born: circa 1865
Career: FOREST (July 1888-May 1890).
Oliver Tolley made ten appearances for Forest in their first season in the Football Alliance (1889-90), scoring one goal (against Sunderland in December - won 3-1). His other goal was claimed in the 2-2 FA Cup draw with Chatham in February 1889. Although a keen and enthusiastic player, he was not retained for the 1890-91 season.

TOWNSEND, Alfred Harold
Outside-left: 15 apps. 4 goals
Born: Nuneaton, 25 August 1902
Career: Cardiff City, FOREST (July 1926), Stockport County (August 1928), Connah's Quay (October 1928-May 1929).
Alf Townsend made his Forest debut in the 2-1 local derby win over Notts County in September 1926 when he partnered Charlie Jones on the left-wing. He spent two seasons at the City Ground before having a handful of League outings for Stockport.

TRIM, Reginald Frederick
Full-back: 73 apps.
Born: Portsmouth, 1 October 1913.
Career: Bournemouth Postal Workers FC, Winton &

Moordown FC, Bournemouth & Boscombe Athletic (juniors, July 1929, professional April 1931), Arsenal (April 1933), FOREST (July 1937), Derby County (December 1943), Swindon Town (July 1946-May 1947), Leyton Orient (trainer, season 1948-49).

An England Schoolboy international (capped in season 1927-28) Reg Trim was a reliable full-back, able to play on both sides of the pitch. He made his debut for Forest in a League game v. Sheffield United (away) in August 1937 and kept his place in the side straight through to the early part of WW2.

TURNER, Alfred D

Outside-right: 9 apps.

Born: Islington, London, circa 1880

Career: Upton Park FC, FOREST (seasons 1902-04), Haringey.

Pacy wing-forward Alf Turner made his League debut for Forest on St Valentine's Day 1903 v. Stoke (away), coming into the side when the right-wing berth was causing something of a problem. He played in six games at the end of that season and in the first three of 1903-04 before Tom Davies entered the action and remained in the position, thus allowing Turner to drift away to pastures new (back in London).

TURNER, Keith John

Inside-forward: one app.

Born: Coventry, 9 April 1934.

Career: FOREST (juniors, August 1952, professional 1954-May 1956).

A League debutant for Forest in a 3-0 defeat against Luton Town at Kenilworth Road on 21 August 1954 (the first day of the new season) Keith Turner was a useful reserve to have around but sadly this was his only chance in the senior side, although he remained at the club until the end of the 1955-56 campaign.

TURNER, Thomas

Left-half: one app.

Born: Whittle-le-Woods, near Blackburn, 2 April 1906. Died: 1980.

Career: Chorley, FOREST (June 1928), Lytham (August 1930)

Tom Turner made his League debut for Forest on 2 February 1929, in the 2-2 draw at Blackpool. He deputised for Bob Wallace who had been out of action with an injury for quite some time and was not quite ready to make his comeback. Wallace did get a recall for the next game and as a result Turner slipped back into the reserves.

UPSON, Matthew James

Defender: one app.

Born: Stowmarket, 18 April 1979.

Career: Luton Town (apprentice, June 1993, professional April 1996), Arsenal (£1 million, May 1997), FOREST

(on loan, December 2000), Crystal Palace (on loan, March 2001), Reading (on loan, September 2002), Birmingham City (£1 million, January 2003).

After gaining England Youth team honours, defender Matthew Upson went on to win 10 Under-21 caps. Very talented, comfortable on the board, he acted as reserve to the likes of Tony Adams, Martin Keown, Sol Campbell and others at Highbury, before establishing himself in the Gunners' Premiership championship winning side of 2001-02.

Upson went on to make his full international debut against South Africa in May 2003.

VAN BREUKELEN, Johannes

Goalkeeper: 75 apps.

Born: Utrecht, Netherlands, 4 October 1956.

Career: FC Utrecht (professional, 1975), FOREST (September 1982), PSV Eindhoven (June 1984 to 1992).

Dutch international goalkeeper Hans Van Breukelen took over between the posts from Peter Shilton and went on to serve the club superbly well for two seasons, amassing 75 appearances before choosing to return to his native country. A fine shot-stopper, he handled the ball; well and possessed a mighty long kick. He won a total of 73 senior caps for his country over a period of 12 years (1970-82) and made more than 300 appearances in Dutch football.

VAN HOOIJDONK, Pierre

Striker: 72+5 apps. 41 goals

Born: Steenbergen, Netherlands, 29 November 1969,

Career: NAC Breda (1990), Celtic (£1.2 million, January 1995), FOREST (£4.5 million, March 1997), Vitesse Arnhem (June 1999), Feyenoord (August 2001), Fenerbahce (cs. 2003).

At 6ft 4ins and 13st 5lbs, Pierre van Hooijdonk was one of the tallest and heftiest footballers in the UK during the late 1990s. A great target man, strong in the air (of course) he was also pretty effective on the ground as well and averaged a goal every two games for Forest, helping them win the First Division title in 1998. He later assisted Feyenoord in their quest for European glory and earlier netted 56 goals in 92 League and Cup games during his time at Parkhead. Listed among the 50 contenders for the coveted European 'Footballer of the Year' award in 2002, he has now won 31 caps for Holland (10 goals scored).

VASEY, Robert Henry

Wing-half: 23 apps.

Born: Tanfield, 16 December 1907.

Career: Consett, FOREST (May 1932), Notts County (June 1936), Brighton & Hove Albion (August 1938). Did not play after WW2.

Bob Vasey was a powerfully built wing-half who made his Football League debut for Forest against Tottenham Hotspur (home) on the opening day of the 1932-33 season.

W

He scored one League goal for each of his other two clubs (in 27 games for County and 15 for Brighton).

VAUGHAN, Anthony John

Defender: 41+5 apps. 5 goals
Born: Manchester, 11 October 1975
Career: Ipswich Town (apprentice, April 1992, professional July 1994), Manchester City (£1.35 million, July 1997), Cardiff City (on loan, September 1999), FOREST (£350,000, February 2000), Scunthorpe United (on loan, March 2002). Motherwell (on loan, January 2003), Mansfield Town (July 2003).

A former England Schoolboy and Youth international, Tony Vaughan made over 70 appearances for both Ipswich Town and Manchester City before joining Forest. A left-sided defender, strong and capable, he did well initially at the City Ground but then fell out of favour during the 2001-02 season and after that was always struggling to reclaim a first-team place.

VAUGHAN, William

Outside-left: 6 apps.
Born: circa 1888
Career: FOREST (seasons: 1908-10)

Bill Vaughan was a reserve with Forest for two seasons during which time he was handed just four senior outings - the first against Woolwich Arsenal in a home League game in March 1910, replacing initially Billy Palmer and later taking over from Jack Horrocks.

VENTERS, John Cook

Inside-right: one app.
Born: Cowdenbeath, 22 August 1910.
Career: Preston North End (August 1928), FOREST (August 1929), Thames FC (September 1930).

After spending a season in Preston's reserve side, inside-forward John Venters' moved to Forest where again he had to be satisfied with second-team football, making just one League appearance for the Reds against West Bromwich Albion on 12 October 1929 when he deputised for Cyril Stocks in a 2-0 defeat. He had failed to make the first team at Deepdale and only played once for Thames.

VOWDEN, Geoffrey Alan

Inside or centre-forward: 108 apps. 48 goals
Born: Barnsley, 27 April 1941.
Career: FOREST (amateur, 1958, professional January 1960), Birmingham City (£25,000, October 1964), Aston Villa (£12,500, March 1971), Kettering Town (player/assistant-manager, July 1974), New York Cosmos (1975). Coached in Saudi Arabia (1976-78) and also at various schools and youth clubs in the Nottingham area. Between 1980 and 1981 he was second XI coach at Sheffield United.

Geoff Vowden started his playing career in the Channel Islands before joining Forest. He developed quickly and became a fine marksman who scored more than 150 goals in just under 500 competitive matches over a period of 14 years. After netting almost 50 times for Forest he moved to St Andrew's and duly paid back the money spent on him with huge dividends, notching almost a century of goals in 253 appearances for Birmingham. On transfer deadline 1971 he switched his loyalties to Villa Park and a little over a year later helped Villa win the Third Division championship. A beautifully balanced player, Vowden could also man midfield if required. He later became a very successful coach.

* Vowden was the first substitute to come off the bench and score a hat-trick, achieving the feat for Birmingham against Huddersfield in September 1968.

WADSWORTH, Harold

Outside-right or left: 35 apps. 10 goals
Born: Bootle, 1 October 1898.
Died: Chesterfield 2 November 1975
Career: Bootle St Matthew's FC (Tranmere & District League), Tranmere Rovers (1914), Liverpool (January 1918), Leicester City (June 1924), FOREST (April 1927), Millwall (June 1928-May 1932).

During his career Harry Wadsworth scored 28 goals in a total of 252 League appearances. At one time he was described as being an 'extremely adroit tactician as well as more than commonly fast and with a trick of swerving when about to be tackled which has baffled many an opponent.' He had a very good season with Forest, averaging just under a goal per game. He made a scoring debut for the Reds in the League game v. Port Vale (away) in August 1927 and was eventually replaced on the left-wing by Bob Morton having been pushed along earlier by Townsend. Before moving to the City Ground he had helped Leicester gain promotion from Division Two and after leaving Forest he was a key member of the Millwall side for four seasons.

His elder brother Walter was a professional footballer between 1914-30, serving with Liverpool, Bristol City and New Brighton among others.

WAGSTAFF, John George

Goalkeeper: one app.
Born: Nottingham, 27 September 1899.
Career: Arnold St Mary's, FOREST (August 1919), Arnold St Mary's.

An immediate post WW1 signing, reserve goalkeeper John Wagstaff made only one League appearance during his career - for Forest against South Shields (away) on 15 November 1919 when he replaced Johnson. He didn't have the greatest of introductions, however, being on the losing side in a 5-2 defeat.

WALKER, Desmond Sinclair
Defender: 387+8 apps. one goals
Born: hackney, London, 26 November 1965
Career: FOREST (apprentice, June 1982, professional December 1983), Sampdoria (£1.5 million, August 1992), Sheffield Wednesday (£2.7 million, July 1993), Burton Albion (2001-02) FOREST (July 2002).
Twice a League Cup winner with Forest in 1989 and 1990, Des Walker also played in the losing side in the 1992 final, a year after scoring an own-goal in the Reds' 2-1 FA Cup final defeat by Spurs. He also helped Forest win the Simod Cup in 1989, the Zenith Data Systems Cup in 1992 and after winning seven Under-21 caps for England he went on to appear in 59 full internationals, He was unfortunately sidelined, for almost the whole of 2001-02, having reached the personal milestone of 800 senior appearances. He regained full fitness and was in superb form in 2002-03 when his vast experience shone through as Forest battled into the play-offs.
Penned as being the ultimate footballing centre-back, Walker, cool, undemonstrative highly skilful, totally unflappable, could be replied upon each and every game he played. Your own 'Mr Consistency' if you like, for he had many long unbroken spells in the side, holding the defence together superbly well with his positional sense and timely interceptions, while his tackles were quite outstanding at times. He was blessed with innate natural speed which opponents found particularly undaunting and even the fans acknowledged this by chanting ' You'll never beat Des Walker.'

WALKER, Duncan Campbell
Centre-forward: 88 apps. 33 goals
Born: Alloa, 12 September 1902.
Career: Dumbarton Union FC, Dumbarton, St Mirren (cs. 1921), FOREST (May 1923), Bo'ness (March 1926), Larkhall Thistle, Thornbridge Waverley.
Dunky Walker once scored a record 56 goals in one season of Scottish football. Thirsty for goal wherever he played, he certainly did the business for Forest, his first two seasons at the City Ground being quite superb. Said to be a 'vigorous forward, quick to seize opportunities' he was also an unselfish player as well as being creative, accurate in heading and shooting despite not being the biggest of players. He took over the scoring mantle at Forest from Pat Nelis and forged a wonderfully partnership up front with Charlie Flood. He made his debut for the Reds on the opening day of the 1923-24 campaign v. Everton, scored his first goal in the second game v. West Brom and finished the season with 17 to his credit, a tally that helped keep Forest in the First Division, but alas his efforts a year later were fruitless as the Reds went down. His last game for the club - before he returned to Scotland - was against Swansea Town in February 1926. The following season Noah Burton led the attack while Walker continued to bulge the nets north of the border!

WALKER, George Henry
Goalkeeper: 304 apps.
Born: Aysgarth, 20 May 1916. Died: January 1976.
Career: Darlington (professional, December 1934), Portsmouth (March 1938), FOREST (April 1947, retired through injury in May 1955).
Harry Walker was an ever-present between the posts when Forest won the Third Division (South) title in 1950-51. During his three-club career he amassed in excess of 400 senior appearances, making 49 in the League for both Darlington and Pompey, winning an FA Cup winners' medal with the latter in 1939 (v. Wolves). He started out as a motor mechanic and as a teenager was well known in athletic circles in the North-east of England, lifting many prizes as a runner before becoming a very fine goalkeeper. Walker was a weighty player, tall and powerful who maintained a high standard of performance for a number of years, also acquiring the nickname of 'Mr Consistency.' At Wembley in 1939 he was 'as safe as houses' and always bred confidence with his judgement and handling. He certainly gave Forest great value before retiring at the age of 39, handing over his duties at the City Ground to Bill Farmer.

WALKER, Thomas T
Inside or outside-left: 7 apps. 5 goals
Born: circa 1870
Career: FOREST (seasons 1894-96)
Despite scoring a hat-trick in Forest's 5-3 win over Sheffield United in the United Counties League in March 1895, Walker failed to hold down a first team place.
It seems as though he was regarded as a reserve team player during his time with the Reds.

WALKER, Victor
Wing-half/inside-forward: 2 apps.
Born: Kirkby-in-Ashfield, 14 April 1922. Died: 1992.
Career: FOREST (August 1943, professional 1945), Stockport County (June 1946-May 1950).
Vic Walker made almost 40 appearances for Forest during the second half of WW2. After leaving The City Ground he scored 10 goals in 94 League games for Stockport. Essentially an attacking player (even from the wing-half position) he had an easy action and was polished if not all that aggressive when the occasion warranted some competitiveness in the centre of the field. He made his 'senior' debut for Forest in the 3rd round, second leg FA Cup encounter v. Watford in January 1946 when he came in at left-half allowing Bill Baxter to move to full-back in place of the injured Bob McCall.

WALKER, William Wilfred
Centre or inside-left: one app.
Born: Walsall, February 1888. Died: circa 1968
Career: Walsall schoolboy football, Walsall Town Swifts (May 1905), Darlaston, Halesowen, West Bromwich

Albion (May 1910), Willenhall Swifts (briefly mid-1911), FOREST (November 1911-May 1912), Willenhall Swifts (July 1912-14).

A tireless forward, Billy Walker made his Football League debut for WBA in December 1910 and went on to score five goals in 34 games during that, his only season at The Hawthorns. He was only a reserve at The City Ground and played in just one senior game for Forest against Glossop (home) on 30 March 1912 (Division 2) when he came in to partner Jack Williams in attack.

WALL, Thomas Henry

Goalkeeper: one app.
Born: Bermondsey, London, 19 May 1909.
Career: Millwall (on trail), Notts County (May 1932), Tottenham Hotspur (briefly in 1933), FOREST (July 1934)

Reserve to Percy Ashton at The City Ground, goalkeeper Tom Wall's only first team outing was in the League Division 2 clash against rivals Notts County in the local derby at Meadow Lane on 29 September 1934. Forest won the game 5-3.

WALLACE, Ian Andrew

Inside/centre-forward: 157+8 apps. 47 goals
Born: Glasgow, 23 May 1956
Career: Yoker Athletic, Dumbarton (June 1974), Coventry City (£40,000, August 1976), FOREST (for a record fee of £1.25 million, July 1980), Brest/France (summer, 1984), Sunderland (January 1985-May 1986), CS Maritimo/Madiera (1986-87), Australian football (1987-88).

Signed for a club record fee when the transfer market was seriously overheating, auburn-haired striker Ian Wallace - brave and aggressive who could be slightly reckless at times - paid back a massive chunk of that huge amount of money by topping Forest's scoring charts three seasons running, 1980-83, when linked up splendidly with first Garry Birtles, and then Trevor Francis, Peter Ward and John Fashanu and others. He made his Forest debut v. Spurs on the opening day off the 1980-81 season and netted his first two goals for the Reds in a 5-0 demolition of Stoke City in his fourth League match.

His dynamic attacking qualities first came to light with Dumbarton and then developed even further at Highfield Road as he rattled in no fewer than 60 goals in 140 senior games for Coventry (being the first Sky Blues player incidentally to net over 20 goals in Division One: 1977-78), although his initial year at Highfield Road was somewhat traumatic, when, just before Christmas 1976, he was involved in a serious road accident when he was hurled through the windscreen of his car. He was out of action for two months with serious cuts and bruising around his eye - and then on his comeback he received another bad eye injury and had to be rushed to hospital.

He bounced back in style by cracking in a hat-trick past future Reds' star Peter Shilton, then of Stoke, the team he seemed to fancy playing against quite a lot! He formed a fine strike-partnership with Mick Ferguson at Coventry

At his best he certainly buzzed around the penalty area with some purpose, taking full toll of any defensive slips by the opposition.

His three full caps for Scotland were gained against Bulgaria, Portugal and Wales (1978-79) and he played in one Under-21 international.

WALLACE, Robert Stewart

Left-half: 269 apps. 2 goals
Born: Greenock, 20 January 1893.
Died: 16 October 1970
Career: Regent Star (Rutherglen), Linfield (January 1921), FOREST (June 1923), Burton Town (June 1931)

A sturdy half-back, Bob Wallace, although born in Scotland, played his first serious football in Ireland with Linfield the team he also skippered. After two-and-a-half years on the Emerald Isle he moved to the City Ground and walked straight into the Forest team at the age of 30, taking over from Noah Burton and going on to form a superb middle-line with Irishman Gerry Morgan and Jackie Belton. He was eventually made Forest's captain and continued playing at left-half until 1931 when he moved into non-League soccer with Burton Town.

WALLBANKS, Frederick

Left-back/half-back/forward/outside-left: 8 apps.
Born: Platt Bridge, near Wigan, 14 May 1908.
Career: Spen Black & Whites FC (County Durham), Crook Town (amateur forms, 1919), Bury (professional, May 1929), Chesterfield (August 1930), Scarborough (June 1931), Bradford City (May 1932), West Ham United (December 1934), FOREST (August 1935), Northampton Town (May 1936). He did not feature after WW2.

Fred Wallbanks was one of five famous footballing brothers who all played soccer in the 1930s/40s - Arthur, George, James, John and William, being the others with James having the better career overall, serving with Barnsley, Norwich City, Northampton Town, Wigan Athletic, Millwall and Reading in that order. Unfortunately Fred never really made the grade as a professional despite his willingness. Once an aspiring wing-half, he later had spells as an inside and then as a centre-forward (initially with Crook) before settling down as a full-back. He appeared in only 29 League games (3 goals scored) during his career. He played once for West Ham (in an FA Cup-tie v. Stockport County); scored 24 goals for non-Leaguers Scarborough (1931-32) and had his best spell with Bradford (15 outings). He made his debut for Forest in September 1935 v. Fulham (home) and his last outing for the Reds came in a 5-0 defeat at Old Trafford (v. Manchester United) three months later. He deputised for Jim Barrington in each of his eight outings for the club.

WALSH, Colin David
Left-winger: 143+31 apps. 37 goals
Born: Hamilton, 22 July 1962
Career: FOREST (apprentice, July 1978, professional August 1979), Charlton Athletic (£125,000, September 1986), Peterborough United (on loan, February 1989), Middlesbrough (on loan, January 1991); quit League football in May 1991.
After gaining honours at Schoolboy and Youth levels for Scotland (12 caps gained for the latter), Colin Walsh went on to represent his country in seven Under-21 internationals and was, in fact, an unused sub for his country v. Wales in 1985.
A positive winger, brave, full of dash and commitment, with an educated left foot, he had a wonderful career that produced a total of more than 450 senior appearances (399 in the Football League). He was a Full Members Cup runner-up with Charlton in 1987, the year he also broke his leg (v. Newcastle United) and then fracturing the same leg against Arsenal reserves in 1988.
Great with free-kicks, he was brilliant at times with Forest for whom he scored on his home League debut against Crystal Palace in December 1980 (won 3-0), having earlier played his first match for the Reds as a substitute v. Coventry City the previous week.

WAPLINGTON, Samuel
Right-half: one app.
Born: Basford, 13 April 1896.
Career: FOREST (August 1919-May 1921).
A reserve half-back, Sammy Waplington took over at right-half from the injured Joe Mills for his only senior game for Forest against Port Vale on 31 January 1920.

WARD, Darren
Goalkeeper: 130 apps. no goals
Born: Worksop, 11 May 1974
Career: Mansfield Town (trainee, July 1990, professional July 1992), Notts County (£160,000, July 1995), FOREST (free transfer, May 2001).
A Welsh international with two Under-21, one 'B' and four senior caps to his credit, goalkeeper Darren Ward joined Forest on a 'Bosman' free transfer in May 2001 after making 302 appearances for the Magpies, helping them win the Third Division title in 1998. Regarded as one of the best 'keepers in the Nationwide League over a four-year period (from 1999) Ward has amassed around 500 senior appearances.

WARD, Denis
Goalkeeper: one app.
Born; Burton-on-Trent, 25 October 1924
Career: FOREST (professional, August 1947), Stockport County (August 1949), Hastings United (1953), Bradford Park Avenue (August 1955-May 1958).
Denis Ward made his Forest debut in the Second Division

v. Luton Town on 13 December 1947 as a replacement for Harry Walker. He later made over 50 League appearances for both Stockport and Bradford PA.
A reserve at the City Ground, along with Laurie Platts (who had been first choice immediately after WW2) Ward enjoyed an ideal keeper's physique; he was a safe handler whose anticipation was first-class.

WARD, Peter David
Striker: 33+6 apps. 7 goals
Born: Derby, 27 July 1955
Career: Burton Albion (1972), Brighton & Hove Albion (May 1975), FOREST (October 1980), Seattle Sounders on loan April 1982). Brighton & Hove Albion (on loan, October 1982), Seattle Sounders (April 1983), Vancouver Whitecaps (April 1984).
Capped once by England at senior level (v. Australia, May 1980) and twice for the Under-21 side, Peter Ward was a quick mover and a voracious snapper-up of half-chances as well as a striker with an individual flair. He netted 79 goals in 178 League games for Brighton before joining Forest for whom he made his League debut against Leeds United at the City Ground in October 1980 (won 2-1). He returned to Hove in 1982 (on loan) and added a further two goals to his tally in 10 games. During his first spell at the Goldstone Ground his efforts were greatly appreciated by the supporters as the Gulls gained promotion to the First Division (1979). He went on to score a few goals in the NASL.

WARNER, Vance
Defender: 5+1 apps.
Born: Leeds, 3 September 1974
Career: FOREST (apprentice, June 1991, professional, September 1994), Grimsby Town (on loan, February 1996), Rotherham United (August 1997-June 2000).
Strong tackling, quite quick, Vance Warner, a former England Youth international, could never really make his mark in Forest's first XI, and after a loan spell with Grimsby Town he went on to appear in 71 senior games for the Millers before his release from Millmoor at the end of the 1999-2000 season.

WARREN, Frederick
Centre-half: 27 apps. 2 goals
Born: Newhall, 1878
Career: Derby Hill Ivanhoe FC, FOREST (May 1902), Ashbourne (August 1905).
Centre-half Fred Warren had one good season with Forest, making 19 League appearances in 1903-04 and scoring one goal. He surprisingly scored for the Reds when making his League debut for Forest in the 1-1 draw at Everton in October 1902 when he deputised for Fred Forman at the heart of the defence. He was a reliable defender with a liking for going forward though quick to get back should danger threaten.

WASSALL, Darren Paul James
Defender: 30+15 apps. one goal
Born: Birmingham, 27 June 1968
Career: FOREST (apprentice, June 1984, professional June 1986), Hereford United (on loan, October 1987), Bury (on loan, March 1989), Burton Albion (on loan, briefly), Derby County (£600,000, June 1992), Manchester City (on loan, September 1996), Birmingham City (£100,000, March 1997), Burton Albion (May 2000).
Versatile defender Darren Wassall played for Forest in the 1992 League Cup final defeat by Manchester United, but was a winner in the Zenith Data Systems Cup final that same year. A strong, tough-tackling defender he never really commanded a regular first-team place at the City Ground, his best season coming in 1991-92 (his last) when he appeared in 22 first-class matches. He made his League debut for the Reds in a 1-1 draw away at Southampton in February 1988.
When he was with Birmingham, Wassall was sidelined for 15 months (until December 1998) after undergoing the last of three Achilles tendon operations.

WATSON, Peter Frederick
Centre & left-half/centre-forward/left-back: 13 apps.
Born: Stapleford, 15 April 1934
Career: FOREST (juniors, summer 1951, professional May 1955), Southend United (July 1959-May 1966).
Centre-half was Peter Watson's chosen position, although during 1956-57 he occupied both the centre-forward and full-back berths for Forest, having failed to gain a regular place in the first XI. However, he made well over 250 senior appearances for the Shrimpers after leaving the City Ground where he had acted as reserve to the likes of initially Horace Gager and then Bob McKinlay. Capable and confident, he was a loyal servant to Forest, staying with the club for eight years. He made his League debut (in place of McKinlay) against Lincoln City (away) in April 1956 (won 3-1).

WEALTHALL, Barrington Arthur L
Full-back: 4 apps.
Born: Nottingham, 1 May 1942
Career: FOREST (juniors, June 1957, professional June 1959), Grimsby Town (May 1962), York City (June 1963-May 1967).
Barry Wealthall - a National Association of Boys' Clubs international, played his best football with York City, making 75 League appearances for the Minstermen during his four years at Bootham Crescent. A well-built defender, and fringe player at the City Ground, he made his League debut for Forest against Cardiff City (at home) in January 1961 when he was chosen to fill in at right-back in the absence of Roy Patrick.

WEBB, Neil John
Born: Reading, Berkshire, 30 July 1963
Career: Reading (apprentice summer 1979, professional November 1980), Portsmouth (£87,500, July 1982), FOREST (£250,000, June 1985), Manchester United (£1.5 million, July 1989), FOREST (£800,000, November 1992), Swindon Town (on loan, October 1994), Grimsby Town (non-contract, August-October 1996), Exeter City, Weymouth (player-coach), Aldershot Town, Merthyr Tydfil, Reading Town (manager, 2000-01), Weymouth (manager, briefly); also played for England Veterans' XI and worked for local radio covering Reading's home matches at the Madejski Stadium. Now employed as a postman in Reading.
Neil Webb was a competitive midfielder who amassed almost 400 League and Cup appearances for his three previous clubs before his big money move to Old Trafford in 1989. He was only 19 years of age when he switched to Fratton Park and was just 22 when Forest boss Brian Clough enticed him to the City Ground. In 1989 he starred in two Wembley triumphs with Forest - helping them win the Simod Cup and the League Cup, scoring in a 3-1 victory over Luton Town in the latter. He was then snatched away by Alex Ferguson but a ruptured Achilles tendon forced him out of action early in the 1989-90 season. He recovered full fitness and at the end of that campaign helped United beat Crystal Palace in the FA Cup final replay. Unfortunately he missed the following year's European Cup-Winners Cup final triumph over Barcelona and was substituted as United lost to Sheffield Wednesday in that season's League Cup final. Nevertheless he earned his place in England's squad for the ill-fated European Championships in Sweden before returning to the City Ground in the winter of 1992, helping Forest regain their top Division status in 1994. He quit competitive football in 1996 with well over 700 appearances under his belt (140 goals scored). His League record was 456 appearances and 114 goals.
Capped initially by England as Youth team player, Webb represented his country in 26 senior internationals and appeared in three Under-21 games, starred four times for the 'B' team and also played for the Football League side. His father Doug was an inside-forward with Reading during the period 1955-67.

WEIGHTMAN
Inside-forward: 4 apps. 2 goals
Born: circa 1868
Career: FOREST (seasons: 1889-91)
Weightman scored on his debut for Forest in a Football Alliance 3-1 defeat away at Sheffield Wednesday in January 1890, when he deputised for Fred Burton. He scored his second goal for the Reds soon afterwards in a 1-1 home draw with Long Eaton Rangers.

WELLS, Peter Arthur
Goalkeeper: 34 apps.
Born: Nottingham, 13 August 1956
Career: FOREST (apprentice, August 1971, professional October 1974), Southampton (£8,000, December 1976), Millwall (on loan, February 1983, transferred May 1983), Leyton Orient (July 1985), Fisher Athletic (July 1989).
Initially reserve to John Middleton, Peter Wells was an agile, brave and daring goalkeeper who made his League debut for Forest v. York City in November 1975, making 23 appearances in the Second Division that season.
Following his transfer to the Dell, Wells became the fifth goalkeeper employed by Southampton during the 1976-77 season. He went on to appear in 160 first-class matches for Saints over a period of seven years, during which time he had to compete with the likes of Terry Gennoe, Chris Turner, Ivan Katalinic and Steve Middleton, and it wasn't until the arrival of another ex-Forest star, Peter Shilton (in 1982), that Wells finally relinquished the 'keeper's jersey at Southampton whom he helped gain promotion to the First Division in 1978.

WEST, Enoch James
Inside or centre-forward: 183 apps. 100 goals
Born: Hucknall Torkard, Nottinghamshire, 31 March 1886.
Career: Hucknall Constitutionals (1900), Sheffield United (late 1901), FOREST (£5, July 1905), Manchester United (June 1910). Suspended sine die, from December 1915.
Enoch 'Knocker' West scored a century of goals for both Forest and Manchester United, the latter in 181 outings. He helped Forest win the Second Division championship in 1907 and was one of a trio of players who scored hat-tricks in that joint record First Division win of 12-0 over Leicester Fosse in April 1909. Two years later he helped United win the First Division title.
Powerful in all aspects of forward play, West replaced Bill Shearman in the Forest attack and he quickly drew up a fine and understanding partnership with Gren Morris. During his time with the club he actually played in every forward position but inside-right was his first choice. He served the club tremendously well, securing five hat-tricks for Forest (four in the League, one in the FA Cup) and, in fact, he became one of the few players to hit four goals in one game for Forest, doing so against Sunderland in November 1907. He struck 14 League goals when Forest won the Second Division title in 1907.
* In April 1915 he was involved in a plot to fix the result of the Manchester United v. Liverpool League game. As a result he was suspended for life (with seven other players). West's was the longest ban in football at that time. It was eventually lifted when he was approaching his 60th birthday - in November 1945 - after almost 30 years! West played for the Football League v. the Southern League in 1912 - his only representative honour. He was also a fine billiards player and could well have become a professional in that field.

WESTCARR, Craig Naptali
Striker: 3+20 apps. one goal
Born: Nottingham, 29 January 1985
Career: FOREST (apprentice, June 2001, professional January 2003).
England Youth international striker Craig Westcarr re-wrote the Forest record books in November 2001 when he made his first-team debut as a second-half substitute against Burnley at the City Ground at the age of 16 years, 257 days, making him the youngest player ever to appear in a Football League game for the Reds. He had a great opportunity to score in that game, firing straight at the 'keeper in a one-on-one situation - but his time will come!

WHARE, William Frederick
Right-back: 322 apps. 2 goals
Born: Guernsey, 14 May 1924. Died: May 1995.
Career: FOREST (professional, May 1947, retired May 1960).
Recommended to Forest by ex-player Billy Walker, full-back Bill Whare played exceedingly well when the Reds captured the Third Division South title in 1951. Six years later he appeared in 13 games when promotion was gained to the top flight and in 1959 he collected an FA Cup winners' medal when Luton were beaten 2-1 at Wembley. Whare actually made his Football League debut in the left-half position in May 1949 but it was at right-back where he made his name. Indeed, his grip on the number 2 shirt meant that the previous right-back, Geoff Thomas, had to be switched to the left to accommodate the impressive Whare. The pair then played magnificently together as partners right through until 1958.

WHEATLEY, Roland
Wing-half: 6 apps.
Born: Radford, Nottingham, 20 June 1924
Died: July 2003.
Career: Beeston Boys Club, FOREST (professional, June 1946), Southampton (January 1949), Grimsby Town (June 1951), Halifax Town (January 1952), Workington (March 1952), Corby Town (July 1952), Stamford (June 1953), Southampton (scout in the Midlands, from 1955 until 1973).
Ron Wheatley originally earned a living working down a Nottingham pit and when WW2 broke out he enlisted as a paratrooper. Wounded during the combat he subsequently struggled to regain full fitness and, having made his Football League debut for the Reds against Brentford at Griffin Park in September 1947, was on the brink of quitting the game after failing to establish himself in Forest's League side when Southampton contacted manager Billy Walker to offer him a life-line - which he greatly accepted. A player with a superb left-foot, but perhaps lacking in speed, he had made only 12 appearances for Saints when doctors diagnosed a heart defect and the beginnings of arthritis. Advised to retire (September 1949) Wheatley was placed in charge of the 'A'

team at the Dell and then confounded the medical experts by returning to first team action. All told he served Southampton FC for some 20 years.

WHITCHURCH, J Herbert
Centre-forward/inside-left: 27 apps. 8 goals
Born: circa 1883
Career: FOREST (August 1905), Ilkeston Town (May 1910).
Versatile forward Bert Whitchurch spent five years with Forest during which time he found himself acting as reserve to the likes of Gren Morris, Tom Niblo and Enoch West, never really having a decent run in the side despite some very promising performances. He made his League debut for the Reds at centre-forward in the 1-1 draw at Blackburn in December 1905 and scored his first two goals in a 3-1 home win over Chesterfield almost ten months later.

WHITE, John W
Right-back: 28 apps.
Born: circa 1879
Career: FOREST (April 1901), New Brompton (August 1903); also Nottingham Forest Committee Member.
A League debutant for Forest v. Sheffield Wednesday in November 1901, Jack White had his best spell in the first team soon afterwards, appearing in 24 consecutive matches including the FA Cup semi-final v. Southampton, before losing his place at right-back to Charlie Craig. Besides being a useful defender, fast, strong in the tackle and physically sound, Jack White was also an active committee member at Forest.

WHITE, Thomas
Defender: 0+1 app.
Born: Brandon, 1953
Career: FOREST (apprentice, June 1969, professional, 1971, forced to retire in 1973 through injury).
A 6ft 2in, 12st defender, Tom White never got a real chance with Forest - his only senior game was as a second-half substitute in a 3rd round League Cup replay against Chelsea at Stamford Bridge in October 1971. Sadly he was forced to retire (through injury) at the age of 20.

WHITEFOOT, Jeffrey
Wing-half: 285 apps. 7 goals
Born: Cheadle, Cheshire, 31 December 1933.
Career: Manchester United (junior, June 1949), professional December 1951), Grimsby Town (November 1957), FOREST (July 1958); retired, May 1968 through injury). Served in the RAF (1951-52).
Jeff Whitefoot - an original 'Busby Babe' - was only 16 years, 105 days old when he made his League debut for Manchester United against the reigning champions Portsmouth at Old Trafford on 14 April 1950 making him the youngest player ever to serve the club at senior level.

Capped by England at Schoolboy level, and later by the Under-23s (v. Italy) wing-half Whitefoot gained a regular place in the first XI during the 1953-54 campaign and two years later collected a League Championship winning medal before losing his place to Eddie Colman. After a season at Blundell Park, he moved to Forest (as a replacement for Bill Morley) and gave the Reds supreme service, amassing a fine record of 285 League and Cup appearances, helping Billy Walker's side win the FA Cup in 1959. He was eventually replaced in the side by Henry Newton.

WIDDOWSON, Thomas Weller
Outside-right/goalkeeper: 9 apps.
Born: Hucknall Torkard, circa 1867.
Career: FOREST (seasons 1890-91)
Short of players, Forest recruited Tom Widdowson (usually regarded as a goalkeeper) to play on the right-wing in their final Football Alliance game of the 1889-90 season. The game was lost 2-0 and afterwards Forest were fined for fielding an unregistered player. However, Widdowson did play for the club again the following season, making a further five appearances in the Alliance and three more in the FA Cup.

WIGHTMAN, Harold
Centre-half: 138 WW1 apps.
Born: Sutton-in-Ashfield, 19 June 1894.
Died: Nottingham, 5 April 1945
Career: Sutton Town (August 1908), Mansfield Mechanics, Eastwood Rangers, Chesterfield (July 1913), FOREST (WW2 guest, September 1915-May 1919), Derby County (July 1919, then assistant-manager season 1928-29), Chesterfield (May 1929), Notts County (player-coach/assistant-manager, May 1930-June 1931), Luton Town (manager, June 1931-October 1935), Derby County (scout, October 1935), Mansfield Town (manager, January-May 1936), FOREST (manager, May 1936-March 1939).
A solid, well-built centre-half, Harry Wightman had his career severely disrupted by WW1, although he did appear in 138 first-team matches as a guest for Forest during the hostilities, helping them win the 1919 Victory Shield (v. Everton). After leaving the City Ground he scored nine goals in 180 League games for the Rams and two in 38 for Chesterfield, the club that had rejected him in 1913.
Wightman later became a respected manager, leading Notts County to the Third Division South championship in 1931. He was George Jobey's assistant at Derby, and as a player helped the Rams gain promotion from Division Two in 1926 while also receiving FA honours v. France and the Combined Universities. He was Forest's first official team manager (prior to that the manager was part of a committee).

WIGLEY, Stephen
Winger: 92+14 apps. 3 goals.
Born: Ashton-under-Lyne, 15 October 1961.
Career: Curzon Ashton, FOREST (professional, March 1981), Sheffield United (October 1985), Birmingham City (player-exchange deal involving Martin Kuhl, March 1987), Portsmouth (£350,000, March 1989), Exeter City (August 1993), Bognor Regis Town (1994), Aldershot Town (March 1995); later returned to FOREST as first team coach.
A speedy winger, good on the ball, Steve Wigley made over 100 appearances under Brian Clough before transferring to Bramall Lane. A good crosser of the ball, a lot of his work (especially at St Andrew's) went to waste and his best efforts came at Fratton Park when he had centre-forward Guy Whittingham to aim at. His career realised a total of almost 400 League and Cup appearances.

WIGNALL, Francis
Striker: 178+1 apps. 53 goals
Born: Chorley, Lancs, 21 August 1939
Career: Horwich RMI, Everton (professional, May 1958), FOREST (£20,000, June 1963), Wolverhampton Wanderers (£50,000, March 1968), Derby County (£20,000, February 1969), Mansfield Town (£8,000, November 1971-May 1973), King's Lynn (player-manager, July 1973), Burton Albion (manager, August 1974), Qatar (October 1975, appointed national coach, 1980), Shepshed Charterhouse (manager July 1981-March 1983).
Frank Wignall scored 107 goals in 323 League games for his four clubs over a period of 15 years. He lost his place to Alex Young at Goodison Park and broke his leg as a Forest player in 1964-65, having earlier scored a hat-trick v. Bolton (February 1964) which coincided with the debut for Forest of Alan Hinton.
After making his League debut for Forest against Aston Villa on the opening day of the 1963-64 season (a 1-0 defeat) Wignall scored his first goal for the Reds soon afterwards in a 2-1 win at Liverpool. And then, along with Colin Addison, he formed an excellent strike-partnership over the next two-and-a-half seasons, Addison contributing 33 League goals while Wignall himself netted 36. Then Joe Baker appeared on the scene (in place of Addison) and he also did the business in terms of goalscoring, aiding and abetting Wignall very well, indeed, before the latter moved to Wolves in 1968. After his spells at Molineux (16 goals in 36 games) and the Baseball Ground (17 strikes in 57 outings) Wignall was signed by Mansfield's chairman Arthur Patrick immediately after Jock Basford had been dismissed and just a few hours before Danny Williams was appointed boss at Field Mill. However, despite his experience and scoring record, he failed to save the Stags from relegation. He did, though, manage Shepshed Charterhouse during a purple patch in the club's history. Much earlier, as a player, Wignall

represented the FA v. Mexico and played for the Football League XI.

WILKINS, Ernest George
Inside/centre-forward: 26 apps. 7 goals
Born: Hackney, 27 October 1919. Deceased.
Career: Hayes, Brentford (professional, February 1938), Bradford Park Avenue (February 1947), FOREST (December 1947), Leeds United (September 1949, retired in May 1950 through injury.).
WW2 severely affected George Wilkins' career. Prior to the hostilities, he had scored seven goals in 29 League games for Brentford whom he served off and on during the war (amassing almost 100 more appearances) as well as guesting for several other clubs including Portsmouth and West Ham United. But when peace returned he took time to re-establish himself in the game, failing to made an impact at Park Avenue. He then averaged a goal every four games for Forest, scoring on his debut for the club in a 4-2 home win over Doncaster Rovers (Division 2) a few days after Christmas, 1947.
On his day Wilkins - short, stocky and sturdy - was fast and clever, described in some quarters as being a 'calculating craftsman' who possessed a 'rattling' good shot (in both feet) and was a dangerous forward to oppose.
Wilkins (who won shoals of medals and trophies as a teenager before leaving Hayes) throughout his career regarded his mother as his fiercest critic, saying that she knew more about the game than many of the male self-styled experts.
George was the father of Ray Wilkins who starred for Manchester United, Chelsea and England.

WILKINSON, Frank T
Half-back: one app.
Born: circa 1873
Career: FOREST (seasons: 1895-97)
Reserve defender at Forest for two seasons, Frank Wilkinson appeared in just one senior game, taking over at right-half in the League fixture against Blackburn Rovers in November 1896. Jack MacPherson was injured and Frank Forman moved to centre-half to accommodate Wilkinson.

WILKINSON, Paul
Striker: 40+3 apps. 8 goals
Born: Grimoldby, near Louth, Lincolnshire, 30 October 1964
Career: Lincolnshire School & Junior football, Grimsby Town (apprentice July 1981, professional November 1982), Everton (£250,000, March 1985), FOREST (£200,000, March 1987), Watford (£300,000, August 1988), Middlesbrough (£550,000, August 1991), Oldham Athletic (on loan, October 1995), Watford (on loan, December 1995), Luton Town (on loan, March 1996), Barnsley (free transfer, July 1996), Millwall (£150,000, September 1997), Northampton Town (free

transfer, July 1998, retired in June 2000). Later coached in Qatar (2001-02). Now runs a garage and car showroom in Nottingham.

Paul Wilkinson was a fast and dangerous striker, possessing exceptional heading ability, a powerful right-foot shot and sufficient strength to hold off the strongest of defenders. An England Under-21 international (4 caps gained) he was a Charity Shield winner in 1986 with Everton whom he also helped win the League title in 1987 (before moving to Forest) and in 1995 was a member of Middlesbrough's First Division championship winning squad. He netted 33 goals in 87 games for Grimsby and 16 in 46 for Everton before joining Forest, making his senior debut for the Reds against Manchester United at Old Trafford a day or so later. He did well alongside Nigel Clough at the City Ground before moving south to Watford. He netted 57 times in 155 games for the Hornets, added a further 66 goals to his tally in 202 appearances for Middlesbrough, claimed just two more goals in 12 loan games and then notched 11 in 55 outings for Barnsley, three in 33 for Millwall and finally one in 20 for the Cobblers, retiring in 2000 with a fine record under his belt of 197 goals in 653 senior appearances (at club level).

WILLIAMS, Brett

Left-back: 49 apps.
Born: Dudley, 19 March 1968
Career: FOREST (apprentice, June 1984, professional December 1985), Stockport County (on loan, March 1987), Northampton Town (on loan, January 1988), Hereford United (on loan, September 1989), Oxford United (on loan, February 1992), Stoke City (on loan, August 1993), Oxford United (October 1993-May 1994).
Brett Williams played at left-back for Forest in their 1992 League Cup final defeat by Manchester United. Loaned out no fewer than five times in six-and-half years, he was never really a regular at the City Ground despite some gritty performances, his best season coming in 1985-86 when he appeared in 13 first-class matches. He made his League debut for Forest against Birmingham City on Boxing Day 1985.

WILLIAMS, Gareth John

Midfielder: 124+11 apps. 3 goals
Born: Glasgow, 16 December 1981
Career: FOREST (trainee, April 1997, professional, December 1998).
A talented young midfielder with plenty to offer, Gareth Williams won his first full cap for Scotland v. Nigeria in April 2002 and has since added a further three appearances. A regular i the first-team lne-up in 2002-03 he looks sure to be a major figure as the Reds seek to find their way back into the Premiership.

WILLIAMS, John

Centre-forward: 4 apps. one goal
Born: Circa 1890
Career: FOREST (seasons 1911-13)
Jack Williams was a reserve centre-forward with Forest for two seasons during which time he was called up for first-team duty on four occasions, making a scoring debut in the home League game against Huddersfield Town on 16 March 1912 when he stood in for Frank Saunders.

WILLIAMSON, Brian William

Goalkeeper: 20 apps.
Born: Blyth, 6 October 1939
Career: Seaton Delaval, Gateshead (October 1958), Crewe Alexandra (July 1960), Leeds United (December 1962), FOREST (February 1966), Leicester City (on loan, August 1967), Fulham (November 1968, retired through injury in May 1970).
Goalkeeper Brian Williamson made 55 League appearances for both Gateshead and Crewe before spending just over five years in Leeds' reserve side, having only a handful of senior outings for the Elland Road club. He was recruited as cover for Peter Grummitt by Forest but with Gordon Marshall also at the City Ground, first-team opportunities dwindled and after a loan spell with Leicester (actually borrowed when Peter Shilton was injured) he chose to move south to Fulham, eventually retiring in 1970 to go into the security business. Williamson, who had the annoying habit of punching almost every aerial ball, made his League debut for Forest against Newcastle in January 1968, playing well in a 0-0 draw.

WILLIAMSON, W

Inside-right: 2 apps.
Born: circa 1870
Career: FOREST (seasons 1890-92)
Williamson played in two Football Alliance games for Forest - in February and April 1892 - against Lincoln City and Crewe Alexandra respectively, taking over from Billy Smith each time.

WILSON, Daniel Joseph

Midfielder: 9+2 apps. one goal
Born: Wigan, 1 January 1960
Career: Wigan Athletic, Bury (September 1977), Chesterfield (£100,000, July 1980), FOREST (£50,000, January 1983), Scunthorpe United (on loan, October 1983), Brighton & Hove Albion (£100,000, November 1983), Luton Town (£150,000, July 1987), Sheffield Wednesday (£200,000, August 1990), Barnsley (£200,000, June 1993, player-manager 1994, retired as a player, May 1995), Sheffield Wednesday (manager, July 1998), Bristol City (manager, June 2000).
Capped 25 times by Northern Ireland, midfielder Danny Wilson, was a most astute footballer with seemingly plenty

of time and space when in possession. A genuine craftsman with adept control and stratagems which were a delight to savour, he amassed more than 760 League and Cup appearances (113 goals scored) during his 20-year playing career. He netted on his League debut for Forest against Aston Villa in February 1983, but never really settled down at the City Ground. His best years were spent at Brighton, Luton and Hillsborough, being a League Cup winner and then runner-up with Luton in 1988 and 1989, (the latter v. his former club Forest), and then a League Cup winner again with the Owls in 1991 (v. Manchester United) and a loser in 1993 (v. Arsenal).

WILSON, David Edward Joseph
Forward: 8 apps.
Born: Wednesfield near Wolverhampton, 4 October 1944
Career: FOREST (amateur, November 1959, professional October 1961), Carlisle United (£8,000, October 1965), Grimsby Town (£10,000, March 1967), Walsall (£10,000, September 1968), Burnley (£15,000, September 1969), Chesterfield (free transfer, June 1971, East London/South Africa (cs. 1975).

Dave Wilson was spotted by the former Aston Villa and England left-winger Eric Houghton and in no time at all he was bedded in at the City Ground, coming through the junior and intermediate ranks with flying colours. Unfortunately he failed to gain a regular place in the first XI, despite a handful of encouraging displays, and after leaving Forest, he went from strength to strength. Over the next 14 years he scored well over 80 goals in almost 350 senior appearances, including a haul of 76 in 294 League outings, as a fast and dangerous forward.

He made his League debut for the Reds just two days past his 18th birthday against Fulham in 1962 (won 3-1).

WILSON, Joseph
Full-back: 92 apps. one goal
Born: Workington, 6 July 1937
Career: Workington (juniors, July 1952, professional January 1956), FOREST (March 1962), Wolverhampton Wanderers (March 1965), Newport County (May 1967), Workington (September 1968-June 1973).

During his career full-back Joe Wilson drew up a fine record of 507 League appearances (10 goals) including 321 in his two spells with his home-town club Workington.

Quite fearless and imbued with an unsurpassed competitive spirit, he was renowned for his powerful tackling. Totally committed he gave wingers a hard time and was generally a reliable performer both at home and away where he was not always the home crowd's favourite visitor!

Wilson made his League debut for Forest against West Bromwich Albion at the Hawthorns in March 1962, and five years later he helped Wolves win promotion from Division Two in 1967.

WILSON, Terence
Defender/midfielder: 131+14 apps. 11 goals
Born: Broxburn, West Lothian, 8 February 1969
Career: Whitburn BC, FOREST (apprentice, July 1985, professional April 1986), Newcastle United (on loan, January 1992). Retired due to injury, March 1994; Dunfermline Athletic (on trial, July-August 1996).

Terry Wilson was both a League Cup and Simod Cup winner with Forest in 1989. He also gained two Scottish Under-21 caps before being struck down at the age of 25 by a serious knee ligament injury from which he never really recovered.

He made his League debut for the Reds as an 18-year-old v. Southampton (home) in September 1987 (as a substitute) and then scored in a 3-0 win to celebrate his full debut against Coventry City (away) a few weeks later. Virtually a regular in the side thereafter (injuries and suspensions apart) Wilson's last senior game for the club was against Arsenal in the 5th round of the League Cup in January 1993.

WILSON, Thomas
Centre-forward: 217 apps. 90 goals
Born: Bedlington, 15 September 1930. Died: 1992
Career: Cinderhill Colliery FC, FOREST (April 1951), Walsall (November 1960, retired in June 1962)

Tommy Wilson was Forest's top scorer three seasons running (to 1960). He helped the team gain promotion to the First Division in 1957 and scored the winning goal (v. Luton Town) in the 1959 FA Cup final. Originally a lively outside-right, he was switched to centre-forward and developed steadily at Forest, helping the reserves win the Midland League title three seasons running: 1952-53-54. As he got older, stronger and wiser, he began to use his physical strength to good effect, scoring goals with commendable regularity. He didn't get too many opportunities in the first team between 1951-54 but after Ronnie Blackman, who had been recruited as a direct replacement for Wally Ardron, failed to impress at the City Ground, Wilson was drafted in to lead the Reds' attack. A lack of goals, however, caused him to lose his place to Peter Higham in 1956 but he bounced back strongly and thereafter maintained a splendid strike-record that saw him average a goal every two-and-half games for Forest. On losing his place in 1960 he moved off to Walsall, retiring in 1962 after helping the Saddlers establish themselves in Division Two following their promotion the previous season. Wilson made his Football League debut for Forest against Luton Town in October 1951.

WINFIELD, Bernard John
Full-back: 408+2 apps. 5 goals
Born: Draycott, 28 February 1943.
Career: FOREST (juniors, June 1958, professional May 1960), Peterborough United (July 1974-April 1975).
John Winfield was initially a wing-half (able to play on

both sides of the pitch) before being successfully converted into a very competent full-back at the City Ground, taking the left-back berth for the first time in September 1966. Capped by England at Under-23 level, he was 6ft tall and turned out to be a wonderful servant to Forest, partnering Peter Hindley in well over 225 senior matches. He made his League debut for the Reds at right-half against Blackpool in February 1962 when he scored in a 4-3 home defeat. His 410th and last outing for the club came in April 1974 away to Aston Villa. He was replaced at left-back by Dave Jones. After leaving football Winfield went into the newsagents' business in Wollaston, later moving to the Nottingham's Victoria Shopping Centre.

WITHE, Peter

Centre-forward: 98+1 apps. 39 goals.
Born: Liverpool, 30 August 1951.
Career: Smith Coggins FC (1966), Skelmersdale, Southport (August 1971), Barrow (December 1971), Port Elizabeth City/South Africa (1972) Arcadia Shepherds/South Africa (1973), Wolverhampton Wanderers (£13,500, November 1973), Portland Timbers/NASL (1975), Birmingham City (£50,000, August 1975), FOREST (£42,000, September 1976), Newcastle United (£200,000, August 1978), Aston Villa (for a record fee of £500,000, May 1980), Sheffield United (July 1985), Birmingham City (on loan, September-November 1987), Huddersfield Town (July 1988, initially as assistant-manager/player-coach), Aston Villa (assistant manager/senior coach to Josef Venglos, January 1991, then reserve-team coach under Ron Atkinson, July 1991), Wimbledon (manager, October 1991 to January 1992), Evesham United (player, February 1992), Community Liaison Officer for the West Midlands and for Birmingham City (1993), Aston Villa (Youth Development Officer, August 1994), Thailand (national coach/manager & football advisor, 1998 to September 2003).

With Forest, striker Peter Withe gained both First Division and League Cup winners' medals in 1978, after helping the team gain promotion to the top flight and lift the Anglo-Scottish Cup a year earlier. With Aston Villa, he also collected a Division One championship medal (1981) as well as European Cup and Super Cup winners' prizes in 1982 (he scored the decisive goal in the final of the former v. Bayern Munich) and netted twice in the 1981 FA Charity Shield game with Spurs. He was capped on 11 occasions by England (as a Villa player).

One of soccer's goalscoring nomads, Withe served with 16 different football clubs at various levels during his 20-year striking career which saw him establish a wonderful record of 232 goals in 640 games (all competitions). Big, strong and fearless, he achieved an awful lot under the guidance and supervision of Brian Clough (himself a former goalscorer) and developed into a splendid target man, being a fine exponent of the chest pass. He played a major role in both Forest's and later Villa's glory years.

His brother, Chris, played for several League clubs, while his son, Jason, started off with West Brom and later served Burnley.

WOAN, Ian Simon

Winger: 237+36 apps. 40 goals
Born: Heswall, 14 December 1967
Career: Runcorn, FOREST (£80,000, March 1990), Barnsley (free transfer, August 2000), Swindon Town (free transfer, October 2000), Columbus Crew/USA (June 2001), Shrewsbury Town (free transfer, January 2002).

Ian Woan played on the wing in Forest's 1991 FA Cup final defeat by Spurs and three years later helped the Reds' reach the Premiership (as runners-up) and likewise in 1998 (as First Division champions). On his day - and when on top of his game - he was hardy, energetic, ever-reliable and could win a match on his own with one piece of brilliance, either by whipping over a defence-splitting pass or smashing home an unstoppable shot.

A player with pace, ability, stamina and a will-to-win, Woan made his League debut for Forest as a substitute against Norwich City (away) in January 1991, helping sew up a thrilling 6-2 win - and he made his full debut in a 1-0 defeat at Luton two months later.

When the 2002-03 season ended - having been part of Shrewsbury's FA Cup giant-killing team with another ex-Forest player, Nigel Jemson - his career record (in England) was impressive: almost 450 appearances and 20 goals scored.

WOLFE, George

Centre-half: 135 apps. one goal
Born: London, circa 1880
Career: Northfleet (1898), Folkestone (1899), Woolwich Arsenal (March 1900), Swindon Town (May 1903), FOREST (August 1905-May 1911)

Defender George Wolfe (who could occupy all three middle-line positions but preferred the centre) played his part in helping Forest win the Second Division title in 1907. Earlier he had skippered Arsenal's reserve side after failing to establish himself in the Gunners' first XI (making only five senior appearances). On leaving London he did much better with Forest, his League debut for the Reds coming against Wolverhampton Wanderers (home) in September 1905 when George Henderson moved to left-half to accommodate him. Described as being 'a resolute, brave, confident centre-half with remarkable sureness of kick' Wolfe spent six seasons at the City Ground, during which time no fewer than six different players challenged him for the pivotal role, George Needham making the most impact.

WOOD, Alexander Lochlan
Left-back: 23 apps.
Born: Lochgelly, Fifeshire, 12 June 1907. Died: 1967.
Career: USA football with Chicago Bricklayers FC, Holley Carburetors FC (Detroit) & Brooklyn Wanderers; then Leicester City (as an amateur, February 1933), FOREST (£750, July 1936), Colchester United (1937-38), Chelmsford City (1938-39). Did not figure after WW2.
Alex 'Sandy' Wood was the only naturalised American in the Football League during the 1930s. He won a Scottish cap as a Schoolboy before settling in the States where he represented the USA v. Uruguay in a full international match. He returned to England in 1933 and signed for Leicester City. He played in 57 senior games for the Foxes, after waiting quite some time before the Home Office authorised his work permit. He vied for the left-back position with Dai Jones at Filbert Street, helping City reach the 1934 FA Cup semi-final before transferring to Forest. At the City Ground he took over from Jimmy Barrington but with John Munro in fine form and pushing hard for a first-team place, Wood eventually succumbed to the former Hearts player and quickly moved to Colchester.

WOODCOCK, Anthony Stewart
Striker: 176+4 apps. 62 goals
Born: Eastwood, Notts, 6 December 1955
Career: FOREST (apprentice, June 1972, professional January 1974), Lincoln City (on loan, February 1976), Doncaster Rovers (on loan, September 1976), 1 FC Cologne /Germany (£650,000, November 1979), Arsenal (£500,000, June 1982), 1 FC Cologne (£140,000, July 1986), Fortuna Cologne (June 1988 to 1990 then coach until 1991), VfB Leipzig (coach, 1994-95).
Twice a League Cup winner with Forest (in 1978 & 1979), scoring v. Southampton in the latter final, Tony Woodcock was also a member of the Reds' League Championship and European Cup winning teams of 1978 & 1979 respectively, having helped the club reach the top flight and win the Anglo-Scottish Cup in 1977. He struggled to get first-team football during his early years with Forest but after gaining experience via loan spells with Lincoln and Doncaster, he came back full of vim and vigour and developed into one of the finest front men in the game. He made his senior debut for the Reds against Aston Villa (away) in April 1974 and he was to return to this same ground a few years later with Arsenal and ram in no fewer than five goals when the Gunners beat Villa 6-2 in a First Division match in October 1983. A vitally important member of Brian Clough's squad, Woodcock loved to run at defenders. He would pick the ball up from a deep position and more often than not would embark on a mazy run down one of the flanks, only occasionally choosing to dart through the middle. He was a difficult customer to contain and provided the perfect foil for Peter Withe, the pair playing superbly well together until

Withe's departure in 1978. After that it was Woodcock and Birtles as the main strike force and they too did splendidly before Woodcock left to play in Germany. In fact, his transfer to Cologne constituted a new Bundesliga record. He returned to England to sign for Arsenal in 1982 and continued to be a force on the international front, going on to win a total of 42 full caps (16 goals scored) up to February 1986, having gained his first six with Forest (1978-79), claiming two goals. During his career he also represented his country in one 'B' and two Under-21 matches. He netted a total of 65 goals in 169 first-class matches for the Gunners, and was voted their 'Player of the Year' in 1983.
Woodcock now lives in Cologne and is a fully soccer qualified coach.

WOODLAND, Thomas
Outside-right or left: 5 apps. 2 goals
Born: Alfreton, Derbyshire, 1880
Career: Doncaster Rovers (April 1902), Chesterfield (August 1903), Worksop (August 1904), Rotherham County (June 1905), FOREST (June 1906), Rotherham County (cs. 1908), Alfreton (1918).A reserve winger with Forest, Tom Woodland could use both feet and had good pace but was a shade erratic with his final ball. He made his League debut for Forest on the right-flank against Burton United in December 1906 (replacing the injured Bill Shearman) but found it difficult to get any more senior outings after that, especially when Bill Hooper began to make his mark.

WOODS, Christopher Charles Eric
Goalkeeper: 7 apps.
Born: Boston, Lincs. 14 November 1959
Career: FOREST (apprentice, April 1975, professional December 1976), Queen's Park Rangers (July 1979), Norwich City (March 1981), Glasgow Rangers (1986), Sheffield Wednesday (August 1991), Reading (on loan, October 1995), Colorado Rapids (free transfer, May 1996), Southampton (free transfer, November 1996), Sunderland (non-contract, March 1997), Burnley (free transfer, July 1997). Retired in August 1998. Goalkeeper Chris Woods made all his seven senior appearances for Forest in the League Cup competition, playing a blinder between the posts when the Reds won the trophy in March 1978 v. Liverpool - having made his debut in the 4-0 3rd round victory over rivals Notts County at the City Ground the previous October. Honoured by England as a Youth team player, he later added one 'B', six Under-21 and 43 senior caps to his tally while also amassing more than 750 appearances for his major League clubs. Standing 6ft 2ins tall and weighing 13st 5 lbs (later rising to 14st 12lbs) he certainly developed into a wonderful 'keeper, being utterly reliable, safe under pressure, highly consistent, a fine shot-stopper and above all he wasn't a show-off. He won a second League Cup winners medal

and also a Second Division championship medal with Wednesday in 1985 and 1986 respectively. With Rangers he gained four Scottish Premier Division titles (1987, 1989, 1990 and 1991) and won three Scottish League Cups (1987, 1989 and 1991). During his five years at Ibrox Park he played in 220 first-class matches.

WOODS, Noel

Goalkeeper: one app.

Born: Nottingham, circa 1943

Career: FOREST (seasons: 1960-62).

Young, untried, goalkeeper Noel Woods made his one and only first-team appearance for Forest in a League Cup-tie against Gillingham on 11 September 1961, doing well in a 4-1 victory. Alas, he never got another chance (with Messrs Grummitt and Armstrong around) and was soon released by the club.

WRAGG, William A

Left-half/left-back: 59 apps. one goal

Born: Knebworth, 1875.

Career: Hucknall Portland, Stannington, FOREST (April 1896), Leicester Fosse (March 1898), Small Heath (January 1901), Watford (August 1901), Hinckley Town (June 1902), Chesterfield (August 1903), Accrington Stanley (July 1904), Brighton & Hove Albion (September 1905).

An FA Cup winner with Forest in 1898, left-half Billy Wragg created the first goal in the final v. Derby County despite carrying a leg injury, suffered early in the game. A versatile performer, who could defend as well as attack and possessed a solid tackle, he was also described as a 'hot shot from the penalty spot.' He made his League debut for the Reds against Liverpool in November 1896 (replacing Alex Stewart) and became an established first-team regular during the second half of that season and retaining his position throughout the next. After that he was switched to left-back before leaving Trentside for Leicester.

WRIGHT, Ernest James

Inside-right/outside-right: 5 apps.

Born: Nottingham, 1881

Career: FOREST (seasons 1902-04)

Ernie Wright made his League debut for Forest on Christmas Day 1903 in the home local derby with Notts County, stepping up a grade after doing well in the reserves. He played at inside-right (in place of Jack Calvey) but had to wait a month before getting another chance in the first XI, this time taking over the right-wing berth from the injured Tom Davies. His last outing was against Blackburn Rovers in a 2nd round FA Cup-tie.

WRIGHT, Ian Edward

Striker: 10 apps. 5 goals

Born: Woolwich, London, 3 November 1963

Career: Greenwich Borough, Crystal Palace (professional August 1985), Arsenal (£2.5 million, September 1991), West Ham United (£750,000, July 1998), FOREST (on loan, August-October 1999), Glasgow Celtic (free transfer, October 1999), Burnley (free transfer, February 2000). Retired in May 2000 to concentrate on being a TV presenter.

Out-and-out striker Ian Wright had a marvellous career as a professional. It spanned 15 years and in that time he accumulated a splendid club record of 625 League and Cup appearances, scoring 323 goals. He also represented England in 33 full and three 'B' internationals, adding another 10 goals to his tally. He is Arsenal's record marksman of all-time (185 goals in 288 outings) and he also holds the record of netting in seven consecutive Premiership matches for the Gunners in 1994-95. Fast, sharp, clever, an excellent header of the ball, Wright could shoot with both feet (but preferred his right) and he had the knack of sniffing out a goal opportunity when nobody else thought there wasn't a hope in hell's chance of finding the net. An instinct striker, forever alert, he simply loved scoring goals - and the fans loved him at Highbury more than anywhere else!

Surprisingly he gained very few club honours. He played and scored twice (as a substitute in the first game) for Palace in their eventual 1990 FA Cup final defeat by Manchester United; he was a Full Members Cup winner with the Eagles the following year; helped Arsenal complete the League Cup and FA Cup double in 1993 and then in 1998 was again a double winner with the Gunners when the Premiership and FA Cup came to Highbury. He made his Football League debut for Palace (as a sub) v. Huddersfield Town in August 1985; he scored his first League goal for the Eagles v. Oldham Athletic in mid-October 1985; his first game for Forest was against QPR (home) in August 1999 (scoring in a 1-1 draw) and his very last League outing was for Burnley v. Scunthorpe united (away) in May 2000. He claimed three goals in nine games for Celtic. Once a goalscorer, always a goalscorer - and 'Wrighty' was amongst the best.

* His son, Shaun Wright-Phillips, plays for Manchester City.

WRIGHT, Thomas James

Goalkeeper: 13 apps.

Born: Belfast: 29 August 1963

Career: Grange Rovers, Ballyclare, Brantwood FC, Linfield, Newcastle United (£30,000, March 1988), Hull City (on loan, February 1991), FOREST (£450,000, September 1993), Reading (on loan, October 1996), Manchester City (on loan, January 1997, signed permanently for £450,000, March 1997), Wrexham (on loan, February 1999), Newcastle United (on loan, August 1999), Bolton Wanderers (on loan, January 2001), Ballymena United (July 2001).

Registered initially as cover for Mark Crossley, Tommy Wright was in the Forest squad during the 1993-94 season when promotion was gained to the Premiership.

After starting his career in his homeland, he followed the path of former Northern Ireland international goalkeeper Willie McFaul to St James' Park and went on to make 84 appearances for the Magpies, gaining the first 22 of his 31 full caps for his country as well playing in one Under-23 and one Under-21 international and representing the Football League in 1993, and also helping United win promotion to the Premiership. Injuries interrupted his days on Tyneside but he always bounced back and on his day and in his prime, he produced some stunning performances. Signed for Forest by Frank Clark (ex-Newcastle) he was again plagued by injury at the City Ground, managing only 13 appearances for the Reds, his debut coming against his future club Bolton Wanderers (away) in September 1993 when the final scoreline was 4-3 to the home side.

He played his 181st and last senior game (with an English club) for Bolton against Forest on 17 March 2001, having appeared in his last Premiership game at the age of 37 years, 32 days for Manchester City against his former club Newcastle on 30 September 2000.

Right at the start of his career, with Linfield, he had appeared in the European Cup competition.

* Wright was a prolific athlete as a teenager, being chosen for his country at the cross-country event. He was All-Ireland champion and was offered a lucrative athletics scholarship in the USA but chose to stay in Northern Ireland as a publican.

WRIGHTMAN

Inside-left: one app
Born: circa 1868
Career: FOREST (season 1889-90)

Reserve inside-forward Wrightman made his only senior appearance for the Reds in a 3-0 1st round FA Cup defeat by Derby Midland in January. He replaced Tinsley Lindley.

YATES, Levi

Centre-forward: 10 apps. one goal
Born: Blackburn: 1890
Career: FOREST (seasons 1912-14). Did not feature after WW1.

A pre-WW1 reserve forward, Levi Yates made his Forest League debut in October 1913. v. Blackpool. He played in five successive games before returning late on to score his only goal for the club in a 2-2 local derby draw with Notts County at Meadow Lane on Christmas Day.

YOUNG, William David

Defender: 64 apps. 6 goals
Born: Heriot near Berwick-on-Tweed, 25 November 1951
Career: Seton Athletic, Aberdeen (1969), Tottenham, Hotspur (£120,000, September 1975), Arsenal (£80,000, March 1977), FOREST (December 1981), Norwich City (August 1983), Brighton & Hove Albion (on loan, March 1984), Darlington (non-contract, September-October 1984). Young later ran an equestrian centre near Newark before taking over a pub - The Bramcote Manor - on the outskirts of Nottingham.

Flame-haired centre-half Willie Young, who stood well over six feet tall, was tough, enthusiastic defender who was chased by Hearts and Coventry City as a teenager before signing as a professional for Aberdeen. He quickly carved a name for himself at Pittodrie, making five appearances at Scottish Under-23 level, the first against Wales in 1972. After moving south to Tottenham (signed by Terry Neill) he became a cult figure at White Hart Lane, going on to make 88 appearances for Spurs. An ungainly figure, he was certainly not a pretty footballer, but his presence at the heart of the defence boosted morale considerably with every team he served and few centre-forwards got the better of him, certainly not in the air. After his transfer across to Highbury, where he linked up again with Neill, he played in three successive FA Cup finals, collecting a winners' medal in the second v. Manchester United in 1979, while also gaining a European Cup-Winners Cup runners-up medal (1980). He then gave Forest good service after being recruited to replace Dave Needham, making his League debut for the Reds in a 2-1 win at Swansea City in mid-December 1981. The following season, with Colin Todd alongside him, he was in excellent form as Forest finished 5th in the First Division. Paul Hart was his replacement at the City Ground in 1983 and when he quit competitive football a year later he had amassed a fine record of 591 club appearances, scoring 46 goals.

YOUNGER, William

Inside-forward: 13 apps. 4 goals
Born: Hollywell near Whitley Bay, Northumberland, 22 March 1940
Career: Seaton Delaval, FOREST (professional, May 1957), Lincoln City (on loan, February 1961), Walsall (June 1961), Doncaster Rovers (December 1961), Hartlepool, United (August 1962), Ramsgate (July 1963).

In his early days with Forest, one reporter said of Billy Younger: '...impressed as a useful schemer, but needs more finishing power.' Indeed, he was a fine footballer but lacked the killer-touch in front of goal. During his career he netted only 12 goals in 79 League outings, including five in eight for Walsall and four in 37 for Hartlepool.

He made his senior debut for Forest in an embarrassing 7-1 home League defeat by Birmingham City in March 1959, making his last in October 1960 v. Sheffield Wednesday.

WARTIME GUESTS

Like every other club in the country, during the two World Wars Forest had several guest players serve with the club, with considerably more being called upon during the WW2 conflict when, in fact, well over 200 players from other clubs assisted Forest, with almost 60 being utilised in 1941-42 and a shade over 50 the previous season.

Here are details of some of those many guest players who donned the red and white colours of Forest. They are listed in A-Z order:

WW1

BENFIELD, Tommy - an inside-forward who served with Leicester Fosse (1910-14, making 111 appearances) and Derby County.

COWNLEY, Fred - a full back with Scunthorpe United & Lindsey before the war and Arsenal afterwards.

GADSDEN, Ernie - a left-back whose career also saw him serve with Mansfield Town (1915-16), Norwich City, Portsmouth, Blackpool and Halifax Town. He retired in 1927.

HARROP, Jimmy - a half-back from Liverpool who also assisted Aston Villa, Sheffield United and Rotherham Town during a career that spanned almost 20 years from 1904. He made over 200 League appearances all told.

HOLFORD, Tom - a top-class centre-half (and occasional centre-forward), an England international, whose career took him to Stoke, Port Vale and Manchester City, helping the latter win the Second Division title in 1910. He made 476 League appearances in all (248 for the Potters) and netted 65 goals. He also had two spells as manager of his former club Port Vale (1914-20 & 1932-35).

JEPHCOTT, Claude - speedy outside-right of West Bromwich Albion who played in the 1912 FA Cup final. He won both First and Second Division championship medals with the Baggies and later became a Director at the Hawthorns.

SHARP, Buchanan (Kenny) - a utility forward who played for Chelsea, Leicester Fosse, Tottenham Hotspur, Nelson and Southport. He netted 57 goals in his career tally of 162 League games.

SHEA, Danny - a dashing centre-forward, capped twice by England, who played League football for West Ham United, Blackburn Rovers, Fulham, Coventry City and Clapton Orient. He won a League Championship medal with Blackburn in 1914, helped Forest win the Victory Shield in 1919 and scored over 120 goals in more than 300 senior games for five major clubs.

WW2

ANTONIO, George - a wing-half or inside-forward of Stoke City who later played for Derby County, Doncaster Rovers and Mansfield Town. He died in July 1997.

ASHLEY, Harry - a WBA reserve who also served with Derby County and Darlington.

BALDWIN, Harry - goalkeeper who played for West Brom and Brighton, as well as for Walsall.

BLENKINSOPP, Tommy - sturdy defender with Grimsby Town, Middlesbrough and Barnsley who, between 1939-53, amassed almost 200 senior appearances and represented the Football League.

BOWERS, Jack - an England international centre-forward, ex-Derby County and Leicester City who, during his playing career, netted 219 goals in 285 League games.

BRAMLEY, Ernie - a well-built right-back from Mansfield Town who made over 100 first-class appearances for the Stags (1938-48).

BRAY, Jackie - an England international and Manchester City left-half who made 260 League appearances in his ten years at Maine Road (from 1929). He later managed Watford and was coach at Nelson.

BROOK, Reg - a sturdy full-back who starred pre-war for Coventry City, Southend United and Bristol City (74 League games).

BROOME, Frank - a quality England international utility forward who played for Aston Villa, Derby County, Brentford, Notts County, Crewe Alexandra and Shelbourne (Ireland). He later managed Exeter City and Southend United, was caretaker-boss at Meadow Lane and coached in Australia and the Middle-East. During his career Broome amassed in excess of 600 first-class appearances and scored some 60 goals.

BROWN, Alan - Huddersfield Town, Burnley and Notts County centre-half between 1934-49, making a total of 158 League appearances. He later managed Burnley, Sunderland and Sheffield Wednesday and coached in Norway.

BROWN, Jackie - Irish international outside-right who played for Belfast Celtic, Coventry, Wolves, Birmingham before the war and for Birmingham, Barry Town and Ipswich Town afterwards.

BURGESS, Ronnie - Welsh international wing-half (32 full caps won) who made over 300 appearances for Tottenham Hotspur (1936-54). He also played for Swansea Town and was later coach and manager of Watford and coach at Fulham.

CAIRNS, Billy - an inside-forward with Newcastle United (1933-44), Gateshead and Grimsby Town. He scored 120 goals in 221 League games for the Mariners up to 1954.

CANNING, Larry - right-winger who played for Aston Villa and Northampton Town and later became a journalist and radio commentator.

CARTER, Raich - a skilful England international inside-forward (13 caps won) who played for Sunderland, Derby County, Hull City and Cork Athletic, amassing well over 500 senior appearances and scoring almost 250 goals (1932-54). He also managed Hull and Cork as well as Leeds United, Mansfield Town and Middlesbrough.

CHADWICK, Cliff - ex-Oldham Athletic and Middlesbrough winger who played for Hull City and Darlington after the hostilities.

CHALLINOR, Jack - left-back who played for Stoke City and Linfield.

CLARKE, Ike - a high-scoring inside or centre forward with WBA and Portsmouth who gained two League championship medals with Pompey. His career realised over 100 goals in senior football.

COEN, Laurie - right-winger with WBA and Coventry City.

COLLINS, Albert - a utility forward who was registered with Chesterfield when he guested for Forest in the early 1940s. After the war he assisted Halifax, Carlisle United, Barrow, Bournemouth, Shrewsbury Town and Accrington Stanley, making well over 165 League and Cup appearances.

COPPING, Wilf - a rock-solid wing-half of Leeds United and Arsenal who gained 20 full caps for England and made more than 350 senior appearances as a professional.

CORKHILL, Billy - Belfast-born wing-half who played over 250 League games in two spells with Notts County (1931-38 & 1946-52). He also assisted Cardiff City and later managed Scunthorpe United and Bradford PA before becoming a Nottingham licensee.

COUTTS, Billy - Scottish-born inside-left who played for Hearts and Leith Athletic before joining Leicester City in 1934.

CRAWLEY, Tommy - a versatile player with Motherwell, Preston North End and Coventry City.

CRISP, George - a pre-war utility forward with Coventry City, Bristol Rovers, Newport County, Colchester United, Merthyr Town and Aston Villa (reserves) who actually signed for Forest in 1939 but had his contract cancelled.

CROOKS, Sammy - an outside-right, capped 26 times by England, who scored 101 League goals for Derby County in 408 games (1927-47). Former chairman of the PFA, Crooks later managed Shrewsbury Town, Burton Albion and Heanor Town among others and was employed as a scout for various other clubs.

CUMMINGS, George - a tough-tackling Scottish international defender who made over 200 League appearances for Aston Villa. He also played for Partick Thistle.

DAVIE, Jim - a versatile half-back with Kilmarnock, Preston North End, Northampton Town and Shrewsbury Town who made over 100 League appearances in all.

DAVIE, Jock - a centre-forward who played either side of the war for Brighton & Hove Albion & Barnsley, scoring 39 goals in 89 League games for Albion.

DEARSON, Don - a Welsh international who served with Birmingham City, Coventry City and Walsall, amassing a total of 266 League appearances.

DRURY, George - an inside-forward who played for Sheffield Wednesday, Arsenal, West Bromwich Albion and Watford.

DUNCAN, Dally - Scottish international left-winger (14 caps won) who played for Aberdeen (briefly), Hull City, Derby County and Luton Town, and later managed the Hatters and Blackburn Rovers. His career produced 114 goals in 404 League appearances (63 in 261 games for the Rams).

EDWARDS, George R - an inside-forward with Norwich City and then Aston Villa, he scored 34 goals in 138 League games for the latter club.

EGAN, Henry - scorer of 20 goals in 34 games for Forest during the 1942-44 wartime seasons, an inside/centre-forward, he played for Brighton & HA, Southend United, Aldershot and Cardiff City before the hostilities, making over 100 League appearances and netting 30 goals.

ELLIOTT, Charlie - a right-back with Chesterfield, Sheffield Wednesday and Coventry City; he made over 100 appearances for the Sly Blues either side of the war. He was also a Derbyshire county cricketer, scoring over 11,000 runs, who later became a Test Match umpire.

FINCH, Lester - an England amateur international left-winger who made his name with Barnet.

FINCH, Roy - a left-winger with Swansea Town, WBA and Lincoln City, he scored 57 goals in 275 League games for the Imps between 1948-59.

GOFFIN, Billy - an inside-forward or outside-left who played for Aston Villa and Walsall.

GRANT, Alick - a goalkeeper who before the hostilities had made five League appearances for Aldershot as well as assisting Doncaster Rovers, Sheffield United and Bury. After WW2 he played for Leicester City, Derby County, Newport County and York City.

GUTTRIDGE, Ron - a full-back with Aston Villa and Brighton & Hove Albion.

HANCOCKS, Johnny - a hard-shooting, fast-raiding outside-left who played for Walsall and Wolves. He netted 158 goals in 343 League games for the Molineux club, gaining both FA Cup and League championship medals. He also won three England caps.

HARDWICK, George - an England international full-back (13 caps won) who played in 143 League games for Middlesbrough and 190 for Oldham Athletic. He also represented Great Britain, managed both Sunderland and Gateshead and coached PSV Eindhoven as well as his former club, Middlesbrough.

HAYCOCK, Freddie - a skinny inside-forward who served with Aston Villa and Wrexham.

HOUGHTON, Eric - an England international winger and penalty expert who netted 160 goals in 301 League appearances for Aston Villa whom he later managed to FA Cup final glory in 1957. He was also boss of Notts County and chief scout at Forest (under his former playing colleague at Villa Park, Billy Walker). Houghton was a Villa director (1972-79) and later vice-president from 1983 until his death in 1996.

HUNTER, James - a dashing outside-right from Preston North End who also played for Mansfield Town and Plymouth Argyle.

ICETON, Jake - a goalkeeper whose League career took in Hull City, Fulham (90 games), Aldershot and Clapton Orient.

IVERSON, Bob - a resolute defender with Aston Villa (135 League appearances) he started his career with Lincoln City and also played for Wolves.

JENNINGS, Dennis - a versatile Birmingham City player (he played in virtually every position) who spent 15 years at St Andrew's, making over 200 senior appearances. He also played for WBA (briefly), Huddersfield Town and Grimsby Town.

JEPSON, Arthur - a goalkeeper with Mansfield Town, Stoke City, Port Vale and Lincoln City who also scouted for Coventry City and Middlesbrough and played county cricket for Nottinghamshire before becoming a Test Match umpire.

JONES, Eric - a stocky winger who played for Kidderminster Harriers, Wolves, Portsmouth, Stoke City, WBA, Brentford and Crewe Alexandra during his career which lasted for 13 years: 1935-48.

JONES, Harry 'Popeye' - an inside/centre-forward, ex-PNE who went on to score 104 goals in 169 first-team games for West Bromwich Albion (1933-43).

JONES, Leslie J - a Welsh international inside-forward (11 caps gained) who played for Cardiff City, Arsenal, Coventry City, Swansea Town and Brighton & Hove Albion as well as Barry Town and Aberdare, and during his 20-year career (1929-49) he appeared in 333 League games and scored just over 100 goals. Later Scunthorpe United manager (1950-51) and also coached at Brighton.

KIRTON, John - a solid wing-half for Stoke City who appeared in more than 200 League games for the Potters and also assisted Bradford City.

LANE, Harry - an inside-forward who played for Birmingham, Southend United (two spells) and Plymouth Argyle between 1929-49, making almost 300 League and FA Cup appearances and scoring over 75 goals.

LEWIS, Jack - pre-war WBA half-back who also played for Crystal Palace (1938-49), Bournemouth and Reading. He died in December 2002.

LINACRE, Billy - after the war he amassed 230 League appearances as a right-winger with Chesterfield, Manchester City, Middlesbrough, Hartlepool and Mansfield Town.

LOWRIE, George - a hard-shooting Welsh international centre-forward with Swansea Town, Preston North End, Coventry City, Newcastle United and Bristol City. He scored 82 goals in his tally of 148 League games.

McNAB, Sandy - a Scottish international left-half who was an FA Cup winner with Sunderland before joining WBA in 1937, later playing for Newport County. His career realised almost 150 League appearances.

McPHERSON, Ian - a Scottish-born winger who served with Rangers, Notts County (two spells), Arsenal and Brentford between 1937 and 1954. He scored 19 goals in 152 League games for the Gunners, winning a First Division championship medal in 1948.

MARTIN, Jackie - a utility forward who made over 80 League appearances for Aston Villa.

MASON, George - a stopper centre-half, he made 330 League appearances for Coventry City (1931-52).

MASSIE, Alex - Scottish international wing-half who played for and managed Aston Villa between 1935 and 1950.
He also assisted Ayr United, Bury, Hearts and Partick Thistle and was boss of Torquay United (season 1950-51) and Hereford United (1951-November 1952).

MERRICK, Gil - England international goalkeeper (23 caps won) who made a record 485 League appearances for Birmingham City (1946-60). Played in the 1956 FA Cup final and later managed Birmingham.

METCALF, Walter - a left-back who played for Scarborough, Sunderland, Brentford and Coventry City who scored once in 77 League games for the Sky Blues.

MIDDLETON, Ray - an England 'B' goalkeeper who made 250 League appearances for Chesterfield (1938-51) and 116 for Derby County (1951-54). He also managed Hartlepool United and Boston United.

MILLS, Percy - a splendid full-back who made well over 400 League appearances for Notts County (1927-39) as well has being associated, albeit briefly, with both Grimsby Town and Hull City.

MORGAN, Billy - a pre-war Coventry City goalkeeper who also played briefly for Wolves reserves.

PARR, Jack - a dogged full-back who played in 112 League games for both Derby County and Shrewsbury Town between 1938-56.

PIMBLEY, Doug - an outside-left with Birmingham City and Notts County.

POTTS, Vic - a full-back who served with Spurs, Doncaster Rovers and Aston Villa, making over 80 League appearances in total.

ROBERTSON, James - an inside-forward with both Bradford clubs, Park Avenue & City.

RUTHERFORD, Joe - the Aston Villa goalkeeper who played for Southport before making more than 150 senior appearances during his 13 years at Villa Park (1939-52).

SHAW, Cecil - a well-built full-back with Wolves and WBA, he made a combined total of 284 League appearances for the two Black Country clubs. He was a penalty-kick expert.

SMITH, Wilf - a full-back or half-back who made almost 100 League & FA Cup appearances for Port Vale.

STARLING, Ronnie - an England international inside-forward and FA Cup winner with Sheffield Wednesday in 1935. He also played for Hull City, Newcastle United and Aston Villa and made over 400 League appearances during his lengthy career (63 goals).

STEELE, Fred - hot-shot centre-forward of Stoke City (140 goals in 224 League games). He also played for Mansfield Town and Port Vale and then as manager, he took the latter club to the 1954 FA Cup semi-finals as well as to the Third Division North championship.

TRIGG, Cyril - a centre-forward and later a full-back with Birmingham City, he scored over 150 goals for them in League, FA Cup and wartime football between 1935-54.

TUDOR, Bill - a Welsh-born centre-half of WBA who also played for Wrexham.

VAUSE, Peter - an outside-left who played for Blackburn Rovers, Blackpool, Darwen and Rochdale before the war, making only 30 League appearances in four years to 1939.

WAKEMAN, Alan - a goalkeeper with Aston Villa, Doncaster Rovers and Shrewsbury Town, whose career brought him just 23 League outings in 22 years (1938-60).

WALKER, Billy - a brilliant goalscorer for Aston Villa and England, he managed Sheffield Wednesday to FA Cup glory in 1935 and later did likewise with Forest in 1959. (see: Forest Managers).

WARE, Harry - a pre-war inside-forward with Stoke City, Newcastle United, Sheffield Wednesday and Norwich City, he scored 38 goals in a total of 152 League appearances.

WARING, Tom 'Pongo' - a dynamic pre-war centre-forward with Aston Villa for whom he scored 167 goals in 226 senior games. He also played for Tranmere Rovers, Barnsley, Wolves and Accrington Stanley and gained five full England caps.

WATSON, Willie - an England international at both football and cricket (4 full caps & 22 tests). He made over 250 League appearances while serving as an inside-forward with Huddersfield Town, Sunderland and Halifax Town (1937-56). He was later manager of Halifax and Bradford City and played county cricket for both Leicestershire and Yorkshire before becoming a Test selector, while acting as player-manager of the MCC tour party in 1963.

WESTLAND, Douglas - a competent goalkeeper who played for Aberdeen, and Stoke City.

WHITE, Fred - a Wolverhampton-born goalkeeper who played for Everton reserves, Sheffield United and Lincoln City between 1935-51.

WIGHTMAN, John - a wing-half who served with Scarborough, York City, Bradford PA, Huddersfield Town, Blackburn Rovers and Carlisle United between 1931-49, amassing 188 League appearances overall.

WILKINSON, Norman - a goalkeeper who made 186 League appearances for Stoke City following his transfer from Huddersfield Town.

WILLIAMS, Bert - an England international goalkeeper (24 caps gained) who appeared in more than 400 League and Cup games for Wolves between 1946-57 having started his career with Walsall. He won FA Cup and League championship medals in 1949 and 1954 respectively.

WITHAM, Dick - a left-back who played for Durham City, Huddersfield Town, Blackpool and Oldham Athletic, appearing in 149 League games for the Seasiders (1933-37).

YOUNG, Alf - An England international centre-half (9 caps won) who played for Durham City before appearing in 309 League and Cup games for Huddersfield Town (1927-39). He joined York City in 1945 and later coached the Danish sides Koge Boldklub and Esbjerg and managed Bradford PA. Young was the innocent victim who was 'wrongly' adjudged to have given away the penalty which resulted in Preston winning the 1938 FA Cup final.

FOREST MANAGERS:

Prior to 1889, the Nottingham Forest team - as with many other clubs - was selected by a committee, usually made up of seven or eight men, including the captain, possibly the vice-captain, secretary and perhaps the trainer. The first two 'managers' of the club - Radford and Hallam - also held the position of secretary.

HAROLD RADFORD: 1889-97

Harry Radford was a dedicated public servant, a professional businessman and father of the former Nottingham bass singer, Bob Radford. He was appointed secretary-manager of Forest at the AGM in July 1889. He held office for six years during which time the club won the Football Alliance in 1892 and as a result gained entry to the Football League (Division One) and reached the semi-final of the FA Cup (also in 1892).

Brought to Forest from the local corporation, he first held the post of club secretary in 1886 and it was due to his ambitions and activities that the Football Alliance was formed (1889). Later his guile and influence encouraged greater things from the club (and indeed the players and team). A far-sighted administrator, he became a representative serving on the FA Council and did much to persuade the Football League to incorporate the Alliance as a 'second' division. He was extremely astute at spotting talent and brought many fine players (some of international class) to the club.

HARRY HALLAM: 1897-1909

Harry Hallam also held the position of secretary-manager (and committee member) and for a while he worked hand-in-hand with Radford. He was in office (in the latter) for 12 years, and at the end of his first season in charge Forest won the FA Cup, beating Derby County 3-1 in the final before a crowd of 62,017 at the Crystal Palace. Forest then reached the semi-final stage a year later (beaten in a replay by Bury) and after suffering relegation, they bounced back as Second Division champions in 1907.

It was Hallam, who also arranged Forest's first-ever overseas tour - to Argentina and Uruguay in 1905 - and saw it as both pioneering and rewarding for himself, the club and the players!

FREDERICK W EARP: 1909-12

Teddy Earp had been a long-serving player (1878-1885) and committee member for Forest and had played in the club's first-ever FA Cup tie. As a manager he was ably supported all down thee line by Board members Bob Cobbin (a future chairman), Bob Marsters (who was to take over as manager himself in 1912) and Noel Watson who was to become manager in 1931. (see EARP, Frederick W).

ROBERT J MARSTERS: 1912-25

Assistant-secretary to Hallam (since 1905) and secretary under Teddy Earp, Bob Marsters bossed Forest (as secretary-manager) for 13 years either side of WW1. The financial state of the club was critical when he took over the reins from Earp in 1912. As it was privately owned, he had to do an awful lot of internal work (juggling things around) to make ends meet. He succeeded and the club survived, although out on the pitch performances weren't brilliant at first, but after the hostilities - and having guided the team to victory in the Victory Cup - things improved and the Second Division championship was won in 1922. Marsters, too, had a good eye for spotting a star player and with the assistance of his good friend and colleague Bob Cobbin, the pair of them ran Forest almost single-handedly, saving the club from disaster in the process. It was Marsters who persuaded legendary goalkeeper Sam Hardy to come back into League football and help the Reds back into the top flight. Marsters served Forest for 21 years (1905-15 inclusive and after leaving the club he became a respected (and frequently visited) licensee in Nottingham

JOHN HENLEY BAYNES: 1925-29

In office for four years, until June 1929, the former Rotherham County and Mansfield Town coach Jack Baynes was introduced as secretary-manager of the club in June 1925, the committee anticipating a change in fortunes (on the pitch) after three lack-lustre campaigns following promotion, Forest having once more been relegated following two finishes in 20th position and one (the last) right at the bottom of the table.

He had limited success. Working with little cash, he found it difficult to attract players of any calibre to the club while at the same time he lost some of his best footballers to other clubs. Forest struggled in 17th position in 1925-26 before claiming 5th spot a year later with some much better displays. However, after two moderate campaigns when the team finished in mid-table, Baynes was eventually replaced in the summer of 1929 by the 39 year-old former Newcastle United inside-forward Stan Hardy, the Forest committee deciding a change was required. After leaving the City Ground, Baynes managed Wrexham for just over two years, from October 1929 until his death in Croesnewyyd Hospital, Wrexham on 14 December 1931 (he had been admitted there in the September to undergo surgery for cancer, and although allowed to return home, he had a relapse and sadly died at the age of 43. He led Wrexham to victory in the Welsh Cup final in the year of his demise. He was born in Yorkshire on 18 February 1888.

STANLEY HARDY: 1929-32

Related to goalkeeper Sam, Stan Hardy's stay in office was all too brief. He was never the man for the job (so it was said) and he disappeared subsequent to an FA Cup-tie with Chesterfield in January 1932...after the team had just ended a disastrous run of nine League games without a win and had slipped alarmingly down the table in the process. Hardy joined Lord Kitchener's army, the Newcastle Quayside battalion of the Northumberland Fusiliers in September 1914 and rose to the rank of lieutenant in the Machine Gun Corps. He was severely gassed in the trenches and never played football again owing to breathing difficulties when running.

NOEL WATSON: 1932-36

Noel Watson, an ex-player and first-class referee, was persuaded to take over from Hardy by chairman Bob Cobbin early in 1932. He was to remain with the club for the next 30 years, serving as secretary-manager (until 1936) and thereafter as secretary (both honorary and paid), as honorary treasurer, becoming as much part of the club as the chairman and manager and indeed of some of the star players. He had Dave Willis, father-in-law of the great Alex James, as his trainer for the first few seasons and they did a good job, Forest rising to 5th place in Division Two in 1933. However, things out on the pitch didn't go all that well during the mid-1930s and after four years in charge, Watson - who was appointed as a Life Member of the club - handed over his duties to the club's first officially designated manager, Harry Wightman.

HAROLD WIGHTMAN: 1936-39

Harry Wightman guested for Forest during WW1, making almost 140 appearances. He was 42 years of age when he took over from Watson at the City Ground and had been in management (at various levels) since 1928. He had laid the foundations for future success at Luton Town (signing Joe Payne) and it came as a shock to the Kenilworth Road club when he resigned in 1935. Unfortunately he failed to do the business with Forest, the team going close to relegation from Division Two in each of his three seasons in charge, finishing a desperate 18th in 1937, 20th a year later and 20th again in 1939 (although he actually left the club six weeks or so before the end of that campaign).
(See under, WIGHTMAN, Harold).

WILLIAM HENRY WALKER: 1939-60

After a marvellous playing career with Aston Villa and England and as manager of Sheffield Wednesday, Billy Walker was appointed boss of Forest in March 1939 and was to remain in office for 21 years, leading the Reds back into the top flight as Second Division runners-up in 1957, having earlier won the Third Division South title in 1951 and seeing the Reds lose in the Midland Wartime Cup final of 1944. He then guided the team to FA Cup glory in 1959, having introduced many fine players to the club in that time.

Born in the Black Country (at Wednesbury) in 1897, he served Villa for18 years from 1915-33 and scored 244 goals in 531 games, helping them win the FA Cup in 1920 and finish runners-up in 1924. He was also capped 18 times by England, skippering his country (and Villa) on many occasions. As manager of Wednesday, he guided them to FA Cup success over WBA in 1935. Before taking over at the City Ground, Walker had managed non-League Chelmsford City. He retired in July 1960 and died in Sheffield in November 1964, having suffered a stroke 12 months earlier.

ANDREW BEATTIE: 1960-63

In charge of Forest from September 1960 to July 1963, Andy Beattie was born in Aberdeenshire in August 1913 and played in 125 League games as a full-back for Preston North End (1935-47), guesting for Forest and Notts County, among others during WW2. He appeared in the 1937 and 1938 FA Cup finals, gaining a winners' medal in the latter. He won seven caps for Scotland and appeared in five wartime internationals. Secretary-manager of Barrow (1947-49), he was then boss, in turn, of Stockport County (1949-52), Huddersfield Town (1952-56, leading the Terriers into the First Division while also looking after the Scotland team in 1954), Carlisle United (1958-60) and also the Scottish national side again (1959-60) before moving into the hot-seat at the City Ground. His three-year stay was not an outstanding success and after leaving the club he managed Plymouth Argyle (1963-64), Wolves (as caretaker-boss, 1964-65) and Notts County (1965-67, having initially been appointed as professional advisor). He was also assistant-manager of Sheffield United (1967), and acted as coach and/or scout for Brentford, Wolves, Walsall, Liverpool and Notts County at various intervals. Beattie, who equalled Major Frank Buckley's record of managing seven different League clubs when he took charge of Wolves in 1964, died in 1983.

JOHN JOSEPH CAREY: 1963-68

Manchester United and Republic of Ireland left-back and captain, Johnny Carey had a wonderful playing career at Old Trafford that spanned 17 years (1936-53) during which time he appeared in 346 first-class games and scored 18 goals, helping United win promotion from Division Two (1938), win the FA Cup (1948) and the League championship (1952). He gained 36 full caps (29 for the Republic of Ireland, seven for Northern Ireland), skippered the Great Britain side v. The Rest of Europe in 1947 and was voted 'Footballer of the Year' in 1948. After retiring he managed Blackburn Rovers (1953-58), Everton (1958-61), Leyton Orient (1961-63), Forest (to December 1968) and Blackburn Rovers (again, first as general manager, 1969, then as manager 1970-71). He was also in charge of the Republic of Ireland for a spell. He guided Blackburn and Orient to runners-up spot (and promotion) from Division Two in 1958 and 1962 respectively. As boss at the City Ground he saw Forest reach the FA Cup semi-final in 1967 (beaten by Spurs) and finish runners-up in the First Division. He bought wisely, securing the services of Terry Hennessey, Joe Baker, John Barnwell and Alan Hinton. Unfortunately he was sacked after the team slipped into the relegation zone halfway through the 1968-69 campaign. Carey died in 1995.

MATTHEW MUIRHEAD GILLIES: 1969-72

A Scotsman, born in Loganlea in August 1912, Matt Gillies was a centre-half who played for Motherwell (as an amateur), Bolton Wanderers, then Arsenal, QPR and Chelsea (as a WW2 guest) and Leicester City, retiring in 1956 to become coach at Filbert Street, eventually taking over as manager in 1958 and retaining his position until December 1968 before moving to Forest in January 1969. He remained in charge of the Reds until October 1972, failing to bring further success to the City Ground. Earlier in his career, he helped Leicester win the Second Division title as a player in 1954 and then guided the Foxes to League Cup glory in 1964 and to runners-up spot in 1965 and to the FA Cup finals of 1961 and 1963, losing to Spurs and Manchester United respectively

DAVID CRAIG MACKAY: 1972

Dave Mackay was one of the greatest footballers of his era. He won just about every honour in the game during his long and distinguished playing career that spanned 20 years. A barrel-chested, hard-tackling wing-half, he started out on the road to glory as a part-time professional with Hearts in the early 1950s.

Born in Musselburgh in November 1934, he was the driving force behind the attack. Tough with a no-nonsense approach, totally committed, never shirking a tackle, going in where it hurt and often coming out on top.

During his seven years at Tynecastle, Mackay won the first of his 22 full caps and represented the Scottish League. He also gained a League championship medal (1958), two Scottish League Cup winners' medals (1955 & 1959) and a Scottish Cup winners' medal (1956). He joined Spurs for £30,000 in 1959 and at White Hart Lane slotted into a 'footballing machine' run by Bill Nicholson. With Danny Blanchflower at right-half and John White at inside-right, the Spurs midfield was the best in the country, emphasised when the double was won in 1960-61, the FA Cup was retained the following season and victory achieved in the European Cup-Winners Cup final in 1963, although Mackay missed the latter triumph with a stomach injury. He won a third FA Cup winners' medal with Spurs in 1967 and when he left the club for Derby County for £5,000 in 1968 he had amassed 364 first-team appearances (63 goals).

At the end of his first season at the Baseball Ground (under Brian Clough) Mackay was voted joint PFA 'Footballer of the Year' (with Manchester City's Tony Book) as the Rams swept to promotion from the Second Division. In May 1971 he was appointed player-manager of Swindon Town; in November 1972 he took charge of Forest but only stayed a short while, returning to his former club Derby as their boss in 1973, a position he held until 1976. A spell out of the game preceded his appointment as Walsall manager in 1977, but after a year with the Saddlers, Mackay switched to the Middle East, taking charge of Al-Arabi Sporting Club (Kuwait). Eight years later he was handed the manager's job at Al-Shabab (Dubai), returning to England in December 1987 to take over the reins of Doncaster Rovers, staying until March 1989. The following month he was appointed manager of Birmingham City and held his position until January 1991 when he handed in his resignation. Mackay's last major appointment in soccer took him to Egypt as coach of FC Zamalek (1991-92).

ALLAN DUNCAN BROWN 1973-75

Another Scotsman, born in Fife in October 1926, Allan Brown was an inside-forward with East Fife, Blackpool, Luton Town and Portsmouth before becoming player-manager of Wigan Athletic in 1963. He took over as boss of his former club, Luton, in 1966 and after that managed Torquay United (1969-71) and Bury (1972-73) before slipping into the hot seat at Forest in November 1973, holding his position until January 1975 when he moved, in the same capacity, to Southport. He returned to Blackpool as manager in 1976, coached in Al-Qadisiya (Kuwait) and then managed Blackpool once more from 1981-82. Capped 14 times by his country, Brown also represented the Football League and was a Scottish Cup runner-up with East Fife in 1950, and then achieved the same award when playing for Luton v. Forest in the 1959 FA Cup final. He also broke his leg twice during his playing days.

As a manager he took Portsmouth to the Third Division title in 1962, guided Luton to the Fourth Division championship in 1968. Under his leadership Forest did hardly anything, having one decent Cup run in 1974.

BRIAN HOWARD CLOUGH: 1975-93

Born in Middlesbrough on 21 March 1935, Brian Clough was an out-and-out goalscorer, who became a brilliant manager. As a player he scored 251 goals in just 274 League games while serving with two clubs: Middlesbrough (May 1953-July 1961) and Sunderland (July 1961-December 1962, a knee injury, suffered against Bury ended his career). He gained two full England caps (v. Wales and Sweden in 1959), collected three more at Under-23 level, played once for the 'B' team and twice represented the Football League. After his enforced retirement he was appointment coach at Roker Park (he had John O'Hare as one of his early pupils) and on leaving Roker Park in October 1965 he became manager of Hartlepool United, thus becoming the youngest boss in the Football League at that time. He switched his managerial duties to Derby County in May 1967, remaining in office until October 1973 when he resigned. He then moved south to Brighton & Hove Albion (November 1973) and after his sojourn on the south coast he went back north to Leeds United, albeit briefly for just 44 days, from August to October 1974. Finally, he bedded in with Forest, taking the hot seat at the City Ground in January 1975. He remained in charge of the Reds until

May 1993, during which time Forest won the League title (1978), the League Cup four times (in 1978, 1979, 1989 & 1990), the European Cup twice (in 1979 & 1980), the Super Cup (also in 1980) and the Zenith Data Systems Cup (1992) as well as gaining promotion to the top flight in 1977 and finishing runners-up in the FA Cup in 1991, the League Cup in 1980, the Super Cup in 1981 and the World Club Championship, also in 1981. As boss of Derby he won the Second Division title in 1969, followed by the First Division crown three years later.

Named 'Manager of the Year' in 1978, he certainly rates alongside the greats of British football management with the likes of Sir Matt Busby, Sir Alex Ferguson, Bill Shankly, Jock Stein and Herbert Chapman. He won virtually everything there was to win in the game. With his side-kick Peter Taylor, who had been his goalkeeper at Middlesbrough, Clough did wonders at Derby (initially on limited resources) and then he turned everything round and upwards at the City Ground. He signed some superb players during his managerial career - Dave Mackay - John O'Hare, Roy McFarland, John McGovern, Alan Hinton, Willie Carlin, Archie Gemmill, Colin Todd and David Nish were among his captures for Derby, while he rebuilt the Forest team with the likes of O'Hare and McGovern, both signed from the Rams, Peter Withe, Frank Clark, Larry Lloyd, Garry Birtles, Peter Shilton and Gemmill (another ex-Ram) while developing the talents of Tony Woodcock, John Robertson, Viv Anderson, Martin O'Neill plus Trevor Francis, the first £1 million footballer, bought in 1979.

Season after season he boosted his squad with experience, bringing in Kenny Burns, Stan Bowles, Frankie Gray, Mark Proctor, Peter Davenport, Hans van Breukelen, Kenny Swain, Paul Hart and Steve Hodge, and adding continuously with quality such as Steve Sutton, Johnny Metgod, Steve Wigley, Hans Segers, his son Nigel Clough, Des Walker, Steve Chettle, Stuart Pearce, Neil Webb, Franz Carr, Gary Mills, Paul Wilkinson, Gary Crosby, Garry Parker, Gary Charles, Brain Laws, Nigel Jemson, Mark Crossley, Scot Gemmill, Kingsley Black, Roy Keane, Steve Stone, Ian Woan and many more, all technically 'Cloughie's' men. He also dabbled successfully with Teddy Sheringham. However, he did have a few failures, Justin Fashanu, Gary Megson and Ian Wallace to name just three. He was allowed some indiscretions wasn't he!

* In February 1989, Clough was charged with bringing the game into disrepute. He was found guilty, fined £5,000 and banned from the touch-line of all Football League grounds for the remainder of that season.
* In December 1989 Clough took charge of his 1,000th League game as a manager.
* In March 1993 he received the Freedom of the City of Nottingham. In May 2003, he followed up by receiving the Freedom of the City of Derby.

FRANK ALBERT CLARK: 1993-96

A full-back with Forest from 1975-79, during which time he appeared in well over 150 games for the club, Frank Clark also played for Crook Town and Newcastle United as well as managing Leyton Orient for eight years (1983-91. He was in charge at the City Ground from May 1993 until December 1996 when fellow full-back Stuart Pearce was given the responsibility as caretaker-manager. (see under, CLARK, Frank Albert).

STUART PEARCE: 1997

After the departure of Frank Clark, England international defender Stuart Pearce, aged 34 at the time, was appointed caretaker-manager at the City Ground prior to the arrival of Dave Bassett in February 1997. (see under PEARCE, Stuart).

DAVID BASSETT: 1997-98

Appointed as Forest's new manager in February 1997 (initially named as general manager), Dave Bassett could do nothing to keep the Reds in the Premiership - but he found the right blend, and gained enough fighting spirit from his players to bounce straight back as First Division champions the very next season, Forest pipping Middlesbrough by three points to take the title following a seven-match unbeaten run from 1 April. Unfortunately he came under severe pressure himself as Forest again struggled in the top flight during the 1998-99 campaign. They were already doomed to relegation, lying in bottom spot with only two wins on the board from 20 games, when Bassett departed on 5 January 1997 to be replaced by Ron Atkinson.

'Harry' Bassett was born in Stanmore, Middlesex in September 1944. He played for Hendon, Walton & Hersham, Wimbledon, Chelsea and Watford, failing to make the first team with any of the last two clubs, having been an amateur prior to August 1974 when he turned pro with the Dons. An FA Amateur Cup winner with Walton & Hersham in 1973, he retired as a player in 1978 and became coach at Plough Lane, taking over as the Dons' manager in 1981 and retaining office until 1987, having briefly been in charge of Crystal Palace (August 1984). From May 1987 to January 1988 he was boss of Watford, managed Sheffield United from February 1988 and then took over the reins at Palace again (in season 1996-97) before trying his luck with Forest. In recent years Bassett has been both team manager (2001-02) and general manager/director of football (2002-03) of Leicester City. As a club manager, he guided Wimbledon to promotion from Division Three in 1981; took them to the Fourth Division championship a year later; led them to promotion from Division Three in 1984 and lifted them to promotion again, this time upwards into the First Division in 1986. He later guided Sheffield United into the First Division in 1989 and then took the Blades a place higher into the top flight in 1990. Palace finished 3rd in Division One when he was in charge at Selhurst Park (1997) but Leicester fell out of the Premiership during his spell at Filbert Street in 2002.

RONALD FREDERICK ATKINSON: 1998-99

'Big Ron' Atkinson was Forest's boss for just over five months, from January to June 1999.

Born in Liverpool on 18 March 1939, he started playing football with the BSA Works team before joining Aston Villa (signed as a professional in 1956). He failed to make an impression at Villa Park, or with Wolverhampton Wanderers (as a trialist) and in 1959 he joined Headington United (later Oxford United) remaining there until 1971. After a spell with Witney Town, he became manager of Kettering Town, and then took charge of Cambridge United (1974), moving up the scale to West Bromwich Albion as their manager in 1978. Thereafter he held the fort at Manchester United (June 1981-November 1986), WBA (for a second time, 1987-88), Atletico Madrid (1988-89), Sheffield Wednesday (1989-91), Aston Villa (1991-94), Coventry City (1995-96, later director of football at Highfield Road) and Sheffield Wednesday (again, 1997-98) before taking control at the City Ground at a time when Forest were in dire straits! He left the Reds following demotion from the Premiership in June 1999. There is no doubt that Atkinson had a fine footballing life - some 43 years to be precise from 1956 to 1999 - and in that time he certainly had his ups and downs. He amassed over 500 League and Cup appearances during his long association with Oxford whom (along with his brother Graham) he helped gain entry into the Football League in 1962 - soon after completing service with the RAF for whom he played in a representative game against an FA XI (1961). He starred in Oxford's Fourth Division championship-winning season of 1968 and then as boss of Kettering he guided them to the titles of both the Southern League North and Premier Divisions, and came within a single vote of getting the non-League team into the Football League! He assembled a very competent side at Cambridge - good enough to win promotion from the Fourth Division in 1977. Indeed, they were on course for promotion to the Second Division when he took over at the Hawthorns in 1978. Atkinson, after guiding the Baggies into the semi-finals of the FA Cup and to the quarter-finals of the UEFA Cup, then made his mark at Old Trafford, immediately signing three splendid players, striker Frank Stapleton and two midfielders, Bryan Robson and Remi Moses for a combined fee of £2.5 million from his former club, West Brom. United twice won the FA Cup during his spell at Old Trafford (1983 & 1985) After a disastrous sequence of results during the early part of 1986-87 Atkinson's reign as United boss ended. During his time with the club he spent over £8 million on new players but sold around £6 million worth of talent in the process, transferring five internationals.

After unsuccessful spells back at the Hawthorns and in

Spain, Atkinson led Sheffield Wednesday into the top flight of English football as well as guiding the Owls to victory over Manchester United in the Rumbelows League Cup final. He then saw Wednesday finish runners-up in the same competition two years later. As manager at Villa Park he again won the League Cup, beating his former club United 3-1 in the final. Thereafter he had mixed fortunes, first at Highfield Road, then back at Hillsborough and of course with Forest, before quitting the game to concentrate on being a TV pundit.

DAVID ANDREW PLATT: 1999-2001
Appointed by Forest as player-manager in July 1999 and remained in office for exactly two years, until the summer of 2001, when he took control of the England Under-21 side (his official title being head coach). (see under PLATT, David Anthony).

PAUL ANTHONY HART: 2001 to date
A former player at the City Ground, Paul Hart was upgraded to team manager in July 2001 following the departure of David Platt at the end of the previous season (See under HART, Paul Anthony).

FOREST CHAIRMEN
1865-66 J S Scrimshaw
1866-68 W R Lymberry
1868-74 J S Milford
1874-79 A Banks
1879-84 S W Widdowson
1884-86 W Brown
1886-94 T G Howitt
1894-95 G Seldon
1895-97 J Cutts
1897-1920 W T Hancock
1920-48 H R Cobbin
1948-55 J H Brentnall
1955-57 G S Oscroft
1957-60 H W Alcock
1960-63 J H Willmer
1964-66 G F Sisson
1966-71 A Wood
1971-73 H Levy
1973-76 J H Willmer
1976-78 B J Appleby, QC
1978-79 S M Dryden, JP
1980-86 G E MacPherson, JP
1986-93 M Rowarth
1993-97 F Reacher
1997-98 I I Korn
1998-2000 P W Soar
2000-2002 E M Barnes
2002 to date N E Doughty

FOUNDER MEMBERS OF CLUB
(the 1865 Committee)
A Barks, W Brown, W P Brown, C F Daft, T Gamble, R P Hawksley, T G Howitt, W L Hussey, W R Lymberry, J S Milford, J H Rastall, W H Revis, J G Richardson, J S Scrimshaw, J Tomlinson.

APPEARANCE-MAKERS & GOALSCORERS
League Appearances
614 Bob McKinlay
464 Jack Burkitt
445 Ian Bowyer
432 Jack Armstrong
423 Grenville Morris
415 Steve Chettle
403 Geoff Thomas
401 Stuart Pearce
398 John Robertson
372 Tommy Graham

League Goals
199 Grenville Morris
123 Wally Ardron
119 Johnny Dent
105 Ian Storey-Moore
102 Nigel Clough
93 Enoch West
75 Tommy Wilson
70 Garry Birtles
69 Tommy Capel
68 Ian Bowyer
68 Bill Dickinson

Senior Appearances (350+)
686 Bob McKinlay
564 Ian Bowyer
526 Steve Chettle
522 Stuart Pearce
514 John Robertson
503 Jack Burkitt
502 Nigel Clough
460 Jack Armstrong
430 Viv Anderson
422 R Sammy Chapman
416 Peter Hindley
410 John Winfield
391 Tommy Graham
389 Bill Thompson
378 Des Walker
372 Martin O'Neill
357 Billy McKinlay
352 Peter Grummitt

Senior Goals (75+)
217 Grenville Morris
131 Nigel Clough
124 Wally Ardron

122 Johnny Dent
118 Ian Storey-Moore
100 Enoch West
97 Ian Bowyer
96 Garry Birtles
95 John Robertson
90 Tommy Wilson
79 Cyril Stocks

FOREST SECRETARIES
1865-66 J S Milford
1866-68 WR Lymberry
1868-88 H S Radford
1888-89 C A Rastall
1889-97 H B Radford
1897-1909 H Hallam
1909-12 F W Earp
1912-25 R G Marsters
1925-29 J H Baynes
1929-31 S Hardy
1931-61 G N Watson
1961-86 K Smales
1987 to date P White

NOTTINGHAM FOREST FC

Formed: 1865
Turned professional: 1889
Ground: City Ground, Nottingham, NG2 5FJ
Ground capacity (2003): 30,602
Previous grounds: 1865 Forest Recreation Ground; 1879 The Meadows; 1880 Trent Bridge Cricket Ground; 1882 Parkside, Lenton; 1885 Gregory Ground, Lenton; 1890 Town Ground to 1898.
Record attendance: 49,946 Forest v. Manchester United (Div.1) 8.10.1967.
Record gate receipts: £499,999 Forest v. Bayern Munich (UEFA Cup) 19.03.1996
First Football League game: 03.09.1892 v. Everton, away (Div.1) drew 2-2.
Biggest League win: 12-0 v. Leicester Fosse, home (Div.1) 12.04.1909
Biggest Cup win: 14-0 v. Clapton, away (FA Cup) 17.01.1891
Heaviest defeat: 1-9 v. Blackburn Rovers, away (Div. 2) 10.04.1937
Highest goalscorer in season: Wally Ardron, 36 (Div. 3 South) 1950-51.
Most League goals in total: 199 by Grenville Morris (1898-1913)
Most League appearances: 614 by Bob McKinlay (1951-70)
Most capped player (with Forest): Stuart Pearce, 76, for England.
Oldest player: Dave Beasant, 42 years, 47 days v. Tranmere Rovers (league) 06.05.2001
Youngest player: Craig Westcarr, 16 years, 257 days, v. Burnley (League) 13.10.2001

Record signing: £3.5 million to Celtic for Pierre van Hooijdonk, 11.03.1997
Record sale: £8.5 million, Stan Collymore to Liverpool, 03.07.1995.

Honours:
Division One champions: 1977-78 & 1997-98 (new)
Division Two champions: 1906-07 & 1921-22
Division Three (South) champions: 1950-51
FA Cup winners: 1898 & 1959
League Cup winners: 1978, 1979, 1989 & 1990
European Cup winners: 1979 & 1980
European Super Cup winners: 1980
Anglo-Scottish Cup winners: 1977
Simod Cup winners; 1989
Zenith Data Systems Cup winners: 1992

FACT FILE
• Nigel Clough scored a hat-trick in four minutes for Forest against QPR on 13 December 1987 - netting in the 81st, 82nd & 85th minutes, the last from the penalty spot, in a 4-0 win (Division 1).
• On 7 May 1938, Forest, reduced to 10 men through injury, drew 2-2 at Barnsley to escape relegation from the Second Division. The Tykes went down instead - by one-200th part of a goal (below Forest) with both clubs on 36 points.
• David 'Boy' Martin scored in eight consecutive League games for Forest during 1936-37 season.
• When winning the FA Cup in 1958-59 Forest were unchanged throughout the competition: the team being Thomson; Whare, McDonald; Whitefoot, McKinlay, Burkitt, Dwight, Quigley, Wilson, Gray, Imlach. Dwight broke his leg in the final v. Luton Town.
• On 21 October 1995, Forest beat Bolton Wanderers 3-2 to establish a then new Premiership record of 23 unbeaten matches, subsequently extended to 25.
• In 1876 Forest became the first club to adopt a team formation comprising a goalkeeper, two full-backs, three half-backs and five forwards.
• Forest played their 1885 FA Cup semi-final against Queen's Park in Edinburgh, Scotland (lost 3-0).
• The referee is said to have used a whistle for the first time during the Forest v. Sheffield Norfolk friendly game in 1878.
• When Forest won the Second Division title in 1921-22 they gained more points (56) than they scored goals (51).

Former Nottingham Forest manager Brian Clough at the official opening of the Brian Clough Stand.
Nationwide League Division One: Forest v Wolverhampton Wanderers 19th September 1999.

Nottingham Forest celebrate after winning 1-0 against SV Hamburg 28th May 1980 and their second successive European Cup Final.

Viv Anderson 1981